Jaguar Books on Latin

Series Editors

WILLIAM H. BEEZLEY, Professor of History, University of Arizona
COLIN M. MACLACHLAN, John Christy Barr Distinguished Professor of History, Tulane University

Volumes Published

John E. Kicza, ed., *The Indian in Latin American History: Resistance, Resilience, and Acculturation* (1993; rev. ed., 2000).
Cloth ISBN 0-8420-2822-6   Paper ISBN 0-8420-2823-4

Susan E. Place, ed., *Tropical Rainforests: Latin American Nature and Society in Transition* (1993; rev. and updated ed., 2001).
Cloth ISBN 0-8420-2907-9   Paper ISBN 0-8420-2908-7

Paul W. Drake, ed., *Money Doctors, Foreign Debts, and Economic Reforms in Latin America from the 1890s to the Present* (1994).
Cloth ISBN 0-8420-2434-4   Paper ISBN 0-8420-2435-2

John A. Britton, ed., *Molding the Hearts and Minds: Education, Communications, and Social Change in Latin America* (1994).
Cloth ISBN 0-8420-2489-1   Paper ISBN 0-8420-2490-5

David J. Weber and Jane M. Rausch, eds., *Where Cultures Meet: Frontiers in Latin American History* (1994). Cloth ISBN 0-8420-2477-8   Paper ISBN 0-8420-2478-6

Gertrude M. Yeager, ed., *Confronting Change, Challenging Tradition: Women in Latin American History* (1994). Cloth ISBN 0-8420-2479-4   Paper ISBN 0-8420-2480-8

Linda Alexander Rodríguez, ed., *Rank and Privilege: The Military and Society in Latin America* (1994). Cloth ISBN 0-8420-2432-8   Paper ISBN 0-8420-2433-6

Darién J. Davis, ed., *Slavery and Beyond: The African Impact on Latin America and the Caribbean* (1995). Cloth ISBN 0-8420-2484-0   Paper ISBN 0-8420-2485-9

Gilbert M. Joseph and Mark D. Szuchman, eds., *I Saw a City Invincible: Urban Portraits of Latin America* (1996). Cloth ISBN 0-8420-2495-6   Paper ISBN 0-8420-2496-4

Roderic Ai Camp, ed., *Democracy in Latin America: Patterns and Cycles* (1996). Cloth ISBN 0-8420-2512-X   Paper ISBN 0-8420-2513-8

Oscar J. Martínez, ed., *U.S.-Mexico Borderlands: Historical and Contemporary Perspectives* (1996). Cloth ISBN 0-8420-2446-8 Paper ISBN 0-8420-2447-6

William O. Walker III, ed., *Drugs in the Western Hemisphere: An Odyssey of Cultures in Conflict* (1996). Cloth ISBN 0-8420-2422-0 Paper ISBN 0-8420-2426-3

Richard R. Cole, ed., *Communication in Latin America: Journalism, Mass Media, and Society* (1996). Cloth ISBN 0-8420-2558-8 Paper ISBN 0-8420-2559-6

David G. Gutiérrez, ed., *Between Two Worlds: Mexican Immigrants in the United States* (1996). Cloth ISBN 0-8420-2473-5 Paper ISBN 0-8420-2474-3

Lynne Phillips, ed., *The Third Wave of Modernization in Latin America: Cultural Perspectives on Neoliberalism* (1998). Cloth ISBN 0-8420-2606-1   Paper ISBN 0-8420-2608-8

Daniel Castro, ed., *Revolution and Revolutionaries: Guerrilla Movements in Latin America* (1999). Cloth ISBN 0-8420-2625-8 Paper ISBN 0-8420-2626-6

Virginia Garrard-Burnett, ed., *On Earth as It Is in Heaven: Religion in Modern Latin America* (2000). Cloth ISBN 0-8420-2584-7 Paper ISBN 0-8420-2585-5

Carlos A. Aguirre and Robert Buffington, eds., *Reconstructing Criminality in Latin America* (2000). Cloth ISBN 0-8420-2620-7 Paper ISBN 0-8420-2621-5

Christon I. Archer, ed., *The Wars of Independence in Spanish America* (2000). Cloth ISBN 0-8420-2468-9   Paper ISBN 0-8420-2469-7

John F. Schwaller, ed., *The Church in Colonial Latin America* (2000). Cloth ISBN 0-8420-2703-3   Paper ISBN 0-8420-2704-1

Ingrid E. Fey and Karen Racine, eds., *Strange Pilgrimages: Exile, Travel, and National Identity in Latin America, 1800–1990s* (2000). Cloth ISBN 0-8420-2693-2   Paper ISBN 0-8420-2694-0

Joseph L. Arbena and David G. LaFrance, eds., *Sport in Latin America and the Caribbean* (2002). Cloth ISBN 0-8420-2820-X Paper ISBN 0-8420-2821-8

Samuel L. Baily and Eduardo José Míguez, eds., *Mass Migration to Modern Latin America* (2003). Cloth ISBN 0-8420-2830-7 Paper ISBN 0-8420-2831-5

Erick D. Langer with Elena Muñoz, eds., *Contemporary Indigenous Movements in Latin America* (2003). Cloth ISBN 0-8420-2679-7 Paper ISBN 0-8420-2680-0

Vincent C. Peloso, ed., *Work, Protest, and Identity in Twentieth-Century Latin America* (2003). Cloth ISBN 0-8420-2926-5 Paper ISBN 0-8420-2927-3

Work, Protest, and Identity in Twentieth-Century Latin America

Work, Protest, and Identity in Twentieth-Century Latin America

Vincent C. Peloso
Editor

Jaguar Books on Latin America
Number 26

A Scholarly Resources Inc. Imprint
Wilmington, Delaware

Scholarly Resources Inc.
104 Greenhill Avenue
Wilmington, DE 19805-1897
www.scholarly.com

Library of Congress Cataloging-in-Publication Data

Work, protest, and identity in twentieth-century Latin America / edited by Vincent C. Peloso.
    p. cm. — (Jaguar books on Latin America ; no. 26)
    Includes bibliographical references.
    ISBN 0-8420-2926-5 (hard : alk. paper) — ISBN 0-8420-2927-3 (pbk. : alk. paper)
    1. Working class—Latin America. 2. Labor movement—Latin America. I. Peloso, Vincent C. II. Series.
HD8110.5.A5W67 2003
305.5'62'098—dc21

2003000608

For the next generation of la famiglia*: Michelle, Chip, Stephanie, and Andrew . . .*
And for the generation that follows: Ian, Patrick, Winston, Calvin, and . . .

About the Editor

Vincent C. Peloso, professor of history at Howard University, is a former editor of *The Americas: A Quarterly Review of Inter-American Cultural History*. His past work includes a volume he co-edited with Barbara A. Tenenbaum, *Liberals, Politics, and Power: State Formation in Nineteenth-Century Latin America* (1996); the book *Peasants on Plantations: Subaltern Strategies of Labor and Resistance in the Pisco Valley, Peru* (1999), winner of the Arthur P. Whitaker Prize; and several related articles. He teaches a course on race, gender, and culture in Latin America and a seminar on Afro-Latins. Peloso's current research focuses on cultural identity in Peru and Latin America after independence, with special emphasis on Afro-Peruvians in the nineteenth century.

Acknowledgments

The central theme of this anthology is the challenge to identify the working class while working-class cultures in Latin America have undergone enormous changes. I owe special thanks to Bill Beezley and Colin MacLachlan, who encouraged me to take on the issues posed by this project, and to Rick Hopper, whose upbeat handling of it proved to be an excellent stimulus. Nevertheless, several distractions made it very difficult to give proper attention to the responsibilities of an editor when this work was under way two years ago. My concentration was broken by a couple of family setbacks that happened coincidentally with the events of September 11. We were fortunate that when we most needed them, a supportive circle of people was organized who called themselves the F. O. M. Meanwhile, our newest hero, Cal, made his presence felt as he grew stronger. The energies generated under stressful conditions spurred me to work harder, and for that reason I dedicate this volume to those awe-inspiring people who are our children, their spouses, and our grandchildren.

I thank Michelle Slavin for handling this project with great cheer, and I appreciate the work of the copy editor, Ann M. Aydelotte, who thankfully was straightforward and meticulous. The journals that hold copyright to the following studies have given permission for their inclusion in the volume, and I thank them for their speedy cooperation:

Alejandro de la Fuente, "Two Dangers, One Solution: Immigration, Race, and Labor in Cuba, 1900–1930," *International Labor and Working-Class History* 51 (Spring 1997): 30–49. Reprinted by permission of *International Labor and Working-Class History*.

Jeffrey D. Needell, "The *Revolta Contra Vacina* of 1904: The Revolt against 'Modernization' in Belle-Epoque Rio de Janeiro," *Hispanic American Historical Review* 67:2 (May 1987): 233–69. © 1987. All rights reserved. Reprinted by permission of Duke University Press.

Anton Rosenthal, "Streetcar Workers and the Transformation of Montevideo: The General Strike of May 1911," *The Americas: A Quarterly Review of Inter-American Cultural History* 51:4 (April 1995): 471–94. Reprinted by permission of the publisher.

Ann Farnsworth-Alvear, "The Mysterious Case of the Missing Men: Gender and Class in Early Industrial Medellín," *International Labor and Working-Class History* 49 (Spring 1996): 73–92. Reprinted by permission of *International Labor and Working-Class History*.

David S. Parker, "Empleados and Obreros: Legislating Social Classes," in D. S. Parker, *The Idea of the Middle Class: White-Collar Workers and Peruvian Society, 1900–1950* (University Park: Pennsylvania State University Press, 1999), 119–33. © 1999 by Pennsylvania State University. Reproduced by permission of Pennsylvania State University.

Catherine LeGrand, "Colombian Transformations: Peasants and Wage-Labourers in the Santa Marta Banana Zone," *The Journal of Peasant Studies* 11:4 (July 1984): 178–200. Reprinted by permission of *The Journal of Peasant Studies*, published by Frank Cass & Company. © Frank Cass & Co., Ltd.

Norman Caulfield, "The Americans and Charro Entrenchment," in Norman Caulfield, *Mexican Workers and the State: From the Porfiriato to NAFTA* (Fort Worth: Texas Christian University Press, 1998), 101–20, 153–55. Photos omitted. Reprinted by permission of the author.

Thomas Miller Klubock, "Copper Workers, Organized Labor, and Popular Protest under Military Rule in Chile, 1973–1986," *International Labor and Working-Class History* 52 (Fall 1997): 106–33. Reprinted by permission of *International Labor and Working-Class History*.

Anthony W. Pereira, "Working for Democracy: Brazil's Organized Working Class in Comparative Perspective," *International Labor and Working-Class History* 49 (Spring 1996): 93–115. Reprinted by permission of *International Labor and Working-Class History*.

Michael F. Jiménez, " 'Citizens of the Kingdom': Toward a Social History of Radical Christianity in Latin America," *International Labor and Working-Class History* 34 (Fall 1988): 3–21. Reprinted by permission of *International Labor and Working-Class History*.

Kenneth M. Roberts, "Labor and Capital in Latin America's Changing Social Landscape," *Journal of Interamerican Studies and World Affairs* 40:2 (Summer 1998): 101–16. © University of Miami. Reprinted by permission of the University of Miami.

Contents

Introduction

Vincent C. Peloso

Reworking Problems

The "boom" in Latin American labor history has a new tone. It has become a polyrhythm, and it calls for different dances and many partners. The upswing in the literature of the past two decades has moved the field onto a new stage.[1] Latin America labor history now gives prominent attention to aspects of work and working-class life that in the past were viewed as sidebars. It focuses less on the job and the workplace and gives more space to the examination of working-class culture. An amplified, more fulfilling picture emerges. The tones, the grit and sweat, the dangers and joys, the details of working-class life move to the foreground. The change is a product of the historian's turn from economics to culture in the study of Latin American labor history.

Studies of working-class culture recognize the immediacy of gender, race, ethnicity, and identity. As findings on these topics are brought to bear on traditional labor themes they shed light on the cultural dimensions of the Latin American industrial labor force and its extension beyond the workplace into the streets. The workers become entwined in the life of the popular sectors of Latin American society. None of the practitioners of this work would deny the importance of the issues that continue to reflect the concerns of the region's traditional labor history.[2] Problems of the mode and forces of production and reproduction, labor union organization, workplace control, movements, struggles, protests, and strikes continue to generate debate and study.

The selections in this volume show that labor historians seek to merge traditional concerns about Latin American labor with a new emphasis. They bring recent findings on identity, gender, race, and ethnicity to bear on traditional labor history. By calling attention to these aspects of the world of labor, the selections provide a glimpse into the larger problem of how society functioned. They also help to enliven the picture of how the working class met society's most basic needs. The results are powerful and illuminating. Several interwoven threads run almost continuously throughout the selections. Gender is one of those threads that crops up persistently in recent labor studies. It is interesting to see the many forms it takes. Likewise, race/ethnicity occurs as a factor in the social relations of workers in several of the selections, as does immigration. Other threads with remarkable strength in these selections are the divisions that arise within the labor movement and within labor organizations and mobilizations, and the divisions that have set workers against one another and against their neighbors. Labor historians have dealt forthrightly with these threads, and they come together to suggest the many modes by which work and culture have mixed over a century to create exclusive as well as inclusive working-class identities.

New Categories and Class Identities

A focus on identity touches the core of many problems in the history of Latin American labor. Even as the working class grew bigger everywhere, it was not always clear who were the workers and who were their friends and allies. But the workers had other identity problems to contend with as well. They struggled with the sense of isolation and detachment that was a common experience when they left the villages and entered the confusing din of the cities, mines, and plantations. In the village a person derived a sense of self from an inherited set of rights and responsibilities, but an industrial job meant that identity came through one's work. At first, the job became life and life became the job. That is how it must have seemed to many workers when they first joined the work force. Those who established families at the same time found life taking on other dimensions.[3]

Identity problems in some instances reflected the larger framework of the world of work. Events early in the twentieth century set the tone for what would become typical patterns in Latin American worker protest. A medical crisis in Rio de Janeiro, a speedup in the routine of streetcar workers in Montevideo, the arrival of immigrants in the sugar fields of Cuba: in each case, a population faced with forces seemingly beyond their control registered their outrage in public and sometimes violent ways. Identities were forged in the confrontations between streetcar workers, cane cutters, and unemployed handymen in these cases and the larger economic structures that demanded their labor without meeting their needs. The workers' opponents, as Alejandro de la Fuente, Jeffrey Needell, and Anton Rosenthal show, were a combination of the newly emerging bourgeoisie and the modern state. In these conflicts, identities of nation and culture were instruments of the state, and the loyalties of workers were tested against those images.

By the end of World War I the demand for industrial labor was strong throughout Latin America. The largest cities in Argentina, Brazil, and Mexico were developing a recognizable industrial core. Elsewhere enormous holes were being carved into the ground to mine copper, lead, and tin, and large stretches of rich lands were being swept clean of the remaining forests to plant sugarcane, cotton, and rice. Oil rigs were going up in every wetland that showed evidence of tar. Both men and women, noticeably for the first time, followed the clouds of dust and smoke to the factories, rigs, and mills. Once again, identity issues plagued society as women found that the workplace left them in a double bind: they were chastised for leaving the hearth unattended but implored to fill out the scarce ranks of labor on the assembly lines. Women throughout the region took up the challenge and found inventive—if exhausting—ways to manage both ends of the new spectrum of workplaces, from the home to the field, the office, or the factory.[4]

Not all women were recognized as workers, to their astonishment, as cultural norms and the needs of labor clashed in a quixotic way, to hear Ann Farnsworth-Alvear tell it. Their greatest supporters revealed their cultural biases as they retained the male dominance of the world of work while they sympathized with the women. In other instances those gender biases helped to redefine work. David Parker shows how the differences between manual labor and intellectual work were gendered in Peru in the 1920s and consolidated in the law. The powerful urge toward gender identity in society reinforced class tensions and consolidated gender prejudices.

The mobilization of immigrant labor that developed anew after World War I recombined identity issues in other ways. De la Fuente and Miguel Tinker-Salas recall the problems created among workers in cane and oil fields by the introduction of immigrants into their midst. Differences of culture and distances from the home community weakened the defenses of the immigrants. When they objected to gross forms of national and cultural discrimination that identified them as different, their susceptibility to national and race claims weakened labor's position. Pay rates were scaled by race or culture, and other noncash rewards were adjusted to feed the obvious prejudices of the workers. Oil camps and cane fields were defined under industrial pressure as men's workplaces and women's work were relegated to the service sectors of these industries. The power of the engine of production that they stoked nevertheless gave these workers a great advantage, and despite the problems entailed in divisions and identities of race and nation they continued to seek cooperation in the interest of justice.

In the pre-World War II era, field work and factory work were viewed as altogether different spheres. Their coexistence within the same national economy was used as evidence that Latin American economies overall were burdened by the disparities and disjunctions between the "traditional" and the "modern" sectors of society. Much recent research has undermined that view of labor in Latin America. Moving beyond those constraints, labor historians now look at work in a fuller sense by studying the interconnectedness of rural and urban forms of industrialization and labor mobilization. Marc Becker, Catherine LeGrand, and María del Carmen Baerga provide excellent cases to demonstrate the new approach. In the absence of opportunities for women, other venues were found for the expression of working-class needs. Becker examines Ecuador, a country whose republican history and culture have until recently not received much attention from historians to bring out the gendered character of its labor history.[5] Here he shows how in Ecuador women of the popular sector were joined by their counterparts of the upper class to mobilize support for bilingual education. These seemingly innocuous programs would offer better alternatives for labor across the workplace spectrum in this highly stratified country. This was not deemed a "man's" issue, and the women struggled bravely on their own. In the context of Ecuadorean national culture their struggle is something special to behold.

Deep Divisions

The selection by LeGrand on banana workers on Colombia's Caribbean littoral illustrates the danger companies felt from the potential of worker-peasant alliances, and they pursued tactics to prevent such alliances. LeGrand portrays the forms of labor organization, protests, and strikes that could be found among a population whose class identity was fuzzy at the edges, moving purposively between peasant and proletariat in the search for advantage and survival. One tactic that the banana producer, United Fruit Company, was unable to use in separating workers from peasants was wage and benefit differentials.

In areas where cultural barriers—including ethnicity, race, and modernity—already were present, however, it was a simple matter for companies to rely on what appeared to be "natural" distinctions as a rationale for unequal wage rates. Tinker-Salas found this to be the case in the Venezuelan oil fields. Baerga's analysis of the needlework trade in Puerto Rico gives a clear picture of the internal divisions that emerged among women to cripple efforts at union organization. When women assumed that gender would unite them in their struggle for a union, their assumptions were undermined by a combination of pressures from the business sector and insuperable cultural divisions along urban-rural lines. Divisions among women workers continued to reflect highly stratified class categories, migration patterns, and company opportunism. David McCreery provided important insight on the issue in his elegantly written synthesis, *The Sweat of Their Brow*: "As with the strawberry workers, the women of the *maquiladoras* [Mexican border assembly factories] sought work for the income it promised and not for personal liberation or fulfillment."[6]

Internal divisions are no stranger to Latin American labor movements. Much of the success of organizational efforts depended on elusive solidarity, the holy grail of labor organization. Ironically, one of the most divisive situations for unionized workers could be found in Mexico after World War II. Although labor's rights had been guaranteed in the famed revolutionary Constitution of 1917, the government patronage implied in those guarantees left the workers tied to the wishes of a regime grown increasingly businesslike. Norman Caulfield points unerringly to one of the major consequences of that fateful link between organized labor and the Mexican Revolution by analyzing the role of the charros, labor supervisors loyal to the revolutionary government rather than to the rank-and-file they ostensibly represented. The conditions in which the charros arose to govern the unions by violence included a vast, unorganized popular sector and a business sector to which the government seemed ever more attuned. As the revolution sought to match its economy to the demands of increasing globalization, the sons and daughters of the early revolutionaries, workers and peasants alike, found their loyalty weakening. Recent events indicate that the experience of the workers and their sympathizers in Mexico is not unique. In Colombia legitimate labor organizers recently found themselves the target of paramilitary assassins. The attacks, in which over 1,200 union organizers reportedly have been killed since 1991, weaken the labor movement and leave the workers prey to the companies. Labor rights and human rights merge in a scenario that calls for a better understanding of the identity of workers.[7]

Globalization and Identity

The forces of neoliberalism and globalization crept up slowly on Latin American workers. Nevertheless, the demands made upon the countries of the region by the tenets of free trade and open markets became evident as early as the 1970s. What was still unclear at that point were the extremes to which states would go to harness this untamed, unpredictable beast. Beginning in the 1960s and continuing into the last decade of the century, regimes responded to the protests of workers—men and women—with violence. It was as if they expected to stimulate the best in workers by lighting a fire under them. That they did, but the outcome was not what the regimes and the world expected. Extreme repression of workers and the students who allied with them was met with a range of responses from popular protests, strikes, and demonstrations through clandestine organization and stubborn counterviolence. In many instances, workers opened their arms to their allies among the popular sectors, and the response very often was supportive. Rachel May's sensitive portrait captures a woman whose lifestyle echoed that of many young people who strove to gain justice for workers during the worst years of Latin America's "dirty wars." She herself, in May's characterization, represented the multiple tasks young workers took on not only to organize against a military dictatorship, in this case Argentina, but also out of necessity. The selection suggests how the idea of work and the meaning of the working class were expanding as neoliberal economics was moving around the globe. May's discussion of an Argentine *militante* is unusual in several respects. For one thing, it provides a glimpse into the multilayered life of a woman worker. At the same time that May reflects on her friend's life, she offers insight into her own, thus making this selection a double-layered testimonial. Through self-reflection, the witness becomes the subject.

The importance of testimony and oral history in the documentation of the lives of workers has risen as scholars have attempted to bring out the individual, human side of labor history. Scholars have in some instances realized that they can provide a channel through which lives may be touched and thereby be made real. Testimony appears in an almost unwitting form in the May essay. Meanwhile, the Tinker-Salas selection puts oral evidence to excellent use by letting the words of oil workers flesh out a picture of oil field culture. In another selection, Baerga offers the evidence of Puerto Rican needlework women gleaned from "testimony" offered at U.S. government hearings.[8] Testimony, testimonial narrative, and oral evidence become particularly important in an age when globalization increasingly signifies the cultural and commercial homogeneity so much desired by a voracious capitalist culture. Some testimonial literature has been available to students of popular culture for years. Witness the testimony of Miguel Barnet, Domitila Barrios de Chungara, Juan Rojas, Rigoberta Menchú, Gregorio Condori Mamani and Asunta Quispe Huamán, and Carolina María de Jesús. One can now add to that list the reflections of Jesús Zúñiga Sotomayor, María Roldán, and Miguel Perdomo Neira.[9] What these figures have in common is a determination to define and come to grips with the world spinning beneath their feet.

Thomas M. Klubock provides evidence of an instance in Chile where the vital mine workers adjusted to an infamously repressive regime by turning to their friends in the wider sectors of society, thereby keeping alive Chilean dreams of democracy. Through the era of repression labor organization suffered and regimes nearly succeeded in snuffing out unions altogether. Surprisingly, however, this was not the case in Brazil, where people experienced some of the more repressive military regimes of the late twentieth century. Yet when the nightmare ended, as Anthony Pereira documents, workers not only rejoiced but also took heart in the results of their efforts to expand their base in the popular sectors. The outcome was a strengthening of the ties between a healthy labor movement and democracy in Brazil.

Pereira notes that the ties between labor and democracy also have depended on the willingness of labor organizations to broaden their understanding of the meaning of work. A successful change in its identity thus appears to be the key to the reproduction of the working class. But this is not a strange or unique view. Looking down the road to the future of the workers in Latin America, the selection by the late Michael Jiménez draws upon a number of cultural markers to hypothesize that as work in the global economy changes, so will the character of the working class. As Jiménez suggests, the allies of workers in the broader society also may change and workers may already have pointed themselves in that direction. Lamentably we will not hear Jiménez's voice on this question again, but there is no doubt that here he has in mind that face of the Catholic Church bound up in the progressive voice of liberation theology.

Reviewing recent literature in the field of labor history, Kenneth Roberts essentially agrees that the meaning of being a worker is changing and identities are not fixed. One might add to these unsettled feelings by directing some thought to the "expanding exodus" from Latin America. This is how emigration from every country in the region is characterized in a recent analysis in the *Washington Post*. The *Post* article noted that the exodus does not merely come to the United States. The estimated 500,000 Ecuadoreans (roughly 4 percent of the population) who left in the past two years went mostly to Europe.[10] Thus far, this movement seems to have been the strongest response to the effects of globalization on Latin American working-class society. At any rate, in the final selection Roberts speculates about the nature of class at this juncture in Latin American history. His thoughts provide a point of departure for further discussion at this early stage in the twenty-first century.

The polyrhythmic beat of Latin American labor history moves in and out of harmony with the tunes played here. Together they resonate strongly across the landscape of the region's cultural expressions. The lyrics may be found in the pages that lie ahead.

Notes

1. See Emilia Viotti da Costa, "Experience versus Structures: New Tendencies in the History of Labor and the Working Class in Latin America—What Do We Gain? What Do We Lose?" *International Labor and Working-Class History* 36 (1989): 3–24; John D. French, "The Latin American Labor Studies Boom," *International Review of Social History* 45 (2000): 279–308.

2. The issues are succinctly summarized in Hobart A. Spalding Jr., "Labor Movements," in Barbara A. Tenenbaum, ed., *Encyclopedia of Latin American History and Culture*, 5 vols. (New York: Charles Scribner's Sons, 1996), 3:366–72. An indispensable bibliographical essay is Ian Roxborough, "The Urban Working Class and Labor Movements," in Leslie Bethell, ed., *The Cambridge History of Latin America*, vol. 11, *Bibliographic Essays* (Cambridge: Cambridge University Press, 1995), 617–34.

3. See Jorge Parodi Solari, trans. James Alstrum and Catherine Conaghan, ed. Catherine Conaghan, *To Be a Worker: Identity and Politics in Peru* (Chapel Hill: University of North Carolina Press, 2000), 99–132, which provides the testimony of a metallurgical worker in Lima of the 1970s and 1980s.

4. See, for example, Susan Besse, *Restructuring Patriarchy: The Moderniza-tion of Gender Inequality in Brazil, 1914–1940* (Chapel Hill: University of North Carolina Press, 1996).

5. See A. Kim Clark, *The Redemptive Work: Railway and Nation in Ecuador, 1895–1930* (Wilmington: Scholarly Resources, 1998); Ronn Pineo, *Social and Economic Reform in Ecuador: Life and Work in Guayaquil* (Gainesville: University Press of Florida, 1996); Erin O'Connor, "Manliness and Nation-Making: Indian Men and the Abolition of Tribute in Ecuador, 1830–1857," paper presented at annual conference of the Rocky Mountain Council for Latin American Studies, Tucson, Arizona, March 30, 2001.

6. David J. McCreery, *The Sweat of Their Brow: A History of Work in Latin America* (Armonk: M. E. Sharpe, 2000), 171. See also the pioneering volumes compiled by Steve Stein, *Lima obrera: 1900–1930*, 2 vols. (Lima: Ediciones El Virrey, 1986, 1987).

7. *New York Times*, April 29, 2001.

8. Testimony, as it appears in Baerga's article, usually is distinguished from the testimonial narrative. On the distinctions between testimonial narrative and oral literature, see John Beverley, "The Margin at the Center: On *Testimonio* (Testimonial Narrative)," in Sidonie Smith and Julia Watson, eds., *De-Colonizing the Subject: The Politics of Gender in Women's Autobiography* (Minneapolis: University of Minnesota Press, 1992), 91–114.

9. I refer to the following literature: Esteban Montejo and Miguel Barnet, ed., trans. Jocasta Innes, *Autobiography of a Runaway Slave* (New York: Vintage Books, 1973); Carolina María de Jesús, trans. David St. Clair, *Child of the Dark: The Diary of Carolina María de Jesús* (New York: Dutton, 1962); Rigoberta Menchú, ed. Elisabeth Burgos-Debray, trans. Ann Wright, *I, Rigoberta Menchú: An Indian Woman in Guatemala* (London: Verso, 1984); June Nash, ed., *I Spent My Life in the Mines: The Story of Juan Rojas, Bolivian Tin Miner* (New York: Columbia University Press, 1992); Domitila Barrios de Chungara with Moema Viezzer, trans. Victoria Ortiz, *Let Me Speak!: Testimony of Domitila, a Woman of the Bolivian Mines* (New York: Monthly Review Press, 1978); Ricardo Valderrama Fernández and Carmen Escalante Gutiérrez, eds., trans. Paul H. Gelles and Gabriela Martínez Escobar, *Andean Lives: Gregorio Condori Mamani and Asunta Quispe Huamán* (Austin: University of Texas Press, 1996); Daniel James, *Doña María's Story: Life History, Memory, and Political Identity* (Durham: Duke University Press, 2000); Parodi, *To Be a Worker*, 99–132; Diana Miloslavich, ed., *The Autobiography of María Elena Moyano: The Life and Death of a Peruvian Activist* (Gainesville: University Press of Florida, 2000); David Sowell, *The Tale of Healer Miguel Perdomo Neira: Medicine, Ideologies, and Power in the Nineteenth-Century Andes* (Wilmington: Scholarly Resources, 2001).

10. "Expanding exodus" was the headline for the article, *Washington Post*, November 30, 2000.

1

Immigration and Race in Cuba

Alejandro de la Fuente

Immigration was a central issue in Latin America at the turn of the twentieth century. The Cuban elite wanted to lead a society that was acceptable to their European and United States cohorts, and a population whose origins were largely African was far from meeting the standard of what constitutes a people worthy of respect in those terms. Cuba shunned its own people in favor of European, especially Spanish, workers who it hoped would stabilize society. But Spaniards came without families, and many who stayed drifted to the cities where they grabbed the most sought-after jobs. Cuba needed labor for its expanding sugar economy, and after the abolition of slavery in 1886 and the fervent participation of Afro-Cubans in the independence war, the elite could hardly dismiss them. Sugar growers put pressure on the state to allow more black workers to migrate from the Antilles to expand the labor force. Thus, in this selection, Alejandro de la Fuente identifies two problems, or "dangers": scarcity of labor, and a cultural disharmony between the Europe-loving upper classes and the workers of African origin. Could the Afro-Cubans be replaced? If so, how? Like their counterparts in other countries in the region (especially Brazil and Argentina), the Cuban landowners sought salvation from racial and cultural divisions in immigration. As De la Fuente makes clear, the Cuban experience shows that working-class society and labor organization took shape in the midst of growing racism and rearrangements of racial identity, and the labor movement arose in the midst of racist and nationalist ideologies that equated whiteness with progress and modernity.

In its morning edition of April 22, 1900, *Diario de la Marina* examined figures released from the 1899 census, noting what it considerd to be its most important feature: One-third of the Cuban population was colored. The columnist elaborated that this situation represented an obvious "danger" for "the white race" living in the island and claimed that the only way to avert a future catastrophe was to further stimulate white immigration to Cuba.[1]

If blacks were perceived as too numerous, workers were not. The other unpleasant fact unveiled by the 1899 census was that, also for the first time since the nineteenth century, the island's total population had declined. This came hardly as a surprise; most estimates considered that the population had declined to between one million and 1,200,000 people— below the official census figure of 1,572,797. Compared to the 1887 census, the net loss was put at some sixty thousand people, although U.S. census authorities believed that the actual figure was higher, surmising that the previous census had underestimated the total population.[2]

The war had also produced a population displacement which further increased the scarcity of labor. Several tens of thousands of members of the liberation army were located, by the end of the war, in areas different from their regions of origin, and without the resources to return to them. In this sense, the disbanding of the army was not only a political and military need, but also a labor question. As Robert Porter wrote, "the disposal of the insurgent troops is so intimately interwoven with the labour problem that it is difficult to separate the two."[3] The situation was not different among civilians, many of whom had found refuge in the cities during the war. Thus, urban unemployment and misery coexisted with the need for labor in other areas of the country. Even if willing to go, many urban residents just lacked the means to relocate to the areas where employment was available.[4]

Plantation owners and other employers bemoaned the disruption of the labor market and the "scarcity" of labor. Sugar interests voiced their concern that, should the situation persist, the crops of 1900 and 1901 would be seriously compromised, not the least because workers were "conscious of the advantages of their position" and determined to obtain higher salaries. Operating in a market with a limited labor supply, employers were unable to impose their own conditions and were forced to bargain with labor. They referred to the "demoralized" condition of workers, to their "exaggerated pretensions" concerning payment and, in the best slavery tradition, suggested that the reestablishment of forced labor was the only viable solution.[5]

Diario de la Marina then reported another "danger threatening Cuba" and insisted that the only way to avert it was by attracting a number of "white families" who would settle in the country and provide the manpower needed during the *zafra* (harvest). Thus white immigrants were seen as the solution to two separate but intimately linked "dangers": the black and labor dangers. Military Governor Leonard Wood summarized this view: "The solution of both the *social* and *economic* problems in the Island of Cuba depends principally on endowing it with a population of 8 or 10 millions of white inhabitants." Such endowment could only be achieved, as Wood himself recognized, by encouraging white immigration.[6]

Immigration to Cuba has been studied before, but less attention has been paid to its effects on native workers, particularly on Afro-Cuban workers.[7] Previous scholars have devoted attention to the immigrants' insertion in the Cuban labor market and society but have overlooked the fact that their success in doing so (in the case of Spaniards) was achieved, to some degree, at the expense of nationals, whose access to some of the best-paid jobs was severely limited. Of course, in a society that put a premium on whiteness, Afro-Cubans were those who lost the most in terms of employment opportunities and social advancement. The immigrants were entering a labor market in which race differences favoring white workers were large already.[8]

Furthermore, immigration was designed to lower salaries not only by increasing the labor supply but also—perhaps primarily—by creating a multiethnic and multinational labor force divided by linguistic, cultural, and national barriers.[9] Race operated along and was subsumed by these national and ethnic divisions, weakening considerably workers' bargaining capacity. That is, the immigrants' presence in the labor market was so prominent that it tended to obscure racial differences among Cuban workers. Instead, "race" was construed as a line separating native and foreign workers, rather than native workers of different racial background among themselves. Cuban historiography has acknowledged the existence of these divisions within the labor movement, but it has paid little attention to their concrete operation and effects and has frequently treated them as a natural outcome of a segmented labor market flooded with cheap immigrant labor.[10]

There is, however, nothing natural about such divisions. True, the existence of a labor force divided on multinational, ethnic, and racial lines created objective organizational problems, but this alone did not guarantee that workers would not unite for the defense of their common problems. Both employers and the Cuban state worked to deepen and reinforce the barriers that separated native and foreign workers, as well as those separating foreign workers of different origin among themselves. Employers promoted open hostility through a policy of ethnically based distribution of employment, promotion, and compensation, as well as by labor to break native workers' resistance—or vice versa. The Cuban state, in turn, reproduced these barriers through its migration policy by targeting "foreign agitators" for repression and through legal proposals designed to protect native workers in the distribution of employment, thus encouraging their animosity toward foreigners.

After briefly reviewing immigration trends, this paper evaluates the impact of these migration policies on the labor market and on workers' attempts to create a unified labor movement. To succeed, the labor movement first had to challenge the narrow nationalist discourse that divided native and foreign workers into two opposing factions, it had to forge a new, cross-national identity based on what they had in common: class. This paper also reexamines the much-argued relationship between race, class, and proletarianization in capitalist societies. The Cuban experience confirms what a number of scholars have recently argued when referring to other cases: Proletarianization coexisted with and in some instances reinforced racial and ethnic divisions and identities within the working class.[11] Not only did race remain a fundamental construct of Cuban society, but a racist ideology equating whiteness with progress and modernity remained equally central to the thinking of the political and economic elites alike. This, however, is just part of the story. At the same time, and despite enormous material and ideological odds, workers of different races and nationalities came together to oppose employers and the state, forging a genuinely cross-national and multiracial labor movement. In the process, a new sense of identity centered on class allegiances slowly emerged as one of the paradigms of Cuban society.

Immigration

Solutions for the two "dangers" mentioned above were only partially compatible, however. Although a steady flow of permanent white immigrants increased the labor supply and was therefore sympathetically viewed by the sugar interests and other employers, the latter were not eager to pay for the resettlement costs of potential immigrants. Nor was there any guarantee that immigrants would always seek employment when needed. Especially in the sugar sector, where labor demands were highly seasonal, the promotion of stable settlement was not, in purely economic terms, the most desirable solution. Companies would have to provide their workers with plots of land, therefore diminishing their own land reserves, and would be forced to supply housing and sanitary services to the workers' families. And there was little guarantee that at harvest time workers would abandon their plots to work for the company, especially for the low wages they offered. For these reasons it was cheaper to recruit temporary workers for the *zafra* and forgo responsibility for their maintenance during the remainder of the year.

Two alternative migration policies quickly emerged as possibilities. Bearing the black "danger" in mind, the Cuban state openly favored the "colonization" solution that advocated the immigration of stable European families to improve—that is, whiten—the composition of the native population. As in any other part of the Atlantic world, the migration policies of the Cuban state operated under the assumption that whiteness was a precondition for progress and were justified within an explicitly racist ideology which denigrated blackness as inferior, atavistic, and savage. But the results were disappointing. Although close to 800,000 entries from

Spain are reported by Cuban government sources between 1902 and 1931, this was not the family-based migration that Cuban authorities had encouraged. Rather, this was basically a movement of single young males who came to the island for several months to work in the sugar harvest. Gender ratios were usually higher than four men per woman, and more than eighty percent of all the immigrants were fourteen to forty-five years old.[12] In 1911, the secretary of agriculture recognized the failure of the colonization initiative and complained that "while large numbers of Spanish men came to Cuba for the winter . . . each year [during the harvest] it was very difficult to induce Spanish families to immigrate." He contended that to guarantee sugar production the introduction of contract labor—the so-called braceros—would have to be allowed.[13]

The free introduction of braceros is what sugar investors had been demanding since the days of the American Government of Occupation (1899–1902) through organizations such as the Círculo de Hacendados, Liga Agraria, and Fomento de la Inmigración. The sugar interests exercised enormous pressure on the Cuban state to liberalize and encourage the introduction of workers and to repeal all the legal obstacles that, following the U.S. immigration laws, prevented the importation of contract labor. By the mid-1910s, the expansion of sugar production had created a demand for labor that neither the colonization attempts undertaken by the Cuban government nor the annual immigration of seasonal workers from Spain and the Canary Islands could meet. The Cuban population had increased more than thirty percent during the first decade of the republic, but sugar production had multiplied sixfold during the same period, from some 300,000 tons in 1900 to more than 1,800,000 tons in 1910. Moreover, the expansion had taken place mainly in the eastern provinces of the island, where population densities were the lowest. Between 1901 and 1913 the proportion of sugar produced in Camagüey and Oriente had doubled from fifteen to thirty percent. In terms of laborers this meant that if the 1902 *zafra* had been made with 4,500 cane cutters, for 1913 some 21,000 would be needed.[14]

The other source of cheap seasonal labor in numbers large enough for the sugar harvest were the islands of the Caribbean. But these workers were black, so it was only reluctantly that Cuban authorities accepted the need to import nonwhite contract labor for the sugar industry. In 1900, the Cuba Company failed to obtain permission to introduce 4,000 Jamaicans for the construction of railway lines in the eastern part of the island.[15] President [Tomás] Estrada Palma (1902–1906) refused to authorize the United Fruit Company to contract Jamaicans for its plantations in Oriente. And in 1912, an authorization granting the Ponupo Manganese Company the right to import 2,000 laborers was later cancelled on the ground that it had not specified that the workers "were to be white."[16]

The perseverance and political influence of the sugar companies ultimately bore fruit, however. A presidential decree authorized the United
Fruit Company to introduce 1,000 West Indians in 1913, and four years
later—in response to the increased demand for sugar generated by World
War I and a conjunctural decline in Spanish immigration—the importation of Antillian workers was fully legalized. According to Cuban fiscal
sources, between 1917 and 1931 some 300,000 Haitians, Jamaicans, and
other workers from the Caribbean region entered the island to work in
sugar plantations. Although the companies were supposed to repatriate
workers after the end of the harvest, many stayed. The Cuban government
had sacrificed whitening to sugar production for, as a popular saying put
it, *sin azúcar no hay país* (without sugar there is no country). According
to the sugar barons, without West Indians there was no sugar.

The Labor Market

The sugar interests and foreign investors succeeded not only in opening
the country's doors to the immigration of contract labor; they also managed to control a growing share of productive lands and other resources.
About sixty percent of arable rural property came to be owned by foreign
companies by 1910. They owned nothing less than fifteen to twenty percent of the national territory by the mid-1920s.[17] This process affected all
Cubans, but it was particularly harmful for Afro-Cubans. Between 1899
and 1931, blacks' control over land decreased by fifty percent both in
terms of number of farms (from twenty-five to twelve percent) and total
farm land (from sixteen to eight percent). By 1931 people labeled as
"black" (including mulattoes) represented about twenty-eight percent of
the Cuban population, but they controlled only 8.5 percent of the farm-
land in the country. As Ramiro Guerra, a well-known white intellectual,
stated in 1929, Afro-Cubans had been "the first victims" of sugar
latifundia.[18]

Proletarianization was just the beginning. Even as proletarians, employment opportunities were restricted in the Cuban countryside for Afro-
Cubans. It was estimated that blacks represented about fifty percent of
the labor force in the sugar plantations by 1899, but employers frequently
asserted that they were almost useless for any productive activity except
cane cutting. "Only in the cutting of cane can the Cuban, and especially
the Cuban negro, be said to excel. This work he understands and finds
congenial." Another observer concurred: "Admittedly the black does not
do well at fruit-raising, and the intricacy of tobacco cultivation is too
great for him to become a successful veguero, or tobacco farmer. In the
cane fields he is at his best as a laborer."[19] After the 1910s employment
opportunities were restricted even in cane cutting due to the massive importation of workers from the Caribbean.

The situation was no better in the cities. Afro-Cubans had to compete for available positions not only with white Cubans, but also with a large contingent of European (mostly Spanish) immigrants—most of whom, to the dismay of the sugar planters, stayed in Havana and other major urban centers. As black intellectual Benjamin Muñoz Ginarte put it, Afro-Cubans were caught "between two great evils: foreigners in the cities and foreigners in the countryside."[20]

White immigrants were indeed well represented in the urban occupational structure. This was due first of all to their concentration in productive age cohorts and the large proportion of men among them: Between 1899 and 1919 the rates of economic activity for this segment of the population were about double those of the general population. But even within the employed population, Spaniards and other white immigrants were disproportionately represented. In the 1907–1919 period they made up fifteen percent of the working-age population but controlled twenty-one percent of the available jobs, and their share was even higher in the urban occupations.

Some economic sectors, such as trade and transportation, were foreign owned and work within them was limited for native workers—especially for Afro-Cubans. Indeed, Spaniards' indices of representation in this economic sector were the highest in the whole occupational structure. Fifty-four percent of all merchants were foreigners (mostly Spaniards) in 1899. This proportion had declined by 1931 to forty-three percent, but this was still well above their representation in the population. Spaniards controlled, for instance, fifty-nine percent of the wholesale trade in the province of Las Villas in the late 1930s and some sixty percent of all mercantile establishments in the city of Matanzas.[21] Conversely, Afro-Cubans were vastly underrepresented in wholesale and retail trades, although their proportional participation more than doubled between 1899 and 1931. Not surprisingly, the first issue addressed by Afro-Cuban journalist Gustavo Urrutia in his influential column *Ideales de una raza* was the "participation of blacks in commerce." Nor is it coincidental that he asked foreign merchants to hire Afro-Cubans for their stores and other establishments.[22]

Transportation, which included urban tramways and the extensive railroad network that covered the island, shared with commerce a major trait: a massive foreign presence. Alberto Arredondo, a black writer and politician, estimated that more than eighty percent of the railways were controlled by foreign capital, and immigrant workers were vastly overrepresented in their labor force. Blacks found it hard to secure some better-paid positions, such as that of locomotive engineer, because unions exercised tight control over the system of promotion. In fact the first black to win this job, in 1901, owed his success to a conflict between the company and the engineers' union.[23] "Those familiar with the labor movement in

Cuba know that a member of the colored race cannot be a conductor in the railways," Communist leader César Vilar asserted as late as 1940. Access to white-collar positions within the sector was even more difficult: All office work was performed by white workers. Nicolás Guillén, the great mulatto poet and writer, recounted how in the 1920s he had tried to obtain a "modest position" in the offices of the railroad in Camagüey with no success: "that company has many black employees, but only in the mechanical shops."[24]

On the urban side, the American-owned tramway companies controlled ninety-eight percent of the market (by number of passengers carried) and generated ninety-seven percent of the jobs in the sector. That they discriminated against native workers is clearly suggested by the fact that only forty-four percent of their total labor force was native compared to eighty-nine percent in the small Cuban-owned companies. This under-representation was true not only in the higher echelons of the company, where only thirty-two percent of the employees were Cubans, but also at the lower end: Native workers represented a meager thirty-four percent of the craftsmen and laborers employed by Havana Electric and other American companies.[25]

Competition for employment opportunities occurred also in more massive and less attractive sectors of the urban labor market. Blacks represented, for instance, a sizable and growing proportion of the labor force employed in the tobacco industry, but they were at a disadvantage for at least two reasons. First, their presence was much more prominent in cigar than in cigarette factories, where salaries were, on average, thirty percent higher. Second, even within the cigar industry Afro-Cubans were concentrated in the worst-paid and least attractive positions. In the mid-1920s they formed thirty percent of the labor force employed in cigar factories, where the average yearly salary was 714 pesos, but only four percent of those producing cigarettes, whose average salary was 935 pesos. Not surprisingly, the distribution of Spanish immigrant workers was exactly the opposite: They made up only ten percent of the cigar workers and nineteen percent of the cigarette workers. Within cigar production Afro-Cubans made up one-third of the worst-paid cigar-makers, but were considerably under-represented among salesmen, clerks, drivers, and other employees; foreigners occupied fifty-two percent of these positions.[26]

This was also true in other areas of production where the foreign presence was prominent. Immigrant workers represented an already high thirty percent of the labor force employed in the alcohol distilleries, but their share of the better-paid positions was much higher. Fifty percent of the technicians, forty percent of the factories' directors, thirty-nine percent of the managers, forty-three percent of the chemists, and forty-two percent of office workers were foreign. Conversely, their proportion in activities such as packing (twenty-three percent) or the unskilled labor force (twenty-five percent) was much lower. Even in the province of Oriente, where they represented only eleven percent of the total labor force in the distilleries, sixty percent of the technicians, fifty percent of the chemists, forty-two percent of the directors, and twenty-seven percent of the managers were foreign.[27]

No wonder Afro-Cubans identified Spaniards as one of the leading causes of their displacement from attractive jobs. A young Afro-Cuban who went to Havana to study in 1916 commented that it was extremely difficult to find a job in any trade because the shops were full of white workers, "most of them from other lands." "Formerly, mason and cigar-maker were synonyms for Cuban. Not today; most construction in Havana is done by Catalan masons and . . . large numbers of Spaniards work in the tobacco factories." The Afro-Cuban journal *Labor Nueva* was categorical: Spanish immigration was harmful not only to blacks, but to all native workers.[28]

In a sense, the journal was right. The indices of dissimilarity in the distribution of blacks and native and foreign whites in the occupational structure were *always* lower among black and white native workers than between natives (of any color) and foreign workers.[29] In other words, differences between native and foreign workers were consistently greater than between white and black Cubans (see table below). It was no accident that plantation owner Edwin Atkins grouped the Cienfuegos dockworkers into two different categories: Spanish lightermen, on the one hand, and "negroes and Cubans," on the other.[30] Atkins identified racial differences among Cubans, but he still saw them as belonging to the same group, at least compared to the white immigrant workers.

Index of Dissimilarity in Occupations, by Race and Nativity, Cuba, 1899–1931

	1899	1907	1919	1931
Native/foreign whites	31.1	27.4	22.8	25.5
Blacks/foreign whites	35.4	34.8	24.8	23.5
Blacks/native whites	20.2	25.2	17.6	9.8

Sources: War Department, Office Director Census of Cuba, *Report on the Census of Cuba, 1899* (Washington, 1900), 438–39, 462; Cuba, *Censo de la República de Cuba bajo la administración provisional de los Estados Unidos, 1907* (Washington, 1908), 514–15, 545–46; Cuba, *Censo de la República de Cuba, año de 1919* (Havana, 1920), 632–33; *Censo de 1931* (Havana, 1938?), tables 16, 21, 24.

The Labor Movement

Atkins's distinction is telling for another reason. "Negroes and Cubans" had traditionally participated together in labor organizations. More often than not, cross-racial alliances characterized the labor movement, and abundant evidence shows that, although some of the old trade guilds were racially segregated, the composition and leadership of most unions was racially mixed.[31] Since 1892, an anarchist-led Labor Congress had held unequivocally that black and white workers shared "the slavery of the shop" and that it would be "stupid and ridiculous" for workers to share the racial prejudices of the "masters," thus condemning any manifestation of racial discrimination within labor organizations and the workplace. In 1903 the Círculo Obrero of Santiago de Cuba criticized a speaker who brought the "racial element" into a discussion of whether workers should participate in politics. "When we refer to workers," one critic noted, "both races are included. He [the speaker] should have said 'Cuban worker.' " The anarchists also criticized any effort to draw black workers into racially separate organizations.[32]

Especially in those sectors in which black workers were well represented, Afro-Cubans frequently held positions of leadership in the unions. Between 1900 and 1933, the presidency of the Stevedores Union of Santiago was occupied by eight blacks and five whites. Around 1910, ninety percent of all the affiliates of the stevedores *gremio* (brotherhood) of Cienfuegos were classified as either "negro" or "mestizo." Among 152 identified delegates to the Labor Congress of 1914, forty-five percent were blacks. Afro-Cubans represented forty-three percent of the Havana delegation, sixty-five percent of that of Las Villas, and eighty-seven percent of the delegates from Oriente. The only female delegate, Maria P. Garbey from Oriente, was black. Of the nine members of the organizing commission, three were nonwhite, including its president, Pedro Roca e Ibarra, a mulatto.[33] One of the main orators in the congress celebrated by the anarchists in Cruces in 1912 was Gregorio Campos, a black labor leader. Even in those sectors to which they had limited access, such as transportation, blacks were not barred from union leadership positions. For instance, the leader of a railway strike in Camagüey in 1919 was Gustavo Vargas Soler, a "full blooded negro" who was also the treasurer of the Railway Company Union.[34]

Cross-racial solidarity in organized labor was also evident elsewhere. Frequently, workers used the facilities of colored societies for their meetings and activities. The Gremio General de Braceros of Lajas (Las Villas) gathered at the Centro Africano, a mutual aid society of former slaves from the region. In Havana, the organization Obreros de la Patria gathered on the premises of the colored society Maine. And the Third Labor Congress, celebrated in Camagüey in 1925, took place in the black club Victoria.[35] When in 1920 the leadership of the Federation of Tobacco Workers gave recognition to a society of cigar-makers in Tampa allied to the American Federation of Labor, opposition arose on the grounds that blacks were not allowed to enter the organization. In the same vein, the Labor Congress of 1920 refused to send delegates to the Pan American

Federation of Labor because "in [Samuel] Gompers's federation our black comrades are rejected, only because they have a skin of a different color." Even during the wave of racist repression that swept the country during the so-called "race war" of 1912, the stevedores in Havana threatened to strike against the American shipping companies because they opposed hiring black workers.[36]

That unions and the labor movement were largely cross-racial is also demonstrated in employers' and officials' statements. Despite the pervasiveness of race in the dominant ideology and its frequent association with turmoil and disorder, employers only rarely presented labor conflicts in racial terms. A striking force of tobacco workers in Remedios (Las Villas) in 1900, for instance, was initially referred to as "a group of 50 colored men," but the incident was subsequently described as "a strike of the tobacco *escogedores*," without any reference to race. Even the U.S. vice consul in Antilla, who remarked that labor troubles in the area "might be classed as 'race agitation' because . . . only one or two white men ha[d] attended the [stevedores'] meetings," implicitly acknowledged that this view did not enjoy much currency.[37]

This does not mean that race was a nonissue in the labor movement, however. Rather, race operated along national and ethnic lines, considerably weakening workers' bargaining capacity. Given that differences based on nationality were indeed larger in the labor market than those dividing white and black native workers, this is hardly surprising. Thus, when an American labor analyst reported in 1902 that tobacco workers were divided in two unions, one for Spaniards and one for Cubans, he referred to this division as "an element of *race antagonism* among the cigar operatives."[38]

Not coincidentally, it was in the tobacco sector where competition for jobs exploded in a massive strike of native workers immediately after the establishment of the Cuban Republic. In November 1902, strikes at twelve cigar factories of the Havana Commercial Company paralyzed their activities; these were soon joined by workers in other factories and sectors. Their main demand was securing Cubans' (especially native children's) access to the tobacco trades; it is therefore remembered as "the apprentices' strike." In a letter to President Estrada Palma, the president of the Liga General de Trabajadores Cubanos explained that workers opposed "the odious privileges in the distribution of jobs" which gave preference to Spaniards, while native artisans and laborers had to emigrate to make a living. More specifically, the strikers and the Liga denounced the fact that Cuban children were "denied the right to learn a trade" and demanded their free entrance into all industries "without distinction of race."[39]

Divisions between Cuban and Spanish workers permeated the labor movement through the 1920s. In 1909, socialist activist Carlos Baliño withdrew from the Partido Socialista de Cuba, led by Spanish socialists, because of their disregard for native workers' rightful struggle for employment opportunities. "There are guilds," Baliño denounced, "where work is so monopolized by Spanish workers that few white Cubans work in the trade, and *not one black*."[40] Divisions arose again in 1911, when several organizations did not support the strike of the workers employed in the construction of Havana's sewer system, where about seventy-five percent of the labor force was foreign. The Socialists, who organized and led the strike, resented the lack of support among Cuban laborers, claiming that their party was opposed to any privilege favoring Spaniards and that one of their main leaders had even rejected dealing with contractors who did not admit the employment of black masons.[41] Some unions, such as the Association of Naval Machinists of Cuba affiliated to the reformist Federación Cubana del Trabajo, remained segregated along ethnic and national lines as late as 1931. Meanwhile, competition for jobs and resources grew parallel to the economic crisis that afflicted the island from the mid-1920s on.[42]

Employers manipulated these divisions to their advantage. Immigrant strikebreakers were used to weaken workers' resistance, and ethnically diverse work forces were hired, and at times isolated, to minimize their capacity to organize. The foreign strikebreaker solution was applied most frequently in those sectors related to the all-important sugar industry: waterfront activities, railroad transportation, and of course sugar production itself. In the case of harbor strikes, American and British shipping companies imported their own laborers, sometimes disguised as crew members; or turned tasks over to Antillians or newly arrived immigrants with no occupation. Three hundred American stevedores were imported, for instance, when a strike developed in Havana's harbor in 1904; more were contracted in 1906 and 1912. After the 1910s, Antillians were clearly preferred. Sixty-five Jamaicans were dispatched to break a stevedores' strike in the western port of Cabanas in 1921, and United Fruit used Jamaicans to counteract native workers' demands for higher salaries.[43]

The employers' view concerning the convenience of having a labor force divided along national and ethnic lines was summarized by a superintendent of the Jatibonico sugarmill: "Owing to the trouble last year . . . we have decided to contract this work with Chinese, and at the same time to house them in the batey [mill town] separate from all other labor. Chinese . . . should put an end to strikes in this department . . . which have been taking place for the last three years."[44]

When social turmoil spread throughout the eastern rural areas due to the Liberal revolt in 1917, a report from the Francisco sugarmill noted that while Cuban workers had used the opportunity to "leave the cane fields," the mill was kept in operation with Antillians: "Our salvation in the matter of cane supply has been the Haitians and Jamaicans. They are all scared." Sugar companies also used West Indians as strikebreakers and to evict native workers attempting to squat in their lands.[45]

If qualified workers were not available to substitute for strikers, they were imported. In 1916, the Cuba Railroad Company responded to a strike freezing all traffic in the crucial sugar region east of Camagüey with a request to their New York office: "Engineers joining the strike. Please get one of the organizations in the United States which make it a business to break strikes to send thirty engineers with their firemen." Fifty-six additional men were also hired in the United States to replace striking mechanics, machinists, carpenters, and car repairers. Ten days later the strike had been brought to an end. On another occasion, the manager of the company brought workers from Mexico to replace those he deemed troublemakers.[46]

These divisionist tactics encouraged hostility among workers of different origins, which occasionally erupted into open violence. In 1916, the Cuban and Haitian cane cutters of the Cuba Company's Jatibonico sugarmill clashed over salaries due to the Haitians' acceptance of wages twenty percent below those demanded by natives. "[T]he Cubans attempted by force to prevent the Haitians from cutting," reported a manager at the mill. A similar conflict was "narrowly averted" in 1922 in an Atlantic Fruit Company mill. Two years later, a full riot leaving one Haitian dead occurred in the town of Sagua de Tánamo (Oriente) when Spanish and Haitian workers battled over limited employment opportunities and salaries. Troubles between Cubans and Spaniards developed also among the Havana dockworkers in 1917, and the native stevedores in Antilla went on strike in 1922 under the leadership of black local leader Antonio Fernández with the motto "Cuba for the Cubans."[47]

To no small degree, employers had succeeded in fragmenting the labor movement along national lines, but instances of cross-national and multiracial cooperation were not uncommon. An early example which is particularly telling was the "apprentices' strike" of 1902 discussed above. Despite the fact that the strikers' main goal was to open opportunities for native children and adults in the tobacco trades and other industries, the movement elicited support among both native workers (both black and white) and foreign workers in other sectors. In the sugar region of Cruces, Spanish anarchists cooperated with Cubans in support of the strike. "We do not ask anyone about his origin, that is, where was he born," Evaristo Landa, a local native mulatto leader, asserted. A Spanish anarchist from the region lamented the fact that cigar-makers of different nationalities were divided in Havana, claiming that in Las Villas they enjoyed "union and solidarity" and that their only goal was "the emancipation of all slaves."[48]

Cooperation between Spanish anarchists and native workers seems to have been common, in keeping with the anarchists' doctrine that workers had no nationality. "The real fatherland," a labor leader from the bakery trades wrote in 1919, "is the perfect union of all workers, without distinctions of race and nationalities." In 1909, the anarchist newspaper *¡Tierra!* responded to the charge that foreigners came to the island to promote labor disturbances with the claim that "workers could not be foreign in any place." Even in those instances in which conflicts and divisions arose, workers' efforts to create unified unions are conspicuous. In a meeting of the cigar-makers, for instance, a Cuban worker accused Spanish anarchists of having sided with the colonial government during the war of independence, but the fact remains that they were all attending the same meeting, that of a cross-national union.[49] As for the Socialists, not only did they claim to be opposed to any national or racial privilege in the distribution of employment, but the group was in fact both multiracial and cross-national. Among the members of the Agrupación Socialista de la Habana listed in a 1911 confidential report, there were eight Cubans, two of them described as "mulattoes," and eleven Spaniards, including people from Galicia, Andalucía, Asturias, Cataluña, and the Canary Islands.[50]

Since Spanish workers were prominently represented in all sectors of the Cuban labor market, any significant strike that developed in the island was almost by definition a multinational event. In the sugar strikes of 1917, not only Cubans and Spaniards but West Indian workers participated. Although the strike started in Las Villas among the sugarmill mechanics, many of whom were white and foreign, they drew support from sectors in which natives and blacks were well represented. In Cienfuegos, the coachmen and chauffeurs paralyzed all traffic and substituted the Spanish leader of their union for a native to avoid the deportation of the former. In several sugarmills, the strike involved occupations in which natives (including blacks) were better represented: "laborers" (*peones, jornaleros*), masons, and carpenters. A report from the Narcisa sugarmill asserted that the strike there had been promoted by "a white and a mestizo" who had come from Cienfuegos. One of the leaders of the whole movement was Vicente Martínez, a Spanish anarchist; another, according to U.S. authorities, was "one William Benjamin, a negro, who is believed to be from Barbados." In Camagüey, several Cuban and Spanish workers were detained, whereas in Havana three Spanish leaders of the anarchist Unión Internacional de Dependientes de Café were prosecuted for deportation.[51]

A "general" strike in March 1919, involving railway workers, public automobiles, waterfront activities, cooks, waiters, cigar-makers, and the building trades, was again a cross-racial and cross-national phenomenon. Out of twenty-five individuals identified by the secret police as leaders of the movement, fourteen were Spaniards and eleven, including blacks such as a tobacco workers' leader, were Cubans. In 1924 sugar strikes hit eastern Cuba and were saluted by the Havana Labor Federation, which declared that workers' interests, "no matter what their nationality," should be "guarded."[52]

It is possible to record instances of West Indian participation in these cross-national efforts of labor mobilization, despite their cultural and linguistic isolation and the seasonal character of this labor force. The case of the Barbadian activist mentioned above is far from exceptional. In 1917, the employees of the Cuba Company in Jobabo, Camagüey, reported that "many Spanish workmen of the central [mill]" had joined with natives and "even the Jamaican negroes" to take advantage of the chaos created by the Liberal revolt and rob, "like a flock of savages," the sugarmill store. Interestingly enough, this cross-racial, cross-national "mob" had conducted its "outrageous looting" while shouting, "Take everything. That which is in Cuba belongs to the Cubans." In their stance against the American company, all workers, regardless of race and nationality, characterized themselves as "Cubans."[53]

West Indians were represented in both the Second and Third Labor Congresses, which took place in 1925, and one of their leaders, Henry Shackleton (a Jamaican), participated in the commission that drafted the charter of the Confederación Nacional de Obreros de Cuba (CNOC). Both events condemned the treatment and exploitation of Antillians and agreed to address immigrant laborers in their countries of origin to tell them the truth about working conditions on the island. Although it is clear that workers wanted to stop immigration, their emphasis was on the "exploiters" who imported the West Indians, rather than on the immigrants themselves, who were referred to as "comrades."[54]

While the reformist sector of the labor movement responded to the deterioration of the economy in the late 1920s and early 1930s with demands to stop all immigration, and "yellow" unions requested the repatriation of Antillians and unemployed foreign workers, the radical wing of organized labor, notably the Communist-controlled CNOC and the Federación Obrera de la Habana, reacted by stressing the need for all workers to unite, regardless of race and national origin. The Communists and their allies understood that to create a truly national labor organization it was absolutely necessary to organize sugar field workers, many of whom were Haitians and Jamaicans. But to forge such an alliance in the midst of an economic depression was a challenge indeed: They had to transcend the narrow nationalism which encouraged blaming immigrants for widespread unemployment and other economic problems.

The Federación Obrera de la Habana opposed the divisionist tactics of the Cuban government, which presented labor conflicts as an imported evil that should be eliminated through the deportation of foreign labor activists. In a 1925 manifesto, the Federación Obrera de la Habana denounced the official campaign depicting foreigners as "monsters who must be exterminated" and native workers as "insensitive slaves" who would be almost grateful for their condition if it was not for the pernicious influence of the immigrants. "Among workers there are no distinctions," they declared, "because they know as a fact what that means." Meanwhile, the Communist-linked Liga Antimperialista advanced a contrasting notion of workers' nationalism: "Cuba must be for the Cubans. This does not mean hatred for the *foreigner*; it means hatred for *foreign capital*."[55] In 1929, the "revindication program" of the Confederación Nacional de Obreros de Cuba included the equality of all workers regardless of race and nationality among its goals, whereas the 1932 political platform of the Communist party devoted a whole section to the issue. The Communists denounced the exploitation and mistreatment of West Indians, the deportation of Spaniards, the discrimination against Chinese, and the persecutions of the so-called "Polish"—Jews and Eastern Europeans established on the island.[56]

At least to a degree, the Communists' efforts to create a multiracial and multinational movement based on class identities were successful. Spanish workers were drawn together with natives into Communist-organized mass demonstrations and "hunger marches." In one such incident in Santiago, "an unidentified Cuban negro" waving a red flag mobilized "a group of unemployed Spaniards" until the police intervened, wounding several of them.[57] West Indians were also attracted by the party's propaganda, and some of the first Jamaican Marxists confronted this ideology while working in Cuba. The longshoremen's union at Nuevitas included Cubans as well as Haitians and Jamaicans, some of whom had become Cuban citizens. The U.S. consul in the area reported in 1931 that "a spirit of unrest was prevalent among them," even though they had been previously apathetic to labor mobilization. Antillian dockworkers also joined natives in a strike at the port of Alto Cedro, Ciego de Avila (Camagüey), according to the testimony of one of the participants.[58]

It was in the sugar sector, however, that the Communists' mobilization efforts proved to be most successful in the long run. In 1932 they organized the Sindicato Nacional de Obreros de la Industria Azucarera, which led some of the most important strikes after the fall of President Gerardo Machado (1925–1933) with the cooperation of native and West Indian workers. As a U.S. observer noted, the Communists successfully mobilized black workers in the sugarmills, regardless of national origin. "The Cuban negro came into close contact with the Haitian negro, converted into a slave working for 10 or 12 cents a day. . . . In some cases the Haitian negro seconded the Cuban negro, forming part of red syndicates." In September 1933, a group of Americans traveling by train to the Miranda sugarmill in Oriente was forced to obtain a pass from a Jamaican worker who signed himself as "corporal of the Red Guard." Thus, Communist leader Rubén Martínez Villena asserted with satisfaction that "a perfect union between white and black workers" had been achieved during the strikes and that the theories blaming the Antillians for the situation of sugar workers had been "discredited again with the active participation of these foreign workers in the common struggle."[59]

Conclusions

The Communists' success in organizing a cross-racial, multinational labor movement largely explains why they became a crucial actor in Cuban politics after the fall of Gerardo Machado's dictatorship in 1933. Furthermore, since the reformist sector of the labor movement had been encouraged and supported by Machado, his fall seriously compromised the viability of reformism, opening the doors for a radical independent labor movement to consolidate its position.

That workers had been able to organize cross-racial and multinational unions in Cuba is nothing short of remarkable. No other country in Latin America had received so many immigrants of different ethnic and geographical origin at the same time. In fact, employers had been so successful in fragmenting the labor market along ethnic lines that differences in the distribution of employment between Cubans and immigrants were consistently higher than among natives of different racial background. Furthermore, employers and the Cuban state had systematically portrayed labor agitation as an imported evil and blamed immigrants for the destitution of Cuban workers.

The emergence of unified labor organizations against these material and ideological odds shows that workers actively resisted the divisionist tactics used by employers and the Cuban state to fragment the labor movement along national lines. Labor unions tended to treat racial and national divisions among workers as employers' strategies. In response, they articulated a notion of nonracialized class identity that tended to underscore the commonality of their grievances and social position.

This was part of a broader process: the emergence of class as the most important point of reference in Cuban politics. After the 1930s, politicians and intellectuals of all colors and ideological creeds tended to agree that domestic conflicts and dynamics were to be understood in class rather than racial terms. Not only a black Communist such as A. Pérez-Medina would assert that "the struggle [was] not one of races but of classes." Similar claims were also made by white and black moderate intellectuals. "In Cuba the racial question is subordinated to the intellectual and economic question," commented a white journalist. Even Afro-Cuban journalist Ramón Vasconcelos, who had headed a daily column devoted to black issues in his youth, subscribed to this view by 1937, stressing that "class consciousness" had become stronger than race identities among blacks.[60]

Ultimately, the public and private elites had failed to avert the "two dangers" that had driven their migration policies. Neither was Cuba white, nor had workers become acquiescent and unpretentious. Quite the contrary, they had identified the essential similarity of their positions in society and had mobilized accordingly to write a new chapter in Cuban history.

Notes

This paper is largely drawn from my Ph.D. dissertation, " 'With All And For All': Race, Inequality, and Politics in Cuba, 1900–1930" (University of Pittsburgh, 1996). The following archival collections are cited:

United States National Archives, Washington, DC (hereafter USNA), including documents from the following collections: Foreign Service Post Records, Record Group 84 (hereafter RG 84); General Records of the Department of State, Record Group 59 (hereafter RG 59); and Records of the War Department, Record Group 165 (hereafter RG 165).

University of Florida, Latin American Library: Braga Brothers Collection (hereafter BBC).

University of Maryland, College Park, McKeldin Library: Cuba Company Papers (hereafter CCP).

1. "El censo," *Diario de la Marina*, April 22, 1900 (morning ed.).

2. Robert P. Porter, *Industrial Cuba* (New York, 1899), 92, 105; Edwin F. Atkins, *Sixty Years in Cuba* (Cambridge, 1926), 306; War Department, Office Director Census of Cuba, *Report on the Census of Cuba, 1899* (Washington, 1900), 77. For modern estimates about the demographic loss caused by the war, see Juan Pérez de la Riva, "Los recursos humanos de Cuba al comenzar el siglo: inmigración, economía y nacionalidad (1899–1906)," *Anuario de Estudios Cubanos* 1 (1975): 7–44; Pérez de la Riva and Blanca Morejón Seijas, "Demografía histórica: la población de Cuba, la guerra de independencia y la inmigración del siglo XX," *Revista de la Biblioteca Nacional José Martí* 13 (1971): 17–27.

3. Porter, *Industrial Cuba*, 88–89. About the disbanding of the Liberation Army, see Louis A. Pérez, Jr., *Lords of the Mountain: Social Banditry and Peasant Protest in Cuba, 1878–1918* (Pittsburgh, 1989), 63–66.

4. "Faltan brazos," *Diario de la Marina*, February 10, 1900 (morning ed.); "Lo que mas importa," *Diario de la Marina*, September 15, 1900 (morning ed.); Porter, *Industrial Cuba*, 86–87.

5. Atkins, *Sixty Years in Cuba*, 306; "Escasez de trabajadores," *Diario de la Marina*, June 19, 1900 (evening ed.); "Invitación," *La Union Española*, February 8, 1900 (evening ed.); "Escasez de braceros," *Diario de la Marina*, January 1, 1901 (morning ed.); "Faltan brazos," *Diario de la Marina*, February 10, 1900 (morning ed.).

6. "Escasez de braceros," *Diario de la Marina*, January 1, 1901 (morning ed.); Cuba, *Military Governor, Civil Report of the Military Governor, 1901*, 15 vols. (Havana, 1902), 5:75.

7. For overviews on immigration to Cuba, see Jordi Maluquer de Motes, *Nación e inmigración: los españoles en Cuba (ss. XIX y XX)* (Barcelona, 1992); Consuelo Naranjo Orovio, "Trabajo libre e inmigración española en Cuba: 1880–1930," *Revista de Indias* 52 (1992): 749–94; Fe Iglesias, "Características de la inmigración española en Cuba, 1904–1930," in *Españoles hacia América. La emigración en masa, 1880–1930*, ed. Nicolás Sánchez-Albornoz (Madrid, 1988), 270–95;

Rolando Alvarez Estévez, *Azúcar e inmigración, 1900–1940* (Havana, 1988); Pérez de la Riva, "Cuba y la migración antillana, 1900–1931," *Anuario de Estudios Cubanos* 2 (1979): 3–75.

8. For an example asserting the "favorable" effects of Spanish immigration, see Maluquer de Motes, "La inmigración española en Cuba: elementos de un debate histórico," in *Cuba, la perla de las Antillas*, ed. Consuelo Naranjo Orovio and Tomás Mallo Gutiérrez (Aranjuez, 1994), 137–47.

9. Charles Bergquist, *Labor in Latin America: Comparative Essays on Chile, Argentina, Venezuela and Colombia* (Stanford, 1986); Julio Godio, *Historia del movimiento obrero latinoamericano* (Buenos Aires, 1979), 47–50.

10. For examples, see Olga Cabrera, *El movimiento obrero cubano en 1920* (Havana, 1969), 37; Instituto de Historia del Movimiento Comunista y de la Revolución Socialista de Cuba, *Historia del movimiento obrero cubano, 1865–1958*, 2 vols. (Havana, 1985), 1:179–80; Efrén Córdova, *Clase trabajadora y movimiento sindical en Cuba 1 (1819–1959)* (Miami, 1995), 91–100. For an example in which these divisions are largely ignored, see Aleida Plasencia Moro, "Historia del movimiento obrero en Cuba," in *Historia del movimiento obrero en América Latina*, 4 vols., ed. Pablo González Casanova (Mexico City, 1984), 1:88–183.

11. For scholarship critical of this idea, see Stanley Greenberg, *Race and State in Capitalist Development: Comparative Perspectives* (New Haven, 1980); George Reid Andrews, *Blacks and Whites in São Paulo, Brazil, 1888–1988* (Madison, 1991); Carlos Hasenbalg, *Discriminação e desigualdades raciais no Brasil* (Rio de Janeiro, 1979); see also George Reid Andrews, "Black Workers in the Export Years: Latin America, 1880–1930," *International Labor and Working-Class History* 51 (1997): 7–29.

12. For a full discussion of these figures, see de la Fuente, " 'With All And For All,' " 58–59.

13. Jackson to the Secretary of State, Havana, January 16 and June 27, 1911, USNA, RG 59/837.55/15 and 18.

14. For sugar production data and the proportion of eastern provinces in the national output, see Ramiro Guerra, *Azúcar y población en las Antillas* (Havana, 1970), 227–30; César Ayala, "Social and Economic Aspects of Sugar Production in Cuba, 1880–1930," *Latin American Research Review* 30 (1995): 95–124; and Alan Dye, "Avoiding Holdup: Asset Specificity and Technical Change in the Cuban Sugar Industry, 1899–1929," *Journal of Economic History* 54 (1994): 628–53. See also de la Riva, "Cuba y la migración antillana," 3–75, esp. 23–27.

15. "La inmigración jamaiquina," *Diario de la Marina*, July 24, 1900 (evening ed.). The Cuba Company denied that it was attempting to introduce Jamaicans: see Charles A. Gauld, *The Last Titan: Percival Farquhar, American Entrepreneur in Latin America* (Stanford, 1964), 44.

16. *United Fruit Company: un caso del dominio imperialista en Cuba* (Havana, 1976), 208–10; Unknown to Craib, no place, September 26, 1913, CCP, Series I, Box 9, 142; Hugh Gibson to the secretary of state, Havana, September 18, 1912, USNA, RG 59/837.55/19. About the Ponupo Manganese Company, see Fe Iglesias, "La explotación del hierro en el sur de Oriente y la Spanish American Iron Company," *Santiago* 17 (March 1975): 59–106.

17. Louis A. Perez, Jr., *Cuba under the Platt Amendment, 1902–1934* (Pittsburgh, 1986); Carlos M. Trelles, "La hacienda y el desarrollo económico de la República de Cuba," *Revista Bimestre Cubana* 22 (1927): 323–42.

18. Ramiro Guerra, "Como nos ven. Nuevas y fecundas orientaciones," *Diario de la Marina*, January 13, 1929.

19. Forbes Lindsay and Nevin O. Winter, *Cuba and Her People of To-Day* (Boston, 1928), 135; Charles M. Pepper, *To-Morrow in Cuba* (New York, 1899), 150.

20. Benjamin Muñoz Ginarte, "Comentos sin comentarios. Al doctor Ramiro Guerra," *Diario de la Marina*, February 10, 1929.

21. Vogenitz to Wright, Cienfuegos, October 18, 1939, USNA, RG 84/800/34; Milton Patterson Thompson, "Cuban Immigration Problems," Matanzas, October 9, 1936, USNA, RG 84/855. For an overview of Spaniards' presence in the commercial sector in Cuba, see Alejandro García Alvarez, *La gran burguesía comercial en Cuba, 1899–1920* (Havana, 1990), 91–104; Naranjo Orovio, "Análisis histórico de la emigración española a Cuba, 1900–1959," *Revista de Indias* 174 (1984): 503–26.

22. Gustavo Urrutia, "Ideales de una raza. La defensa," *Diario de la Marina*, April 22, 1928; Urrutia, "Ideales de una raza. La cuestión económica del negro," *Diario de la Marina*, July 17,1929.

23. Alberto Arredondo, *El negro en Cuba* (Havana, 1939), 57; Foreign Policy Association, *Problems of the New Cuba* (Havana, 1935), 475–76; Victor S. Clark, "Labor Conditions in Cuba," *Bulletin of the Department of Labor* 41 (1902): 663–793.

24. Andres M. Lazcano y Mazón, *Constitución de Cuba*, 3 vols. (Havana, 1941), 2:516. For the Ferrocarriles del Norte de Cuba, an American-owned company, not only the twelve high employees of the general administration were white, but among the 101 employees in the departments of accounting, fares, shops, and others there was not a single Afro-Cuban employed. See Ferrocarriles del Norte de Cuba, *Boletín Quincenal, edición extraordinaria* (1923); Nicolás Guillén, "El camino de Harlem," *Diario de la Marina*, April 21, 1929.

25. "Datos cubanos. Movimiento de las empresas de tranvías eléctricos durante 1924–25," *Revista Bimestre Cubana* 22 (1927): 274.

26. "Datos cubanos. Movimiento de las fábricas de tabaco en el año de 1924," *Revista Bimestre Cubana* 22 (1927):108; Cuba, *Comisión Nacional de Estadística y Reformas Económicas, Estadística en relación con la elaboración de cigarros y tabacos en el año 1926* (Havana, 1928); Arredondo, *El negro en Cuba*, 63. For an overview of the tobacco industry, see Jean Stubbs, *Tobacco in the Periphery: A Case Study in Cuban Labour History* (Cambridge, 1985).

27. "Datos cubanos. Resumen de la estadística de destilerías y su producción," *Revista Bimestre Cubana* 22 (1927): 757–59.

28. "Cuartillas traspapeladas," *La Prensa*, January 11, 1916; Ramiro Neyra y Lanza, "La prensa y la inmigración antillana," *Labor Nueva*, April 16, 1916, 6–7.

29. The index of dissimilarity measures differences between two population groups. In Table 1 it measures differences in the occupational distribution of immigrants and native whites and blacks. To calculate this index, the absolute values of the differences in distribution for each group are divided by two. An index of perfect equality equals 0, an index of 100 indicates total inequality. For an example of the use of this index in a similar context, see George Reid Andrews, "Racial Inequality in Brazil and the United States: A Statistical Comparison," *Journal of Social History* 26 (1992): 229–63.

30. Atkins, *Sixty Years in Cuba*, 315.

31. Instituto de Historia, *Historia del movimiento obrero*, 1:122; Clark, "Labor Conditions," 770–72; Pepper, *To-Morrow in Cuba*, 152.

32. "Manifiesto del Congreso Obrero de 1892," in Instituto de Historia, *El movimiento obrero cubano. Documentos y artículos*, 2 vols. (Havana, 1975), 1:75–85; Marcelino Ojeda Mayor, "Por la verdad y el obrero," *El Cubano Libre*, Sep-

tember 17, 1903; "La bancarrota de los ídolos y el trabajador consciente," *¡Tierra!*, November 27, 1909; "Politiquerías," *¡Tierra!*, December 4, 1909.

33. "Presidentes del Gremio de Estibadores y Braceros de la Marina de Santiago de Cuba," *La Voz Obrera*, May 1, 1933; Rebecca Scott, "Labor and the Exercise of Political Voice: Santa Clara, 1899–1906," paper presented at "Race at the Turn of the Century," a conference at New York University (April 1996), 10. The figures concerning the Labor Congress of 1914 were gleaned from photographs published in *Memoria de los trabajos presentados al Congreso Nacional Obrero* (Havana, 1915).

34. John Dumoulin, "El movimiento obrero en Cruces, 1902–1925," in *Las clases y la lucha de clases en la sociedad neocolonial cubana*, 4 vols. (Havana, 1980), 2:27; William Brackett to the Commanding Officer, Marine Camp, Camagüey, January 11, 1919, USNA, RG 165/2056-112.

35. John Dumoulin, "El primer desarrollo del movimiento obrero y la formación del proletariado en el sector azucarero. Cruces 1886–1902," *Islas* 48 (1974): 3–66; "Obreros de la Patria," *La Lucha*, October 9, 1909; Evelio Tellena, *Congresos obreros en Cuba* (Havana, 1973), 154.

36. Blas Rodríguez Pascual, "Obreros y burgueses. El odio de razas entre los torcedores," *La Opinión*, March 25, 1920; Juan Cubero García, "A los trabajadores y en particular a los torcedores," *La Opinión*, April 2, 1920; Arturo Juvanet, "Por la justicia y el derecho," *La Opinión*, April 13, 1920; Cabrera, *El movimiento obrero*, 152; "Conflicto en puerta," *La Correspondencia*, July 18, 1912. I thank Rebecca Scott for sharing the last reference with me.

37. "Asuntos varios. En Remedios," *Diario de la Marina*, August 25, 1900 (evening ed.); Jos. Wells to the Secretary of State, Antilla, June 17, 1921, USNA, RG 59/837.504/211.

38. Clark, "Labor Conditions," 768–69 (my emphasis).

39. "Huelga general," *La Lucha*, November 2, 1902; "La huelga de los aprendices," in Instituto de Historia, *El movimiento obrero*, 1:193–95; "La huelga general. La Liga General de Trabajadores Cubanos," *La Lucha*, November 14, 1902. See also Córdova, *Clase trabajadora*, 91–95; Instituto de Historia, *Historia del movimiento obrero*, 1:137–39. The Liga had petitioned the government concerning Cuban apprentices since June. See "La Liga de Trabajadores," *La Lucha*, June 17, 1902.

40. Instituto de Historia, *Historia del movimiento obrero*, 1:150 (emphasis in original).

41. "La huelga del alcantarillado de la Habana," in Instituto de Historia, *El movimiento obrero*, 1:289–92; Instituto de Historia, *Historia del movimiento obrero*, 1:163–64; Partido Socialista, "Manifesto to All Workers," enclosed in Victor Berger to the Secretary of State, Washington, DC, February 19, 1912, USNA, RG 59/837.0132/1.

42. Flaxer, "Memorandum on Labor Unions," in Guggenheim to the Secretary of State, Havana, June 18, 1931, USNA, RG 84/850.4/747; "Extranjeros, y no nativos, son los obreros con que cuenta obras públicas," *Union Nacionalista*, September 7, 1928; "Capataces extranjeros atropellan inicuamente a los obreros cubanos," *El Globo*, May 16, 1927.

43. "La huelga de bahía," *La Lucha*, July 9, July 19, 1904; "Movimiento obrero. Los estibadores," *La Lucha*, July 16, July 17, 1906; Beaupré to the Secretary of State, Havana, May 8, 1912, USNA, RG 59/837.5401/23; "Noticias del puerto. Jamaiquinos," *Diario de la Marina*, March 11, 1921; "Estibadores cesanteados injustamente," *La Lucha*, August 15, 1928.

44. Frank Garrett to George Whigham, Jatibonico, October 22, 1913, CCP, Series 1, Box 9, 135.

45. F. Gerard Smith to Leandro Rionda, Francisco, February 15, 1917, BBC, RG 10, Series 10a, Box 8; "Cincuenta haitianos de la 'Sugar States' cometen más atropellos con los terratenientes de Cueto," *Diario de la Marina*, June 29, 1928.

46. Unknown to Galham, Camagüey, November 30, 1916, and M.K. to George Whigham, Richmond, November 29, 1916, CCP, Series 1, Box 23, 913 and 204; Griffith to the Secretary of State, Santiago de Cuba, December 12 and 15, 1916, USNA, RG 59/837-504/1 and 2; DeGraux, "Labor Situation," December 4, 1918, USNA, RG 165/2056-65.

47. Craib to George Whigham, Jatibonico, December 20, 1916, CCP, Series 1, Box 20, 264; Dickinson to the C.B. Hurst, Antilla, June 13, 1922, USNA, RG 59/ 837.00/2232; "El antagonismo que desde hace tiempo viene separando a los españoles de los haitianos fue causa de una horrible batalla," *La Lucha*, July 4, 1924; "Strike Conspiracy Develops in Havana," *The Havana Post*, October 13, 1917; Jos. Wells to the Secretary of State, Antilla, June 17, 1921, USNA, RG 59/ 837.504/211.

48. Dumoulin. "El primer desarrollo," 59–60.

49. Lino Castelló, "Francisco Lamuño," *El Hombre Nuevo*, October 13, 1919; "Argentina, Cuba, España," *¡Tierra!*, November 20, 1909; "El mítin de Martí," *¡Tierra!*, November 27, 1909. See also Dumoulin, "El primer desarrollo," 34–35.

50. Jackson to the Secretary of State, Havana, July 13 and August 5, 1911, USNA, RG 59/837.108/2 and 5.

51. "La huelga de Cienfuegos se intensifica," *La Lucha*, October 12, 1917; "El estado de la huelga en las Villas," *La Lucha*, October 13, 1917; "La huelga de las Villas continúa sin solucionar," *La Lucha*, October 15, 1917; "Huelguistas arrestados," *La Lucha*, October 22, 1917; "Un centro de conspiración," *La Lucha*, October 22, 1917; Van Natta to the Chief of Military Intelligence, Havana, November 26, 1917, USNA, RG 59/837.00/1444; Charles Winnans to Gustave Scholle, Cienfuegos, October 22, 1917, USNA, RG 59/837.504/26; John Dumoulin, *Azúcar y lucha de clases, 1917* (Havana, 1980), 82.

52. "Report on the Cuban Strikes since January 1, 1919," Havana, March 26, 1919, USNA, RG 165/2056-171; Crowder to the Secretary of State, Havana, November 24, 1924, USNA, RG 59/837.00/2583. On the sugar strikes of 1924, see Instituto de Historia, *Historia del movimiento obrero*, 1:217–19.

53. "Horrible ejemplo de ferocidad," *La Discusión*, March 25, 1917.

54. Tellería, *Congresos obreros*, 128, 137–42, 188; "Actas del Congreso de funda-ción de la CNOC," in Instituto de Historia, *El movimiento obrero*, 1:407–41.

55. "Nueva protesta de la Federación Obrera de la Habana," "La viril protesta obrera" and "Manifiesto protesta de la Liga Antimperialista," all in Mirta Rosell, ed., *Luchas obreras contra Machado* (Havana, 1973), 83–84, 95–98, 108–10 (em-phasis in original).

56. Instituto de Historia, *Historia del movimiento obrero*, 1:256–57; "Plataforma electoral del Partido Comunista de Cuba," in *Luchas obreras contra Machado*, ed. Mirta Rosell (Havana, 1973), 188–211. On the CNOC's program see Policía Judicial, "Memorandum," Havana, July 17, 1930, USNA, RG 84/800B. For the relationship between Communists and Eastern Europeans, see Sección de Expertos to Federico Rasco, Military Commander of Havana, November 13, 1931, USNA, RG 84/800.1/1143.

57. Edwin Schoenrich to Guggenheim, Santiago de Cuba, July 13, 1931, and Guggenheim, General Conditions Report for July 1931, Havana, August 8, 1931, USNA, RG 84/800/4 and 809.

58. Wakefield, "Political Situation in the Nuevitas Consular District," March 17, 1931, USNA, RG 84/800; Carlos González Echevarría, *Origen y desarrollo del movimiento obrero camagüeyano* (Havana, 1984), 87; Rupert Lewis, *Marcus Garvey, Anti-Colonial Champion* (Trenton, 1988), 106–7.

59. "Memorandum: Racial Problem of Cuba," enclosed in Welles to the Secretary of State, Havana, September 29, 1933, USNA, RG 84/800/143; Welles to the Secretary of State, Havana, September 30, 1933, USNA, RG 84/800/324; Ruben Martínez Villena, "Las contradicciones internas del imperialismo yanqui y el alza del movimiento revolucionario," in Ministerio de Eduación, *Documentos de Cuba republicana* (Havana, 1972), 176–93.

60. A. Pérez-Medina, "The Situation of the Negro in Cuba," in *Negro, An Anthology*, ed. Nancy Cunard (New York, 1970), 294–98; Matilde S. Menéndez, "¿Racismo o política?," *La Correspondencia*, February 28, 1936; Gastón Mora y Varona, "La cuestión social," *Diario de la Marina*, February 24, 1929; Ramón Vasconcelos, "Al margen de los días. Complejos," in Municipio de la Habana, *Las comparsas populares* (Havana, 1937), 33–37.

2

Rebellion against Vaccination in Rio de Janeiro

Jeffrey D. Needell

Jeffrey Needell raises in this selection one of the central problems of this volume on "work, protest, and identity." He notes that the Brazilian government—the established, staid Rodrigues Alves regime—wanted to modernize the nation in part by cleaning up disease in the population. The most scientific method available at the time for doing so was vaccination. We would think now that this was a harmless means for achieving a socially good end, relieving disease among the working poor. Who could possibly object? Yet, as Needell incisively shows, vaccination was anything but neutral. The political opposition quickly seized upon the announced government program for its own ends. What seemed like a beneficial federal project suddenly polarized the people of Rio de Janeiro into class opponents and threatened the existence of the government. Needell recognizes the central irony that the object of the government's efforts, the least well-off sector of the population, was the group most threatened by its authoritarian methods. As a sort of "cloning" of another day, the way in which vaccines were produced did little to instill confidence in a population already feeling threatened by the advances of science. Later, when rumors circulated that social conventions about sexual privacy would be crudely swept aside to carry out the program, vaccination proved to be the straw that broke the camel's back.

Significantly, Needell notes that the most important political allies of the Rio workers were sectors of the military, who believed that republican ideals had been thwarted ever since the republic was founded. The volatile combination of a divided military, middle-class reformers, aroused workers, and an open and competitive press nearly toppled the Rodrigues Alves regime. Needell's detailed knowledge of Rio and his careful sorting out of the events open a window on working-class life in the capital at the turn of the twentieth century. The selection also raises questions about race and immigration. With whom can the workers identify—their fellow workers only, or their fellow workers and their allies in the middle class? Can the interests of the workers ultimately be met by such allies with their own agendas?

Francisco de Paula Rodrigues Alves's "modernizing" administration (1902–1906) imposed a new urban plan, portworks, and drastic measures against disease on Rio de Janeiro. In 1904, in a crisis linked to the administration's obligatory smallpox vaccination plans, a popular revolt dominated the capital and cleared the way for a nearly successful military coup. The historiography to date has either neglected this revolt or (more recently) focused on one aspect to the exclusion of the other. Here, I point to the *Revolta Contra Vacina* as the culmination and conjuncture of more general and more radical conflicts and resistance within Brazil's Old Republic (1889–1930)—a failed revolution against one sort of "modernization" which gives another meaning to the events and indicates another perspective on Rio's *belle époque*.

In October 1904 an opposition newspaper in Rio posted a portrait of a man suffering from a grisly tumor that had distorted his arm and chest. The paper, the *Correio da Manhã*, did this "so that our public may evaluate well what it is risking with obligatory vaccination." The daily then went on:

> And what is the reason for this shocking change? What? Simply vaccination, the great destroyer of human happiness, of human health, and of human life. Vaccination, the propagator by all means of illness, . . . the monster that pollutes the pure and innocent blood of our children with the vile excretions expelled from sick animals, of a nature that contaminates the system of any living being.[1]

This quotation was part of a sustained effort on the part of the opposition paper to galvanize the Carioca population to reject the obligatory vaccination program directed by Dr. Oswaldo [Gonçalvesl Cruz during the Rodrigues Alves administration. Most of the press opposed *obligatory* vaccination, as did many prominent opposition politicians, professional organizations, academic institutions, and the Positivist church. By November's first week, a Liga Contra Vacina Obrigatória, explicitly modeled on an earlier British organization, had been put together by more radical leaders to rally popular resistance. Many of the same men, militant republicans, politicized army officers, and opposition journalists who figured in the Liga, also reached out to organized workers by addressing huge meetings at the Centro de Classes Operárias. In the second week of November, as word of the government's regulations for obligatory vaccination spread, the heated political milieu finally exploded.[2]

On November 10, in the aftermath of a mass meeting, a police officer arrested a few youths with whom he had had an angry exchange. On his detachment's return with the prisoners to headquarters, it was surrounded and attacked, and had to be rescued by well-prepared police cavalry, who charged and dispersed enraged crowds for the better part of the evening. The same pattern of public meetings, hostility, violent police repression, and riots marked the afternoons and evenings of the next three days.

The crowds mobbed streets and squares, broke streetlamps, and fought police sabers, revolvers, and rifles with paving stones, knives, straight-razors, revolvers, and rifles of their own. Streetcars soon stopped running, since they served too well as barricades which were repeatedly thrown up in the narrow streets of the Old City. Rio's historic center, and the nearby working-class slums near the northern docks (see map). Indeed, by November 12, the army and navy were called in to reinforce the police garrisoning strategic points in the Old City and the outlying working-class districts. The endangered positions included the local police stations, the Gazómetro (which, if taken, would leave the city's gas lighting without fuel), and, of course, the streets leading from the Old City to Catete—the presidential palace where, during the next two days, Rodrigues Alves's ministers periodically rushed to confer with the president about their vain attempts to regain control of his capital. Rio was effectively in the hands of the masses.[3]

One of the men who came to see Rodrigues Alves on the 14th angered and dismayed the president profoundly. General Olímpio da Silveira, though polite, offered the president a scarcely veiled ultimatum on behalf of elements in the army. Rodrigues Alves rejected it pointedly. On General Silveira's return to the Club Militar, traditional focus of the army's more political activities, he reported the president's response to the civilian and military conspirators awaiting him. The general's mission had been an attempt to force administration concessions under the threat of military rebellion; now it was decided to take the fatal step and compel the government's fall. Together, the military and civilian conspirators went ahead with plans hastily put together that day at the club.[4]

By late afternoon and early evening, these plans had had uneven success. The military school of Praia Vermelha, a source of youthful, violent, radical idealism for a generation, had been made ready by the conspirators, and now rose up at the call of Senator Lauro Sodré. The senator, an army officer, had been the most prominent opposition figure at the Liga and the Centro de Classes Operárias. In the Senate, representing Rio itself, he had long censured the administration and had urged the radical recasting of the republic back to its betrayed ideals. Now, joined by General Silvestre Travassos, he organized the cadets to march the short distance to Catete, to depose Rodrigues Alves, and to set up a new government, with himself as its leader.[5]

While Lauro was successful in arousing the military school, however, his agents at the tactical school of Realengo, in the North Zone of the city, suffered a complete reverse. Just when they called on the cadets to revolt, the head of the school, forewarned and aided by loyal officers, attacked and imprisoned all but one of the conspirators who were to have led the cadets from Realengo to the northwestern edge of the Old City at the Praça da República, across from the army's general headquarters. There

RIO DE JANEIRO

ZONA NORTE

ZONA SUL

1 = Cidade Velha (Old City)
2 = Morro do Castelo
3 = Morro de S. Bento
4 = Morro da Conceição
5 = Campo de Santana
6 = Morro do Livramento
7 = Saúde
8 = Saco da Gambôa
9 = Gambôa
10 = Saco de Alferes
11 = Saco de S. Diogo
12 = Mangue
13 = Cidade Nova (New City)
14 = São Cristovão
15 = Morro do Senado
16 = Morro do S. Antônio
17 = Morro de Sta. Teresa
18 = Lapa
19 = Morro da Glória
20 = Flamengo
21 = Botafogo
22 = Leme
23 = Praia Vermelha
24 = Site of cadets' battle
25 = Gatete Palace
26 = Praça Tiradentes
27 = Largo de São Francisco
28 = Army General Headquarters
29 = Laranjeiras

scale
1 km

This sketch of Rio de Janeiro is based on an eighteenth-century map, when the Old City had reached its traditional limits; hence, the New City and residential districts are marked only by numbers here, along with the dockside slum areas. Further, an original geographical feature, the tongue of water/marshland (the Mangue) which originally penetrated to within a short distance of the Old City is still represented. By 1902, of course the Mangue had been partially filled in and inadequately canaled. The railroad is designated with a cross-hatched line (++++); major new boulevards and severely altered old streets are shown by a broken line (‐ ‐) to give the reader an idea of the impact of the reforms. The Largo de São Francisco and the Praça Tiradentes noted were favorite sites for demonstrations and rioting. Gâvea and Realengo are too distant to be shown here.

they were to have joined those army units expected to adhere to their triumphant cause, before proceeding to help Lauro, who was to attack Catete in the South Zone. However, these two coordinated moves, one to pull in the army from the north, the other to lead the attack to depose the president in the south, were now out of step. The northern thrust had been parried—the coup's success was now to be decided wholly in the south.[6]

Precious time was lost at Praia Vermelha as cadets sought ammunition for a reserve in their attack. This search gave loyal officers time to warn the president of the uprising and to attempt to organize a palace defense and a small, mixed unit of military police and other loyal soldiers to meet the cadets en route from the military school. The president, upset at the delays and the paucity of troops sent to his defense by his generals in the Old City, then prepared, with family, staff, and ministers, to await his fate. Late that night, the cadets, with Lauro and Travassos in the van, finally began their march, strengthened by the adhesion of two other units on their way. Then, unexpectedly, they met the demoralized, exhausted loyalist forces on a dark street leading from Praia Vermelha into the residential district of Botafogo. There was less than a half-hour's exchange of fire, which brought little honor to the loyalists and disaster to the rebels. On the one hand, the government forces fled headlong in disorder, quickly spreading rumors of defeat in their rout. On the other hand, however, the charismatic leadership of the coup was eliminated—Lauro, felled by a bloody scalp wound, was unable to lead. Even Travassos, badly wounded, with his horse shot from under him, could not go on. The two rebel leaders were taken in by friends living nearby, and the cadets retreated to their school.[7]

Catete, in the immediate aftermath of the exchange, heard only the rumors of defeat brought back by the retreating loyalists. The president was urged to flee the beachfront palace to a nearby battleship; everyone in his entourage assumed Lauro's forces would soon overrun them. Rodrigues Alves refused to abandon the city. Shortly afterward, word came of the cadets' retreat; only then did army reinforcements finally arrive. The administration had survived.[8]

From November 15 to 18, the army and navy wrested the capital from its masses. The morning of the 15th was taken up with the peaceful surrender of Praia Vermelha—the next few days were more difficult elsewhere. There were industrial workers' revolts in suburban factories and street battles in town. Even while the Old City was being disputed over barricades between the military and roving groups, a more fearsome threat loomed. In one of the oldest Afro-Brazilian districts, the hilly dockside slum called Saúde, streetfighters had built an ordered series of barricades and organized a disciplined resistance, complete with military-style communications, chosen leadership, and a battle standard—the red flag. Reporters noted a great sign posted near the flag, with the words "Porto Arthur" written there. The streetfighters, mindful of the siege highlighting the ongoing Russo-Japanese War, were apparently warning of their determined resistance. Indeed, when the army began the painful task of taking Saúde back street by street, barricade by barricade, the streetfighters counterattacked, led by "Prata Preta" (Black Silver), Porto Arthur's commander. They failed. In terrible hand-to-hand combat, Prata Preta himself, isolated in the retreat, was captured, straight-jacketed, and taken to jail under heavy guard (as much to protect him from the police as to prevent his escape). Porto Arthur's defenders, retreating before the army's pressure by land and threatened by bombardment from a navy ironclad positioned just off dockside, faded away into the maze-like squalor of the slums. Only sporadic street or factory conflicts, progressively contained, remained. By the 18th, the revolt was effectively over.[9] A period of repression followed, armed by an official state of siege. Imprisonment, beatings, interrogation, and internal exile were the order of the day. The trial of Lauro and a number of officers and opposition leaders took place over the next several months. The plan for obligatory vaccination, however, was put aside by the Rodrigues Alves administration. Smallpox continued to decimate the population during the course of the next few years.[10]

Contemporary response to the revolt generally fastened on its putative leadership, Lauro and his associates, and their coup attempt of November 14. Friends of the administration accused them of being dictatorial cynics, even monarchists, misleading the idealistic cadets and engaging in criminal demagoguery with regard to the masses. More neutral or opposition writers tended to decry Lauro and his followers' tactics as misguided and irresponsible, criticizing the use of violence (rather than constitutional redress), the sacrifice of the cadets, and the provocation of easily misled urban masses. What little analysis was actually spent on those masses typically turned on superficial characterizations of their actions as the function of atavism, ignorance, criminality, and barbarism. Class and race prejudice, redolent of the social Darwinism of the epoch, tended to obscure any alternative approaches: the people revolted because they were savage. The police report, attempting a more politic and "scientific" distinction, dwelt on the central role of Rio's marginal elements and explicitly distinguished such "prostitutes," "pimps," "drunks," "vagabonds," "thieves," "professional troublemakers," and "crooks" from the responsible, respectable working class.[11]

Like some bad dreams, the revolt of 1904 was quickly repressed and largely forgotten. It is only noted in passing by chroniclers, and even then in a way which continues the emphasis on the coup's leadership and its apparent political concerns—it is recorded as the *Revolta Contra Vacina*. Only occasionally (or in the description of the revolt) is the role of the common people indicated (and distorted) by using the term *quebra lampiões* (streetlamp breakers) to designate those most active in the street violence. The fact that the revolt's successes were (and remain) unparalleled in Brazilian history has generally gone unremarked. Nor have the underlying reasons for the revolt, even on the part of Lauro and his followers, been given proper analytic attention until relatively recently. As for the Cariocas who, for several days, met their enemies in bloody combat or defied them from smoldering barricades—their story has only recently been given the possibility of investigation.

Thus, the traditional historiography, as Nachman has observed,[12] has left 1904 as its elite and middle-sector contemporaries bequeathed it—a focus on the leadership; observations on the constitutional and medical issues of compulsory smallpox vaccination; and an account of the ferocity of the popular violence and government repression (though, for the most part, blatant racial and class prejudices have been shed or disguised). Revisionists, at least, have pointed to the context of the revolt, but they have not explored its origins at length. Even Melo Franco's discussion (1973), doubtless the best published account to date, makes only the scantiest reference to the possible underlying causes for mass violence, though he advances our understanding of the conspiracy headed by Lauro with the greater precision possible through primary research.[13]

Since Melo Franco's work, little has been published which breaks new ground on the revolt. In 1977, Nachman offered a brief article demonstrating the revolt's links to the enduring tradition of positivist radicalism in the Old Republic.[14] In 1986, Meade published a fresh account of the people's role, a focus which, while based on exemplary research on the poor, did not allow for a fully developed contextual analysis or satisfactory handling of other elements involved.[15] For the most part, those who wish to comprehend the revolt of 1904 must turn to primary source research, recent theses and monographs touching on related problems, and Lahmeyer Lobo's statistical analysis of Rio's history (1978). The theses are, with the exception of Maram's (1972), recent indeed. Benchimol, Keremitsis, Porta Rocha, Costa, Adamo, and Meade have written theses and dissertations since 1980 focusing on urban reform, Carioca labor, public health, popular culture and resistance, the plight of people of color, and community response, which give us the fragments of a framework for understanding the masses' role in the revolt. What I and others (the Casa de Rui Barbosa's Equipe de Pesquisas) are adding is the necessary comprehensive analysis of the revolt itself, garnered from these and untapped contemporary records.[16]

The Carioca *Belle Époque*

The revolt must first be placed in its immediate context—the Carioca *belle époque* of 1898–1914. This era emerged after nearly two decades of urban and national upheaval. The struggle for abolition (ca. 1880–88) and for the republic (ca. 1870–89) had brought street violence, middle-sector politicization, and elite division to the city during the 1880s. The 1890s intensified such symptoms, as the underlying struggle over the nature of the new republic and the impact of alternating policies of inflation and deflation galvanized the city. The period was one in which the nation's direction was disputed by two different groups. On the one hand, the victors of 1889—radical republicans (*jacobinos*) among the urban middle sectors and the army's officer corps, often positivist-influenced or positivists—were attempting to use the state to remake Brazil. Influential in the early republic's government, they sought an authoritarian, centralized, "modernizing" regime in which Brazil's progress would be quickened and more opportunities would be brought to the urban middle sector and working class by promoting an expanded meritocratic bureaucracy and a nationalist, paternalist industrial program. On the other hand, the badly divided traditional elites, tied to regional plantation agriculture and its associated complement of commerce and credit, were trying to regain power. They were struggling, first, to reestablish elite consensus in the wake of certain regions' agricultural decline and other regions' increasingly clear preeminence, and, second, to reassert their traditional agroexport bias as national policy. Both tasks involved the ouster of the radicals. The second necessarily implied an end to the radicals' statist interventionism, and the promotion, instead, of only limited intervention, to encourage foreign credit and, with it, facilitate infrastructural expansion, access to cheap labor, and foreign investment and trade.[17]

In the mid-1890s, the leaders among the great planter interests of São Paulo found the opening through which to lead the reorganizing agroexport elites against the *jacobinos*, who had coalesced around the government of Marshal Floriano [Vieira] Peixoto (1891–94). Floriano, struggling against a desperate revolt in the south, needed Paulista support and turned to the moderate Paulista Republicans; he received the weight of their firm backing, in exchange for allowing the "election" of a Paulista president in 1894. It was the beginning of the end. In the next two administrations, those of Prudente [José] de Morais [e Barros] (1894–98) and Manuel [Ferrez] de Campos Sales (1898–1902), both Paulistas, the republican radicals were routed—broken as a power in national politics and rooted out, with federal connivance, from all but one of those state governments where they had gained power in the early 1890s. The exception, Rio Grande do Sul, remained a beacon to Florianistas among the military and the Carioca middle sectors, though its national representation, headed by Senator Pinheiro Machado, would, over time, seek more to win power within the emergent structure than leverage to remake it. Indeed, under Campos Sales, the notorious *política dos governadores* delivered the state governments over to the local reorganized machines controlled by each state's agroexport oligarchy, in exchange for acquiescence to the national government's new political and economic direction (which favored, above all, the two most powerful coffee states, São Paulo and Minas Gerais).[18]

It is under Campos Sales that Rio began its *belle époque*. It was clear that the nation had once again been bent to the will of the "conservative classes." Campos Sales's political victory for the oligarchies signaled domestic stability at the expense of radical ideology and broader political participation. His personal negotiations with Lord Rothschild brought new credit to Brazil at the expense of a savage deflationary policy that brought recession by 1900. Naturally, however, the return to oligarchical control and foreign credit also brought a sense of relief and delighted anticipation to those associated with traditional elite circles. Fashionable weeklies began publishing light literature and society gossip. The Jockey Club and the Club dos Diários enjoyed a period of resurgence, merger, new members, and new pleasures. Indeed, when Rodrigues Alves came to power as the third Paulista president and the first without credentials earned in the early republican movement, an official ball was held at the Casino

Fluminense, old seat of the monarchy's high society. It was the first such affair since the celebrated one at the Ilha Fiscal in 1889—where D. Pedro II had been the host.[19]

Personally, Rodrigues Alves was hardly interested in a renaissance in high society. He hoped to build from the secure political and fiscal base left him by Campos Sales to provide the limited intervention traditionally preferred in Brazilian liberal economic thought. He planned to promote national change along European lines by encouraging immigration, building infrastructure, and securing more foreign credit, and he focused on the reform of Rio as the centerpiece of such promotion. Rodrigues Alves proposed to dramatically strengthen Rio's role as the nation's port-capital —symbolic and functional neocolonial nexus between North Atlantic civilization and economy and a "modernizing" Brazil.[20]

There were three hinges to this portal to the future. One was the ambitious, sophisticated program of disease control and eradication directed by Oswaldo Cruz, who promised to rid Rio, Brazil's threshold, of the illnesses (yellow fever, plague, and smallpox) that had made it notorious among immigrant laborers and foreign capitalists. The second was Rio's Europeanization, by way of the building, improvement, beautification, and rationalization of the city's streets and public places according to the Parisian model synonymous with Haussmann, reforms placed in the practiced hands of Rio's prefect, Francisco Pereira Passos. The third was the construction of Rio's modern port, a practical necessity for Brazil's major entrepôt; a port, moreover, linked to the burgeoning commerce, industry, and labor of the Old City and the North Zone by Parisian-style boulevards. This last reform was undertaken by the minister of industry, transport, and public works, Lauro Müller, who delegated the complicated planning and construction to the clique of engineers and entrepreneurs associated with the Club de Engenharia and headed by [Gustavo André] Paulo de Frontin and Francisco Bicalho. This was Rodrigues Alves's dramatic "modernizing" program, one which spoke to the triumph of the traditional elites' vision of Brazil as a progressive but agroexport participant in the North Atlantic economy. It was one which rested on victories wrested from nearly a generation of conflict; it was a program central to the meaning of the Carioca *belle époque*. This was the context of the revolt of 1904—a revolt that was the negation of the *belle époque* and this particular "modernization" in political and symbolic terms.[21]

Opposition and Radical Conspiracy

Traditional discussion and recent research alike point to the roots of elite and middle-class opposition to Oswaldo Cruz's obligatory vaccination. There was strong, but probably minority, resistance to vaccination itself, and general resistance to the obligatory aspect, a resistance obvious even in periodicals normally favorable to Rodrigues Alves and his policies. The Positivist church, although it never called for nor participated in violence, was the most marked opponent to vaccination on two counts: it was especially adamant against obligatory innoculation on the doctrinaire ground of constitutional principles, and it also mustered scientific arguments against the practice. Individuals from the medical community, the press, and the congress also spoke out against vaccination per se. Their resistance to vaccination was based on misgivings (expressed sometimes soberly, often quite emotionally) regarding its safety and efficacy. It is important to recall that these were hardly a function of obscurantism—although vaccination had become an established method by that time, there were still international and learned debates over the practice. The more general opposition, however, was to forced inoculation, central to Oswaldo Cruz's plan—a plan based on foreign, successful precedent. This opposition, like that of the positivists, was founded on constitutional grounds: the sanctity of the individual's rights against the coercive powers of the state. Objections on both counts were presented in the press, in congress, and in petitions from various groups and institutions, one of which, counting more than 10,000 names, was submitted by various unions. It was all countered publicly by administration champions and effectively ignored by the president and his allies until far too late.[22]

The Rodrigues Alves administration presumed that such opposition was generally a cover for political sabotage of the administration and its program, or, at best, a mere misguided obstacle to crucial reforms. It now seems clear that the administration was both terribly wrong and correct. It was wrong in that even politically neutral or proadministration elements opposed the measure because of strongly felt medical fears and ideological values, or because of a more sensitive reading of the impolitic, explosive potential of the administration's interventionism.[23] Here, in effect, one finds the roots of the general atmosphere of middle-sector and elite resistance to the policy. However, if grown in isolation, these would have flowered only in protest and anger in the press and in the congress. The roots of the revolt itself were elsewhere. For the administration was also correct in sensing that, just barely beneath much of this public outcry, there was determined political opposition seeking an issue with which to destroy the Paulista government and the forces it embodied.

It is important to remember that the *belle époque* was a victory over the radical officers and urban middle-sector elements, the *jacobinos* and Florianistas. Such men had not disappeared after 1894—they had fought rearguard actions in the form of riots, a foiled military school revolt in 1897, and, in the same year, the near assassination of Prudente de Morais, who afterward had adroitly hamstrung them politically. Thereafter, the principal *jacobino* leaders had retreated to a few congress seats or the press to maintain an energetic opposition and bide their time. Future leaders of the 1904 revolt, such as Lauro Sodré, Barbosa Lima, and Alfredo Varela, were figures of recognized polemical gifts and were closely associated with the victories and defeats of the 1890s.[24]

Lauro, above all, enjoyed a singular moral preeminence among long-time Republicans, often regardless of their political position vis-à-vis the Paulista administrations. A member of the positivist military circles who made the coup of 1889, former secretary to the "Founder of the Republic," Benjamin Constant [Botelho de Magalhães], Florianista governor of Pará, defeated presidential candidate of 1898, Lauro was generally respected as *imaculado*, a republican hero untainted by corruption or self-seeking. His birthday celebration in 1904 took on something of the quality of a national republican holiday, as he was flooded with thousands of telegrams and honored with processions and passionate speeches. He had made himself, and was recognized as, the charismatic leader of those disappointed with the administrations that followed Florianos. Indeed, Lauro, with support in the congress and the press, championed a return to the ideal republic of which the conspirators of 1889 had dreamed, and he organized a congressional movement for constitutional reform. The senator, with the avid support of such firebrands as Barbosa Lima, was thus generally accepted as the spokesman for the radical republican forces in retreat after 1894. His natural following was the traditional one: die-hard Florianistas and *jacobinos* in the military (especially the military schools in Rio) and in the economically vulnerable middle sectors (lesser bureaucrats, liberal professionals, radical polemicists, and politicized students), as well as elements of the working class (particularly a minority of government employees).[25]

There was another element in the traditional elite who backed Lauro's movement, if only for a time: the monarchists. This surprising adherence, however, was strictly opportunistic. The monarchists, though they had helped to fund the radical paper, *Commercio do Brasil* (edited by Lauro's cohort, Alfredo Varela), were hoping to add to the problems of the republic, just as they had done in the previous few years by supporting abortive workers' strikes and violence. Their game was seemingly to break the republic down in order to rebuild the monarchy. However, in the more violent phase of *Commercio do Brasil*, just before the revolt, monarchist aid evaporated. There is some proof that the restorationists declined to continue participating in the struggle when it became apparent that Lauro would not countenance their participation in the government he planned to head after deposing Rodrigues Alves. Though the police attempted to taint Lauro's coup with monarchism, it is doubtful that they persuaded anyone then, and the evidence to date would persuade no one now.[26]

The roots of the revolt of 1904, centering on the coup of November 14, thus lie in the ongoing attempts of *jacobino* military elements to retake power and destroy the regime of the Paulista-led oligarchies. From their past efforts and published positions, it is clear that these *jacobinos* hoped to institute a paternalist and authoritarian republic of national regeneration, favoring state interventionism and protectionism, with urban middle-class and working-class support. These were not anti-"modernists"; rather, they were different "modernizers," favoring a much more radical and inclusionary path than the Paulista-led oligarchies. The latter envisioned only the relatively limited change congenial to the traditional agroexport interests; Lauro and his followers envisioned a dramatic pattern of change initiated by a strong state. They proposed to break with the old Brazil by promoting a more diversified economy, where the state not only intervened to strengthen export agriculture, but favored industry and addressed the needs and interests of the masses and the new urban groups which had been emerging since the 1890s. The authoritarian, reformist regimes men such as Lauro helped construct in various states (notably Pará, Pernambuco, and Rio Grande do Sul) in the 1890s (regimes attempted, again, in the ephemeral *salvacionista* movements in the 1910s) give one a concrete sense of their intentions.[27]

Lauro may have begun to gather support for a coup as early as the aftermath of his unsuccessful presidential campaign in 1898. He attracted support with increasing success, especially after the election of Rodrigues Alves. Both the president and his policies were just too repellent for many old Republican purists. It was not simply that the new president, like Prudente and Campos Sales, represented the oligarchies' reascendency; it was that Rodrigues Alves, unlike the two earlier Paulistas, was a man without any link to the republican movement of 1870; indeed, he had been a stalwart of the monarchy's Conservative party and a member of the emperor's honorary council. The radical and republican milieus were fired to the point where bitter charges, conspiracy, and threats electrified the political atmosphere. Over the course of the administration, it became evident in congress and in the press that something familiar was crackling in the air again. The police, under the thoroughly "modern" administration of Dr. Antonio Augusto Cardoso de Castro, put the obvious opponents of the regime—radical, labor, and monarchist alike—under the close watch of a widespread network of police agents. What obligatory vaccination added to this situation was a lightning rod.[28]

As Nachman has made clear,[29] the principal leaders of the coup had no real animus toward Oswaldo Cruz's solution to smallpox—Barbosa Lima, for example, as the Florianista governor of Pernambuco, had even promoted obligatory vaccination. The issue, however, could be used as a fuse to ignite general opposition to the administration, and to produce the catalytic explosion of popular violence required for military cover and diversion. They also worked successfully to associate the movement leading up to the coup with symbolic celebrations and rhetoric, linking it and its leaders to the consecrated republican *golpe* of 1889. Thus, though

Cardoso de Castro had frantically prepared to fend off a coup as early as mid-October (he assumed October 17, Lauro's highly politicized birthday celebration, was to be the occasion for the conspirators' move), he would have done better to remember the republican calendar. The conspirators were exploiting the issue of vaccination, the complaints of the army, and the larger issue of the regime's betrayal of the republic's ideals, gradually building toward a November crescendo. By then, after several last weeks of demonstrations commemorating Lauro's birthday, celebrating the republic's founders, and recalling the events and actors linked to the Proclamation of November 15, they would be prepared to act. The coup was to be launched by participants in the military parades normally held on the 15th, the perfect date for the republic's would-be redeemers. But, as it happened, matters were taken out of the conspirators' hands by their most powerful ally. Before Lauro could seize state power, the Carioca masses had already begun to threaten it.[30]

The Carioca Masses

Recent research allows us to go beyond the word "masses" to analyze the identity and characteristics of the Cariocas who went into the streets on November 10. Even before abolition there were two main racial categories among the urban poor: the Afro-Brazilian and the fluctuating, immigrant (largely Portuguese) component. The main sources of wages, excluding suburban agriculture, were various forms of labor in the homes, in the shops and the tenements, and on the streets and docks, as domestics, artisans, vendors, unskilled heavy laborers, carriers, and stevedores—as well as unskilled and artisan labor in small factories, for Rio since mid-century had been the nation's center for (mostly secondary) industry. Another factor was locale: the working poor and the under- and unemployed lived as close to their work (or hope of work) as they could afford. Thus, some crowded into the decaying old townhouses and mansions and the slowly increasing number of new tenements that characterized shelter in the Old City and the New City, where commerce and most of the factories were. Others lived on the hillsides and on the twisted streets that lay between the city's hills and northern shoreline. These areas were near the docks that had grown up over the last century and the two main railheads (one at the shore, the other at the frontier between the Old City and the New— both connecting commerce and industry to hinterland plantations).[31]

Over the last 30 years of the nineteenth century, little had changed structurally for the poor. What did change was the impact that ever increasing numbers had on their already desperate conditions of life. Especially after abolition, the population flow into Rio was striking. About 20 percent of the city's population in 1890 was foreign-born, about 25 percent made up of native migrants. Immigrants from Portugal remained plentiful; the censuses indicate that, unlike São Paulo, where Italian immigrants tended to predominate, the Portuguese made up perhaps two-thirds of the foreigners in Rio in 1890 and 1906. In 1906, that meant that about 16 percent of the population was first-generation Portuguese. After Portugal, the single greatest source of newcomers was the rural areas of the northeast and southeast of Brazil, areas in economic decline. These regions were also the origin of most of the Afro-Brazilian portion of internal migration, and Afro-Brazilians (Carioca and migrant) made up more than a third of the city's residents in 1890 and 1906. Together with their children, Portuguese peasants and the Afro-Brazilians of the old plantation areas thus characterized the poor who swelled the population of the capital, tripling it between 1872 and 1906 from 274,972 to 811,443.[32]

The opportunities presented to these people had changed only slowly, with the relative shrinking of domestic service, the spurt in industrialization, and the continued, slow fading of agriculture. Some 117,904 people (14.5 percent) were domestics in 1906; 115,779 (14.3 percent) were industrial workers (between them, they made up about 45 percent of the economically active). Those still working the land were only 21,411 (2.6 percent); day laborers already outnumbered them, at 29,933, as did those workers who had no known "profession" (65,492, or 8 percent). Among the industrial workers, the largest categories included those involved in construction (31,800), clothing and accessories (31,710, 18,187 of whom were women), metallurgy (7,144), energy (5,301), and textiles (2,934, 1,010 of whom were women). Foreigners (including Portuguese) were numerically important in agriculture (6,313), metallurgy (2,768), food preparation (1,923 of 3,585), clothing and accessories (13,977), construction (16,954), energy (1,649), day labor (16,015), and domestic service (25,432). The industrial census of 1907 suggests that most workers labored 12 hours a day; it also notes the presence of children, with some 2,859 in 315 industries (though one assumes far more were probably involved; the figures were voluntary and child labor common enough in similar industrial situations elsewhere), and that most factories were small or medium sized—of the 726 enterprises registered, 216 had from 1 to 5 workers, 306 had from 6 to 40, and only 204 had more than 40. This industrial park, which employed roughly two times the number of people in 1907 that it had in 1890, was in fact still largely made up of small manufacturing and artisanal units with little division of labor and mechanization, although the relatively few large factories employed very large numbers of workers (e.g., the 1907 census notes that 22 textile factories employed an average of 467 workers).[33]

It was in the poor parishes of the city that industry flourished, along with commerce, construction, and day labor, so the poor continued to flood into them. Even before the 1890s, when the population and industry grew dramatically, the pattern of overcrowding had intensified steadily.

Between 1872 and 1890, the Old City's population grew 52 percent, and the three poorest parishes, São José, Sant'Ana, and Santa Rita, grew 100 percent, 75 percent, and 42 percent, respectively. Benchimol cites figures showing that an average of 14.7 persons per building in 1872 had increased to 32/35 in 1890, with an obviously greater proportion of this crowding taking place in the Old City center. While the 1906 census cannot be cited in this regard because it was made after the reforms central to the discussion here, the agony of the 1890s and early 1900s may be imagined by simply noting that the city's population grew from 522,651 to an estimated 691,565 between 1890 and 1900. If one bears in mind that shelter had already been considered problematic by the 1850s, and that cheap housing and the number of dwellings in the Old City and New City were never considered adequate by any of the many commissions investigating them over the next half-century, the scope of the problem is glimpsed. Indeed, by the 1870s, the poor began to build their own shelters on the hills separating most of the city from the docks. The most famous, called Favela, was founded in the late 1890s, and would later be used as a generic name for all such shantytowns. The other solution, increasingly sought by those with better wages, was flight to the north zone, to São Cristóvão or further, necessitating travel to work by increasingly expensive railway or streetcar.[34]

For the masses who continued to live in the traditionally poor, distinctively Afro-Brazilian districts, New City, Gambôa, Saúde, and certain Old City streets, conditions were infernal. *Casas de cómodos* (rooming houses) were made of late colonial- and imperial-period townhouses and mansions, which were converted by dividing and redividing every room into several, using wooden boards or merely lines of sacks. There, industrial workers, jacks-of-all-trades, teamsters, cashiers, laundrywomen, seamstresses, and prostitutes crowded to sleep. They used the common corridors and spaces under staircases for cooking, with the out-of-work and dirty and naked infants and young children underfoot, and prostitutes, seamstresses, and laundrywomen plying their trades close by, all in the noise and filth and hot and humid air. As for the *cortiço* (tenement), one contemporary noted its hot, low, dark rooms and relative lack of privacy, and commented that "there are *cortiços* where one penetrates with one's handkerchief over one's nose and whence one leaves nauseated."[35] As for the favelas, this same investigator reported that the homes were no higher than a man, with floors of beaten earth and walls and roofs made of opened kerosene cans, the boards from boxes, and a multitude of other odds and ends, without water or suitable space, lumped together along the narrow, winding paths up the hillside. Here were prostitutes and bully boys and the poorest of the industrial workers. It is little wonder that such conditions, when combined with the malnutrition common to such poverty, made the traditional parishes of the poor the main killing ground of the gastrointestinal illnesses and communicable diseases common to the era, sicknesses which regularly killed infants and adults by the thousands, year in and year out.[36]

Such wretched poverty was maintained, and could worsen, with under- and unemployment. Besides the obvious impact, there is also an indirect impact of a large pool of under- and unemployed. Such a pool often helps keep wages down for the labor force as a whole, and limits the success of labor organization. This may well have been the case here, especially considering the size of such a pool in Rio. Although the 1906 census does not register unemployment as such, noting only the professions declared by working men and women, it does have certain suggestive categories. Besides those for day laborer (*jornaleiros, trabalhadores braçaes*, etc.), 29,933, there were "professions badly specified" (*profissões mal especificadas*), 6,595; "unproductive classes" (*classes improductivas*), 27,888; and "unknown professions" (*profissões desconhecidas*), 65,492. These were all distinguished from those who were apparently not economically active ("without declared profession"—*sem profissão declarada*), comprised of those younger (182,646) and older (109,556) than 15 years of age (the older, one assumes, being women who did not work and the aged who could not or no longer had to). Setting aside this last category, a total of some 129,908 people might well be defined as without steady or full-time gainful employment. This category is larger than those employed in either domestic service or industry, the two most numerous categories, and comprised 16 percent of Rio's population and 25 percent of those economically active.[37]

Good, steady work was difficult to get. Industrial employment had steadily increased, but unevenly with respect to race, national origin, and job security. As Adamo[38] has shown, the European immigrant had a much greater chance of securing factory employment, retaining it, and, most important, being promoted, than Afro-Brazilians. Moreover, no matter where the urban poor worked, their livelihood was directly affected by the financial policies and disasters of the government, events whose impact on the city's economy was immediate and quite consequential. The last half century, with the increasing growth of urban and national commerce, urban population, urban investment, and foreign capital dependency, had increased the scope and frequency of such impact. There were major periods of inflation and capital investment in the mid-1850s and 1888–95; there were major depressions or recessions in 1857, 1875–79, and 1895–1902. The last boom-and-bust cycle had been especially hard on wage earners. Their money bought relatively less from 1888 to 1898. Although many, particularly those in construction and unskilled labor, did well in 1898–1902 and received salary increases, the more skilled workers (for example, the artisanal workers common among the industries) generally received no increases. Exchange and credit problems of the 1880s had brought much of the insecurity and hardship which plagued the urban wage earners and middle sectors, and added fire to the movements for abolition and the republic. The boom-and-bust cycle of the decade or so before 1904 was a good deal more traumatic and, in the case of Campos Sales's deflationary austerity, was correctly perceived as being the work of the administration, which left office amidst violent popular anger.[39]

It seems clear, then, that by the time of the Rodrigues Alves administration, the Carioca masses, riven by racism and beset by poor housing, constant illness and disease, precarious employment, and vagaries in the amount and value of their wages, were in a wretched, rebellious condition. To speak of political alienation and hostility is an understatement, particularly in the case of the Afro-Brazilian population. The vitality and the repression of their distinct culture, as well as the poverty and racial abuse they had suffered for generations, formed only the backdrop to the new anguish they must have endured in postabolition Rio. For, although the censuses do not specify racial distinctions, it is logical to assume that it was the most recent native rural migrants, largely Afro-Brazilian, who, handicapped by racism, illiteracy, lack of marketable skills and urban-industrial socialization, suffered most. They doubtless made up a disproportionate number of the under- and unemployed, the marginalized people who inhabited the favelas and worse slums. We know that it was there that the Afro-Brazilian cultural traditions were maintained, and that it was from there that working people were recruited for the heaviest unskilled work of docks, streets, and factories—when they could get it.[40]

Higher-ranking workers, including artisans, skilled factory workers, and shop staffs—likely Rio-born or immigrant, and less disproportionately Afro-Brazilian in origin—earned more, but were just as subject to the tenuous economic health of the city. From this relative minority, some artisans, stevedores, railroad workers, and skilled factory workers were organized into Rio's first unions. Indeed, these groups, a sort of labor elite, generally led by middle-sector organizers of confused *jacobino*, positivist, socialist antecedents, had recently become increasingly militant. It was precisely over the last decade or so, with all of the interlinked problems already noted, that workers' strikes and riots had become numerous—indeed, in 1903, the capital witnessed its first May Day labor parades and a major textile strike. The police were increasingly monitoring the largely Afro-Brazilian stevedores' union, which was elaborating international ties to the stevedores of Montevideo and Buenos Aires by 1904. They were also observing the work of Dr. Vicente de Sousa, a Bahian-born mulatto and veteran of abolitionism. This physician and professor was the most successful of the era's labor organizers; in many ways, his general background seems to be typical. Vicente de Sousa was a man of the middle sectors, of positivist, *jacobino* inclinations, who supported the coup of 1889 and who had studied socialism during the 1890s, committing himself to a reformist, multiclass perspective on the workers' plight. He then worked successfully to organize labor, promoting a sort of socialist paternalism which articulated well with his earlier perspectives. In 1902, he helped found the ephemeral Partido Socialista Coletivista. By 1903, he was president of the Centro de Classes Operárias (1902–1904) in the Old City, the great meeting place of a number of constituent workers unions. Moreover, since neither his nor other pioneering workers' organizations noted here were the handiwork of foreign agitators, the police could not simply deport the "troublemakers." In this phase, at least, Carioca labor militancy (unlike that of São Paulo) was often the accomplishment of just such native ideologues, who organized among the poor according to their own lights, without direct ties to foreign socialist or anarchist experience.[41]

The masses' perception of the *belle-époque* program of Rodrigues Alves must be understood in this context. The changes rarely brought positive elements into their lives. Although some enjoyed temporary employment in construction and allied industries, the reforms generally worsened harsh, grinding conditions for the poor and exacerbated a rising tide of hostility and militance. In 1901, there had been riots touched off by an increase in streetcar fares and by Campos Sales's repression. In 1902, violent demonstrations had marked the end of Campos Sales's regime. In Rodrigues Alves's second year, 1903, there was the textile strike just noted, the largest strike in Brazilian history, which had spread to a general strike before suppression. That same year, there were also riots (led by civilian and military *jacobinos*) sparked by the coming of foreign-born, rather than native, Benedictines.[42] Now, over the course of 1904, Rodrigues Alves's program made life suddenly worse in a matter of months. The urban reforms and the boulevards linking the new portworks to the city quite purposely destroyed as much of the decrepit housing as was economically possible. The street widening and the new streets and boulevards that smashed through the Old City, the dockside area, and the New City destroyed a world. They snapped the shoestring economies of thousands of Cariocas and brutally uprooted them. The very poorest retreated up into the hillside shantytowns. Those who could found refuge in certain unreformed pockets of the New City. Others added to those flooding into the north zone, where the population increased by 116.1 percent between 1890 and 1906. In the Old City and the New City some 1,600 buildings were destroyed, and an estimated 20,000 people were forced to leave, presumably with enormous difficulty and trauma for themselves and those who now had to share their small space with the refugees. For no real effort was made to find or build new dwellings. The prefect, Pereira Passos, long an advocate of authoritarian reforms to order and sanitize working-class housing, did build some multiple residences to accommodate workers—but they were so few (and their residents so select) as to be ridiculous. The poor, as usual, had to take care of themselves.[43]

If the poor had reason to look on such administration policies with less than a sanguine eye, the same can be said with respect to the administration's related program of disease control. The two phases (yellow fever and plague eradication) completed before obligatory vaccination goaded the population mercilessly. For example, Oswaldo Cruz's plans for yellow fever (derived from the model of U.S. success in Cuba) turned on a strategy of dramatic and authoritarian tactics, carried out with precise military-style organization and in conjunction with the housing destruction. Despite the obvious benefit to the population, the doctor's prescription doubtless fostered bitterness and suspicion. Cruz divided the city into sections and then, armed with the appropriate legal dispensations, sent in teams of officials and sanitary police to inspect every building, force the cleanup of mosquito breeding grounds, and designate which buildings were too amenable for such breeding to be allowed to stand. These were promptly torn down. The procedure for plague eradication was similar: it involved rat killing and unannounced visits to buildings to ensure that the residents maintained the required conditions and, as with yellow fever, registered the diseased. In both cases, then, the poor were physically forced to stand aside while the public physicians, sanitary police, and public health officials entered and ransacked their homes, designating some for destruction, and reserving the rest for periodic invasion, threats, and meddling.[44]

With the smallpox vaccination campaign, even worse was threatened. It was not simply that one's home was to be invaded by police and other agents. Now, every man knew that he would be forced to allow these strangers to innoculate the women of his household; modesty was sure to be outraged. Barbosa Lima, in a scandalous speech in the Chamber of Deputies, asked the aged gentleman presiding what his response would be to obligatory innoculation in the buttocks. If this mortified Barbosa Lima's associates, one can barely imagine the indignation and fear even the thought aroused in the poor men and women who had no reason whatever to expect discretion or respect from Dr. Oswaldo's squads. Moreover, as the editorial at the beginning of this essay indicates, the opposition radicals exploited the fears and ignorance of the poor with inflammatory articles. They focused skillfully on the vaccination's purported ill effects and on antivaccination arguments of the elite and middle classes, which appealed to constitutional principles and more forcefully, surely, to the norms of an unchallenged patriarchal tradition of masculine protection. Nor, apparently, was mendacity neglected. During the revolt, supposedly, a few of the streetfighters interviewed testified that they had heard that the vaccination serum was to be injected into their women's groin area and that it was drawn from the bodies of rats.[45]

Impoverished, overcrowded, poorly and irregularly employed, wracked with disease, profoundly alienated from the governing elite, traumatized by migration, the loss of home, and government abuse, and now, finally, threatened in the integrity of their wretched households with the violation of women, it is little wonder that the Carioca masses turned to violence in 1904.

After all, it was not the first time. Violence among the poor in Rio was endemic; in many of the forms that came into play in 1904, it was also traditional. The papers reported daily the seemingly pervasive violence that punctured life in the favelas, bars, and streets. Indeed, sensationalist coverage of crimes of passion, bar fights, personal disputes, muggings, and random murder and mayhem, with brief moralistic (or cynical) commentaries, was apparently the delight of the literate population there and then, as it is here and now. What is worth remarking is that there were certain sorts of people who traditionally specialized in violence, some of whom were well known individually, and that public violence against authority had a long history in the city.

Certain figures repeatedly surface in the popular press in barfights, election-day intimidation, and so on; men known by colorful sobriquets (Poxface, Kid Johnny, and the like) and given the traditional designation *desordeiro* (disorderly). Such men were dangerous with the club, the knife, the straight-razor, and their feet, hands, and head; they practiced the delicate, dangerous, deadly moves of Rio's traditional Afro-Brazilian martial art and folk ballet, *capoeira*. To be sure, the *capoeiragem* of 1904 was not the highly organized gang warfare of the monarchy. Then, the city's parishes had often had distinct, secret societies of *capoeiras* (the term signified both the art and its practitioner), each gang, or *malta*, belonging to one of the two old divisions of Nagoas and Goyamas. Such *maltas* had not only fought and danced with one another in public, but had hired themselves out to the great political chiefs of the day as bodyguards and bully boys, especially during election struggles in the city parishes. Now, such public organization and traditional connections were in decline. Many *capoeiras* had been organized to defend the monarchy (and, thus, to attack republican open meetings) in 1889, and were recruited into the Black Guard. In 1890, the new republic's provisional government attempted in turn to liquidate the *capoeiras*, and the police rounded up the most noted. By 1904, then, *capoeiragem* still existed, but without the public prominence and well-known traditional Afro-Brazilian trappings. Petty parish politicians, not imperial party chiefs, called them out for municipal elections. The rumor of gangs worked its way intermittently into the press, but now the emphasis was on the personal reputation of individual *desordeiros*, not *maltas* and their parish wars.[46]

Other forms of violence were also traditional to Rio. The earliest period of national history was punctuated with terrible riots that the police were unable to stifle. In some of these, *capoeiras* played a part, but not the major one. Numerous periods of political tension ignited in riots in which the Carioca multitude fought pitched street battles against the police, building trenches and barricades as shelter against their traditional, better armed foe. The records indicate that such events were well known in the First Reign. In the Second Reign street violence, under republican and abolitionist auspices since the 1870s, became a common threat again. The hardships of the lower middle class and the working masses gave new strength to the street violence of the 1880s, and continued to feed that of the 1800s. In that last decade, some *jacobinos* cultivated popular fury and directed it against Portuguese workers, shopkeepers, merchants, and native-born monarchists alike—and now, not only civilian firebrands but young officers joined in the rioting.[47]

It is legitimate to ask whether immigration from Portugal and rural Brazil might have diluted the strength of this Carioca tradition of street violence by bringing in population foreign to it. The answer is initially ambiguous: the poor Portuguese immigrants might definitely undercut such a tradition, while the Afro-Brazilian might strengthen it. We have no direct evidence either way, and must rely on inference. A Portuguese, for example, might understandably refrain from joining traditionally Lusophobic *jacobinos* and more reasonably hope for the real relative opportunity for social mobility present in the case of white workers. He might also be counting on familial or old-country village relations to help him advance in commerce, traditionally dominated by his countrymen through just such patterns of mobility. Finally, Portuguese immigration had slowed dramatically by 1900. Those already in Rio were probably in a relatively more stable, upwardly mobile position than recent immigrants; certainly, their relative strength in, say, the industrial work force was dropping. Matters for the Afro-Brazilian migrants, who were still flooding in, remained different and harsh. Such migrants more likely took more of the economy's body blows and might well respond to *jacobino* nativism in a racial and economic situation favoring European immigrants. They might also be prone to embrace the established patterns of Carioca violence because it was something born of an environment whose values they quickly assimilated. It is important in this regard to recall that the Afro-Brazilian migrants generally came from the same areas, generation after generation, and lived in the same urban districts on arrival, where they would undergo shared hardships and doubtless respond in shared ways as they were absorbed into the preexisting Afro-Brazilian community. This was something of a world apart, with its distinct cultural heritage sharply distinguished from the European immigrants' and the urban elite's Europhile ways. Coming to the city in wave after wave, migrants constantly reinforced that milieu's rural, African, and servile origins, while learning the community's response to suffering such new and old city-dwellers bore alike: accentuated racism, poverty, oppression, petty violence, and socioeconomic instability. Moreover, it is central to underscore that the last ten years exacerbated the problems and fed the Carioca tradition of violence, this time fortified by political and labor militance. Thus, although there is no way to prove it, one may reasonably conclude that while many Portuguese in the working class may have held back from the revolt, the Afro-Brazilians were almost certainly in its vanguard.[48]

Finally, one cannot neglect the fact that violent individuals and violent mass response were not only traditional in Rio but reinforced by state violence. On the one hand, the army provided a school for mayhem. Its ranks were generally made up of poor criminals and the unemployed, brought to the colors by press gangs. Violent recruitment, training in violence, and constant billeting close to, or within, the favelas and tenements of the city made the army's recruits and veterans a constant pool of violent potential among the Carioca masses. On the other hand, the police provided this multitude with both a goad to violence and a traditional enemy. Although recruited from the poor themselves, they showed no mercy; they were notorious as being among the city's most violent thugs and *capoeiras*. Uniformed or plain-clothes agents, they commonly acted as just another gang of bully boys, but one licensed to beat, maim, rob, extort, and kill. At constant war with the *desordeiros* and preying on the masses among whom the *desordeiros* had their place, the police were hated by the Carioca poor with good reason and a terrible passion.[49]

So neither tensions, traditions, nor training were lacking in 1904. The masses, both the elite of organized workers and the larger group of under- and unemployed, had reasons, experience, and their own leaders for battle. What made 1904 different from years gone by was a larger vision of the possibilities of violence and the hope of effecting social change. These would both be provided by the conspirators linked to Lauro Sodre.

Achievements of a Failed Revolt

All the evidence agrees on the revolt's leadership: Lauro, Barbosa Lima, Alfredo Varela, and Vicente de Sousa. The generals, other officers, and civilians who met at the Club Militar on November 14 were tools of these men, trusted agents, or ambitious opportunists. It is safe to assume that Lauro, deciding to use the disruptive potential of mass street violence, a potential evident since 1880, agreed to ally his cause to that of his old comrade, Vicente de Sousa. As noted, the latter, like Lauro, was associated with 1889 and was a man of positivist, *jacobino* background. Now, his unprecedented achievement as the founder of the Centro de Classes Operárias, joining industrial artisan, railroad, and dockworker unions into one umbrella organization, provided the conspirators with a new weapon against the oligarchs' republic. The roles of Barbosa Lima and Alfredo Varela focused on middle-sector and elite agitation. Each seconded Lauro in increasing the tensions in congress; Varela added to this the editing of his extremist opposition paper. The others, as suggested, joined either out of loyalty to the old cause or for reasons of thwarted or whetted ambition, and were involved in the mechanics of the coup.[50]

Sousa and his Centro provided the crucial link to the masses. By October 1904, all the pieces were in place, and the leadership, building the pressure and heightening the tensions, used the vaccination issue to ready the middle sector for opposition and the military, radicals, and urban poor for action. The Centro was the staging area for that action. In public meetings there the leadership played to the public with the inflammatory speeches and tactics that precipitated violence. The founding of the Liga Contra Vacina at the Centro on November 5 was the penultimate step. It formally linked the leadership to cadets, middle-sector radicals, students, and organized workers in an organization of legitimate opposition that provided the oratorical platform for launching the revolt. The last step was short—from the call for violent resistance, out the Centro's door to the agitated thousands of *jacobino* militants and desperate throngs in the hall and the streets.[51]

There, in the streets, the revolt was entirely within the Carioca tradition; what varied was its scope and success—and the latter was the result of the former. Public meetings, heckling, hostility, and armed clashes— these were nothing new, nor were the locales—Cariocas had always massed at the plazas and then stormed down the main streets of the Old City, building barricades and pitting themselves against the police. The *desordeiros*, often leading the action now, were commonly the most terrible antagonists in such melées, and streetcar barricades were a part of Carioca rioting since at least 1880. What was different now was the numbers involved and their determination.[52]

Some 4,000 people attended the last league meeting of November 12, immediately before 500 or 600 marched on Catete and other groups of hundreds began widespread violence and rioting in the Old City. More than 24 streetcars were destroyed that day. By the 13th, whole sections of the Old City's center were barricaded and held. Groups of a thousand or more were cited in action on other days of the revolt. Groups were attacking parish police stations and taking streets not only in the Old City but on the hillsides and in other working-class parishes. After the 14th, strikes and violence broke out in factories in the south zone at the Gâvea and Laranjeiras, and large sections of the north zone became battlegrounds.

Then, too, the violence was hardly the complete anarchy often recorded afterward. It often mixed strategic and symbolic violence and, to a
great extent, was clearly purposeful within a larger plan. As a rule, the
only passersby who were robbed, beaten, or shot were victims of the police; the streetfighters generally reserved their stones for the carriages of
the ministers and officials most responsible for repression. Many of the
stores sacked were those stocked with food and liquor, arms and kerosene. On one occasion, wealthy commuters from the elite resort of
Petrópolis, on docking at their ferry building, were received by a mob—
but the latter touched none of the wealthy physically; they apparently
wanted symbolic vengeance. They allowed the rich to leave unmolested,
but attacked the property of the ferry company. Other destruction was
just as symbolic, though it often served practical military purposes as
well. Property associated with the police, public transportation, the administration, and the urban reform construction seems to have been singled
out for attention. Although streetcars were probably a special target as the
property of the hated companies that the north zone workers blamed for
the high cost of transportation, they also made excellent barricades. As
for the constant destruction of streetlamps, telegraph and telephone wires,
and the attacks on the Gazómetro, these were tactical; without light, the
streetfighters were safer; without telephone and telegraph, the authorities
were less able to coordinate repression.[53]

It also seems clear that the streetfighters, who were, after all, occasionally joined by uniformed army officers, and who cheered the army
whenever its units appeared (ostensibly to aid the police), saw themselves
in alliance with the military. They apparently expected the coup that the
speeches and the obvious military links of the leadership made patent. It
is worth noting here that, indeed, the army, though its units were sent to
defend positions against the streetfighters on the 12th, was rarely trusted
with offensives against them until after the cadets' failure signaled the
coup's collapse. On those occasions when they were sent against the masses
before the 15th, they proved unenthusiastic, if not sympathetic. More indicative still is one memoir which recalls seeing many important officers
waiting hidden near the military school on the 14th, to see which direction the fortunes of war might blow. Rodrigues Alves's own dismay at the
lack of military support sent him by the generals on the evening of the
14th has already been noted.[54]

The violence of the streetfighters, then, although it obviously corre-
sponded to their own particular hatreds and anger in many details, was
directed toward a larger goal. As evident from their actions and the context just noted, their mission was to distract, divide, and tire the government's loyal forces and thus provide the military and psychological milieu
propitious for Lauro's coup. In this, they were successful. Indeed, too successful; they apparently forced the leadership to change plans. By taking

over the city streets and neutralizing the police, the streetfighters placed the government in an emergency situation in which the armed forces had to be called on and the military parade celebrating the republic's proclamation on November 15 had to be canceled. This parade, as noted earlier, was going to be the crucial medium for launching the planned coup. Now, the conspirators, meeting at the Club Militar, had to figure out how to bring the military out against Rodrigues Alves from their barracks or, worse, from the field, where they were now deployed against their popular allies. They seemingly fell back on the paradigm of November 15, 1889. Then, the cadets of Praia Vermelha and regular troops from the north zone, organized by republican, positivist militants, had come out at the call of a general of great personal prestige and struck together at the imperial government in the person of its prime minister and his cabinet. Now, after organizing among both cadets and the military, the conspirators again turned to the military school cadets; once again, a combination of the cadets' militance and army solidarity would launch attacks north and south against the government, in the person of its president and his assembled ministers. If only the cadets of Praia Vermelha (not to mention those of the Realengo school or the wavering army units in the Old City) had been able to strike quickly, matters might easily have gone Lauro's way. If the cadets had had their proper arms and ammunition and had marched immediately, all the evidence suggests that they might well have reached Catete unopposed, indeed, quite possibly reinforced, and have received the surrender of the palace's demoralized defenders. The army might well have gone over completely at such a juncture, and the day been won. But though the *desordeiros*, radicals, workers, and marginalized Cariocas had made this feasible, it was not to be. They were, in the end, dependent on Lauro's success, and Lauro failed.[55]

By November 14, the streetfighters began fortifying sections of the hillside shantytowns and dockside slums. These preparations, it will be recalled, centered on the Afro-Brazilian district of Saúde, where they called their barricaded trenchworks "Porto Arthur." They obeyed the commands of a well-known *desordeiro*, Horácio José da Silva, "Prata Preta," who had been elected to command. He did so with military precision; possibly he and others were veterans. Behind the barricades, cornets sounded, mock-up cannon were set up, and dynamite bombs were prepared (some real, some fake, for effect, like the cannon). And it was all done under the red flag the streetfighters unfurled, doubtless to signify adherence to the kind of socialist sindicalism men like Vicente de Sousa had injected into the Carioca milieu over the past decade. Until the ironclad turned its big guns against them, and until their hoped-for ally, the army, began its street-by-street attack, the streetfighters seemed to have maintained their readiness for battle. In the end, however, after Prata Preta's failed counterattack, they decided against striking the pose of some sort of tropical commune, with its terrible bloodbath: they left Porto Arthur. Unhappily, Rodrigues Alves was quite willing to play out the roles of 1870 Paris—if the *desordeiros* abandoned the role of communards, the president, as will be shown, was quite willing to take up something of the role of Thiers.[56]

The Triumph of the *Belle Époque*

The so-called Revolta Contra Vacina was, in essence, two revolts against the Paulista regime and its "modernizing" policies, each with distinct participants and agenda: two revolts, one of which consciously, and the other perhaps unconsciously, fought under the useful banner of a constitutional and medical issue of little real moment. The leadership launched their coup to remake the republic; the streetfighters among the masses, as far as we can discern, fought for a new social order or, at least, fought back against their immediate oppressors. Ostensibly, both leadership and masses won—obligatory vaccination, after all, was abandoned for several years. In reality, both lost. And each lost to the "modernizing" oligarchs' regime in separate ways which are worth noting.

The radical opposition lost in its bid for power and was further marginalized politically. They would never offer another real challenge to the Old Republic and its oligarchies—at least, not in Rio. Though Rodrigues Alves was bitter to see Lauro and other surviving conspirators and cadets amnestied in 1905, the larger questions of power had been answered in favor of the forces he represented. Save for vaccination, his policies triumphed. Rio became "modern," trade, immigration, and investment were successfully cultivated, and "progress" and "civilization" were assured. The *belle époque* had triumphed.[57]

If the leadership and cadets paid a small price for their failure, the poor paid terribly for their success. There was no amnesty for them. Hundreds arrested in the fighting were sent to the Ilha das Cobras compound just offshore, in a process of capture and imprisonment involving fearful beatings. After the revolt was smoldering and then cold, the police took their vengeance and the *belle époque* its toll. The police swept through the favelas, "beating" their target areas the way beaters flush out English sportsmen's quarry. There, and in raids in the various refuges to which the *desordeiros* fled, the police selected their enemies and the most dangerous-looking unemployed and sent them, along with beggars, poor prostitutes, and noted pimps to the Ilha das Cobras. Under the state of siege that an accommodating congress granted the administration thrice in succession, the rights of such prisoners could be trampled on, and they were. The wealthy foreign dealers in the white-slave trade were deported. For the native sons, Rodrigues Alves's government took a page from the French bourgeois who triumphed over the Paris commune. The streetfighters, beggars, unemployed, and prostitutes were sent to a kind of Brazilian Devil's Island—the recently acquired Territory of Acre, in the steaming tropical rain forests drained by tributaries of the Amazon. The newspapers record that between 539 and 855 or more prisoners—men and women—were sent there in three or four levies between the end of November and the first week of January, on coastal packet-boats the opposition would later aptly compare to the slaveships of the Middle Passage. Rio had been purged of the dangerous and the unsightly; the government had singled out people for elimination, just as it had eliminated so much of old Rio, the traditional, Afro-Brazilian port-capital—both were condemned by the values and needs of the elite's vision of modernity.[58]

The Brazilian-dominated unions that survived or succeeded those of 1904 would be moderate in their politics; indeed, like the radical leadership of 1904, native-born workers would generally no longer offer a substantial threat to the status quo. Their great struggle soon became unknown to most Cariocas, successfully captured and dismissed by middle-class and elite chroniclers as a kind of tropical Luddite reaction to the blessings of "modern" science—savage, barbaric, the work of political opportunists and atavistic masses.[59]

We have seen that it was far different and far more. The revolt of 1904 was a coordinated effort by at least two distinct groups to remake the Brazilian path: to destroy the oligarchical government, to strike back at its oppression and the savage attrition of its works, and, possibly, to erect an authoritarian, inclusionary, paternalist order dedicated to "modernity" without marginalization or the continued hegemony of the agroexport elites. But this unique attempt, mercilessly crushed, left no trace, no tradition. The alliance between ideological middle-sector leaders and the workers, marginalized, and *desordeiros* bore no fruit—only a distorted memory.

Each of the two elements went its separate way. After the amnesty that freed Lauro, his colleagues, and the cadets, there was tremendous acclaim for the senator—he was lionized by elements of the city's elite and middle sectors opposed to the particular policies of Rodrigues Alves (though none acclaimed the use of violence, nor the failed revolt). On his release, he enjoyed a fevered reception at the Teatro Lírico, traditional social center for the elite and the stage of the fantasy triumphs of opera. A subscription had raised the money for a sword of gold, which was presented to Lauro on that occasion.

One wag remembered, however, someone whom everyone else at the theater was apparently trying to forget. This wit observed that Lauro's sword would have been more fitting if it were made of silver—of *prata*. In two generations, this acid allusion to Prata Preta and the streetfighters of Saúde would go unnoticed.[60] The last contemporary reference I found to the *desordeiro* leader formed part of what its author described as a "Dantesque nightmare." In December 1904, a proadministration paper recorded this description of a group of those exiled to Acre. It says more, perhaps, about the "modernizers" than about their *desordeiro* enemy:

> From below decks of the ship came muffled sounds, shouts, curses, blasphemies. . . . There, piled up in the greatest promiscuity, were children and old people, blacks and whites, native-born and foreigners, some lying down, others standing, with both hands bound securely to the cableheads, trying to breathe, making superhuman efforts to take in the pure air of the exterior, which penetrated through only with difficulty. . . . The 334 convicts, almost all naked, fought with the enormous rats in the dark, who attacked them boldly and covered them with bites . . . without support, the prisoners rolled over one another, hurting themselves and slipping in the nauseating mud of feces and vomit. . . . Next to the hatches, riflemen pointed their weapons below, maintaining the respect of the miserable. Thus passed the first day, but other days followed and nothing changed the situation of the unhappy; on the contrary, their evils were aggravated with the sinister apparition of a terrible black, Prata Preta—a true demon: This black, tall, muscular, among the strongest present, immediately took a certain supremacy, taking on the office of chief below decks. Armed with a thick piece of rope, he began to beat his companions in misfortune bestially, ferociously, only stopping when the blood ran in jets.[61]

Plainly, Afro-Brazilian Rio was being exorcised in 1904—the city was "civilizing itself"[62] indeed.

Notes

1. "Perigos da vaccina," *Correio da Manhã* (hereafter, *CM*), Oct. 13. 1904, p. 1.

2. The Oswaldo Cruz campaign is discussed below. On the opposition see, e.g., Gil Vidal, "A terceira discussão," *CM*, Oct. 1, 1904, p. 1; "Vida operaria," *CM*, Oct. 1, 1904, p. 3; "Preparativos para a violencia?,' *CM*, Oct. 6, 1904, p. 1; "Vaccina ou morte," *CM*, Oct. 7, 1904, p. 1; "Vaccinação obrigatoria," *CM*, Oct. 10, 1904, p. 1; "Apello ao povo contra a vaccinação obrigatoria," *CM*, Nov. 5, 1904, p. 1; "Liga Contra a Vaccinação Obrigatoria," *CM*, Nov. 6, 1904, p. 1; "O dever do povo," *CM*, Nov. 7, 1904, p. 1; "Liga Contra a Vaccinação Obrigatoria," *CM*, Nov. 9, 1904, p. 2; *Gazeta de Noticias* (hereafter, *GN*), Nov. 12, 1904, p. 1; Menelau, "Chroniqueta," *A Avenida* (hereafter, *AA*), Oct. 29, 1904, p. 2; *AA*, Oct. 29, 1904, p. 5; Vital do Valle, "Notas e apanhados: Vaccinação obrigatoria," *AA*, Nov. 12, 1904, p. 15; "A vaccina," *Rua do Ouvidor*, July 16, 1904, p. 2; ibid., Aug. 13, 1904, p. 2; José [Araujo] Vieira, *O boto abaixo: Chronica de 1904* (Rio de Janeiro, 1934), 84–86, 88–89.

3. This synthesis is based on the analysis of the era's four major dailies: *O Paiz* (mass circulation, progovernment); *O Jornal do Commercio* (elite circulation, progovernment); *Gazeta de Noticias* (mass circulation, progovernment); and *Correio da Manhã* (mass circulation. opposition).

4. *Jornal do Commercio* (hereafter, JC), Nov. 16, 1904, p. 2; *O Paiz* (hereafter, OP), Nov. 17, 1904, p. 2; Dr. A. A. Cardoso de Castro, chefe de policia do Districto Federal, "Relatorio apresentado ao exm. sr. dr. J. J. Seabra, Ministro da Justiça e Negocios Interiores," Ministerio da Justiça e Negocios Interiores, *Relatorio apresentado ao Presidente da Republica dos Estados Unidos do Brasil pelo Dr.*

J. J. Seabra, Ministro . . . *em Marco de 1905* (Rio de Janeiro, 1905), 1, 18–19, 36–39, 40; Francisco de Paula Rodrigues Alves, "1904: Movimentos de novembro," ms. quoted *in toto* in Afonso Arinos de Melo Franco, *Rodrigues Alves: Apogeu e declíneo de presidencialismo*, 2 vols. (Rio de Janeiro, 1973), 1, 408–409; Dantas Barreto, *Conspiracões* (Rio de Janeiro, 1917), 11–14.

5. *JC*, Nov. 20, 1904, p. 2; General Lobato Filho, *A última noite da Escola Militar da Praia Vermelha: (Contribuições para a história)* (Rio de Janeiro, 1945), chs. 1, 2, 6, 7 [N.B., Lobato Filho was a rebel cadet]; Cardoso de Castro, "Relatorio," 13, 18–19, 20–21, 34–43, passim; see *CM* citations in n. 3 for a record of Lauro's activities before the rising.

6. *OP*, Nov. 15, 1904, p. 2; *JC*, Nov. 15, 1904, p. 1; Cardoso de Castro, as cited in n. 5; "O anno politico: Brasil," in *Almanaque brasileiro Garnier para o anno de 1906*, 314–315; Lobato Filho, *A última noite*, 96–98.

7. *OP*, Nov. 15, 1904, p. 1; *JC*, Nov. 15, 1904, p. 1; *GN*, Nov. 15, 1904, p. 2; Lobato Filho, *A última noite*, 91–113; Rodrigues Alves, "1904," 410–412; Emmanuel Sodré, *Lauro Sodré: Na história da República* (Rio de Janeiro, n.d.), 89–90.

8. Rodrigues Alves, "1904," 411–412. Cf. Vital do Valle, "Notas e apanhados," *AA*, Nov. 26, 1904, p. 3.

9. *OP*, Nov. 15, 1904, p. 2, Nov. 16, p. 2, and Nov. 17, p. 2; *GN*, Nov. 15, 1904, pp. 1–2, Nov. 16, 1904, pp. 1–2, and Nov. 17, pp. 2–3; *JC*, Nov. 15, 1904, p. 2, Nov. 16, 1904, p. 2, Nov. 17, 1904, p. 2, and Nov. 18, 1904, p. 2.

10. The repression began even earlier; *CM* was suspended Nov. 16–17 and Nov. 18–Dec. 14, 1904. Arrests of principal suspects began before Nov. 18 (see *CM*, Nov. 18, 1904, p. 2 and Dec. 28, 1904, p. 2; *GN* as cited in n. 9). On the immediate repression thereafter, see *JC* or *OP* through early Jan. 1905. On the subsequent smallpox toll, see Nancy Stepan, *Beginnings of Brazilian Science: Oswaldo Cruz, Medical Research and Policy, 1890–1920* (New York, 1976), 90, who reports some 9,000 dead of smallpox in 1908 alone.

Note that the rising in Rio was echoed by an abortive revolt in Salvador's ninth battalion on Nov. 18 (see *JC*, Nov. 20, 1904, p. 1; *OP*, Nov. 19, 1904, p. 1).

11. See, e.g., *JC*, Nov. 16, 1904, p. 2; *OP*, Nov. 15, 1904, p. 1, Nov. 17, 1904, p. 1, and Nov. 19, 1904, p. 1; *GN*, Nov. 16, 1904, p. 1; "Notas e noticias: Agitação inutil," *GN*, Nov. 13, 1904, p. 1; O. B., "Chronica," ibid.; "Notas e noticias: Os acontecimentos de hontem," *GN*, Nov. 14, 1904, p. 1; "Notas e noticias: Tentativa malograda," *GN*, Nov. 16, 1904, p. 1; "Notas e noticias: A licção dos factos," *GN*, Nov. 20, 1904, p. 1; Sancho Alves, "Commentarios," *Kósmos*, 2:3 (Mar. 1905), 1–2; Vital do Valle, "Notas e apanhados: Vaccinação Obrigatoria," *AA*, Nov. 12, 1904, p. 15; Til do Tal, "Sabbatinas," ibid., Nov. 19, 1904, p. 2; Vital do Valle, "Notas e apanhados: Prevenção d'A *Avenida*," ibid., p. 3; "O anno politico: Brasil," *Almanaque brasileiro*, 314–315; Cardoso de Castro, "Relatorio," 12, 14, 16–17; "Chronica politica," *Os Annaes*, 1:17 (Nov. 24, 1904), 110.

12. Robert G. Nachman, "Positivism and Revolution in Brazil's First Republic: The 1904 Revolt," *The Americas*, 34:1 (July 1977), 20.

13. Melo Franco, *Rodrigues Alves*, I, 392–436, especially 395–404. Nachman ("Positivism and Revolution," 20–21, nn. 1–4) lists these traditional and revisionist sources: Glauco Carneiro, *História das revoluções brasileiras* (Rio de Janeiro, 1965), I, 136–150; Lobato Filho, Dantas Barreto, and João Cruz Costa, *O positivismo na República* (São Paulo, 1956), 37–44; João Camilo de Oliveira Torres, *O positivismo no Brasil* (Petropolis, 1934), 282–286; Edgar Carone, *A República Velha (evolução política)* (São Paulo, 1971), 196–221; José Maria Bello, *A History of Modern Brazil, 1889–1964*, J. L. Taylor, trans. (Stanford, 1966).

14. Nachman, "Positivism and Revolution," especially pp. 22–37, discusses the position of the Positivist church and analyzes the relationship of the foremost conspirators and positivist republican militancy. He also points to the impact of the urban reforms on the masses as crucial to the revolt, although he does not explore the issue (21–22, 25–26).

15. Teresa Meade, " 'Civilizing Rio de Janeiro': The Public Health Campaign and the Riot of 1904," *Journal of Social History* (Dec. 1986) [ms. photocopy in author's possession through authors' exchange]. Meade's contribution is in excellent archival research and a good discussion of the plight of the poor.

16. See Sheldon Leslie Maram, "Anarchists, Immigrants, and the Brazilian Labor Movement, 1890–1920" (Ph.D. diss., University of California, Santa Barbara, 1972); Eulália Maria Lahmeyer Lobo, *História do Rio de Janeiro (do capital comercial ao capital industrial e financeiro)*, 2 vols. (Rio de Janeiro, 1978); Jaime Larry Benchimol, "Pereira Passos—Um Haussmann tropical: as transformações urbanas na cidade do Rio de Janeiro no início do século XX" (M.S. thesis, Universidade Federal do Rio de Janeiro, 1982); Eileen Keremitsis, "The Early Industrial Worker in Rio de Janeiro, 1870–1930" (Ph.D. diss., Columbia University, 1982); Oswaldo Porto Rocha, "A era das demolições: Cidade do Rio de Janeiro, 1870–1920" (M.A. thesis, Universidade Federal Fluminense, 1983); Nilson do Rosário Costa, "Estado e políticas de saúde pública (1889–1930)" (M.A. thesis, Instituto Universitario de Pesquisas do Rio de Janeiro, 1983); Samuel C. Adamo, "The Broken Promise: Race, Health, and Justice in Rio de Janeiro, 1890–1940" (Ph.D. diss., University of New Mexico, 1983); Meade, "Community Protest in Rio de Janeiro, Brazil, During the First Republic, 1890–1917" (Ph.D. diss., Rutgers University, 1984). See also Boris Fausto, *Trabalho urbano e conflito social (1880–1920)* (São Paulo, 1977), 13–62, passim; Nicolau Sevcenko, *Literatura como missão: Tensões sociais e criação cultural na Primeira República* (Rio de Janeiro, 1983), 51–68 and his pamphlet, *A revolta da vacina: Mentes insanas em corpos rebeldes* (São Paulo, 1984); Jeffrey D. Needell, "Making the Carioca *Belle Époque* Concrete: The Urban Reforms of Rio de Janeiro under Pereira Passos," *Journal of Urban History*, 10:4 (Aug. 1984); and José Murilo de Carvalho, "A revolta da vacina" (preliminary draft presented in the Seminário Rio Republicano, Rio de Janeiro, Oct. 4, 1984) [ms. photocopy in author's possession through authors' exchange]. Sevcenko's suggestive pamphlet, as such, lacks the documentation so notable in his book; more important, its focus skirts the role of the conspirators and their linkage to the masses and blurs some simple facts. Murilo de Carvalho's work, focusing on the workers' role and making apt comparisons with nineteenth-century Parisian revolts, is complementary to mine. Murilo de Carvalho, heading one group of the Equipe de Pesquisas of the Centro de Estudos Históricos, Fundação Casa de Rui Barbosa (Rio de Janeiro), has brought sophisticated methodology to bear on his team's extensive primary source research.

17. See Needell, "Making the Carioca *Belle Époque* Concrete," 399–400, 405–406 and "The Origins of the Carioca *Belle Époque*: The Emergence of the Elite Culture and Society of Turn-of-the-Century Rio de Janeiro" (Ph.D. diss., Stanford University, 1982), 45–68. With respect to the *jacobinos* and positivism, it must be noted that such radical positivists were distinct from members of the Positivist church. The latter was a formal organization, whose members refrained from political partisan activity per se—*jacobinos* were positivists as individuals, and were very partisan indeed.

18. Ibid.; Sevcenko, *Literatura como missão*, 41–51, 63–65; June E. Hahner, *Civilian-Military Relations in Brazil: 1889–1898* (Columbia, SC, 1969), 125–

134, 140–144, ch. 7; Joseph L. Love, *Rio Grande do Sul and Brazilian Regionalism, 1882–1930* (Stanford, 1971), 99–105, 151–152. Rio Grande radicals were distinguished by integration with one faction of the state's divided oligarchy (ibid., ch. 2, p. 75).

19. Needell, "Origins of the Carioca *Belle Époque*," 62–68, 115–128, 132–133, passim; Melo Franco, *Rodrigues Alves*, I, 241; Luiz Viana Filho, *A vida de Rui Barbosa* (São Paulo, 1943), 209.

20. Needell, "Making the Carioca *Belle Époque* Concrete," 400, 405-406.

21. Ibid., 400–406. For the dominant concept of "modernization" and the *belle époque* in Rio, see 403–410 and also Needell, "Rio de Janeiro at the Turn of the Century: Modernization and the Parisian Ideal," *Journal of Interamerican Studies and World Affairs*, 25:1 (Feb. 1983), 83–103.

22. For contemporary responses to obligatory vaccination, see the citations in n. 2, above. For traditional analyses, see, e.g., Bello, *A History of Modern Brazil*, 181–182; Lobato Filho, *A última noite*, 68; Carneiro, *História*, 136–138; Melo Franco, *Rodrigues Alves*, I, 390–395, 417–420; Sodré, *Lauro Sodré*, 85-87. For recent research, see Nachman, "Positivism and Revolution," 21-24; Stepan, *Beginnings of Brazilian Science*, 88–91; Costa, "Estado e políticas," 75, 78–79, 82, 84–87; and Meade. See also Donald B. Cooper, "Brazil's Long Fight Against Epidemic Disease, 1849–1914, With Special Emphasis on Yellow Fever," *Bulletin of the New York Academy of Medicine*, 51:5 (May 1975), 672–696 and his "Oswaldo Cruz and the Impact of Yellow Fever on Brazilian History," *The Bulletin of the Tulane University Medical Faculty*, 26:1 (Feb. 1967), 49–52.

23. See, e.g., regarding neutral or proadministration opposition, the case of the established lawyer, Villela dos Santos, seeking a writ of habeas corpus against obligatory vaccination in *GN*, Nov. 12, 1904, p. 1; the reasoned arguments against the legislation on political grounds in Menelau, "Chroniqueta," *AA*, Oct. 29, 1904, p. 2; cf. ibid., p. 5 (provaccination); the provaccination, antiobligatory comments in "A vaccina," *Rua do Ouvidor*, July 16, Aug. 13, 1904, p. 2. See also Nachman's review of the Positivist church's position, "Positivism and Revolution," 22–23.

24. Melo Franco, *Rodrigues Alves*, I, 390–399; Nachman, "Positivism and Revolution," 23–37. Again, note the distinction that must be made between these men, often positivist or positivist-influenced, and members of the Positivist church, which abstained from politics and violence.

25. Melo Franco, *Rodrigues Alves*, I, 399–400; Nachman, "Positivism and Revolution," 33–35; Sodré, *Lauro Sodré*, 34–66, 69–99; Lobato Filho, *A última noite*, 69–86; *CM*, Oct. 18, 1904, pp. 1–2. On the *jacobinos* and Florianistas, see Hahner, "Jacobinos versus Galegos: Urban Radicals versus Portuguese Immigrants in Rio de Janeiro in the 1890s," *Journal of Interamerican Studies and World Affairs*, 18:2 (May 1976), 131–133, 135–139; and Sevcenko, *Literatura como missão*, 63–64; Benchimol, "Pereira Passos," 365–371.

26. Melo Franco, *Rodrigues Alves*, I, 396, 403–404; Nachman, "Positivism and Revolution," 27–30; Edgar Carone, *A República Velha, I: Instituições e classes sociais* (1889–1930), 4a ed. (São Paulo, 1978), 386–388; Cardoso de Castro, *Relatorio*, 9, 11–12, 14–15, 18, 41–42, 45–46; *JC*, Nov. 19, 1904, p. 2; *OP*, Nov. 19, 1904, p. 2.

27. See the speeches and editorials given full play in *CM* during Oct. and Nov. 1904. See also Lobato Filho, *A última noite*, 69–73, 82–86; Hahner, "Jacobinos versus Galegos," 131–132, 142; Nachman, "Positivism and Revolution," 31–37; and his "Positivism, Modernization, and the Middle Class in Brazil," *HAHR*, 57:1 (Feb. 1977), 7, 10–16, 22–23; but cf. Sodré, *Lauro Sodré*, 55–57, 58–59, 65–66. Note, especially, Lauro's Pará administration (see Sodré, 54–74, passim, and

Nachman, "Positivism, Modernization, and the Middle Class," 10–16, passim). Nachman points to links between Brazilian positivism and post-1920 ideology, from Plínio Salgado's *integralismo* to Getúlio Vargas, in both of his pieces. On the *salvacionista* movement, see Love, *Rio Grande do Sul*, 156–157, 159, 163.

28. "Os Acontecimentos," *Os Annaes*, 1:7 (Nov. 24, 1904), 111–112; Cardoso de Castro, *Relatorio*, 8–13, 15, 34–40; Lobato Filho, *A última noite*, 67–73. On the police, see also "Dr. Cardoso de Castro," *Rua do Ouvidor*, May 2, 1903, pp. 1–2. Rodrigues Alves's election was the work of Campos Sales, who, although he recognized the importance of "historical" republican credentials (as did Rodrigues Alves), writes that he preferred a successor he could trust to carry on his financial policies through competent administration, above the partisan considerations of the 1890s; see Campos Sales, *Da propaganda á presidencia* (São Paulo, 1908), 366–368. Cf. Dunshee de Abranches, *Como se faziam presidentes: Homens e fotos do início da república* (Rio de Janeiro, 1973), 304–307, 322, 326–328, 334–335, 341, 343–347, who relates that Rodrigues Alves, then governor of São Paulo, was indicated by northern politicians and São Paulo's machine principally to avoid the candidacy of a certain northern political chief, and was then embraced by Campos Sales, who wished to take the credit and had become personally uncomfortable with the most obvious alternatives.

29. Nachman, "Positivism and Revolution," 32–33; Sodré's son tells us that his father had had the family vaccinated but opposed obligatory vaccination (*Lauro Sodré*, 85).

30. For opposition articles on vaccination, see n. 2; for the rest, see, e.g., "Pelo exercito: É demais," *CM*, Oct. 2, 1904, p. 1; "A miseria no exercito," *CM*, Oct. 4, 1904, p. 2; "Preparativos para a violencia?" *CM*, Oct. 6, 1904, p. 1; "Campanhas de assassinato," *CM*, Oct. 10, 1904, p. 1; "Eleições e governo," *CM*, Oct. 11, 1904, p. 1; "Que sera?: Greve?— Revolução?—Agitação policial—O Sr. Cardoso de Castro em campo—Promptidão absoluta," *CM*, Oct. 18, 1904, p. 1; "A Bernarda," *CM*, Oct. 19, 1904, p. 1; "Escravidão," *CM*, Oct. 21, 1904, p. 1. See also the coverage of the "civic pilgrimage" celebrating Benjamin Constant [Botelho de Magalhães], *CM*, Oct. 19, 1904, pp. 1–2. On the conspiracy, see n. 28 and Carneiro, *História*, 148–149; Nachman, "Positivism and Revolution," 24–36, passim; Melo Franco, *Rodrigues Alves*, I, 394–403.

31. See Benchimol, "Pereira Passos," chs. 4, 7, and especially pp. 144, 145, 147, 151, 153, 165–172; Keremitsis, "The Early Industrial Worker," ch. 2, especially pp. 17, 24, 28, 50, 54; Lahmeyer Lobo, *História do Rio*, I, 227–231. Note that slaves made up a fifth of the workforce in 1872, with most involved in agriculture, domestic service, and artisanal activities (Lahmeyer Lobo, *História do Rio*, I. 231). A study of domestic labor can be found in Sandra Lauderdale Graham, "Protection and Obedience: The Paternalist World of Female Domestic Servants, Rio de Janeiro, 1860–1910" (Ph.D. diss., University of Texas, 1982).

32. See Adamo, "The Broken Promise," 7, 11, 13–15, 18, 21–24 and ch. 1, passim. The 1906 census did not pick out race: Adamo estimated it by computer extrapolation (see pp. 11–12, n. 14). The reliability of the apposite censuses is discussed on p. 9. The basis for extrapolation was censuses in which respondents identified themselves racially; in a racist society, one should expect respondents to "whiten" themselves, hence these figures are probably too low. See also Republica dos Estados Unidos do Brasil, Directoria Geral de Estatistica, *Recenseamento do Rio de Janeiro (Districto Federal): Realisado em 20 de setembro de 1906* (Rio de Janeiro, 1907), 388–389; Lahmeyer Lobo, *História do Rio*, II, 469; Benchimol, "Pereira Passos," 339–341.

33. *Recenseamento*... *1906*, 104, 236–237; Lahmeyer Lobo, *História do Rio*, II, 508, 572; Benchimol, "Pereira Passos," 345, 388–389. In the 1870 census, of the urban population of 235,381, there were 53,160 domestics (23 percent); 13,560 people employed in agriculture (*lavradores*) (6 percent); and 41,381 people (18 percent) employed in *manufactura, artes e officios*—some 80,717 (34 percent) were *sem profissão conhecida* (*Recenseamento*... *1906*, 100). In comparing the figures and proportions, bear in mind that the commercial and professional-liberal sectors of the economy had grown significantly by 1906 (see Benchimol, "Pereira Passos," 350, 351–352), and that the category *manufactura, artes e officios* includes artisans and the like, as well as industrial workers per se. The 1907 industrial census is in Lahmeyer Lobo, *História do Rio*, II, 572–576. One supposes the great difference between the figures for textile employment in 1906 and 1907 has to do with census categories; 1906 distinguishes "textiles" from "clothing and accessories"—1907 apparently includes much of 1906's clothing and accessories in its "textiles" category.

34. Porta Rocha, "A era das demolições," 92, 101–102; Benchimol, "Pereira Passos," chs. 7, 9, pp. 359–364, passim; Adamo, "The Broken Promise," 31–40; Keremitsis, "The Early Industrial Worker," 41–53; Sevcenko, *Literatura como missão*, 51–59. Beyond the commission reports, analyzed in Benchimol, an excellent contemporary description is Everardo Backheuser, "Onde moram os pobres," *Renacença*, 2:13, 2:15 (Mar., May 1905), 89–94, 185–189.

35. Backheuser, "Onde moram," 92. More graphic descriptions made Alusío de Azevedo's novel, *O cortiço* (1890), a naturalist classic.

36. Backheuser, "Onde moram," 92–94; on illness, beyond Cooper, Costa, Benchimol, and Stepan the best quantitative and medical analysis is Adamo, "The Broken Promise," chs. 3, 4.

37. *Recenseamento*... *1906*, 104. On the impact of the under- and unemployed on Rio's labor force, see Fausto, *Trabalho urbano*, 26–28.

38. Adamo, "The Broken Promise," ch. 2.

39. Sevcenko, *Literatura como missão*, 59–61; Lahmeyer Lobo, *História do Rio*, I, 209–222, II, 453–468, 471–508; Rebecca Baird Bergstresser, "The Movement for the Abolition of Slavery in Rio de Janeiro, Brazil, 1880–1889" (Ph.D. diss., Stanford University, 1973), chs. 1–3, passim; Hahner, "Jacobinos," 129–130; Francisco de Assis Barbosa, "A presidência Campos Sales," *Luso-Brazilian Review*, 5:1 (1968), 3–26.

40. On the repression of cultural expression and the disproportionate hardships of the "nonwhite" population, see Adamo, "The Broken Promise," chs. 5, 6, and passim; and Alison Raphael, "Samba and Social Control: Popular Culture and Racial Democracy in Rio de Janeiro" (Ph.D. diss., Columbia University, 1979). On the African quality of this culture, see Needell, "Making the Carioca *Belle Époque* Concrete," 385, 408–410. Note also the cumulative impact of the African slave trade, which continued to Brazil until 1855; as late as 1872, the number of Africans in Rio and the Province of Rio de Janeiro was at least 67,235 (6.4 percent of the total); in Rio alone, there were 10,973 (3.9 percent of the city's total); see Stanley J. Stein, *Vassouras: A Brazilian Coffee County: 1850–1890* (New York, 1970), 296; and Robert Conrad, *The Destruction of Brazilian Slavery: 1850–1880* (Berkeley, 1972), 287. Surely, bearing in mind the traditional, rural, African roots of Bahian and Fluminense Afro-Brazilian culture, central to popular culture in turn-of-the-century Rio through migration, to speak of a distinctive culture and alienation or hostility among the emancipated or the children and grandchildren of slaves vis-à-vis the Europhile, urbane elite is not an exaggeration. On the

cultural aspects of Afro-Brazilian resistance, see Porto Rocha; on the culture per se, see, e.g., Raphael, "Samba and Social Control," Ary Vasconcelos, *Panorama da música popular brasileira na belle époque* (Rio de Janeiro, 1977), or José Ramos Tinhorão, *Pequena história da música popular* (Petrópolis, 1974).

41. Fausto, *Trabalho urbano*, 14–15, 26–27, 31–32, 35–37, and especially 41–62, shows, in his discussion of Paulista labor and Carioca "*trabalhismo*," the way in which Carioca workers were often organized by déclassé intellectuals, often Florianistas or self-taught "socialists," in unions or clubs of ephemeral influence and impact. Cf. Hahner, "Jacobinos and Galegos," 136–140. Maram, "Anarchists," 3–5, 10–13, 16, 17–18, 21–23, 54–55, 57–58; as in his "Labor and the Left in Brazil, 1890–1921: A Movement Aborted," *HAHR*, 57:2 (May 1977), 254–255, 259–260, 268, 270–271; and in his "The Immigrant and the Brazilian Labor Movement, 1890–1920," in *Essays Concerning the Socioeconomic History of Brazil and Portuguese India*, Dauril Alden and Warren Dean, eds. (Gainesville, 1977), 179–180, 182–185 n. 15, 186–188, 189, 191, tends to focus on the post-1906, immigrant-led, anarchist movement, yet still provides an idea of the weaknesses besetting the nascent Carioca industrial proletariat. Murilo de Carvalho ("A revolta da vacina," 41–42) claims an important element among Carioca industrial workers, organized in the Federação das Associações de Classe (FAC), was anarchist in orientation (cf. Fausto, *Trabalho urbano*, 120–121) and suggests that its actions in 1904 were separate from those of Vicente de Sousa's Centro de Classes Operarias (CCO). This has not, however, been documented. It is also unclear that the FAC's membership was of a wholly distinct origin compared to the CCO's. Although the FAC was largely made up of artisan and factory workers, it did include dockyard workers, and, while the CCO was linked to government employees and dockyard workers traditionally associated with *jacobino* union organization, it also had artisan and factory worker elements. On women in the work force, see Hahner, "Women and Work in Brazil: 1850–1920: A Preliminary Investigation," in *Essays Concerning the Socioeconomic History*, 87–117, especially 100–117. For contemporary accounts, police activities, and the stevedores, see, e.g., M. Curvello, "O movimento socialista no Brasil," *Almanaque brasileiro . . . 1905*, 272–277; Cardoso de Castro, "Relatorio," 13, 16, 18, 37; and his "Relatorio apresentado ao Exmo. Snr. Dr. J. J. Seabra Ministro da Justiça e Negocios Interiores pelo Chefe de Policia do Districto Federal. . . . ," in *Ministerio da Justiça e Negocios Interiores, Annexos ao relatorio apresentado ao Presidente da Republica dos Estados Unidos do Brasil pelo Dr. J. J. Seabra . . . em março de 1904* (Rio de Janeiro, 1904), 15, 29–30; "Vida operaria," *CM*, Oct. 1, 1904, p. 3; "Vida operaria," ibid., Oct. 7, 1904, p. 2; "Os estivadores," ibid., Oct. 19, 1904, p. 3; "Os estivadores," ibid., Oct. 22, 1904, p. 2; "Vida operaria," ibid., Nov. 1, 1904, p. 1; *GN*, Nov. 17, 1904, p. 2.

42. See Lahmeyer Lobo, *História do Rio*, II, 503–504, 505–506; Carone, *República Velha*, I, 219–220; Maram, "Anarchists," 54–55; "Augmento de passagens," *CM*, Oct. 11, 1904, p. 1; Cardoso de Castro, "Relatorio" (1904), 16–22; F. de A. Barbosa, "A presidência Campos Sales," 16; Murilo de Carvalho, "A revolta da vacina," 22, 39–40.

43. See Needell, "Making the *Belle Époque* Concrete," 401–403, 408; Backheuser, "Onde moram"; Benchimol, "Pereira Passos," 359–364, ch. 14, passim, and 592–609; Porta Rocha, "A era das demolições," ch. 4. I differ here from Murilo de Carvalho ("A revolta da vacina," 44–45) on the impact of the economic situation and housing.

44. Costa, "Estado e políticas," 68–79. Murilo de Carvalho points out that the issue of "invading the hearth" was central to the signed petitions against vaccina-

tion sent to Congress by thousands of organized workers ("A revolta da vacina," 7, 23).

45. Costa, "Estado e políticas," 79, 82, 84-87; Vieira, *O boto aboixo*, 170; "A terceira discussão," *CM*, Oct. 1, 1904, p. 1; "Vida operaria," ibid., p. 3; "Vaccinação ou morte," ibid., Oct. 7, 1904, p. 1: "O dever do povo," ibid., Nov. 7, 1904, p. 1; Menelau, "Chroniqueta," *AA*, Oct. 29, 1904, p. 2; *GN*, Nov. 15, 1904, p. 2.

46. Elisio de Araujo, *Estudo historico sobre a policia da Capital Federal: 1808–1831* (Rio de Janeiro, 1898), 56–62, 113–123, 133–135; Thomas Flory, "Race and Social Control in Independent Brazil," *Journal of Latin American Studies*, 9:2 (Nov. 1977), 203–204; L. C., "A capoeira," *Kósmos*, 3:3 (Mar. 1906), 56–57; Dunshee de Abranches, *Actas e actos do governo provisorio* (Rio de Janeiro, 1907), 361–366; Medeiros e Albuquerque, *Minha vida: Da infancia a mocidade: Memorias: 1867–1893*, 3a ed. (Rio de Janeiro, 1933), 123–129; R. Magalhães Junior, *Deodoro: A espada contra o império*, 2 vols. (São Paulo, 1957), II, 182–187; on contemporary response, see, e.g., "Grande conflicto," *CM*, Oct. 10, 1904, p. 2; "Reclamações," ibid., Oct. 26, 1904, p. 3; Menelau, "Chroniqueta," *AA*, Oct. 29, 1904, p. 2.

47. Araujo, *Estudo historico*, ch. 5, passim, 135–137; Mello Moraes Filho, *Factos e memorias* (Rio de Janeiro, 1904), pt. 4, ch. 10, and pt. 5, ch. 11; Bergstresser, "Abolition of Slavery," chs. 1–3, passim; Graham, "The Vintem Riot and Political Culture: Rio de Janeiro, 1880," *HAHR*, 60:3 (Aug. 1980), 431–449; Hahner, "Jacobinos versus Galegos," 128, 132, 140–141, 143; O. B., "Chronica," *GN*, Nov. 13, 1904, p. 1. The basis for Lusophobia lay in the traditionally dominant Portuguese role in Carioca commerce and the active sympathy the Portuguese government appeared to show for the fallen Braganza dynasty's cause.

48. On the Portuguese, cf. Maram, "Labor and the Left," 257–258; and his "Immigrant and Brazilian Labor," 190–191; Hahner, "Jacobinos versus Galegos," 120–128, 130, 139, 148. Murilo de Carvalho ("A revolta da vacina," 35–37, 55n.) notes Portuguese participation in 1904, despite the alienation from Carioca traditions of violent resistance I suggest here. Indeed, as Maram notes, the Portuguese-dominated workers' movement in Santos was quite militant; Santos, however, did not have the ongoing, violent tradition of Lusophobia noteworthy in Rio. Indeed, regarding the 1904 events, it may well be impossible, even given the superb research done by Murilo's Equipe de Pesquisas, to ever know precisely the extent of Portuguese involvement or that of any other group. For example, both my own research and Murilo's comments suggest that the police arrest records are hardly a record of activism in the revolt, since the police arrested whomever they pleased, especially after the 18th. Neither do reports of the dead and wounded necessarily prove Portuguese involvement in the revolt. Although they do detail nationality, one cannot presume casualties are proofs of participation—the papers regularly report the damage done to passers-by during the disorders. As for occupation, the list of 90 casualties, dubious for the reason just noted, is hardly helpful—the occupations of less than 50 are noted. The best indications are in the analysis of the workers' petitions in Murilo de Carvalho, which suggest the participation of organized labor. However, such petitions are not the sort of thing the marginalized or the *desordeiros* were likely to sign. On the urban Afro-Brazilian culture, see the references in n. 40, above. I found no reference to Lusophobia in the published propaganda of the movement; thus, this paragraph deals with the putative memory, or "unofficial" expression, of such prejudice in *jacobino*-mass relations.

49. Frank D. McCann, "The Nation in Arms: Obligatory Military Service During the Old Republic," in *Essays Concerning the Socioeconomic History*, 217–219; Jose Murilo de Carvalho, "As forças armadas na Primeira República: O poder

desestabilizador," in *História geral da civilização brasileira*, tomo 3: *O Brasil republicano*, Boris Fausto, ed. 2 vols. (São Paulo, 1977), II, 189–191; Adamo, "The Broken Promise," 188–194; cf. Cardoso de Castro, "Relatorio" (1904), 5–7; *AA*, Oct. 29, 1904, p. 26.

50. Cardoso de Castro, "Relatorio" (1905), 18, 38–39; *JC*, Nov. 16, 1904, p. 1; *OP*, Nov. 17, 1904, p. 2; Lobato Filho, *A última noite*, 68–69, 70–80; Dantas Barreto, *Conspirações*, 12–15; Nachman, "Positivism and Revolution," 24–33; Fausto, *Trabalho urbano*, 43–51 and passim; "Vida operaria," *CM*, Oct. 7, 1904, p. 2.

51. See the elements involved in the first meeting of the league and the speech in which Lauro made clear the larger political issues: "Liga Contra a Vaccinação Obrigatoria," *CM*, Nov. 6, 1904, p. 2; see also the introductory "Appello ao povo," ibid., Nov. 5, 1904, p. 1. An excellent analysis of the actions of the mass participants vis-à-vis urban workers is Murilo de Carvalhos, "A revolta da vacina," 35–42 and passim.

52. See, e.g., O. B., "Chronica," *GN*, Nov. 13, 1904, p. 2; Graham, "Vintem Riot," 436–437.

53. On these last two paragraphs, see *CM*, Nov. 13, 1904, p. 1, Nov. 14, 1904, p. 2, and Nov. 15, 1904, p. 2; *GN*, Nov. 13, 1904, pp. 1–2, Nov. 14, 1904, pp. 1–2, and Nov. 15, 1904, pp. 1–2; *JC*, Nov. 15, 1904, p. 2. My interpretation here owes something to the studies of mass and urban violence appearing in *Past and Present* since the 1950s and associated with E. J. Hobsbawm, E. V. Thompson, George Rudé et al. Meade and, especially, Murilo de Carvalho are more heavily indebted to this approach, since they focus on the masses' role,

54. See the accounts in *CM* cited in n. 53, above; the "fictional" memoir of Vieira, *O boto aboixo*, 171–172; on the waiting officers, Dantas Barreto, *Conspirações*, 41; and Rodrigues Alves, "1904," in Melo Franco, *Rodrigues Alves*, I, 409–411.

55. On the conspirators' expectations and strategy, see Cardoso de Castro, "Relatorio" (1905), 30–39; Lohato Filho, *A última noite*, 79–81, 98, 100. Cf. the contemporary accounts and memoirs of the coup of 1889 in Ernesto Senna, *Deodoro: Subsídios para a história* (Brasilia, 1981). Murilo de Carvalho, "A revolta da vacina," 41–42, argues for a clearly disassociated factory revolt after Nov. 15, distinct from the larger movement of the CCO. I agree that, after that date, the various components of the Carioca masses continued with their several agendas, but I disagree that this proves they were without earlier links to Vicente de Sousa or Lauro's hopes.

56. The *CM* being closed down, the best coverage of Porto Arthur is in *OP*, *GN*, and *JC*. See *JC*, Nov. 15, 1904, p. 1, Nov. 16, 1914, p. 2, and Nov. 17, 1904, p. 2; *OP*, Nov. 15, 1904, p. 1, Nov. 16, 1904, p. 2, and Nov. 17, 1904, p. 2; *GN*, Nov. 15, 1904, p. 2, Nov. 16, 1904, p. 2, and Nov. 17, 1904, pp. 2–3.

57. The amnesty occurred at the end of 1905, largely as a maneuver to embarrass the president by elements who were successfully undermining his personal power; see Melo Franco, *Rodrigues Alves*, 427–435.

58. The repression is covered in the progovernment dailies, which uniformly accepted the measures as salutary: see, e.g., *OP*, Dec. 11, 1904, p. 2, Dec. 16, 1904, p. 2, Dec. 21, 1904, p. 2, Dec. 30, 1904, p. 2, and Dec. 31, 1904, p. 2; *JC*, Nov. 20, 1904, p. 2, Nov. 21, 1904, p. 2, Nov. 23, 1904, p. 2, Dec. 24, 1904, p. 2, Dec. 25, 1904, p. 2; *GN*, Nov. 26, 1904, p. 2, and Nov. 27, 1904, p. 2; cf. Melo Franco, *Rodrigues Alves*, I, 424–426.

59. Post-1904 labor militance was largely immigrant anarcho-syndicalist in origin; see the references in n. 41. On the memory of 1904, see the responses

cited in n. 13; cf. Bello, *A History of Modern Brazil*, 181–183 or Melo Franco, *Rodrigues Alves*, I, 391–393.

60. Melo Franco, *Rodrigues Alves*, I, 434. I have the cited comment from a quotation Melo Franco takes from Rodrigues Alves's notebook, where the president apparently took pleasure in the jibe. Melo Franco, however, seems not to understand the point—Porto Arthur and Prata Preta do not appear in his narrative.

61. "Os degregados do Acre," *CM*, Dec. 28, 1904, p. 1, quoting *A Noticia*, Dec. 27, 1904. Prata Preta was apparently on the first packet-boat sent out.

62. This is a reference to Figueiredo Pimentel's celebrated contemporary phrase, "O Rio civiliza-se" and to the elite fears and hopes linked to the urban reforms which Figueiredo Pimentel championed. See Needell, "Making the Carioca *Belle Époque* Concrete," 403, 410, 421.

3

General Strike in Montevideo

Anton Rosenthal

In this lively selection, Anton Rosenthal analyzes an important event in the history of Latin American labor. As he points out, in this episode gender and class situations intercede and allow—as in the Needell essay about Rio—insights about how broadly workers have influenced the lives of many other people among the salaried sectors of society. The new, modern middle class of Montevideo expected to live like its European counterparts, and the arrival of European immigrants and the opening up of new industries at the turn of the century were accompanied by urban reforms. Progress was the catchword not only for the middle-sector managers and clerks but also for the workers in the various industries. They all crossed paths in the new city centers and they all went home by trolley car. The shared experiences blurred the sharp distinctions that had existed earlier between workers and their middle-sector neighbors.

As Rosenthal makes clear, unlike factory workers and office personnel, trolley workers were always in the limelight, and when they aired their grievances the riding public could hardly be unaware. In the same way that the daily ups and downs of trolley workers' lives were evident to everyone, so were their poor living conditions. Overcrowded housing, despite the move from conventillos *(high-rise slums) to the rim of the city, and unhealthy conditions followed the workers wherever they settled. Finally, it is worth noting that while the poorly organized trolley workers received little sympathy from their passengers a few years before the general strike, the growing conviction that the companies were treating their employees unfairly shifted public opinion. Female riders were notably sympathetic, and the press got into the act. As the image of the companies turned from progressive to repressive, the stage for an unusual outpouring of sympathy for the general strike was set.*

The first general strike in Uruguayan history, which completely paralyzed Montevideo for three days in May 1911, provides a useful vantage point from which to view the transformation of the third largest capital in South America from a sleepy "Belle Epoque" horse town into a modern, cosmopolitan city. Coming many years after general strikes in Buenos Aires, São Paulo and Rio de Janeiro, the 1911 Montevideo conflict appeared to erupt virtually overnight, at a moment when the labor movement itself was in some disarray, and caught the city by surprise. Merchants closed their doors, transport ground to a halt, and theaters and cinemas remained dark as the city became strangely quiet. An estimated 50,000–60,000 workers in 37 unions left their jobs in factories, breweries, *frigoríficos*,[1] stores, and newspapers.[2] In the words of a journalist for a conservative daily paper, "every sign of activity vanished from the city as completely as if it had been stricken by a pestilence—as in truth it was."[3] The anarchist labor confederation, which organized the mass strike, took over control of the streets and the food supply, and vehicles were only allowed to run with its authorization, thus inverting the city's power structure, at least temporarily.

Considering its novelty and the fear and hope which it provoked in different sectors of the urban populace, the 1911 strike has received surprisingly little interest from historians. It has been treated primarily in the context of the populist reformism and pro-labor sympathies of the major political figure of the era, José Batlle y Ordoñez, as he began his second presidency in 1911. His infamous balcony speech on the eve of the strike urged workers to struggle for their rights but also to respect the law. It inflamed the conservative press which denounced him as a radical, but the speech actually had little lasting impact on the workers themselves.[4] Labor historians have recorded the strike as a small milestone for its role in regenerating a movement that had stagnated due to police repression and union busting, and they have also emphasized its impact on the general political culture, including the development of anarchist and socialist movements.[5]

But the strike has far greater historical importance than these political approaches have been able to uncover. By shifting the focus to the true center of the strike, the streetcar system, this article intends to show how a group of aggrieved trolley workers was able to attract the support of tens of thousands of residents in the most powerful demonstration of collective resistance to foreign capital and an industrial work regimen seen in the city up until that time. Without the benefit of an established union, streetcarmen used networks outside of elite control and their unique positions as publicly visible workers to mobilize women, newsboys, students, bakers, linotypists, barbers, tailors, and even police in defense of their demands for improved working conditions under the banner "a little more bread and a little more liberty."[6] This article offers an analysis of the strike from the level of the street in order to reveal the fluid nature of class relations in an urban milieu that was no longer artisan but not yet industrial. It also demonstrates how the streetcar emerged as an essential part of the city's physical and mental landscape in the opening years of the 20th century and how the residents' dependency upon it led to sharp social conflict.

The Streetcar and Social Change

The electric streetcar came to Uruguay relatively late, arriving in November 1906 amidst great fanfare, elite-orchestrated celebrations and public displays of curiosity and fascination with the lighted vehicles. There were many speeches and editorials praising the trolley as a symbol of progress which would allow the capital to renovate slums, expand and prosper in the 20th century.[7] There was also an underlying hope that the civil wars of 1897 and 1904 which had pitted rural landowners against urban modernizers would at last fade into history, allowing merchants, industrialists and the new middle class to bring about changes that would put the capital on par with its European counterparts.

The end of the civil conflicts in Uruguay unleashed another wave of immigration from Italy and Spain which fed directly into Montevideo as the port of entry. Under this impetus, the capital grew by great leaps in the period prior to World War I and became the most dominant primary city on the continent, housing one-quarter of the nation's citizens.[8] As new areas of the city were opened up to accommodate these immigrants and new industries were begun which provided jobs, the mass transit system was increasingly employed to convey workers to factories, clerks to offices, mourners to funerals, shoppers to large downtown stores and families to Sunday amusements.[9] Within a few years of its inauguration, the electric streetcar system provided regular service seven days a week, nearly 20 hours per day, on routes extending over 157 miles from the port and the Ciudad Vieja to the suburbs and adjacent towns of Pocitos, the Prado, Unión, Maroñas and Villa Colón.[10]

The expansion of the trolley system, in turn, set off a chain of other civic improvements, including the construction of sewers, the paving of streets and the extension of street lighting. Together these helped foster a boom in land sales and construction as developers created new neighborhoods on the northern and eastern fringes of the capital. The number of permits for new buildings nearly tripled in the period immediately after the *eléctricos* were inaugurated.[11] Carlos Maeso observed in 1910 that

> The establishment of electric trolleys which cross nearly all of Montevideo's streets and avenues as well as its surrounding areas, has accelerated considerably this building progress, uniting areas previously separated from the central zones.[12]

Amid this construction and civic improvement, a vibrant center-city nightlife developed, with the trolley serving as the vehicle connecting a network of cafés, theatres and stores.[13] In 1908, the first full year of electric streetcar service throughout the city, theatres, biographs [movie theaters] and other arenas attracted over 2 million spectators, thus significantly augmenting the trolleys' clientele of daily commuters and Sunday beach- and park-goers.[14] In a short time, Montevideo's residents became completely dependent upon the streetcar, with ridership doubling between 1906 and 1910, thus beginning a period of growth that would last until the mid-1920s.[15]

The streetcar also insinuated itself into the mental life of the city. Its increased speed led to a perception of shrinking distances for people in all social classes and a certain democratization of leisure. The Prado, previously a summer getaway for the city's elite, required only a one-half hour trip on the trolley from the city center after electrification. This new speed effectively converted the enormous tree-laden park into a place of leisure for the middle and popular classes, and thus opened up their sense of urban space.[16] Slowly, the neighborhood-based identities of Montevideo's residents gave way to a shared experience of the increased movement and general rush of the city as people used the trolley to cross its different zones. The northern beach at Capurro, the eastern beach at Pocitos and the central beach of Ramirez, as well as the various parks, the race-track, the zoo and the Sunday street fairs, all acted as magnets for residents from across the city. At the end of their outings, their last shared experience was the crowded trolleys which took them home.

The streetcar also became a focus of collective representations of the city. It appeared prominently on postcards which celebrated the changing architecture of the city and which were sent across town, to the interior of the country, to Buenos Aires and even across the ocean to Milan, Barcelona and Paris. It was featured in cartoons in the daily press and it was linked by merchants and newspapermen, in advertising and stories, to the tourism they desired and promoted. At the other end of the social spectrum, the streetcar was satirized during *carnaval* as early as 1909[17] and memorialized in at least one local tango after electrification. By the time of the 1911 general strike, the eléctrico had emerged as the nexus of a new city and a key part of its evolving self-image as a capital with a dynamic future. It had become an indispensable part of everyday life for the vast majority of Montevideo's residents. As the new urban order became subject to the antagonistic demands of different social sectors, the streetcar was also turned into a scene of conflict.

The Streetcar as a Workplace

In the period prior to the First World War, Montevideo's working class underwent a process of transition from the customs of artisanry to an industrial discipline.[18] Perhaps the clearest example of this shift from artisans to industrial workers were the men who worked on the streetcar

platforms. The slow rhythms of horse-drawn trams run by 7 small companies in the second half of the 19th century disappeared with the arrival of
the cleaner, quieter, faster, and larger electric cars.[19] The days of horse
tram guards having the time to flirt with female passengers along their
routes were ended in the name of an efficiency promoted by the new streetcar combines.[20] The 2 foreign concerns that had seized control of the streetcar network by 1907 instituted a strict program of reforms which attempted
to create machine-like workers.[21] La Sociedad Comercial, incorporated
as the United Electric Tramways of Montevideo, Ltd. in London with
British capital, and La Transatlántica, which was created primarily by
German capital, sought to become models of modernization in
Montevideo. The old horse drivers had to give up their traditional neck
scarves and rural attire for the button-down look of the electric motormen while conductors (known locally as *guardas)* were forced to wear
elaborate, heavy, standard-issue uniforms in all seasons.[22] But the uniforms were just a symbol of a new regimen which included a code of
behavior that replaced the easy familiarity of streetcarmen and passengers with strict attention to traffic, tickets and regulations. The code made
conductors into policemen and subjected motormen to fines and imprisonment for infractions.[23] Motormen found themselves whisked off to jail
for weeks or months following an accident, even if they were not to blame.[24]
The increased speed of the electric trams and the promulgation of new
service schedules resulted in a tyranny of the clock which made trolley
crews virtual prisoners on their cars, unable to leave even to eat or relieve
themselves during a long shift which could last from 5 to 8 hours.[25] On
some occasions they worked 10- or 11-hour days that were spread out
over 15 hours with rest periods, and one striker claimed that it was common practice for crewmen to work 13 1/2 hours without stepping off the
platforms in a station.[26] Nor were conditions in the other branches of the
streetcar system much better. Mechanics and smelters routinely clocked
14-hour days in the workshops while line workers were exposed to bad
weather and the dangers of automobile traffic for very low wages.[27] In the
middle of the 1911 strike, mechanics issued a manifesto that complained
of being treated "like soldiers" by superiors in the Goes station, being
obliged to work on holidays for no more than 1.30 pesos per day.[28]

The complaints against the arbitrary authority of the streetcar companies were not new and in fact predated the inauguration of the trolleys.
Coachmen and guards struck in February 1906 on several horse tram lines,
complaining of long hours and appealing to the public to judge their act
as "a logical protest against the abuses of capital."[29] A newspaper editorial in support of the strike claimed that this was the most recent incident
in a 10-year-long history of demands for better conditions and pay.[30] In
December 1906, just after the inauguration of the La Comercial line,
motormen and conductors balked at a new requirement by the company

that they submit to physical examinations for which they were in turn charged 2.50 pesos. No doubt one of their fears was that they might be discovered to have tuberculosis, at that time the leading cause of death in Montevideo and widespread among the working class. Such a diagnosis meant dismissal from their posts.[31] They held meetings to protest the examinations and other measures such as on-call status and undefined wage schedules.[32] The following year, further agitation by trolley workers led to the firing of 40 La Comercial crewmen and the public voicing of complaints concerning uniform deposits, excessive hours, the replacement of licensed motormen by apprentices and the employment of a military-style discipline.[33] The company kept the strike limited to one station where it collapsed. In general, the tough attitude of both companies with regard to control of the workplace meant that worker resistance tended to be individual and passive rather than collective and active up until 1911.

The position of the workers was further complicated by the fact that riders were not necessarily their allies. A letter from a monthly ticket-holder to *La Razón* in 1907 complained that motormen were poorly dressed and sometimes smoked, an infringement of the clean, modern image of the trolley which the companies promoted and the middle class grew to expect.[34] As time went on, the riding public became not only a part of the surveillance of the trolley as a workplace, but also a spectator of the enforcement of the new regimen. The public form of chastisement practiced by inspectors on conductors for non-compliance with regulations resulted in humiliation and a general seething among the latter.[35] In their first newspaper, launched in 1910, streetcarmen criticized the poor treatment they received from their station chiefs and equated their own position with that of slaves, claiming that the pay was so low they could barely meet the needs of their families.[36] The companies, however, continued to turn a deaf ear to such worker complaints and dismissed workers who were involved in organizing activities, thus maintaining a high level of fear in their workforce.[37]

Streetcar Workers and Urban Networks

The motormen and conductors of the two electric streetcar lines occupied a critical place in the daily life of the city and played a very ambiguous role in the evolving urban social order. They served as a bridge between industrial workers and artisans, while belonging to neither group. Every day, they came into contact with mechanics, blacksmiths and electricians in the company stations and in the nearby cafés, while they ran up debts with neighborhood artisans such as bakers, butchers, tailors and barbers until they received their fluctuating biweekly pay.[38] They found themselves charged with enforcing order while at the same time subject to a strict disciplinary system and the frequent abuse of authority on the part of their superiors. In this way, trolley men existed in the seams of urban society, as both "soldiers" and company representatives, "slaves" and skilled workers, private-sector employees and public servants.

As we have seen, platform personnel were virtually in the street all day long and into the night. They worked in all types of weather and on holidays, when demand for their services was the greatest. The streetcar network, like electricity, gas and sanitation services, was deemed essential to the life of the city. Trolley crew members, attired in their distinctive uniforms, were always personally visible, and the rules and power relations of their jobs were publicly revealed and commented on by passengers. Accidents, with motormen automatically being taken off to jail, and incidents involving rule infractions, leading to shouting matches between guards and inspectors or passengers or policemen, were all part of the urban landscape by 1911. They resulted in a workplace that differed markedly from the more private world of factories and offices. Conductors and motormen were responsible for public safety, the maintenance of social order within the cars and the efficient operation of the transport system, but had very limited authority and received wages that were in line with the rest of the city's semi-skilled workers.

The streetcarmen also had more physical mobility than any group of industrial workers. They crossed paths with nearly all sectors of Montevidean society, except the very rich who could afford private carriages, taxis or autos and the very poor who could not muster the streetcar fare. Factory workers, merchants, students, teachers, clerks, musicians, seamstresses, mothers with children, pickpockets and politicians rode the trolleys. On the crowded back platforms, guards entered into discussions with these passengers and with mailmen, news vendors, police transporting criminals and others who took the cars as a part of their daily jobs. On the front platforms, motormen came into contact with passengers leaving parcels and luggage on their way to their seats and also with the action in the street itself, from which they were not separated by glass barriers. They kept up a dialogue with their environment both verbally and through the medium of the trolley warning bell which they had to sound each time they entered and left an intersection.[39] The crews moved from one end of the city to the other, since most lines were funneled into the narrow confines of the Ciudad Vieja and the Customs House and then back out to the various districts, like a slingshot. Motormen and guards thus had ties to a particular station and its neighborhood, but spent much of their day in other parts of the city. In this way they came to know Montevideo completely and intimately, perhaps even better than policemen confined to a single precinct.

At the same time, the platform jobs were so specialized that crewmen had very few options once they entered into the streetcar service. Motormen had to undergo an unpaid apprenticeship of a month and then pass an exam for a certificate before entering into their posts.[40] Once achieved, this training and licensing was not transferable to any other occupations. In fact, motormen had some difficulty even moving between the two electric trolley companies in Montevideo because the cars were manufactured in different parts of the world and featured different equipment.[41] At the other platform, guards tended to come from, or exit to, occupations that were tied to the street, such as news vendors, policemen, itinerant merchants, or more scandalous positions, such as a healer's assistant or fortune-teller, none of which paid well or offered a secure future.[42] Compared to these limited options, the industrial part of the streetcar workforce, those who labored in the powerhouses, maintenance shops and the stations, and numbered about one-third of the total employees, had much greater occupational mobility, being able to cross into small workshops or other factories.

Few other enterprises in Montevideo concentrated as many workers in their domain as the electric streetcar system. Taken as a whole, the workforce of the two streetcar companies was formidable, consisting of 1,944 workers in 1910.[43] But unlike the large workforces of the frigoríficos (1,230 workers) which were concentrated in the Cerro, west of the bay and away from the main city, and the railroads (3,860 workers nationally), which had their workshops in the far northern suburb of Peñarol, the streetcarmen were distributed in neighborhoods throughout Montevideo. As a consequence of this dispersion and of their interaction with the populace, their discontent was more difficult to contain. At the same time, trolley workers were far more concentrated than other types of workers. Shoemakers (2,156 workers) were dispersed among 46 different factories, the 699 bakers were employed in 109 bakeries and 1,491 carpenters worked in 80 furniture shops.[44] The result of this concentration was that one streetcar company's directives or changes in conditions had an immediate impact on a very large number of workers whose grievances could be disseminated quickly throughout the metropolis. The intransigence of the two electric car companies on issues of union recognition, workplace conditions and discipline, struck a dissonant chord with the city's working class and thus helped pave the way for a truly mass strike. The public nature of their work, their concentration in just two large companies, their physical mobility and occupational immobility, and the ambiguous roles they played as enforcers and victims of a new urban order placed trolley personnel in a key position to realize what quickly became a city-wide protest of the abuse of authority in May 1911.

The Streetcar Strike

The immediate background of the events of May 1911 was formed by a rent protest in the working-class neighborhood of Villa Muñoz, the annual celebration of May Day, and the meeting of the third congress of the anarchist labor federation, the first one to be held in five years.

The district of Villa Muñoz had been constructed as a working-class area in 1889, known as Barrio Reus al Norte, located 10 to 15 blocks north of the main artery of Avenida 18 de Julio at the eastern limits of the city proper. It was designed as an alternative to the crowded and unhealthy *conventillos* of the center city and was so well received that it was featured on postcards at the turn of the century, alongside the city's parks, beaches and major buildings. By 1911, however, under the pressures of renewed immigration, the neighborhood of 3,000 residents had become very crowded and the living conditions had deteriorated markedly.

> Villa Muñoz in that year was considered the most unclean zone in Montevideo. The barrio was located in a ravine and the winds, which could drag along and dissolve the miasmas that developed, did not reach it. Typhus and smallpox left a trail of victims there. Many died without even receiving aid.[45]

At the same time, rents shot up astronomically after the State Mortgage Bank auctioned off the individual properties. Street protests began in April and continued into May, with speeches by various anarchists and workers denouncing the rent increases and the poor sanitation.[46] This discontent eventually merged with that of the streetcar workers whose strike was welcomed and furthered in this discontented neighborhood.[47]

The May Day celebration focused on the issues developed in the Villa Muñoz protests, especially the high cost of living. *La Razón* estimated that 8,000 people took part in the march to the main wharf and that 10–12,000 demonstrators gathered there to hear speeches by Argentine labor leaders and local anarchists. Unions carried banners that read "Respect the liberty of the citizen" and "Down with forced vaccination" while José Castelli, an Argentine anarchist, told them that there could not be a celebration of labor while workers were dying of hunger and while exploiters and exploited continued to exist.[48] The trolley workers did not observe May Day, continuing to work and in at least one case, getting involved in an altercation with other workers following the hurling of insults. Yet two days beforehand, mechanics, guards and motormen of both companies had held a meeting to constitute a society of resistance and they publicly claimed the adherence of 500 members.[49] It is likely that they felt additional resentment of the companies for not allowing them to celebrate May First.

Immediately following May Day, the Federación Obrera Regional Uruguaya (FORU) held its third congress in Montevideo. It was a three-day event and its debates were widely reported in the daily and worker press. The congress was dominated by anarchists who combined a short-term desire to improve working conditions with a long-term goal of anticapitalist revolution, a position paralleled by much of the city's working-class press. Delegates to the FORU discussed the Mexican Revolution, the high cost of living and the necessity of unionization, and they adopted a strategy of "direct action" which advocated the use of boycotts, sabotage and general strikes.[50] This did not go unnoticed by the state. Towards the end of the congress Castelli was arrested on a murder charge from Argentina and his extradition quickly became a *cause célèbre* among the Montevideo working class, serving as a starting point for the political networks that would sustain the coming strikes.

Following the close of this congress, streetcarmen continued to organize their union secretly.[51] As in the past, the companies tried to short-circuit their efforts by dismissing workers whom they identified as activists. On the night of May 10, at least 600 tram workers turned up for a meeting to protest the latest round of firings. They issued an ultimatum to the companies to reinstate nine workers within 48 hours or face a walkout.[52] The following day, the newborn union claimed a membership of 1,000 workers, but the companies refused to budge, viewing the ultimatum as a challenge to their ability to freely conduct business.[53] In this way, the terms of the conflict were etched in stone from the first moment. The key concerns of the workers were dignity and security and those of the companies were discipline and control.

The shadowy presence which lurked in the background of this strike was the fear of destitution in the new Montevideo. While the state did not compile statistics on rates of unemployment during this period, it is clear that many people were desperate for work.[54] The pro-business *Uruguay Weekly News* observed, "It does not seem to us that the lot of the motormen on the trams can be a very hard one, for the companies have no difficulty in getting as many men as they require."[55] In fact, the union not only had to face the threat of its members being replaced by strikebreakers drawn from rural areas of Uruguay, but also by trained streetcarmen recruited from nearby Buenos Aires and its suburbs.[56] The trolley workers themselves recognized the fear of being fired as the main impediment to founding and sustaining a union.[57] They also had to worry about the use of a blacklist by the two companies.[58]

In spite of these fears, trolley workers held increasingly large meetings during the first ten days of May, moving out of the secret phase of union-building, since they had been betrayed by some of their co-workers.[59] Their plan to formulate a program of improvements to be submitted during the summer months (December–February) when traffic reached its peak was undercut by the companies which fired everyone suspected of union activity, thus precipitating a walkout.[60] The meeting of May 10 at the FORU offices drew 600–900 workers who demanded that the companies reinstitute the men. On the afternoon of the following day, the trolleymen went out on strike, in response to the companies' refusal to rehire the union organizers. Motormen and guards fanned out to the city's seven trolley stations to notify their co-workers of the action. Cars were abandoned in the stations and many passengers were stranded half-way home.[61]

The striking trolley workers drew up a list of 16 demands which, in addition to the rehiring of the organizers, included the institution of an 8 to 81/2 hour day, accident insurance, revision of work regulations, payment of interest on the mandatory cash deposit for uniforms, double pay for forced overtime, rest periods, free transit passes for all groups of streetcar workers including shop mechanics, replacement of dangerous hand brakes with air brakes, establishment of a closed shop and wage increases for certain categories of employees.[62]

From the first moments of the strike, the trolley workers received assistance from other sectors of the working class. Newsboys were among the most conspicuous in their support of the strike, perhaps because the streetcar was their workplace as well. Always dashing onto and around the streetcars in their daily struggle to sell enough papers at two centésimos apiece to live on their own or help their families, news vendors were familiar with trolley crews and saw firsthand how they were treated by police and inspectors. Newsboys also were subject to injury in boarding and leaving trolleys, and so had a special relationship to motormen and guards, placing their lives in their hands and trusting in their quick reactions and street awareness.[63] In the first days of the trolley strike, newsboys helped to distribute news of the strike throughout the city and were also part of the crowds that attempted to halt the passage of streetcars. *The Montevideo Times*, in a typically British fit of outrage, complained and insinuated,

> A most scandalous phase of the affair is the open manner in which the street newsboys have made themselves partisans of the strike and seek to molest men and passengers by stone-throwing, abusive language and so forth. There is no doubt that they have been instigated to do this, and are possibly even paid for doing so, for they seem to prefer it to selling newspapers.[64]

As the strike progressed, other groups showed their support of the streetcarmen in a variety of ways. Bricklayers tossed bricks from construction sites at passing trolleys while students were arrested for hurling insults at scabbing crewmen or boarding cars to enter into dialogues with them in the hope of convincing them to abandon work.[65] A variety of artisanal gremios and industrial unions also contributed funds and goods to help the families of striking trolley workers, including tailors, linotypists, butchers, milkmen, vegetable sellers and electric light workers as well as the Socialist Party, streetcar workers from Buenos Aires and horse tram workers on the Norte line in Montevideo.[66] A sanitation worker was arrested for boarding a trolley and yelling "carnero" (sheep/scab) at the motorman while a baker was arrested for speaking at a meeting of trolley workers, an indication that sectors of the working-class population were willing to lose their liberty for symbolic acts of support even before the general strike developed.[67] Women were also conspicuous in their public support of the streetcarmen. The main daily newspaper ran a photo showing a crowd of women and children with a wooden sheep hung in effigy at an intersection, greeting each passing trolley with shouts and laughter.[68] At the Goes station, a woman made a scene by demanding that her husband, a ticket inspector pressed into service as a motorman, stop working and come home. She was supported by onlookers who blocked his trolley and he gave in to her entreaty as the crowd applauded.[69] All of these incidents taken together led the press to conclude that the public supported the strike.[70]

The streetcar strike became a collective experience for Montevideo's residents unlike any other one of the new century. The organization of the city was disrupted; mail had to be delivered using ambulances; horseraces, plays and soccer matches were cancelled and attendance at cafés dwindled. As streetcars ran infrequently and also became dangerous targets, people took to walking the long distances to work and offices, joking that the strike would make the shoemakers rich. Meanwhile the press remarked on how unanimated the city had become and described the disappearance of trolleys in emotional terms:

> Yesterday, under the rain, the city lived under a heavy and desperate monotony. It was a grey, moody, silent day. The sadness and solitude were deep. No electric car was seen crossing the streets. Nothing of rolling iron wheels nor of vibrating cables. The banging of the gong, the shaking of the trolley, sounds so familiar to our ears, were not heard all day.[71]

In a stunning counterpoint to this silence, noise was heard from a previously mute source, the streetcar workers themselves, who had been suffering quietly for years. Suddenly, they began to talk directly to the city as a whole. Manifestos and open letters were launched explaining the reason behind the strike action, noting the wealth of the foreign companies and disparaging the lack of dignity accorded by the managers to their workers.[72] A manifesto from the strike committee pointed out that in some months workers were unable to feed their children or clothe their wives due to fines levied by the companies and municipal inspectors. It complained of policies such as that forbidding workers to contract debts which it characterized as "despotic" and an assault on "our human dignity."[73] A handbill which invoked nationalism issued this call:

> Mothers that have children! Children that have parents! Men that have nerves! To the street, to the street! Everyone that has an ounce of conscience, impede the circulation of even a single streetcar, in so that the working class will be more respected. Workers! Give us your hands and

> everyone united will make the companies consider their workers as free
> men and not as slaves.[74]

Beyond manifestos and letters, the daily assemblies of hundreds and eventually thousands of workers led segments of the press to interview workers and quote them verbatim on the issues of the day. *La Razón* and *El Día* were exemplary in this type of coverage, letting trolley workers speak directly to their city and framing the terms of conflict along the lines of respect, moral duty and safety, rather than simply wages. A La Comercial motorman explained to an interviewer that the hand brakes in use needed more force than was humanly possible to apply, resulting in accidents in which drivers suffered internal injuries. He demanded the use of electric brakes, with which the cars were equipped but which the company did not want to use due to the additional expense of operation.[75] A mechanic pleaded for the restoration of free passes while a conductor laid out the subservience of crewmen to the companies:

> –Are there other problems?–For us? I could talk to you until tomorrow about them. They make us arrive in the stations a quarter of an hour before work begins. But if we are late one minute they hit us with a three-day suspension. If we are late an hour, the suspension is for eight days and a recurrence will bring a 15-day suspension. Another late arrival will result in being fired. During the last summer, those suspended without pay were still made to remain on duty in the stations. This is an inequity which is double punishment![76]

By framing the conflicts in these terms, transport workers struck a chord with the rest of the urban working class as well as parts of the middle class. The trolley workers undercut the image of the companies as the guardians of progress and knowledgeable organizers of urban transport. The result was that at least some sections of the middle class became sympathetic to the strikers.

The period between May 11 and May 21 was a standoff. The companies refused to yield to what *The Montevideo Times* described as "an open declaration of war against capital."[77] On the other side, crew members were joined by mechanics and even inspectors in a very effective walkout that drew increasing support from other unions. Service was reduced to skeleton crews who operated with police and military guards on the platforms and each day the number of cars operating decreased. Riders caught in rainy and windy weather turned to the old horse-drawn trams, disparagingly called " cockroaches," seeing these as safer and more dependable than the electric replacements. But these relics of the nineteenth century could not sustain the phenomenal demand and horses began to collapse and die in the street from overexhaustion. The League Against Cruelty to Animals forced the Tranvía del Norte to put more horses on each car, thus reducing its overall service.[78]

On May 21, facing the hostility of an impatient public and the municipal government (which had levied fines on them for failing to provide services according to their concession contracts), the company managers agreed to a few of the strikers' requests concerning pay increases, reduction of the workday to nine hours and deposits on uniforms. The workers, facing fatigue and shortage of resources, as well as threatening visits to their homes by supervisors, backed off of their demands for a closed shop and the fired activists graciously decided to step aside.[79] That day, thousands of workers participated in a public demonstration organized by the FORU and the Socialist Party. The marchers, composed of union members carrying red and black banners and estimated at between 6,000 and 20,000 strong, filled nine city blocks and listened to speeches that "violently condemned the attitude of the capitalists."[80] That evening, the streetcarmen approved the accord and decided to return to work the next day. The trolley strike appeared to have been settled peacefully with the workers gaining a limited victory.[81]

The General Strike

When the trolleymen showed up for work on the morning of May 22, some of them found that they were not going to be rehired. At first there was great confusion as dozens of workers in different stations, believing that they had been laid off and that the victimization was general, began to gather at the headquarters of the labor federation. The companies claimed that in fact they had made no agreement with the strikers but had instituted the reforms unilaterally. The managers said that they had an obligation to continue employing workers hired during the strike and that they did not have the funds to carry both loyal workers and strikers on the payroll. Given the recent profitability of La Sociedad Comercial, the now impoverished workers were irate.[82] This proved to be the trigger for a mass strike, the indignity which would coalesce the city's working class into action. Between 2 P.M. and 3 P.M. the trolley men abandoned work as the cars pulled into their respective stations or in some cases were left in the middle of the street. They then stationed themselves at corners and key locations throughout the city, including the stock exchange, admonishing other workers to join them.[83] Some waved red banners as a signal for a general strike.[84]

The following day, May 23, Montevideo was completely shut down as the FORU declared a general strike and sent its delegates to organize alternative services and maintain order. Tens of thousands of workers joined in the action and trolley cars were attacked with tar or burned as the companies tried to force the issue by running them with scab labor.[85] The entire character of the city changed and violent incidents became more common. In a matter of hours, the power relations in the city were

inverted, with workers controlling the space of the streets and the movement of vehicles. Private autos needed the permission of the labor confederation to move through Montevideo. Milk was dumped rather than
allowed to be brought into the center city from the railroad station. Servants on their way to markets were not permitted to continue. Funeral
processions were prohibited if they involved the use of hearses. The streets
filled with garbage and ships were stuck in port, unable to unload their
goods.[86]

> Thereafter very little moved in Montevideo. Workers dressed in Sunday
> clothing took the day off. Newspapers weren't printed. The garbage col-
> lectors joined the strike. The Federacion Obrera issued passes to doc-
> tors and authorized meat deliveries to hospitals.[87]

Commercial establishments closed and there was no business as usual for
three days. This transformation was a shock and was met with equal parts
fear and humor. A writer in *La Razón*, commenting on the lack of cigarettes and soda in cafés, remarked that the usual clientele were having to
take their drinks straight, "with a consequent loose tongue, shining of the
eyes and weakness in the legs."[88] A woman riding a La Transatlántica trolley on Avenida Agraciada, carrying a plate of food under a napkin, got up
and asked the motorman if he was hungry and before he could answer she
proceeded to push the plate in his face, no doubt taking inspiration from
a contemporary biograph film.[89]

The attitude of the government shifted as the streetcar-strike-turned-
general-strike began to take on the appearance of an urban insurrection.
In the days prior to the general strike, various government branches had
taken actions which were widely interpreted as support for the workers, a
clear break with the anti-labor policies of the previous national administration. The municipal government had fined both foreign streetcar companies for failure to provide the services spelled out in their concessions
and was either slow or careful in its licensing of new motormen employed
to break the strike. Both of these strategies were designed to bring the
companies to the negotiating table. The police, for the most part, sought
to avoid confrontations with strikers in the streets, though there were cases
of harassment. In any case, the unions and the FORU were allowed to
meet freely in early May. Batlle, as President of the Republic, even spoke
to a demonstration of workers from his balcony, encouraging them to organize in order to improve their conditions while his newspaper, *El Día*,
ran editorials highly critical of the companies.[90] Yet when Batlle's government was unable to push the streetcar companies into a settlement favorable to the workers and the latter took over Montevideo, effectively
challenging the authority of the state, Batlle ordered the military occupation of the city with a consequent ban on public assemblies, an act clearly
hostile to the labor movement.[91] On the morning of the twenty-third, a

march of strikers was dispersed by the police and on the afternoon of the twenty-fourth, an illegal demonstration in support of the general strike was disrupted by police and soldiers on horseback, resulting in scores of arrests and injuries.[92] In the words of an Italian diplomat summing up the actions, "many windows and some heads were broken."[93] Gradually the workers' euphoria gave way to caution and fear as the military occupied the streets and the city became silent and dead once again.[94] Batlle's action revealed the limits of his populism at the same time as it made clear the splits in the labor movement between socialists who wanted to use the state and anarchists who rejected the state no matter what its form.

On May twenty-fourth, Juan Cat, the Uruguayan manager of La Comercial, issued a letter to the Minister of the Interior explaining that some of the strikers would have to wait until the new shorter work schedule went into place on June first before being reemployed. This amounted to 21 people and the rest were guaranteed their old jobs. On the night of May twenty-fifth, with food in short supply and scores of workers under arrest, the trolley workers' union sent a note to the FORU requesting that it end the general strike. The ensuing debate among union delegates at the Centro Internacional pointed out that the government was not able to force the foreign companies to cede to the tram workers' demands, thus making the general strike strategically invalid. With this, the general strike was ended and streetcar service was slowly resumed on May twenty-sixth, still under military guard. On May twenty-seventh, the system offered the first night service in 16 days and Montevideo returned "to its habitual calm."[95]

The historiography of the general strike has completely ignored its epilogue, leading to a romanticization of the conflict. Since the workers had not obtained any guarantees from the companies, perhaps trusting in the perceived protection offered by the state through its intervention in the strike, they left themselves open to post-strike victimization. This was not long in coming. Both *La Razón*, which disapproved of the strike, and *El Tranvía*, the workers' organ, concurred that there were provocations of ex-strikers by loyal workers and strikebreakers in the days after the settlement. Returning workers alleged that their superiors were using double standards in monitoring the two sets of workers, giving a free hand to the loyal workers and going by the book with the ex-strikers. The latter found themselves discriminated against in the awarding of shifts, cited for minute or imaginary infractions, suspended for simply greeting ex-strikers, and eventually fired.[96] By mid-June, tempers had reached a boiling point and another strike broke out in a section of the La Comercial system after two guards were fired. The company, which apparently had been training replacements in the interim, used this as a pretext to fire 130–135 workers, purging its workforce of union activists.[97] The union, still unrecognized, apparently collapsed a few months later, since it had to be reconstructed when the next major conflict broke out and there is no evidence that its newspaper lasted into the new year. It took the trolley men seven more years before they could mount another serious challenge to the company's authority.

Conclusion

Montevideo's first general strike reveals the centrality of the streetcar to the city's daily life. By throwing urban power relations into relief in a way analogous to a solarized photograph, the 1911 strike makes visible the ties which existed among elements of the working class just below the surface of press reports and official studies. The trolley workers occupied a particular niche in the social and physical structure of the city which allowed them to act as the vehicle for the city's first mass strike. The networks that they formed both with the riding public and the diverse and changing working class served as the necessary support to generalize their grievances to the entire city and to sustain them for weeks against two intransigent foreign companies. They were in the right place (literally riding a primary agent of change) at the right time (a mid-point of industrialization) in the city's transformation from horse town to metropolis. By focusing on actions in the streets, plazas and union halls during this urban crisis, rather than on the actions and pronouncements of politicians, we can see the sharpness of the social conflict that was obscured by the myth of Uruguay as the Switzerland of South America, exempt from the problems of its neighbors.

This suggests several considerations which should be taken into account in rewriting the history of general strikes in Latin America. First, that space and class are closely connected and should be evaluated together, particularly in an urban context. The streetcar workers in Montevideo derived a certain power from the knowledge bestowed on them from their physical mobility, from the visibility of their workplace and from their dispersal throughout the city. They may have been poorly treated by supervisors, police, municipal inspectors and company managers, but they also possessed the weaponry to react to these outrages, in the form of collective action which cut across neighborhood boundaries and even class lines.

Following from this point, general strikes need to be discussed in terms of the occupations of their primary actors. What will probably emerge from such an analysis is a picture of transport workers at the forefront of most early mass strikes in the region. Port workers were very active in the labor movements of Buenos Aires, Callao and Valparaíso, for example, while Ecuador's first general strike was led by railroad workers, trolley workers and employees of Guayaquil's utility companies. Mexico City experienced a general strike during the Revolution led by

streetcarmen. This pattern may be explained by the importance of transport to the maintenance of the region's export economies, but it also has
to do with the high degree of concentration of the workforce in the transport industry and the key social roles that these particular workers played
in the lives of the affected cities. If nothing else, transport workers need
to be accorded their rightful place as significant actors in the history of
the region's labor movements. Labor historiography has tended to emphasize the story of export workers' struggles while ignoring those in the
transport industry.[98]

Third, the general strike in Latin America needs to be reconceptualized
as a process which includes not only the relatively short period of complete shutdown of factories and services in a single city and the inevitable
government and elite response, but also the localized strikes which initiated the movement, the long-term preparation which laid the groundwork
for solidarity and the final resolution of labor conflicts which occurred
often weeks after the general strike. If we view the general strike as more
than a simple two- or three-day event, the complex organizational underpinnings of what is often a potentially revolutionary challenge to authority become more visible. We can also step away from the perception of
contemporary observers that general strikes were spontaneous mob actions or the overflowing of vague democratic aspirations, and see them in
the context of elaborate traditions of resistance with both ideological and
psychological roots. As we have seen, the 1911 strike in Montevideo was
not the first expression of discontent by streetcar workers in that city. The
fact that it was organized secretly at the start shows that they had learned
from their unsuccessful challenges to the companies in 1907 and 1910
and also that they drew on some of the experiences of conflict during the
horse-tram era. The 1911 strike, in turn, became part of the tradition of
resistance on which trolley men built when they launched the general strike
of 1918, a far more violent conflict that resembled an urban civil war.

Lastly, general strikes have to be seen as qualitatively different events
in labor history, rather than simply large strikes. They have significant
long-term psychological impacts on their urban participants which have
not been fully explored in the historiography. Barrán and Nahum recognized this in observing that "The general strike was the first event which
obliged the inhabitants of Montevideo to experience it and feel it in accord with their social position."[99] The general strike was a lived event
which helped to define the identity of the city as part of the modern world,
a sort of rite of passage toward a metropolis, but which also made clear
the deep social divisions that resulted from waves of immigration and
compressed industrialization beginning in the previous century. As Temma
Kaplan points out in her study of Barcelona, the general strike was an
urban ritual which involved the use of powerful symbols as well as the
physical control of public space by the marginalized.[100] In the case of

Montevideo, the electric streetcar was a key urban symbol, not only connoting technological advancement and the "opening up" of the city, but also dependency on foreign enterprise and a "policed" public space. Viewed from the level of the street, which the strike demanded, the trolley system was a vulnerable network run by, and sometimes controlled by, hungry and desperate men. After the events of May 1911, no one looked at the streetcar or the city in quite the same light.

Notes

[1. Meatpacking plants.]

2. The estimate of the number of strikers comes from the first issue of the trolley workers' newspaper, *El Tranvía*, I:1, June 10, 1911, 4 and Héctor Rodríguez, *Nuestros Sindicatos (1865–1965)* (Montevideo: Centro Estudiantes de Derecho, 2nd edition, 1966), p. 18. The number of unions comes from *The Uruguay Weekly News*, May 28, 1911, p. 3.

3. *The Montevideo Times*, May 27, 1911, 1.

4. For examples of political treatments of the strike see José Pedro Barrán and Benjamín Nahum, *Batlle, Los Estancieros y el Imperio Britanico: Las Primeras Reformas, 1911–1913*, vol. 4 (Montevideo: Ediciones de la Banda Oriental, 1983), pp. 61–64, and Milton Vanger, *The Model Country* (Hanover, NH, and London: Brandeis University Press, 1980), pp. 122–132. Carlos M. Rama, writing about the history of social conflict in Uruguay, misrecords the date of the strike and then discusses it primarily in terms of how Batlle responded to it in "La 'Cuestion Social'," *Cuadernos de Marcha*, No. 22, February 1969, 71. Juan Oddone fails to mention it in his survey of the period, "The Formation of Modern Uruguay, c. 1870–1930" in the *Cambridge History of Latin America, c. 1870 to 1930*, vol. V (Cambridge: Cambridge University Press, 1986), pp. 453–474.

5. See for example German D'Elia and Armando Miraldi, *Historia del movimiento obrero en el Uruguay: Desde sus orígenes hasta 1930* (Montevideo: Ediciones de la Banda Oriental, 1985), pp. 99–104. H. Rodríguez, p. 18 misrecords it as occurring in 1913 and devotes only a paragraph to it. Francisco R. Pintos, *Historia del movimiento obrero del Uruguay* (Montevideo: Suplemento de "Gaceta de Cultura," 1960), p. 95, points to an explosion of strikes in late 1911 and 1912 as an indication of the impact of the May 1911 conflict on the wider labor movement. F. Lopez D'Alesandro, *Historia de la izquierda uruguaya*, vol. 2, second part, 1911–1918 (Montevideo: Ediciones del Nuevo Mundo, 1991), pp. 14–19 is concerned with how socialists and anarchists viewed the strike. Lucía Sala de Touron and Jorge E. Landinelli, "50 años del movimiento obrero uruguayo" in Pablo González Casanova, ed., *Historia del movimiento obrero en américa latina* (Mexico: Siglo Veintiuno, 1984), p. 256 also devote only a paragraph to it and see its importance within the context of the struggle for the 8-hour day.

6. *El Día*, May 15, 1911, "La Gran Huelga." Alternatively this slogan was given as "a little more bread and a little more respect."

7. For details on this event and the debates it unleashed see Anton Rosenthal, "The Arrival of the Electric Streetcar and the Conflict over Progress in Early 20th Century Montevideo," *Journal of Latin American Studies*, May 1995.

8. The Department (or province) of Montevideo had a total population of 309,231 in 1908 and an estimated 338,175 on December 31, 1911. Ricardo Alvarez Lenzi et al., *El Montevideo de la expansión (1868–1915)* (Montevideo: Ediciones

de la Banda Oriental, 1986), p. 18; *Anuario Estadístico de la República Oriental de Uruguay, 1911–1912* (Montevideo: Tipografía Moderna, 1915), p. 14. Juan Rial, "Estadísticas historicas del Uruguay, 1850–1930" (mimeo, Montevideo: CIESU, 1980), p. 108, notes that in 1908 the population of the city proper was just under 300,000 and constituted 25 percent of the nation's population, but gradually rose to a proportion greater than one-third. James R. Scobie, "The Growth of Latin American Cities, 1870–1930" in *The Cambridge History of Latin America*, volume IV (Cambridge: Cambridge University Press, 1986), pp. 245 and 249, writes that by 1930, Montevideo was the premier primary city in all of Latin America, at 33.0 percent of the national population, compared with 18.3 percent for Buenos Aires and 16.5 percent for Havana.

9. *La Democracia* (all newspapers published in Montevideo unless otherwise noted), December 7, 1906, 7.

10. W.H. Koebel, *Uruguay* (London: T. Fisher Unwin, Ltd., 1911), p. 307.

11. Ministry of Industries, *Uruguay in 1915* (Montevideo: A. Barreiro y Ramos, 1915), p. 204.

12. Carlos M. Maeso, *El Uruguay a través de un siglo* (Montevideo: Tip. y Lit. Moderna, 1910), p. 46.

13. Luis Enrique Azarola Gil, *Ayer, 1882–1952* (Lausanne, Switzerland: Imprimeries Réunies S.A., 1953), p. 158; *El Día*, May 15, 1911, "La Gran Huelga."

14. Maeso, *Uruguay*, p. 51.

15. Eduardo Acevedo, *Anales Históricos del Uruguay*, tomo V (Montevideo: Casa A. Barreiro y Ramos, 1934), p. 458 and Banco de la República Oriental del Uruguay, *Sinopsis económica y financiera del Uruguay* (Montevideo: Impresora Uruguaya S.A., 1933), p. 11.

16. W. H. Koebel, *Uruguay*, p. 161; Alejandro Michelena, *Rincones de Montevideo* (Montevideo: Arca, 1991), p. 94.

17. *Uruguay Weekly News*, February 28, 1909, 4.

18. An industrial census in 1913 records the existence of 2 breweries, 2 match factories, 13 mills, 5 chocolate factories, 2 phone companies, a gas company and an electric company which operated alongside 109 bakeries, 40 brick factories, 80 furniture workshops, 46 shoe factories and 96 blacksmith shops. *Boletín de la Oficina del Trabajo*, No. 5, January 15, 1914 (Montevideo: Ministerio de Hacienda, Tall. Graf. "Escalante"), 153–159.

19. The horse-drawn cars and horses were sold off by the major trolley companies almost immediately after electrification, but one tram line remained under horse traction until 1925. This was the Norte Tranvía which was owned by the Ferrocarril del Norte and served only a small section of the city with 25 cars. *Boletín Mensual de Estadística Municipal*, Montevideo, Año IX: Nos. 89–100, January–December, 1911, 7.

20. Máximo Torres (Carlos Maeso), *Divigando . . .* , (Montevideo: Imp. y Lit. de "La Razón," 1895), p. 38.

21. A telling filler run in the trolley workers' newspaper after the 1911 strike reads: "A worker without a stomach, genitals or brain, who does not eat, nor think, nor feel the sweet affections of love; an automatic worker, artificial, made 'of steel,' who works without rest mechanically: such would be the preferred worker, dreamt [of] by the vampires in their desire for profits." *El Tranvía*, 1:7, July 29, 1911, 2.

22. La Transatlántica Compañía de Tranvías Eléctricos, *Reglamento* (Montevideo, no date), pp. 3–4. There are no statistics on the numbers of horse-tram personnel who moved into jobs on the new electric lines, but references in the daily and worker press (in stories on strikes, accidents, firings and retire-

ments) to long-term employees who served prior to 1906 suggest that the percentage was not insignificant. See for example *La Razón*, May 16, 1911, 8 and June 21, 1911, 1. The battle over uniforms, the collars of which had to be kept buttoned even in the summer, lasted until the 1940s when traffic personnel finally attained a lighter summer uniform. Omar M. Gil Soja, *18 y 41* (Montevideo: Arca, 1993), p. 87.

23. Junta E. Administrativa, *Reglamento de Tranvías Eléctricos* (Montevideo, 1910); *La Democracia*, May 17, 1911, 1–2.

24. *El Tranvía*, 1:13, September 13, 1911, 1.

25. *El Día*, May 12, 1911, "La huelga del dia" and *La Razón*, May 12, 1911, 2. Motormen were suspended for bringing their cars into the stations even a few minutes early. *El Tranvía*, 1:14, November 15, 1911, 4.

26. *La Razón*, May 12, 1911, 2.

27. *El Socialista*, April 16, 1911, 6.

28. *La Razón*, May 15, 1911, 8. The peso was roughly at parity with the U.S. dollar at this time; Reginald Lloyd, *Impresiones de la República del Uruguay en el Siglo Veinte* (London: Lloyds Greater Britain Publishing Co., Ltd., 1912), unnumbered page.

29. *La Democracia*, February 3, 1906, 4 and February 6, 1906, 3.

30. *La Democracia*, February 6, 1906, 1. Strikes occurred on the horse tram lines in 1895 and 1901, involving limited violence; see Carlos Zubillaga and Jorge Balbis, "Dossier de documentos sobre el movimiento obrero uruguayo" (typescript, CLAEH), volume I, document 42 and volume II, document 85.

31. *El Día*, May 17, 1911, "La Gran Huelga"; *Anuario Estadístico de la República Oriental del Uruguay*, 1911–12, pp. 43–51.

32. *La Democracia*, December 29, 1906, 4.

33. *La Tribuna Popular*, June 19, 1907, 4, June 21, 1907, 2, June 22, 1907, 1, June 23, 1907, 4.

34. *La Razón*, February 6, 1907, 1.

35. *El Tranvía*, 1:14, November 15, 1911, 5.

36. *El Combate*, 1:1, June 1, 1910, 1.

37. *El Combate*, 1:1, June 1, 1910, 2.

38. *La Democracia*, May 17, 1911, 1–2. Crew personnel were paid by the hour and they had no guarantees of how long they would be employed in a given two-week period. Pay was reduced as much as 40 percent by fines and subject to interruptions for sickness and time spent in jail after accidents. For these latter causes, as well as for funerals and marriages, workers organized mutual aid collections on paydays in the stations. *El Tranvía*, 1:8, August 15, 1911, 5 and 1:15, November 30, 1911, 3–4. Individual responses included moonlighting as chauffeurs, coachmen and painters. *La Razón*, May 16, 1911, 18.

39. *Uruguay Weekly News*, January 6, 1907, 1.

40. *El Día*, May 17, 1911, "La Gran Huelga."

41. *El Día*, May 13, 1911, "La Gran Huelga."

42. *El País*, January 9, 1920, 8; Víctor Soliño, *Crónica de los años locos* (Montevideo: Ediciones de la Banda Oriental, 1983), pp. 79–81.

43. Maeso, *Uruguay*, pp. 206–208.

44. *Boletín de la Oficina del Trabajo*, No. 5, January 15, 1914, 153–157.

45. Universindo Rodríguez Díaz, *Los sectores populares en el Uruguay del novecientos, primera parte (1907–1911)* (Montevideo: Editorial Compañero, 1989), p. 39.

46. Rodríguez, *Los sectores*, pp. 39–40; *La Democracia*, May 9, 1911, 4.

47. *La Razón*, May 12, 1911, 2.

48. *La Razón*, May 2, 1911, 3.

49. *La Razón*, May 2, 1911, 3, 8.

50. *La Democracia*, May 9, 1911, 4; *La Razón*, May 3, 1911, 7.

51. *El Tranvía*, 1:1, June 10, 1911, 1.

52. *La Razón*, May 11, 1911, 2.

53. *La Razón*, May 11, 1911, 8.

54. Raúl Jacob, "Crisis y mercado de trabajo: Una aproximación a la problemática de los anos veinte y treinta," Serie Investigaciones Numero 16 (Montevideo: Centro Interdisciplinario de Estudios Sobre El Desarrollo/Uruguay, no date), p. 42.

55. *Uruguay Weekly News*, May 14, 1911, 7; this view was echoed after the strike by the workers, *El Tranvía*, 1:11, September 30, 1911, 2.

56. *La Razón*, May 20, 1911, 10.

57. *El Combate*, 1:1, June 1, 1910, 2.

58. *El Tranvía*, 1:4, July 8, 1911, 1–2.

59. *El Tranvía*, I:1, June 10, 1911, 1.

60. *La Razón*, May 11, 1911, 2.

61. *La Razón*, May 12, 1911, 2.

62. *El Socialista*, I:9, May 14, 1911, 2–3.

63. *La Razón*, June 23, 1911, 2.

64. *The Montevideo Times*, May 14, 1911, 1.

65. *The Montevideo Times*, May 19, 1911, 1 and May 20, 1911, 1; *La Razón*, May 12, 1911, 2.

66. *La Razón*, May 16, 1911, 2, May 17, 1911, 2, May 19, 1911, 8 and May 20, 1911, 3, 5 and 10; *El Día*, May 13, 1911, "La Gran Huelga."

67. *La Razón*, May 17, 1911, 2; *El Día*, May 15, 1911, "La Gran Huelga."

68. *El Día*, May 15, 1911, "La Gran Huelga."

69. *El Día*, May 13, 1911, "La Gran Huelga."

70. *La Prensa* (Buenos Aires), May 15, 1911, 8.

71. *El Día*, May 15, 1911, "La Gran Huelga."

72. *El Día*, May 16, 1911, "Asamblea de Huelguistas."

73. *El Día*, May 15, 1911, "La Gran Huelga."

74. Great Britain, Public Record Office, FO 371/1276/23908, "Pueblo Todo de Montevideo."

75. *La Razón*, May 13, 1911, 2.

76. *La Razón*, May 13, 1911, 2.

77. *The Montevideo Times*, May 16, 1911, 1.

78. *Uruguay Weekly News*, May 21, 1911, 2. Traffic jumped from 10,616 passengers on May 11 to 18,814 on May 12 and remained high throughout the strike, garnering high returns for the company. *La Razón*, May 20, 1911, 3. Overall traffic for the entire month of May decreased by over 2 million, but increased by nearly 100,000 riders over April for the Tranvía del Norte, a 42 percent rise. Traffic in the same period declined by 39 percent on La Transatlantica and by 38 percent on La Comercial. *Boletín mensual de estadística municipal del departamento de Montevideo*, IX:92 and 93, April and May, 1911, 7. Electric trolley workers did not at first ask the horse-tram personnel to join their strike, since they worked for different companies and did not share the same economic grievances. This changed during the general strike as the Tranvía del Norte also closed down as an act of solidarity.

79. *El Tranvía*, I:1, June 10, 1911, 3.

80. *La Prensa* (Buenos Aires), May 22, 1911, 10; *El Tranvía*, I:1, June 10, 1911, 3; *The Montevideo Times*, May 23, 1911, 1.

81. It should be noted that the correspondent of *La Prensa* alone foresaw this as a temporary truce which left the main grievances of the workers unanswered, May 23, 1911, 10.

82. In 1910 the company reported that revenues increased by 18 percent while expenses decreased by 2 percent. *South American Journal*, June 17, 1911, 724.

83. *The Montevideo Times*, May 23, 1911, 1.

84. D'Elia and Miraldi, *Movimiento obrero*, p. 101.

85. *La Democracia*, May 27, 1911, 2; *The Montevideo Times*, May 23, 1911, 1.

86. *Uruguay Weekly News*, May 28, 1911, 3.

87. Vanger, *Model Country*, p. 127.

88. *La Razón*, May 26, 1911, 4.

89. *La Razón*, May 26, 1911, 4.

90. Barran and Nahum, *Batlle*, pp. 61–63.

91. *La Democracia*, May 27, 1911, 2.

92. *La Democracia*, May 27, 1911, 2.

93. Carlo Umiltá quoted in Juan Antonio Oddone, *Una perspectiva europea del Uruguay* (Montevideo: Universidad de la República Oriental del Uruguay, 1965), p. 91.

94. Barrán and Nahum, *Batlle*, p. 60; *The Montevideo Times*, May 27, 1911, 1.

95. Oddone, *Una perspectiva*, p. 91.

96. *El Tranvía*, I:10, September 15, 1911, 5, I:15, November 30, 1911, 1; *La Razón*, June 6, 1911, 2 and June 7, 1911, 5 and 7.

97. *La Razón*, June 21, 1911, 1.

98. See, for example, Charles Bergquist, *Labor in Latin America* (Stanford: Stanford University Press, 1986).

99. Barrán and Nahum, *Batlle*, p. 60.

100. Temma Kaplan, *Red City, Blue Period* (Berkeley: University of California Press, 1992).

4

Women, Men(?), and a Strike in Colombian Mills

Ann Farnsworth-Alvear

*Among the more dramatic developments in Latin American industrializa-
tion after World War I was the entry of women into the workforce. A process that was not missing from the earlier period, it now began in earnest.
Mill owners sought females, especially children, whose fingers they supposed would more nimbly and more cheaply run the machines than the
men.* It is important to note, however, that the central feature of Ann
Farnsworth-Alvear's analysis of a strike by women in Colombia is not
that they were omitted from the modern conception of the working class;
it is that they were excluded from it. In the Medellín textile strike of 1920
the press reported events as though no men were involved (clearly not
true), and they discussed the women as a special case, to be handled as a
group apart from workers who, by definition, could only be men. This
finding boldly calls attention to the problem of gender in Latin American
history. It issues a challenge: which is more relevant to an understanding
of women in the workforce, paternalism or class? Are there elements of
both? Can we better understand female workers in relation to other women
alone or in relation to men and society in general? Did these strikers
threaten the social order as women or as workers? Finally, who were their
allies in this instance—the members of the press, the Church reformers,
the political parties, or the government? There are no conclusive answers
to these questions.*

In February of 1920, four hundred women and about one hundred men
struck Colombia's largest textile mill, the Compañía de Tejidos de
Medellín. From the beginning, the women's actions radically expanded

---

*See, for example, Juan Norberto Casanova, *Ensayo económico-político sobre
el porvenir del la industria algondonera fabril del Perú* (Lima, 1849); and the
broader analysis of Casanova's development views in Paul Gootenberg, *Imagin-
ing Development: Economic Ideas in Peru's "Fictitious Prosperity" of Guano,
1840–1880* (Berkeley: University of California Press, 1993), 45–57.

observers' understandings of what "a strike" might be. First, the striking women made unexpected demands; not only did they want higher wages and a ten-hour day but also the dismissal of two sexually abusive foremen. Second, they used gender as a weapon, shaming male strike-breakers with direct sexual taunts. At this, reporters expressed both surprise and condescension. The local correspondent for a Bogotá daily, *El Correo Liberal*, described the scene with bemusement:

> Armed with sticks and stones, the girls went up resolved to take the pants off those of the opposite sex who attempted to go to work. They sang cheerfully, raising high on a pole the fundamental insignia of their sex, some skirts.
>
> Mr. Editor: Excuse me if today I don't report as usual. This is charming. In my job as a reporter I never imagined such a thing as a strike of 500 señoritas.[1]

Every subsequent public representation of the strike, from newspaper reports to negotiators' statements to later commemorative articles, focused on the women's flamboyant action. There were clues that some men (although not all) had participated in the strike and that a few had played leading roles, but these were generally ignored. A degree of male solidarity would seem a logical necessity, however, as men formed a substantial minority of the workforce. In 1920–1921 female employment at the Bello mill ranged from 360 to 420; the number of male workers varied between 132 and 175. Yet the only men in strike reports were those feminized by the women's mockery; any others found themselves erased, as the month-long labor action became a strike of "500 *señoritas*."

Why should a feminist historian care that men, for once, had been erased from the historical record? Beginning my research on working women in Medellín's textile mills, I was thrilled to find a strike of *señoritas*. I was not unduly concerned that the city's *anuarios estadísticas*, for example, included statistics only on female workers. It seemed odd to have such wonderful, year-by-year data on the numbers of women in industry with no way to know if any men worked alongside them in the textile mills, cigarette and shoe factories, bottling plants, and food-packing houses. But I could fill in with the occasional census and, besides, I cared more—just as the record-keepers had—about the women workers than about their male counterparts.

Slowly, however, I began to sense a trap. Elite observers had created a historical record that separated women from "the working class," defined as masculine. Accepting that separation would prevent me from asking what gender difference and class position had meant to working women themselves. It would also limit my understanding of the 1920 strike. The more I struggled to glean evidence of women's activism by reading "against the grain" of condescending reports, the more likely I was to miss the importance of the distortion involved in such reports. That distortion, like reformers' detailed records on "women workers," was a key event in itself and part of the local definition of a new category, the woman worker or *la mujer obrera*. By separating working women and their problems from class politics, elite observers limited the meaning of women's activism, confining it within a romantic narrative of pity and protection. This was a double-edged sword. The women won their strike by manipulating (and mocking) the language of female vulnerability, but they lost exactly that claim to class identity most associated with the act of striking one's workplace.

By paying attention to the language in which reporters and others wrote about the strike and about *la mujer obrera* more generally, this paper analyzes how that category developed in local discourse.[2] Even in 1920, the woman worker was a familiar image; she had already been separated, symbolically, from "the working man" and from the "social question" of class. Catholic reformers and writers on the Left used her to stake their moral claims in the firm ground of sexual hierarchy; society women sponsored charitable projects aimed at guarding her chastity; and the local legislature required that an inspector visit those establishments that employed women, keeping statistics on this new work force but also assessing the moral safety of each workplace. The gender anxiety that surfaced in strike reports had its roots in this emerging discourse about working women's sexual vulnerability. Telling the story of the strike thus requires a history of imaginary beings, the pitiable "women workers" who drew observers' sympathies, as well as of the real women—and men—who surprised reporters with their assertiveness and daring.

My purpose is not only to trace the systematic distortions of reporters and reformers, but also to ask where bourgeois values intersected with working women's own moral vision: In what ways did the strikers accept, reject, manipulate, or ignore the discourse created about them? Pointing out the smoke and mirrors that shrank aggressive women to charming *señoritas* and made male strikers disappear is only part of the process of understanding the strikers' demands and the possible meanings of their public gestures.

The "*Mujercitas*" of Bello

The reporter who found himself too charmed to report as usual also expressed surprise that anything so interesting would happen in Bello—this little town on the outskirts of Medellín, the capital of Antioquia province, whose only distinction was the mill that city investors had built on its swift-flowing creek about fifteen years earlier. "The peaceful population of Bello," he began, "which seems more like an ox put out in pastureland, grazing, than the capital of a municipality, is today a theater of happenings. You heard me: happenings, in Bello."[3] Like other educated

Antioqueños, he separated the still-rural communities on the city's outskirts from Medellín itself, which was rapidly losing its small-town feel.[4]
By the mid-1920s, the city's eight textile mills employed more than nine
hundred workers, almost five hundred people worked at three cigar and
cigarette factories, and hundreds more held semi-industrial jobs in food-
packing plants and smaller workshops.[5] Medellín's population had grown
to one hundred twenty thousand, and urban services like electricity, water
and sewage piping, and street cleaning were slowly being extended even
to working-class neighborhoods. A railroad line and the first telephone
cables brought outlying parishes like Bello closer to the city, while the
local and national press had expanded and made itself modern with telegraph correspondents and the regular inclusion of photographs (our reporter headed off to Bello with a Kodak camera). All of this made a town
like Bello a new kind of "theater" for a strike.

Although the country saw its first strike, or the first action by waged
workers using the word "strike," only in 1910, Colombian workers mounted
at least thirty-three strikes between January of 1919 and February of 1920.
There were four in Medellín in January and early February of 1920.[6] Nationally and locally, the idea and the fact of strikes suddenly became common knowledge, and the social meaning of waged work began to be debated
in terms of "classes," "the social question," and "revolution." True to form,
the oligarchic parties tried to contain the social conflict within the structure of Liberal vs. Conservative politics, although the more prescient party
politicians recognized the need for a bipartisan front against the new dangers of anarchism and socialism. Liberal newspapers tended to recognize
workers' right to "just treatment" in the face of the governing Conservatives' hostility, and they often supported strikes. Conservatives backed
Catholic unions and workers' societies, but they denounced strikes and
class-based rhetoric as anti-Christian and threatening to the social order.[7]

Even in this politicized world, the Bello strikers enjoyed almost un-
qualified solidarity. Press reports were uniformly supportive, while Socialists, Liberals, local priests, and Conservative politicians involved
themselves on the women's behalf.[8] Understanding this apparent anomaly
requires unpacking the obvious: that men in different parts of the world
of politics responded similarly to a strike of "*señoritas*." Because the
women framed it as a denunciation of sexual abuses and a demand for
respectful treatment, male observers were constrained either to support
their action or insist they were lying *en masse*—something the factory
owner attempted only briefly. The strikers' gender-based claims separated
their action from politics as such. Socialists and left Liberals treated it as
an inspiration to male workers, and elite politicians described it as an
exception among work stoppages, but they agreed that this strike was not
like other strikes.

Leaving aside the language of class and politics associated with strikes, reporters filed anecdotal, serialized stories that relied upon romantic images of maidens injured yet valiant. A writer for the Liberal daily *El Espectador*, who signed himself "*el curioso impertinente*" (the curious and impertinent one), offered engaging descriptions of his own emotions along with sympathetic portraits of the women and caricatures of the villains. "The virility of these girls," he wrote, "submissive slaves until yesterday, attracts me, fascinates me. I'd break a thousand pens, if I knew how to fence with pens, in their defense."[9] Inviting the public to share this experience, the young reporter described his leave-taking on the first day of the strike in the personal language of a novel or travel diary:

> I undertake the return to the Station between the fire of a roasting sun and the yellow dust of the highway. At every step I turn my eyes back toward the factory and my young man's enthusiastic and sentimental heart flies to those hundreds of little women who have had the gallant and fertile madness to confront the resistance and the fury of capital . . . without more luggage than a good provision of rebellion and dignity.
>
> The hoarse whistle of the locomotive warns me that haste is useless. The smoke draws a black pencil-stroke between the green of the fields and the blue of the skies. I outfit myself with a horse and at a stretched-out gallop I quickly breathe the heavy air of the capital [Medellín]."[10]

Reporters' rhetorical fancies inspired them to create a heroine, a Joan of Arc leading this army of *mujercitas*. They found her in Betsabé Espinal, "a very pretty, very upright girl, who they say is most dexterous at her weaving job," who was the subject of flowery descriptions, interviews, and lyric poems in both the Liberal and Socialist papers.[11] *El Luchador* compared her to a goddess, an abject victim, a rebelling slave. She was luminous and sexual:

> As Betsabé spoke, erect atop a stool which served her as a tribunal, her brilliant black eyes darted over the multitude . . . lightning bolts of rage and flashes of just indignation. As her lungs swelled, giving a rhythmic motion to her bosom, it seemed that her heart was fighting to force its way out of her chest.

With a flattering photograph, they published an interview with Espinal and painted a sentimental picture of her devotion to her aging mother, who was "crazy—perhaps from hunger" and whose "double suffering" she could never earn enough to lessen.[12] And although Espinal herself offered the names of other strike leaders, including Adelina González and Teresa Tamayo, who had initiated the work stoppage after presenting a formal petition to the manager, reporters repeatedly returned to Espinal's extemporaneous oration as the beginning moment of the strike.[13] Devoted to her aging mother, she embodied the chaste, hard-working *obrera*. Her example corroborated the public vision of the strike as "a fight between a weakness that petitions with justice and an obstinate strength that refuses to yield."[14]

The gendered metaphor of female weakness before an inflexible force often became a titillating narrative of sexual implication. Seeking sensation, "*el curioso impertinente*" launched "a general interrogation" with a group of *obreras* of the specific charges against Manuel de Jesús Velásquez.[15] The women offered examples: The foreman had fired a boy who "understood" why he called women into his office alone; he favored certain girls; he punished and forced the retirement of those who would not "give in to his presumptions." Our reporter, however, insisted on details, asking questions and demanding verifiable cases. He reproduced his conversations, complete with suggestive ellipses, for his readers:

> —He threatened a certain señorita with a fine if she left the work room [. . .] she stayed alone with [him] and . . .
> —And . . .
> —Yes, it is known for certain. Poor thing [. . .]
> —This is not enough for me [. . .] I need someone to be more concrete, someone to confirm if it is possible.
>   Knowing looks. Vacillations. Blushes.
> —He, —ventures one girl finally— he put my niece in the Home for Repentant Women [*Casa de Arrepentidas*].[16]

This is enough to stop "*el curioso*" short; he expresses emotional confusion and withdraws from the scene: "I desired but did not expect an affirmation so complete, so categorical. I am disconcerted, disturbed . . . and I opt for touching my hat and taking my leave."[17]

Later reports referred darkly to "incalculable abuses" and "very dirty threads that should be brought to light" and confirmed five cases of "violent seduction" by Manuel de Jesús. One writer accused the foreman of having "thrown various *obreras* into the dreadful depths of prostitution" and intimated that these "crimes" had been committed "in the very work rooms of the factory," evoking a visual image which fed directly into the reformist discourse of the factory as a primary site of sexual depravity. Symbolically, the themes of sexual perversion and virginity came together in an odd description of the strikers as "tame sheep, some of whom have been led astray by their own shepherd dogs."[18]

Images of female violation, and sexual and physical struggle, also summoned orientalist and racist visions. Manuel de Jesús was labeled a "*Sultán*" and a " *Nabab*," and one fervent writer celebrated the striking women as "these purest of virgins, fugitives from the harem."[19] Physical descriptions of Manuel de Jesús and another foreman, Jesús María Monsalve, hinged on racial identifications: "*el curioso impertinente*," for example, depicted Velásquez as "more than dark" and as having "large lips," and the striking women apparently called the foremen "snitching blacks" (*negros lambones*).[20] In one aside, Velásquez's name appeared with the parenthetical addition of "a. [alias] the forgotten Indian."[21] The exact meaning of *"negro"* (or *"indio"*) in this context is somewhat elusive, as the word has a kind of discursive instability in Colombia. Nor is it at all clear whether or not the foremen were "in fact" black. What *is* clear is that racial language was used as part of a larger attempt to discredit the factory and win sympathy for the innocence and purity of the strikers. Given that the strikers were certainly not homogeneously "white," the opposition between the "black" villains of the piece and their pure "white" victims (sheep!) was symbolically drawn.

That opposition, furthermore, made "gentlemen's" support for the strikers a defense of their racial honor as well as of their gender. *El Espectador* sounded this theme implicitly, with references to "the noble and gentlemanly tradition that inspired Don Quijote" and calls to defend the striking women "if anything is left of our noble Castilian blood." Invocations of "the race" and "the Latin soul," together with descriptions of the foremen as *"Sultáns," "Nababs,"* or "Black Chiefs," thus underscored the script of sexual danger and virgins in distress through which reporters told the story of the strike.[22]

This discourse of sexual danger translated directly into a call for chivalry, with the masculine dominance that implied. The editors of *El Correo Liberal* and *El Espectador* reminded readers of "the natural weakness of the strikers" and cautioned that at risk in the Bello conflict were "the tears, the sufferings, the hunger and even the honor of a group of Antioqueña mothers and girls." Their helplessness required that the paper's readers involve themselves on behalf of these "suffering women": "The very special character of this occasion, in which . . . a weakness and a strength fight in open and equal struggle, authorizes us to place ourselves on the side of the former; and almost more than it authorizes us, it obliges us."[23]

The city's socialist paper, *El Luchador* (The Fighter), expressed the same sentiments in a workerist idiom, appealing to readers to defend "these indomitable women" in page after page of fiery polemic.

> For these proud and rebellious slaves, vagabonds from the dungeon of Don Emilio Restrepo [the mill's owner], where their souls were outraged and where every minute, every hour that passed was a danger to their virtue and their honor. . . . For these masculine females who, when the vacillating *men* fell back one step . . . went forward twenty . . . every one of the *Luchadores* has an immense heart with which to love them and a strong arm to defend them.[24]

For both socialist *"luchadores"* and Liberal gentlemen, then, defending femininity was a matter of masculine honor; the gender inversion of striking women denouncing vacillating men required that real men rally to the women's cause and thus restore threatened gender roles.

The flip side of chivalry was anxiety about gender inversion, and images of the sexual world turned upside down dominated reports of the Bello strike. The eighteen or so men who remained at work were reviled and made ridiculous by reporters who contrasted their "cowardice" to the courage of "gallant and heroic women."[25] "Let them cry like women that which they could not defend like men," railed a columnist in *El Luchador* who denounced "the fact that some of those who belong to the ugly sex (colloquially, men) did not take part in the strike."[26] Reporters hailed "the virility of these girls" and described them as having "manly hearts" and "more character than the fearful men."[27] Yet this textual inversion expressed a central contradiction. The striking *obreras* challenged the opposition between masculine strength and feminine helplessness, but by describing them as more "like men" than the men, press reports sustained the power of that opposition.

Of course, this carnivalesque tension, one that disrupted gender roles while at the same time affirming "natural" difference (by emphasizing the unnaturalness of a momentary inversion), emerged not only in press accounts but also in the women's strategies of protest. If reporters responded to the strike with sexually charged rhetoric and sensational descriptions of manly women and emasculated men, they did so because the strikers consciously manipulated sexual images. In addition to the visual insult of presenting male strike-breakers with skirts, the women taunted them verbally. As a typically theatrical report of a dialogue between strikers and scabs described the scene:

> —Girls, make way—says the gentleman Mayor to the *obreras* grouped at the factory gate—so that the workers can enter.
> —Of course, Don Gabriel. With pleasure.
> —Let's make way girls, so that the LADIES can go to work.
>   The path was made. And eighteen MEN, one by one, filed through that double row of human flowers, pretty girls who watched them . . . with pity.[28]

The sexual ridicule, symbolic inversion of roles, and manipulation of visual images contained in the Bello strikers' skirt-bearing do not make their protest exceptional. Rather, the strikers' playfully subversive tactics fit a pattern of women's street protests identified by historians in a variety of cultural contexts. Jacqueline Hall and Temma Kaplan, particularly, have drawn attention to working-class women's manipulation of gender-laden symbols and to the often creative ways their protests mock male authority.[29]

Striking women generally left intact the sexual hierarchy. Denouncing male strike-breakers as "women" by offering them female clothing, for example, relied upon but did not question society's denigration of women. Analyzing an incident at a cigar factory in Tampa, Florida, in which female strikers called men who remained at work "females" and offered them skirts, exactly as the women in Bello did, Nancy Hewitt points to the ambiguity of the action. "Was offering their skirts to men a derogation of femaleness?" she asks, "or was it an attempt to shock reluctant comrades by flaunting the role reversal?"[30] Clearly, it was both; but there is another point to be made about such demonstrative transvestitism. In waving skirts before male scabs, striking women symbolically took off their own female dress. Furthermore, they visually demonstrated the socially defined, rather than anatomical or innate, character of gender roles. The skirt made the woman, and it could symbolically unmake the man.

As it worked in Bello, a skirt hoisted on a pole was not only a sign ridiculing the men; it was also a flag of female presence—the "insignia" of women's sex. Seen from the women's perspective (rather than from that of masculine pride), it may have signified a demand for inclusion as much as a gesture of exclusion. Certainly, the gesture recognized going out on strike as a "masculine" thing to do, but it also highlighted the women's own claim to a work-based identity. By striking and urging men to strike with them, the women undercut the dichotomy between womanhood and political action—even as they manipulated it.

What did male strikers make of the skirts and shouted taunts? They may have felt valued, as men, by comparison to unmanly strike breakers, or they may have felt threatened—newspaper sources provide few clues. Rather, reporters wrote about the strike as though *they* were the only men present. Noticing this suggests a motive for the textual erasure of male strikers: Male observers could then safeguard their own sense of gender hierarchy by positioning themselves as the women's protectors.

¡Pobres Obreras!

By framing the strike within a narrative of protection, reporters drew upon locally available images of *la mujer obrera* as innocent, sexually vulnerable, and wholly deserving of pity. Such images were part of a growing campaign for charity and protective legislation, one waged by local proponents of Catholic Social Action, including Jesuits and other clerical activists, charitable ladies' societies, political conservatives, and various lay organizations. The first local debates about female labor, for example, took place around an ordinance for "factory policing" proposed in 1917. Like the 1920 strike, discussions of the proposed ordinance centered on working women's vulnerability and anxieties about woman's place. The Catholic paper, *El Social*, argued for the legislation in a long series titled "¡Pobres Obreras!," in which the author urged his readers to descend with him into the "hell" of working-class life:

Various times, we have solicited that our beloved readers descend to the abyss of the working classes . . . but in the black and fathomless abyss of the proletariat it is not the *obreros* that inspire in me the most compassion. In it is another group that inspires in me pity much more profound, if that were possible.

It is the *obreras*! It is the *obreras* that share all the miseries of the obreros, that suffer all the misfortunes that they do, *and . . . some more.*[31]

This pity was reserved not for male workers' wives and daughters, because they were poor, but specifically for female workers who suffered these other, more terrible trials. More precisely, it was for factory workers, not maids or female coffee-pickers or serving girls:

The factory is woman's enemy. Enemy of her body and of her soul; exhauster of her health and poisoner of her virtue . . . the almost inevitable mix of women with men, and what is worse, the dependence on them; finally, like a dark backdrop for so many stains, the lowness of the wage, these make an *obrera* of the factory a miserable woman compelled to languish physically and morally.[32]

Here and elsewhere, *El Social* reflected the ambiguous position of the international Catholic church, accepting the inevitability of female waged labor (and thus the need for protections) but nonetheless denouncing the woman worker as "a dislocated being," forced by circumstance to violate heaven's mandate. Man was cursed to work, woman to bring forth children in pain (reproductive labor being defined as nonwork).[33] The idea of their "dislocation" and the corollary female vulnerability ensured a romanticized distortion of any independent action by female workers.

Descriptions of working women's slave-like exploitation, bodily weakness, docility, and threatened purity also permeated the liberal and socialist press in 1917–1919. Like Catholic reformers, liberals and socialists emphasized the unnatural violation of gender roles and focused on women workers' sexual vulnerability. This was often implicit and couched in cliché, as with the contrast between "men's work" and the (inevitably sexual) association between femininity and slavery: "They are worked like *machos* and paid like *esclavas*."[34] But it also appeared in elaborate prose descriptions; according to a writer in the socialist *El Luchador,*

At six in the morning they bustle like bees[,] these poor women who have to work ten or twelve hours to be able to bring a crust of bread to their mouths, and to be able to cover their bodies with a rag . . . laboring hard and intensely and perhaps submitting to the mistreatment of an overseer.[35]

By suggesting the women's nakedness, the writer did more than simply associate femaleness with passivity and helplessness; his was a sexualized description. Such images of beauty despoiled and innocence destroyed became standard fare. "To think," despaired *El Luchador,* that these fragile beings, "whom nature clothed in supreme delicacy . . . will go like fugitive butterflies to be kept prisoners in the unyielding nets of a factory, of its slavery."[36] A terrible fate awaited them, warned another gothic piece describing the suffering of one "Flor María": "When I met Flor María, she bloomed with her twenty years. She was beautiful, of a queenly beauty. Her body . . . her hair. Her intensely black eyes seemed magnificent gems . . . more than all this, she was as good as an angel and as sweet as a child."[37]

Upon the death of her loving father, however, the angel delivered "her weak and fragile body to the hard labor of the factory." This sealed her fate. As the writer put it, "Not long ago she crossed my path. She laughed like a mad woman. Her eyes no longer shone. . . . Poor Flor María!"[38] Industrial work consumed every marker of femininity: youth, beauty, fragility, modesty. And arguments for protective legislation—like the strike reports that called upon male readers to act in support of Bello's valiant *mujercitas*—centered on these markers of femininity rather than on the complexity of women's actions and experiences at work.

Passed in 1918, the Ordinance on Factory Policing contained various articles that were not gender specific, such as a prohibition against hiring children under ten and limits on the widespread practice of fining workers for disciplinary infractions, but it was explicitly focused on moral regulation. In its final form, and in most attempts at enforcement, factory policing was defined as the protection and control of female sexuality. Arguments before the departmental assembly made this explicit. As the bill's author, Government Secretary Francisco de Paula Pérez, insisted:

> It is necessary that the policing gaze penetrate to the factories, to the end that places of work not become places of seduction . . . so that in giving themselves over to their labors [women workers] do not hazard their virtue; so that in weaving productive pieces for the commercial market they do not also weave the dishonor of their lives.[39]

Although a piece of labor legislation, the Ordinance on Factory Policing maintained the furthest possible distance from the language of revindication emerging in the growing Colombian working-class movement. It maintained that distance from workers in exactly the same way that strike reports made the Bello action an unassailable cause, by dividing female factory workers (pitiable beings in need of protection) from the more threatening, class-based image of *los obreros*. Its first article required that factories employing both women and men hire matrons, later called *vigilantas*, to guard against any kind of immorality. To enforce this and other provisions, a factory inspector would be appointed to visit those workplaces employing women. Not incidentally, this resulted in male workers' virtual disappearance from the statistical record. Because they were based

on data the inspector collected, the city *anuarios* included data on working women's hours, wages, place of origin, civil status, etc., but no
corresponding figures for working men.[40] While confusing from a labor
history perspective, a mandate to visit only mixed-sex workplaces was
self-evident within the terms of debate that produced the 1918 measure.

The inspector was charged with policing not only the relations between women workers and their employers and supervisors but also their
interactions with male workers. Seeking to protect women from their male
co-workers as much as from those overseeing their work, the ordinance
aimed to legislate and make real this discursive separation between female and male workers. Inspector Daniel Vélez (1920–1927) concentrated
special attention on conversation between male and female workers, pursuing silence as the only answer to mixed-sex workplaces and demanding
that the *vigilantas* be inflexible and ever present.[41] Records from his office indicate the scope of reformers' attempts to control gender boundaries in the new workplaces. In 1922, for example, the inspector made a
special visit to one factory upon hearing "that the matron, through her
pusillanimity, authorized chatting between men and women workers."[42]
At another, he praised the "strict vigilance" which reigned, specifically
noting that "conversations among workers are not permitted, that is to
say, between men and women workers—Morality thus proceeds very well."[43]

Even when enforcing aspects of the ordinance unrelated to sexual
morality, the inspector referred to gender claims. Not only did sanitation
standards require modern toilets, they must be separate for women and
men so "that morality [does] not suffer damage."[44] Not only was a certain
technician insubordinate, he was also disrespectful of women and had
called the *obreras* "mares, tramps and other apostrophes."[45] When a mechanic was accused of allowing himself "inconvenient expressions" with
the *obreras* of Tejidos Hernández, Vélez expressed particular outrage that
women workers should be exposed to his intemperate odor: "[H]e presents himself in the work-rooms with that sickness known as a hangover
and the *obreras*, some of whom are even *from very good families*, find it
necessary, because of their poverty, to suffer the nauseous breath of said
individual."[46]

The problem was not only his smell but also his vulgar proximity to
obreras, defined as ladies. Inspector Vélez blurred the line between feminine delicacy and morality, just as reformist discourse assumed a kind of
frailty belied by women's competent and daily labor. In this, as in their
rhetoric about the working-class family, the inspector and other Catholic
activists represented working-class women by evoking a bourgeois conception of femininity: Women should be clean, protected, modest, silent, and
chaste. This rhetorical strategy further separated the categories of *la mujer
obrera* and "the working class."

Vélez's reports to the assembly stressed his perseverance: "I am pleased," he wrote in 1926,

> To manifest to you that during this year . . . not one of the obreras was dishonored in a factory building, neither by a [white-collar] employee *nor by a worker*. An official must carry out multiple inquiries . . . and through interposed persons, to succeed in obtaining [such a] result in the matter of morality.[47]

He assured the legislators that their "policing gaze" had entered the shadowy world of the factories; he also framed his success in terms of working women's vulnerability not as workers but as women. Again and again, Vélez placed women in the same position vis-à-vis men of their class and their more powerful supervisors and employers. The language of vulnerability and protection had a sexual emphasis that worked to obscure the class issues inherent in the swirling debates over "the social question" and the now-present reality of strikes in the small-town atmosphere of Medellín.

The constant application of the adjective "poor" to women workers, as in *¡Pobres Obreras!*, has a special meaning here. As Mauricio Archila has argued, the 1910s and 1920s mark a transition in the language and self-identification of radical Colombian workers, a category that included artisans and the craftsmen they hired but also, and increasingly, waged workers in general. In these decades, they gradually moved away from the broad *pobres*, deriving from Christian tradition and tinged with racial classifications from the colonial period, and toward the more politically combative identifications of *obreros* and *pueblo*.[48] Separating workers from "the poor," Archila argues, made them part of an active citizenry and enabled them to make demands as workers, persons with skills and strengths (and votes), rather than as the passive receivers of charity. But this turn away from the language of protection and succor was a masculine self-definition. Indeed, the increasing distance between *pobre* and *obrero* may have deepened the symbolic connections between pity and femaleness. The discourse associated with female factory labor hinged on women's vulnerability not as *obreras* in a specific relationship to the economic system but as women at risk by their proximity to men—not only male supervisors or employers, but also male workers. If workers were powerful, even dangerous male figures, the females lost among them stood the more in need of protection. Their frailty and sexual vulnerability were the logical flip side of fears about the changing meaning of class in Colombia, as well as the natural extension of gender anxieties about women working for wages. Thus, a strike would likely be more charming to a young gentleman's heart if the spectacle involved *obreras* standing at a distance from their male counterparts.

Nonfictional Women

This rhetoric of vulnerability had power. It swayed legislators and slowly moved local industrialists toward the moralistic paternalism for which Medellín became well known in the 1940s. It also ensured women's gradual exclusion from textile jobs, as I have argued elsewhere.[49] Thus the hackneyed images of *pobres obreras* that circulated in debates over female labor in Medellín cannot be called unreal. That imaginary women played a more obvious role in historic causality than "real" people points to the limits of a strictly bottom-up approach to working-class history; it is a small example of the reasons historians have begun to make the linguistic turn. Nevertheless, an argument about discourse becomes meaningless without an assessment of its distance or closeness to the contradictory experiences of the nonfictional people being spoken about. It is not enough to notice that actual men and women are missing from texts obsessed with frail but heroic *señoritas*. Stopping there would be doubly inadequate in cases where the objects of discourse speak and act publicly, changing the term of discussion—as did the Bello strikers.

Capitalizing on its novelty and the amusement generated by a strike of *mujercitas*, reporters shaped their stories to tell a certain kind of story about the strike; but they faced constraints that the legislators and Catholic polemicists did not. A reporter might be overtly condescending, as in one account: "the girls vociferated, they talked and talked: imagine for yourselves a strike of 500 women," but the women's action had forced him not only to notice their speech but also to include sentences about their demands in the first person.[50] Nonfictional women and men pushed against the narrative that reporters created and against the erasures they perpetrated.

Mixed in with *El Luchador*'s flowery rhetoric about "these purest of virgins, fugitives from the harem," for example, were a few more prosaic accounts of strike meetings, and these included male speakers. The paper published the minutes of a strike meeting stating that the workers had named two representatives: "Rubén Hernández for the men and the *señorita* Betsabé Espinal for the women." The minutes themselves were taken by a man, one Manuel S. Osorio.[51] Similarly, *El Espectador*'s reporter, so charmed by the picturesque scene in Bello, did include one reference to the involvement of a foreign technician and, with it, a mention of other, unidentified "men." In the informal style of his reports from Bello, he reproduced a conversation with the strikers:

> [Reporter]—Do you know . . . that the dyer, Francisco Charpiot, was fired from the factory today because he figures as the director of the strike?
> [Strikers]—Him director of the strike? When! And you say he's been thrown out? Fine, we won't go back to the factory if he doesn't go back. . . . We won't go back—*affirm the men*.[52]

With Charpiot there is a paper trail, as the mill's administrator wrote to the Belgian firm that had sent him, informing them of his dismissal for having "promoted" the strike.[53] Questions about the other men must remain speculative: Did men regularly join striking women on the street, only to be generally ignored by reporters? Were they present when the women and girls waved their skirts at another group of men?

Other kinds of sources provide glimpses of workers' daily experiences in Medellín's mixed-sex workplaces. Unsurprisingly, nonfictional *obreros* and *obreras* bear little relation to either the melodramatic depictions of Catholic polemicists or the "fugitive butterflies" appearing in liberal and socialist reports of the strike. First, the factory's "nets" were hardly so unyielding. Although records for the Bello mill are spotty before the 1930s, a personnel log from nearby Coltejer (a mill that obervers considered to be better managed and to have a more stable workforce) indicates that a third of all workers remained at their jobs less than a year. Sixty-three percent of women and eighty-seven percent of men stayed less than three years. Coltejer's log also reveals that most left when they wanted to and because they wanted to. Workers left over reassignments, "to travel," or because they disliked a work-mate. A good number quit because they objected to being scolded: Carmen Morales, for example, "left hot under the collar because of the director's reprimand," while Julia Mora called the *vigilanta* a tattle-tale and walked out.[54] More frequently, however, people simply didn't show up, leaving the supervisor to jot down "left without notice" and to surmise that they had gone to another factory, knowing, as the workers did, that quitting a particular factory did not mean being without work.[55] The same complaint—that workers felt free to come and go—appears in the inspector's notes on a visit to another mill, Tejidos Unión. Seeing a sign saying that workers would not be paid for the morning hours if they failed to return after lunch, the inspector pointed out its illegality; the mill administrator, however, refused to rescind the policy, insisting that "the *obreras* cause grave damage" by doing exactly that.[56] Such evidence of women's (and men's) independence, ease of movement, and willingness to talk back sits uneasily with attempts to portray them as long-suffering victims.

Second, there is as much evidence of workers' disruptiveness and insubordination as of their supposed vulnerability. Because he was so often short-handed, Coltejer's manager complained regularly of workers who "took advantage of being needed."[57] In 1928, for example, he noted that Margarita Hoyos "has for some time now had a bad attitude, bad attendance, and has been talking back—she took advantage of our necessity because of the lack of workers—*Ungrateful*." When they needed extra workers, employers rehired workers with a record of bad behavior or whom they had previously fired. In the 1920s, Fabricato rehired a fifteen-year-old boy despite a previous entry that he was "lazy, dirty, [and] a liar," according to his employee card.[58] People who did get fired had often been directly insubordinate, like María Flórez, who called the *vigilanta* an "H.P." (*Hijeputa* or *Hija de Puta*, a "bastard" or "daughter of a whore").[59] Or they were women who flouted the norms of feminine behavior; a sixteen-year-old girl working at Fabricato, for example, was fired and labeled a "*corrompida*" (corrupted woman) because "her way of talking caused a scandal in the work-room and because she was "*badly inclined*," according to the manager.[60]

Working women, like their male counterparts, could also be violent. Angela Ríos held a *vigilanta* accountable after work hours; her entry reads as follows: "Fired for being troublesome, disobedient, chattery, and insufferable. She behaved loutishly as she waited for the *Señora Vigilanta* and beat her and roughed her up in the middle of the street."[61] Similarly, a twenty-one-year-old woman working at Fabricato was suspended for a week "for having mistreated a *vigilanta*"; furious, "she said that she would quit for good—After this she punched the *vigilanta* she had mistreated three times right there in the work-room."[62] At Coltejer, Eduardo Arango attacked a foreman: "he shouted at him and threatened him with a knife in the work-room, causing a huge commotion."[63] However rarely such physical attacks may have occurred, their defiant signal must have been amplified by the next day's gossip and remembered as shop-floor lore. Oddly, such wildly undisciplined workers fit well with the disparaging, sometimes racist descriptions offered by hardline elitists concerned about the deficiencies of Colombian workers, but there was no place for them in the more positive images put forth by socialists and left-leaning liberals. Catholic reformers, like Inspector Vélez, similarly found it convenient to trim unruly workers (especially unruly women) out of their pleas for protective legislation.

But nonfictional women will strain the "disorderly rebel" mold of a feminist historian as quickly as they break stereotypes of frailty. One of the truths of the 1920 strike was, precisely, that women found themselves sexually vulnerable. Despite its inherent condescension, reformist intervention had some positive meaning in women's lives. Medellín's inspector sought to control working women's sexuality as much as he sought to stop sexual molestation, but his concern nevertheless addressed one of the most serious problems faced by female factory workers, one not faced by their male co-workers. In 1922 he demanded that the manager of Tejidos de Rosellón fire a male worker who "had tried to corrupt an *obrera*, the fact being proven with juried declarations."[64] In 1923, Laura Rosa Sánchez complained to the inspector "that Luís Angel, the administrator of the factory [Tejidos Unión], had ruined her while she was working in the factory," and the inspector noted that "Twenty-nine days ago she gave birth in the hospital and is dying of hunger with the baby girl—she's 18 and a bit years old. He gave her $2.00 [pesos] a week. . . . They say he's got two in the factory that he has ruined."[65] In each instance, the inspector's intent (often unsuccessful) was to obtain the man's dismissal, not to aid the woman in her plight.[66] Yet the very fact that such cases reached the inspector's ear suggests that a woman had complained or sought remedy or that a co-worker had. Coupled with the fact of the Bello strike, in which mill workers protested sexual abuses publicly, indications that they called upon the inspector to take action against certain administrators suggest a point of convergence between the moralizing project of Catholic reformers and working women's own efforts to shape the moral world of the factory.

If reformers set out to control female sexuality as much as to protect working women, it does not follow that their discourse had no anchor in working women's experiences. Indeed, the points at which reformist rhetoric echoed working-class language may have provided a seal of "authenticity" necessary to the success of bourgeois-reformist discourse. By denouncing an abusive manager or a lecherous foreman the inspector may have said publicly, from a position of power, some of the things that working women discussed among themselves. The 1920 strike is itself the best example. The striking women did not simply manipulate a normative language of sexual morality; rather, they acted to ensure that accepted sexual norms would provide on-the-ground protection from sexual harassment.

Nevertheless, the strike itself underscores the gap between working women's understanding of their sexual vulnerability in the mills and the concerns of their reform-minded protectors. For male legislators and polemicists, the perils of being female separated women workers from their male counterparts, and protecting them meant enforcing that separation. Bello's strikers, however, pursued respectful treatment for "their sex" without dividing that claim from others not based on gender. In addition to their central demand for the dismissal of the three abusive foremen, the striking women and men demanded—and won—an increase of forty percent in piece rates and the reduction of work hours to the nine hours fifty minutes prevailing at other mills. They also insisted that the mill administrator rescind a bizarre regulation against wearing shoes to work.[67] More generally, they forced a public discussion of working conditions, denouncing the supervisors' practice of fining workers for daily infractions and complaining to reporters about being forced to work when ill.[68] Their actions combined claims made in the "male" register of economic value and public respect with the traditionally female demand of restitution for the loss of young women's reputations. If the strike was about working women's honor, the range of demands advanced suggests that the strikers defined their honor more broadly than did reporters or Catholic reformers.[69]

Conclusion

In Bello, as in other strikes documented by feminist labor historians, shared outrage at sexual molestation mobilized working women in their own defense.[70] The women challenged entrenched notions of male bravery and female timidity by deriding male strike-breakers as "women" while demonstrating that women could also be independent, rebellious, and persevering. They manipulated the discourse of pity associated with *la mujer obrera*, but their actions resisted formulations which limited female claims to those made in the name of virginity or maternity. If elite commentators painted them as helpless maidens needing male protection, Bello's working women and men defended themselves as *obreras* and *obreros* needing fewer arbitrary fines, better wages, shorter hours, *and* respectful supervisors. Their actions united moral and material claims—crossing a boundary between gendered sets of symbols. Any reconstruction that takes as its subject the "women workers" of Bello runs the risk of recreating the fictional creatures of strike reports and of separating what their action combined. In Medellín, for example, the feminists, historians, and labor educators who make reference to the Bello strike tend to do so in a romantic and celebratory language that conforms almost exactly to the presumptions of early newspaper reports.[71] The point is not that feminist historians should not celebrate women whose actions can inspire an ongoing hope but rather that appropriating a gendered fiction will not rewrite a script that erased not only the men but also those women who might not have conformed to reporters' typecasting.

Reading for the contradictions in representations of the strikers' public action means bringing the men back in, not as leads, but as supporting actors. Otherwise, the only male roles in a history of this strike will be those of the villainous supervisors and the self-satisfied onlookers of different political persuasions who rushed to the women's aid. The women will remain invisible, along with the younger or older brothers, boyfriends, and workmates with whom they talked or argued about the strike. The Bello strike was a small drama in a small town on the far outskirts of industrialism, but it demonstrates one of the most difficult problems for feminist labor history: The category we most often use, "women workers," obscures working women as subjects.[72] The strike is also a cautionary tale (yet another one!) about heroism, the language of the male subject in history. Feminists have turned away from attempts to include women in narratives of male workers realizing themselves in history precisely because those narratives (themselves unsustainable) obscure the larger effects of gender in industrial societies. Inevitably, we are like the reporters and reformers whose writings we mine for clues. Rushing in to save working people, women and men, from posterity's condescension, we trade in fictions about who they were.

Notes

1. *El Correo Liberal*, February 13, 1920. I thank Alberto Mayor for generously sharing this and other articles on the Bello strike.
2. My starting point is Joan Scott's observation that as historians of women's work, "we start the story . . . too late, by uncritically accepting a gendered category (the 'Woman Worker') that itself needs investigation because its meaning is relative to its history." Joan Wallach Scott, *Gender and the Politics of History* (New York, 1988), 175. Excellent analyses of the discourse associated with "women workers" include Sandra McGee Deutsch, "The Catholic Church, Work, and Womanhood in Argentina, 1890–1930," *Gender and History* 3 (1991):304–22; Patricia Hilden, "The Rhetoric and Iconography of Reform: Women Coal Miners in Belgium, 1840–1914," *Historical Journal* 34 (1991):411–36; Asuncion Lavrin, "Women, Labor and the Left in Argentina and Chile, 1890–1925," *Journal of Women's History* 1 (1989):249–77. See also Scott's own " 'L'ouvrière! Mot impie, sordide . . .': Women Workers in the Discourse of French Political Economy, 1840–1860," in *Gender and the Politics of History*.
3. *El Correo Liberal*, February 13, 1920.
4. A fascinating example of how Antioqueño intellectuals begin to reimagine the region's small towns through a modernist lens is Fernando Gonzalez's novel *Viaje a Pie* (Bogotá, 1967; orig. pub. 1929). For a discussion of regional literary production in this period see Raymond L. Williams, "Novela y Cuento," in Jorge Orlando Melo, comp., *Historia de Antioquia* (Medellín: Suramericana de Seguros, 1988).
5. To the figures on textile employment in the *Anuario estadistico de Medellín, 1922*, I have added the available figures for Fabricato, in Luz Gabriela Arango, *Mujer, religión e industria: Fabricato, 1923–1982* (Medellín: Universidad de Antioquia, 1991), 301, and for Montoya Hermanos y Cia, in Inspector de Fábricas, Acta no. 1362, 10 April 1922), which were not listed. See also Fernando Botero, *La industrialización en Antioquia: génesis y consolidación, 1900–1930* (Medellín: CIE, 1985), 174.
6. In Medellín in January and early February, tailors struck for ten days, shoemakers for nine, glass workers for seven, and railroad workers at the Cisneros station for two days. Mauricio Archila, *Cultura e Identidad: Colombia, 1910–45* (Bogotá, 1991), 222, 435–36.
7. For discussions of the political ramifications of the working-class movement, see Archila, *Cultura e Identidad*, as well as Charles Bergquist, *Labor in Latin America: Comparative Essays on Chile, Argentina, Venezuela, and Colombia* (Stanford, 1986), 342–43. Also: Ivan Darío Osorio, "Historia del sindicalismo," in Melo, comp., *Historia de Antioquia*.
8. The Liberal papers *El Sol, El Correo Liberal*, and *El Espectador* strongly supported the strikers, as did the Socialist papers *El Luchador* in Medellín and *El Socialista* in Bogotá. Among politicians of national standing, both Alejandro López and Pedro Nel Ospina involved themselves in negotiations behind the scenes, as did the Archbishop of Medellín. Pedro Nel Ospina to Ricardo Restrepo C., AGPNO/C/26, Collection of the Fundación Antioqueña de Estudios Sociales, folio 395; Emilio Restrepo to Illmo. Sr. Arzobispo de Medellín y Reverendo P. Gabriel Lizardi, S.J., March 5, 1920, Copiador 16, 352, Archivo Fabricato (AF); and Alejandro López to Alfonso Mejia, March 12, 1920. I thank Professor Alberto Mayor for sharing a copy of López's letter with me. See also Secretario de Gobierno to Don Emilio Restrepo, February 18, 1920, Archivo Histórico de Antioquia (AHA), S. 8570, 28.

9. *El Espectador*, February 14, 1920.

10. Ibid.

11. Ibid. See also *El Espectador*, March 1, 1920, which published a long ballad dedicated to "vuese finosura/Besthabé," and *El Luchador*, February 17, 1920.

12. Ibid.

13. Ibid. *El Luchador*, February 14, 1920, reported that González and Tamayo had been "ready to fight and capable of detaining the *obreras* and *obreros* who didn't care to accept the strike," but that Betsabé Espinal had argued for "the freedom of the obreras that have stayed at work, [and that] the rest of the obreras applauded her." The socialist paper thus tried to present her as a fair, morally upright defender of the obreras rather than as a "striker."

14. This description was offered by a "group of gentlemen" who met in the offices of *El Correo Liberal* and published a manifesto in solidarity with the strikers; see *El Espectador*, March 2, 1920,

15. *El Espectador*, February 14, 1920.

16. Ibid. Ellipses in brackets are added; others appear in the text.

17. Ibid.

18. *El Correo Liberal*, February 13, 1920.

19. "Sultán" appears in *El Socialista*, February 17, 1920 and *El Espectador*; "Nabab" in *El Correo Liberal*, February 13, 1920; and "harem" in *El Luchador*, February 25, 1920.

20. *El Espectador*, February 14, 1920, and *El Correo Liberal*, February 13, 1920. In the latter report Teódulo is described as being so surprised and frightened by the women's rebellion that he appeared "so pale he was almost white."

21. *El Luchador*, February 17, 1920.

22. *El Espectador*, February 26, and March 10, 1920. Also *El Luchador*, February 17, 1920.

23. *El Espectador*, March 5, 1920. Men from the two Liberal papers joined in producing this "Manifesto" of solidarity with the strikers.

24. *El Luchador*, February 25, 1920.

25. *El Espectador*, February 23, 1920.

26. *El Luchador*, February 17, 1920. Readers in Medellín likely would have remembered that a local magazine of caricature had offered hilarious sketches of "el sexo feo" a few years earlier. Luz Posada de Greiff, "La Prensa," in Melo, comp., *Historia de Antioquia*.

27. *El Espectador*, February 14 and 23 and March 5; *El Luchador*, February 14 and 20, 1920.

28. *El Luchador*, February 27, 1920; emphasis and ellipses in original.

29. Jacquelyn Dowd Hall, "Disorderly Women: Gender and Labor Militancy in the Appalachian South," *Journal of American History* 73 (1986):362; Temma Kaplan, "Female Consciousness and Collective Action: The Case of Barcelona, 1910–1918," *Signs* 1 (Spring 1982):551–52. I am also drawing on Kaplan's more recent work comparing the public theater of the *Madres* of the Plaza de Mayo, the housewives who denounced the poisoning of Love Canal, and the Nigerian women who challenged the British in the "women's war" of 1929, in "Making Spectacles of Themselves: Women's Rituals and Patterns of Resistance in Africa, Argentina, and the United States," conference paper, "El Trabajo de las Mujeres: Pasado y Presente," Universidad de Málaga, December 1–4, 1992.

30. Nancy A. Hewitt, " 'The Voice of Virile Labor': Labor Militancy, Community Solidarity, and Gender Identity among Tampa's Latin Workers, 1880–1921," in Ava Baron, ed., *Work Engendered: Toward a New History of American Labor* (Ithaca, 1991), 158–59.

31. *El Social*, July 8, 1917. (Ellipses in original, my emphasis.)

32. *El Social*, July 22, 1917.

33. *El Social*, July 8, 1917. For a good summary of the Catholic position, see Deutsch, "The Catholic Church."

34. *El Luchador*, November 28, 1919.

35. *El Luchador*, November 28, 1919.

36. *El Luchador*, January 24, 1920.

37. Jorge Isaacs, *María* (Madrid: Espasa-Calpe, 1983). See Doris Sommer's analysis of the importance of this novel in her *Foundational Fictions: The National Romances of Latin America* (Berkeley, 1991).

38. "Cuadros de Miseria," *El Luchador*, November 8, 1918. This same narrative of innocence lost to the factory appeared in a 1948 novel by the Conservative intellectual Jaime Sanín, which described the transformation of Helena, a farmer's daughter who loses her virginity while working at Coltejer and becomes a sophisticated woman of loose morals. Jaime Sanín Echeverri, *Una mujer de cuatro en conducta*, 5th ed. (Medellín, 1980). I would like to thank the author for discussing the novel and for sharing so generously his memories of Medellín with me, his foreign-born niece.

39. "Que la mirada policiva penetra a las fábricas," Secretario de Gobierno, *Memoria a la Asemblea de 1917* (Medellín, 1917), 7–13.

40. Medellín, *Anuarios Estadísticas, 1916–1935.* The inspector's manuscript, "Acts of Visitation," held in bound volumes at the Archivo Historico de Antioquia, does provide piecemeal data on the number of men employed at each mixed-sex workplace. Data on men was thus "missing" only at the level of published and publically accessible data.

41. Administradors were given notice that they would be required to hire more *vigilantas* and that matrons must be present around the clock. Actas no. 1513, February 19, 1927, S. 8944; no. 121, June 12, 1920, S. 8930; and no. 428, April 26, 1922, S. 8932, Archivo Departmental de Antioquia (AHA). See also Daniel Vélez to Secretario de Gobierno, July 5, 1920, S. 8562, AHA, which informs him that the *matrona* at the shoe factory Rey Sol was so only in name, and a similar letter from Vélez's predecessor, Joaquín Emilio Jaramillo to Administrador de la Fábrica de Tejidos Hernandez, July 19, 1919, S. 8562, 28, AHA.

42. Acta no. 1533, August 9, 1922, S. 8934, AHA.

43. Actas no. 427, August 18,1927, S. 8949 and no. 1476, July 7,1922, S. 8934, AHA, in which he editorializes that "chatting . . . is prejudicial to conserving morality."

44. Secretario de Gobierno, *Memoria a la Asemblea de 1923* (Medellín, 1923), 74.

45. Inspector de Fábricas, "Fábrica de Tejidos Rosellón," 21 July 1920, Signatura 8930, 56, AHA.

46. Acta no. 705, June 19, 1920, S. 8929, 220, AHA. My emphasis,

47. Secretario de Gobierno, *Memoria a la Asemblea de 1926* (Medellín: Imprenta Oficial, 1926), 254. My emphasis.

48. Archila, *Cultura e Identidad*, 385–92.

49. Ann Farnsworth-Alvear, "Gender and the Limits of Industrial Discipline: Textile Work in Medellín, Colombia, 1905–1960" (Ph.D. diss., Duke University, 1994). See also Arango, *Mujer, religión.*

50. *El Correo Liberal*, February 13, 1920. Michel-Rolph Trouillot uses precisely this example, of "a strike," to demonstrate to seminar students how workers' action in collectively not coming to work intervenes palpably in the world of discourse. Journalists and historians alike are unable to describe the action without reference to the idea of a collective work-stoppage. Personal communication.

51. *El Luchador*, February 17, 1920. This was not an article but a reproduction of the minutes.

52. *El Espectador*, February 14, 1920. My emphasis.

53. Emilio Restrepo to Sres. Leopold Cassella & Co. (Frankfurt), 2/16/1920, Copiador 16 (1919/20), 307, AF.

54. Entries for Julia Mora Alvarez and Carmen Morales Alzate in *Libro de Personal*, 1918–34, Hemeroteca Coltejer, 151, 153. Subsequent references to "entries" are to this source.

55. It was very common for workers to claim they were sick and needed a few days off and then to turn up working in another factory. See entries for Marco Holguin Ortiz, 116, and Rosario Franco, 83. Or they claimed that a relative was sick, as with Carlos Jaramillo, who went to work elsewhere and, wrote the director, "I found out he bad-mouthed about the factory in the street," 129. Often, people did not return to the mill after the Christmas holidays; see the entry for Ana Molina, whose sister said she'd gone to work in a shoe shop, 153. See also entries for Josefina Ocampo, 177; Ines López, 138; and Margarita Hincapié, 116.

56. Acta no. 715, June 22, 1920, S. 8929, AHA,

57. There are numerous entries containing the phrase "se aprovechó de la necesidad" or "se cree necesaria." See, for example, the entry for Luis Vasco, who was dismissed for "grosero y altanero," with the note that "este sambo mal educado se aprovechó por la necesidad que había de trabajadores." "Sambo" was of course a term of racial denigration.

58. From an *hoja de vida* stacked with others in the "Sala Histórica," AF.

59. Entries for Ernestina Rios, 204; María de la Paz Florez Villa, 83; and María Villa, 253. Other references to "boca sucia" include Rosalina Ruíz, 205.

60. From an *hoja de vida* at Fabricato. This included as part of the data I collected for a statistical sample of personnel records at different Medellín firms. Sample data in my possession.

61. Entry for Angela Rios, 204. See also similar entries for Sofia Tabares, 232, and Alejandrina Mejía, 151.

62. See note 60.

63. Entry for Eduardo Arango Gutierrez, 2 (unnumbered), 173.

64. Acta 458, July 3, 1922, S. 8932,103. In 1923, an administrator at the Fábrica de Bello was accused "of having wanted to corrupt two *obreras*," but the inspector concluded that he was innocent and had observed "exemplary" conduct. Acta 597, April 19, 1923, S. 8932, AHA.

65. This appears on a loose note (8 1/2" by 4") in S. 8935, AHA, and includes another woman's name, "Ester Bustamente," but it is not clear if the information came from Bustamente or what other involvement she may have had in the case.

66. See Acta 1875, April 3, 1923, S. 8935, AHA.

67. The full text of the agreement which ended the strike appears in Emilio Restrepo's letterbook; 3 March 1920, Copiador 16, 347, AF.

68. *El Espectador*, February 26, 1920, and various pieces in *El Luchador*.

69. An exception is Inspector Vélez's relentless persistence on the issue of fines. In his monthly *actas de visita* and his annual reports he denounced—as backward and un-Christian—those employers who docked workers' pay as a disciplinary practice.

70. In addition to Kaplan's cited work, see Rose Glickman, *Russian Factory Women: Workplace and Society, 1880–1914* (Berkeley, 1984), 166; Jan Lambertz, "Sexual Harassment in the Nineteenth Century English Cotton Industry," *History Workshop Journal* 19 (1985):29–61.

71. See, for example, Jorge Bernal, "Características de la primera generación de obreras antioqueñas: del infierno de la explotación a la primera gran huelga," *Relecturas* Ano II, no. 5, 19. This was a publication of the Escuela Nacional Sindical in Medellín.

72. Scott, *Gender and the Politics of History.*

5

Laws against a "Working" Middle Class in Peru

David S. Parker

One of the most obvious examples of how legislation and social forces influenced the relationship between workers and potential sympathizers appeared as a chapter in David Parker's book, The Idea of the Middle Class. *He studied the construction of "middleness" as a class in Peru during the 1920s and 1930s. It is particularly interesting to see how laws gradually created the distinction between employee and worker to the extent that employees became associated with the "middle class," an almost inevitable social distinction that North Americans seem to take for granted. At stake was a vital idea—that association with "intellectual" labor (done by employees) versus manual labor (done by workers) gave one respectability. This selection raises at least one further consideration: the legal distinction seems not only to have driven an apparently immovable wedge between the "middle" and lower, or popular, classes, but it also drove out of the middle and into the worker category the advanced sector of the workers, artisans, and craftsmen who in the nineteenth century had seen themselves as an evolving "middle" (read respectable) sector of society. The legal division also created the conditions for further distinctions within the working class. Employers, at first reluctant to get involved, began to use the law to their advantage as craftsmen and artisans disdained any association with the unskilled labor sector (whether or not they were organized). Such divisions, consciously created or not, made the organization and coordination of labor and labor movements all the more difficult. It weakened, Parker notes, "collective opposition" by the workers.*

President [Augusto B.] Leguía, members of Congress, the Chamber of Commerce, the press, and most other participants in debate over the Law of the Empleado had been confident that they understood exactly whom it was designed to benefit. Advocates of the legislation repeated again and again that the purpose of Law 4916 was to relieve the suffering of the middle class: those members of respectable families who after serving their employers loyally for years still found themselves impoverished and forgotten in their old age. Indeed, opinion makers viewed the empleados' plight as particularly desperate *because* they were *gente decente*, people for whom poverty also meant indignity and shame. Implicit throughout the congressional debate was the assumption that an empleado was intrinsically different from an obrero, who neither deserved nor needed similar protection.

When judges apply legislation to specific cases, however, abstract assumptions must confront practical realities, often with unexpected results. The Law of the Empleado proved no exception. If in theory empleados and obreros were distinct species of human beings, in practice the line of separation was exceedingly difficult to locate. Yet the location of that line was critical, not only because empleados received new benefits that obreros did not, but also because empleado status carried an important symbolic meaning. Classification as an empleado for the purposes of Law 4916 provided compensation for time of service and a degree of protection from dismissal, but just as important, it conferred a stamp of respectability that obreros were expressly denied. Public debate over the legislation had explicitly and repeatedly invoked the image of the empleado to define the middle class, and vice versa. With the passage of Law 4916, therefore, the juridical category (empleado) increasingly became confused with the social category (middle class), with the effect that for the first time in Peru's postcolonial history, law challenged custom for the right to determine a critical social boundary.

The creation of the legal distinction between empleado and obrero—and by implication, between middle class and working class or between *gente decente* and *gente de pueblo*—had four major effects. First, it ignited a firestorm of litigation, as all who could make a reasonable claim to empleado status, and many who could not, tried to win a favorable classification. Arbitrators found themselves charged with the task of determining case by case who was an empleado and who was not. Second, the judges hearing those claims established nonmanual labor as the primary consideration in distinguishing an empleado from an obrero. While this followed both the letter and the spirit of the law, its effect was to privilege nonmanual work—formerly only one indicator of respectability—as the defining characteristic of the middle class. The implicit message was that artisans and skilled laborers no longer enjoyed a favored position over the rest of the working class. Third, the concrete and symbolic benefits of asserting empleado status created an incentive for nonmanual workers to distance themselves from the mass of obreros. In this way the Law of the Empleado reinforced the hierarchical ordering of the workplace, and undermined potential solidarity between manual and nonmanual workers. Finally, Law 4916 became the precedent upon which all future empleado legislation was built, while the laws affecting obreros followed an entirely different juridical path. This legal separation affected the shape of Peruvian labor relations for decades to come.

Defining the Empleado

The majority of arbitration cases under Law 4916 arose in response to contested firings. The person who lost his or her job would go to an attorney—often one of the freelance *tinterillos* who peddled their legal expertise on the sidewalk outside the labor office—and submit a formal brief [*expediente*] respectfully explaining the particulars of the case. Claimants usually sought payment of their severage package: the three months' salary for *despido intempestivo*, the *indemnización* for years of service, or both, depending upon the circumstances. Each side then supplied supporting evidence and named arbitrators, who convened with the board's third member, typically a mid-level ministry functionary. These government delegates, who had the deciding vote, found themselves ruling on complicated legal questions, and their determinations provided one basis for the jurisprudence of Law 4916. The arbiters were not always well prepared for the task, and contradictory rulings were not uncommon; however, their decisions provide a telling glimpse at how they conceptualized the empleado-obrero division and, in effect, how they defined the middle class.

During the four and one-half years that passed between the promulgation of Law 4916 and publication of its *reglamento*, no question challenged arbitrators more than that of who was and who was not an empleado. Blue-collar workers and domestic servants tried to win rulings in their favor, sometimes in the cynical hope of scamming severance pay out of the system, but often with the sincere conviction that they deserved to be considered empleados. On the other side, many employers sought to deny empleado status to people legitimately covered by the law, either to circumvent legislation with which they did not agree, to evade onerous compensation costs, or in a few cases to belittle employees whose services they did not value. In other words, while some disputes over empleado status were nothing more than legal maneuvers for benefits, others proved to be meaningful individual struggles for dignity, respect, and consideration as members of the *gente decente*. In those cases the arbitration tribunals played a significant role in the formation and definition of Peru's social classes.

The government delegates found that the text of Law 4916 did not adequately define who was an empleado and that everyday wisdom offered only ideal types, not objective classifications that held up to legal scrutiny. The widely shared idea that obreros and empleados were inherently different failed to account for hundreds of workers in the gray areas between empleado and obrero, or between commercial and domestic employee. Moreover, the rise of new occupations played havoc with customs and vocabularies of stratification whose origins traced to an earlier, less diversified economy.[1] Complicating the arbitrators' task was the highly imperfect fit between the impersonal criteria used to define certain occupational categories as the work of empleados and their own commonsense perception of specific claimants as either respectable members of the middle class or not. As it turned out, many of those whose jobs seemed to meet the technical requirements of empleado status did not, as individuals, fit the accepted profile in terms of their social origins, race, education, or living standard. They were often not the people for whom the law had been designed, *gente decente* in need of financial help to maintain the position "demanded" by their social circle. Nevertheless, because the arbitrators tried to adhere to impersonal standards, low-level empleados like our fictional Arturo Rosales and others with even less of a claim to membership in the middle class used the tribunals to claim benefits that the legislators had never really intended for them. When successful, these socially marginal and sometimes dark-skinned employees received more than just severance pay and an insurance policy—they also won a certain mark of respectability. In a twentieth-century analogy to the colonial *cédulas de gracias al sacar*,[2] the pursuit of empleado status through litigation became a way to raise one's social standing.

In theory, the fundamental principle that defined an empleado was the degree to which the duties performed on the job were intellectual as opposed to manual. In the cases of bank tellers, insurance agents, commercial accountants, and retail clerks, classification was a relatively simple matter. But things were not so cut-and-dried when it came to trained technicians, night guards, foremen, hacienda administrators, errand boys in commercial establishments, and many other positions that combined manual skills with a degree of authority or initiative. In these cases both sides emphasized the elements that best made their case. For example, the Cerro de Pasco Copper Corporation wrote about the highly skilled manual job of *calderero* [boilermaker]: "This job is clearly a craft [*oficio*] in whose practice intervene almost exclusively aptitudes acquired by experience and by habit, without the necessity of special studies. . . . There is no doubt that the work of *calderero* is a work of obreros, . . . characterized by the preponderance of mechanical skills and habits over intellectual abilities."[3] Similarly, when Fernando Wiese petitioned against the application of Law 4916 to employees of the Gran Hotel Bolívar, he took special care to note that hotel and restaurant personnel carried out "exclusively mechanical labors."[4] Workers' arguments were the mirror image of those of their employers. An apartment building superintendent, for example, made sure to provide extensive written documentation proving that his job involved not only cleaning and maintenance but also the nonmanual tasks of collecting rents, screening new tenants, and dealing with public utility companies.[5]

In their assertion of empleado status, some claimants understandably embellished their job descriptions in ways that exaggerated the intellectual requirements. A doorman pointed out the occasions on which he took money to the bank or made purchases for his employer, a mechanic called himself a "mechanical employee" [*empleado mecánico*], and in one intriguing case the most senior of three telephone repair workers gave herself the title "chief of repairs section."[6] Employers of course played the same game, declaring in one instance that a highway construction engineer performed services "of a technical nature" and in another that a highly trained draftsman only worked as a day laborer.[7]

When the job description alone was not sufficient basis for a ruling, arbitrators turned to secondary factors in determining the worker's condition, and both claimants and employers quickly learned which elements would help or hurt their case. One such consideration was the method of payment. By tradition, empleados received monthly salaries while obreros were paid day wages [*jornales*], and they appeared on separate payrolls. If accompanied by other evidence, being on the salary payroll [*planilla de sueldos*] could bolster one's case for empleado status. Several industries, however, particularly in mining and construction, put as much of the workforce as possible on the daily payroll [*planilla de salarios* or *planilla de jornales*], sometimes in keeping with long-standing tradition but sometimes in a cynical effort to deny legitimate empleados their new benefits.[8] Because inclusion on the salary payroll was an important symbolic mark of status as well as an argument for consideration under Law 4916, some empleados considered transfer to the day payroll as sufficient grounds for quitting. Indeed, when the Cerro de Pasco Copper Corporation attempted to shift several job categories off the *planilla de sueldos*, the resulting litigation turned into a *cause célèbre* for Peruvian employees.[9] The government eventually ruled that the mode of payment in no way determined the status of the worker, but in practice payment by salary versus *jornal* remained important in borderline cases. Similarly, the wage paid sometimes made a difference: a high day wage might argue for empleado status, while a low monthly salary could support an assertion that the individual was either an obrero or a domestic servant, as one employer successfully argued: "[T]he scant abilities of the claimant are sufficiently proven by the salary he received, compensation enough for his useless services."[10] In another case a department-store employee with the catch-all title of majordomo proved that his duties were not those of a domestic servant because his salary was "equal or superior to that of other employees of the firm."[11]

If claimants could demonstrate that otherwise manual jobs entailed a good deal of responsibility, they might justify empleado status. Such was the argument made by warehouse guards and night watchmen who won some early arbitration cases before the 1928 *reglamento* explicitly excluded them from Law 4916.[12] One watchman, Victoriano Gallués, was able to argue that he could not be an obrero because he customarily worked a twelve-hour shift, far more than the obrero's legal eight-hour day.[13] Sometimes seemingly minor characteristics of the work regime might come into play, as in the case of a salesperson in a family-owned bakery who argued that she was not a domestic servant because she went home for lunch instead of eating on the premises.[14] And finally, Lima was not without its sharp labor lawyers, who called upon the most ingenious arguments to win empleado status for their clients. All Cerro de Pasco Copper workers, for example, carried ID cards in Spanish that labeled each as "empleado # N" of the company. The word "empleado" was no doubt a literal translation of "employee," used by that U.S. mining concern for its more generic English meaning, covering both manual and nonmanual workers. Some miners, however, successfully used their ID cards as material evidence to prove, as if by the company's own admission, that they were indeed empleados and not obreros.[15]

Law and Respectability

Significantly, a description of the job was often not enough to settle the obrero-empleado conflict, so the tribunals tended, albeit against the letter of the law, to take the claimants' personal qualities into account. Education was the most crucial factor. Any technician with a formal degree had a much better chance of proving empleado status than his self-taught counterpart, and debate over qualifications was common. One sugar mill owner argued that his technicians "have not graduated from any university or specialized school, they are mere *empíricos*, self-taught by experience, who carry out a manual and mechanical labor, in keeping with their abilities."[16] In another case an engineer argued that his employer's attempt to classify him as a manual worker was a "pretext [that is] totally futile, as . . . I am an Electrical Engineer graduated in Chicago, and 1 will present . . . the diploma that certifies my status as a professional."[17] At the other end of the spectrum, it was next to impossible for an illiterate to justify empleado status, no matter what the job. In the case of one worker in a warehouse, the company argued: "Never has this individual been able to carry out the job of warehouse administrator, since he barely knows how to write his own name; he has only been occupied in the carrying of packages."[18] Another company explicitly equated empleado status with literacy: "The first condition necessary to be a commercial employee is to know how to read and write, but Camargo does not know how to read or write, therefore he could never have been an empleado."[19]

In the years before the clarifying *reglamento*, analogous cases sometimes received conflicting judgments. One reason for this, beyond the normal imperfection of the legal process, was the influence of how arbiters viewed the claimant as a human being. The fact that night watchman Victoriano Gallués won empleado status when other watchmen were deemed obreros or domestic servants may well be explained by the fact that Gallués was a Spanish immigrant, not an Indian or mestizo like most of the others.[20] In Peru, unlike Argentina or Brazil, European birth in and of itself argued strongly for consideration as one of the *gente decente*, and this greatly bolstered his case. By the same token, indigenous blood greatly hurt one's chances, and many of the employers' references to a worker's illiteracy, "lack of culture," or drunkenness appear to have been a shorthand code to discredit the "wrong sort" of people. In short, the most effective petitions emphasized both the characteristics of the job and the qualities of the worker in order to provide as unassailable a case as possible.

One arbitration brief went so far as to cite workplace politics in order to drive home the idea that obreros and empleados were inherently different kinds of people:

> [Lawyer] David Torres Balcazar argued that José León was neither an obrero nor a *sobrestante* [foreman] but rather a *chequeador* ["checker"], whose occupation consists of ordering the transfer of cargoes from the warehouse to the convoy in order to send them on to their destination, recording each package on an *ad hoc* list; that he was the one man responsible in case of the loss or misdirection of cargo; that he earned a monthly salary of 85 *soles*, paid fortnightly, as were the other empleados; . . . that a checker works overtime and even on holidays without receiving overtime pay, and that in past strikes the checkers have never intervened on the side of the workers nor have they taken the obreros' side in their negotiations with the company.[21]

While it was rare for claimants to refer to their political or strike behavior in order to argue empleado status, the strategy pursued by José León's attorney underscored how Law 4916 rewarded and reinforced the empleados' argument that they were innately distinct from obreros. The empleado organizations frequently promoted this attitude, in fact. For example, in at least two cases where predominantly manual workers sought to win designation as empleados, former SEC president José M. Ramírez Gastón agreed to represent *employers* in the dispute, and argued that neither claimant was protected under the Law of the Empleado. Not surprisingly, Ramírez Gastón won the cases.[22] In the end, as nonmanual labor came to be enshrined as the essential characteristic of the respectable middle class, the big losers were artisans and skilled technicians, especially those whose comfortable income and lifestyle had once won them a certain consideration as *gente decente*. Exclusion from the Law of the Empleado in effect defined artisans out of the middle class.

The 1928 clarifications of Law 4916 sought to put to rest the conflict over the definition of the empleado by devoting three pages to detailed lists of the kinds of occupations included and excluded from empleado benefits.[23] The *reglamento* reasserted that intellectual effort determined empleado status more than any other factor, but in practice the technical distinction between manual and nonmanual work continued to be colored by judgments about which occupations and individuals were respectable and which were not. In short, some arbitration rulings continued to be based on race, education, salary, and other ostensibly irrelevant issues because people still thought of "empleado" as shorthand for "middle class" or *gente decente*.

The juridical consecration of the manual-nonmanual distinction could not help but erode the grounds for alliance between obreros and empleados, especially if an empleado like José León could use the demonstrated lack of solidarity with obreros as evidence to prove his status and claim his benefits. In fact, there were empleados who cited the new legislation expressly to discredit and demean those "below them" in the hierarchy, as in this letter from factory timekeeper César Augusto Zevallos to his company director:

> I can only protest, Mr. Superintendent, that in order to fire me from my position you have invoked the affirmations of a drunken watchman, whose word could never prevail, given his sad condition of domestic (in accordance with paragraph "A" of article 2 of the *reglamento* of Law 4916), over the affirmations of a man of honor and a conscientious employee, who in his thirteen years of service to the company has never given his superiors any reason for complaint.[24]

By giving legal force to customary prejudices about the characteristics of decent empleados versus the unwashed working masses, Law 4916 turned the obrero-empleado distinction into a new arena of conflict, creating or reinforcing artificial barriers between the manual and nonmanual worker to the benefit of the latter and the detriment of the former. Ostensibly progressive labor legislation thus crystallized and preserved a castelike conception of society, with roots deep in Peru's colonial heritage.

Divide and Conquer? The Legacy of Law 4916

The divisive impact of the Law of the Empleado, so clearly demonstrated in the cases of José León and César Augusto Zevallos, has led several students of Peruvian labor legislation to discern a conscious strategy by employers and the State to divide and conquer the Peruvian working class.[25] If we look at the origins of the law, however, the evidence supports no such conclusion. Neither in public debate nor in private correspondence concerning Law 4916 was this possibility even remotely hinted at. On the contrary, the legislators' guiding assumption was that obreros and empleados were *already* entirely separate castes, lacking any logical shared interest. So ingrained was this belief that at no time during debate over the bill did a single legislator bring up the problems that might arise in distinguishing empleados from obreros. Only once did a senator discuss whether obreros should be covered by similar legislation, and as we saw earlier, he was quickly silenced by another, who simply asserted that the condition of the empleado was entirely different from that of the obrero.[26] The virtual consensus on this intrinsic, almost biological, distinction contrasts notably with neighboring Chile, where the question of how to define an empleado dominated parliamentary debate over similar legislation, also passed in 1924.[27]

Nevertheless, if we look beyond the original passage of Law 4916 to consider its practical implementation over subsequent decades, the divide-and-conquer scenario becomes somewhat more convincing. When empleado legislation was first enacted, many employers did everything they could to classify borderline and not-so-borderline personnel as obreros. This was clearly anything *but* a strategy of using grants of empleado status to co-opt loyal workers and sow division within the labor force. Employers often doggedly resisted creating new categories of empleados, even at the risk of fostering greater worker solidarity. Starting in the 1940s, however, management behavior gradually began to change. The concession of empleado status to individuals or to entire occupational categories became an increasingly normal element of labor relations. By the 1950s and 1960s, large numbers of manual workers, especially foremen and skilled technicians, had been declared empleados, in direct contravention of the letter and spirit of the original law.[28]

What had happened? Three complementary explanations come to mind. Employers, who had once bemoaned the severance provisions of Law 4916 as costly and radical, gradually came to accept them as inevitable. Companies grew accustomed to setting aside a small portion of their payroll each year for employee compensation, and procedural changes in the administration of Law 4916 greatly reduced the number of arbitration cases, frivolous or not.[29] Second, labor laws passed between the 1930s and 1960s began to raise some of the benefits provided to obreros, thereby reducing the relative costs of granting empleado status. But perhaps most important, the empleado-obrero distinction fit extraordinarily well into new personnel management techniques pioneered by corporations in the United States after World War II and exported to Latin America in the 1950s and 1960s. These strategies emphasized the creation of a minutely graded system of internal stratification, where each job had a strict hierarchical ranking reflected in title and salary. Workers were tracked onto well-established career paths, whereby loyalty and effort found their constant reward with each new promotion, however small.[30] The system fostered the illusion and to a lesser degree the reality of upward mobility, offering promotion to *empleado* as the culmination of a successful blue-collar career. The system also fragmented the workforce and depersonalized supervisory control, creating incentives for productivity and obedience while undermining workers' collective opposition culture. Or at least that was what employers hoped.

A 1970–71 study of the Cerro de Pasco Copper Corporation illustrates one extreme case of a company making the obrero-empleado distinction an integral part of a strategy of worker socialization and control. In its mining camps and smelting complex in Peru's central highlands, the company provided empleados with separate schools, hospitals, clubs, dining halls, and cinemas; superior housing made of brick instead of adobe; better working conditions; the ability to buy scarce luxury goods; and many other similar privileges.[31] At the same time the company expressly promoted the idea that any worker, no matter what his social origins, could eventually gain promotion to empleado after years of effective and loyal service. In a Cerro de Pasco propaganda film, a poor Indian boy is hurt in a soccer match, cured by a passing company doctor, given a company scholarship, taught in a company school, and after years of study and hard work for the company as an obrero, crowns his career with a promotion to empleado.[32] The U.S.-owned and managed Cerro de Pasco, with its deeply ingrained American corporate culture, was clearly atypical in Peru. We have no example of a nationally owned firm propagating the same kind of Horatio Alger mythology so at odds with the vision of empleados and obreros as inherently separate castes. Nevertheless, when we remember Cerro de Pasco's intransigent refusal to obey Law 4916 in the 1920s and 1930s, we begin to understand the magnitude of the change that had occurred, as the company realized the utility of the distinction as a way to divide and discipline its workers. There seems little doubt that by this time Peru's employers and labor officials had come to see practical advantages in the obrero-empleado division, a division that they in turn championed, nurtured, and utilized for their own ends.

To the extent that workers continued to long for promotion to empleado, these policies were a success. Far more problematic, however, is the idea that management enjoyed unilateral control over who was promoted to empleado and who was not. After all, anything that can be given by owners can also, under the right circumstances, be *taken* by workers, and empleado status was no exception. From the 1940s on, labor unions often demanded elevation of their specialization to empleado status and transfer to the *planilla de sueldos*.[33] Government labor officials regularly received petitions from groups of organized workers throughout the 1940s, 1950s, and 1960s requesting that their occupation be considered the work of empleados.[34] There were even cases of strikes being settled only after management acceded to a demand that one job category or another be reclassified.[35] In operation here is the age-old debate over co-optation: we could say that astute employers reclassified their foremen as empleados in order to buy them off, or we could say that foremen called the shots by demanding elevation to empleado as the price of their loyalty.

While the question of co-optation remains a complicated one, there seems little doubt that the obrero-empleado split served over the long term as a useful tool to divide workers and weaken collective resistance. One of the most important effects of the division was the tendency for obreros and empleados to organize in separate unions. Peruvian labor law did not expressly forbid the creation of *sindicatos únicos* (joining obreros and empleados), but governments frequently used the formal union certification process to discourage unification. Even in the absence of overt government pressure, separate unions made practical sense, given that empleados and obreros were covered by different legal regimes and dealt with completely different labor and social security bureaucracies. Union leaders spent their entire careers learning the intricacies of one or another set of regulations and procedures; few could master both. In times of labor conflict, however, the existence of separate unions doubtless strengthened the employers' hand. All things being equal, employee unions were less likely to strike, particularly if middle and upper managers were voting members of the organization. And even in those cases where white- and blue-collar unions shared the same demands and fought the same battles against management, empleado unions might still be tempted to settle separately. After all, in a factory or mine where obreros greatly outnumbered empleados, management could make strategic concessions to empleados, even quite generous concessions, at a comparatively low cost.

While the ultimate effectiveness of the divide-and-conquer strategy cannot fully be gauged, the fact remains that empleado status continued to matter, at least through the 1960s. Neither the improvement in benefits for obreros nor the rising numbers of clearly blue-collar "empleados" tarnished the idea that being an empleado signaled or at least facilitated one's entry into the middle class. In a poll taken in the early 1960s, students in Peruvian secondary schools were asked how much money it would take for them to accept obrero, rather than empleado, status. Only 13.3 percent said that they would choose to be an obrero with the same salary as an empleado; 31.1 percent replied that they would only agree to be an obrero, rather than an empleado, if as obreros they were paid 300 *soles* extra per *week* (at a time when the official minimum wage was 750 *soles* a *month*); and a full 35.6 percent declared that they would not accept being an obrero under any circumstances.[36] Flawed as such polls tend to be, they lead inexorably to the conclusion that empleado status retained its symbolic importance, an importance rooted at least in part in its connection to the idea of the middle class.

Conclusion

The legal distinction between obrero and empleado proved to be the most lasting and important legacy of the empleados' struggles and legislators' initiatives of the 1920s. Unequal benefits packages led to separately administered labor and social security systems, which in turn fostered separate unions. The obrero-empleado division widened the social distance between manual and nonmanual workers, magnifying distinctions between the two while simultaneously turning the line of demarcation into a motive for individual and collective conflict. In its original form, the distinction was a direct outgrowth of the vision of the middle class that empleados had successfully promoted since before 1919: the idea that empleados and obreros were different types of people, with different needs. Only later, particularly in the 1950s and 1960s, did employers and government officials finally come to appreciate the utility of the division as a way to divide workers and undermine labor militancy.

Notes

1. Archivo General de la Nación. Lima, Peru (hereafter AGN), Inspección Fiscal de Bancos, "Informes," 1926, O.L. Series, Doc. no. O.L. 845–1527.
2. Royal certificates of honorary "purity of blood," awarded to successful mestizos, mulattoes, or descendants of non-Christians, in essence making them legally white.
3. Víctor M. Aguilar v. Cerro de Pasco Copper Corporation, 1926, no. 85, AGN, Expedientes Laborales Varios 1919–46 (ELV).
4. Henry Grandjean v. the Gran Hotel Bolívar, 1927, no. 641, AGN, ELV.
5. Emilio Cisneros v. Geo. L. Sellé, 1927, no. 308, AGN, ELV.
6. Victoriano Gallués v. Compañía Peruana de Vidrio, 1927, no. 624, AGN, ELV; Tomás Viacava v. Empresas Eléctricas Asociadas, 1925, no. 1633, AGN, ELV; Otila Casagrandi v. Compañía Peruana de Teléfonos, 1926, no. 34S, AGN, ELV.
7. Miguel Acosta Cárdenas v. Empresa Agrícola Chicama, 1926, no. 47, AGN, ELV; S. E. Deza v. Cerro de Pasco Copper Corporation, 1926, no. 500, AGN, ELV.
8. Walter Simm v. The Foundation Co., 1928, no. 1398, AGN, ELV.
9. *La Defensa*, no. 3 (16 April 1927), p. 1.
10. Enrique Viacava v. Arturo Morelli, 1930, no. 1558, AGN, ELV.
11. Leoncio Calixto v. A. F. Oechsle, 1925, no. 335, AGN, ELV.
12. Valerio Camargo v. Cerro de Pasco Railway Company, 1928, no. 384, AGN, ELV; Antonio Fontana v. Juan Nosiglia, 1927, no. 554, AGN, ELV; Peru, Ministerio de Fomento, *Ley del empleado no. 4916 y sus ampliatorias no. 5066 and 5119, reglamento de las precedentes leyes* (Lima: Imprenta "El Tiempo" [1928?]), p. 19 (art. 2, secs. A and B).
13. Victoriano Gallués v. Compañía Manufacturera de Vidrio del Peru, 1927, no. 624, AGN, ELV.
14. Maria Castillo v. Juan B. Mazzi, 1930, no. 270, AGN, ELV.
15. César Castillo v. Cerro de Pasco Copper Corporation, 1927, no. 282, AGN, ELV; Carlos Coni v. Cerro de Pasco Copper Corporation, 1927, no. 346, AGN, ELV.

16. Hermanos Castañeda v. Hacienda Pomalca, 1927, no. 1723, AGN, ELV.

17. Saul Bonilla Collazos v. Compañía Minera Santa Inés, 1928, no. 159, AGN, ELV.

18. Eulalio Podestá v. la Casa Sanmartí, 1927, no. 1162, AGN, ELV; Cirilo Vásquez v. Empresas Eléctricas Asociadas, 1927, no. 1614, AGN, ELV.

19. Valerio Camargo v. Cerro de Pasco Copper Corporation, 1928, no. 384, AGN, ELV.

20. Victoriano Gallués v. Compañía Manufacturera de Vidrio del Perú, 1927, no. 624, AGN, ELV.

21. José E. León v. Empresa del Ferrocarril Central del Perú, 1924, no. 851, AGN, ELV.

22. Jorge M. Lucich v. Sociedad Maderera Ciurlizza Maurer, 1926, no. 901, AGN, ELV; César Vargas Machuca v. Cerro de Pasco Copper Corporation, 1928, no. 1634, AGN, ELV; Cecilio Carrión Bazán v. Cerro de Pasco Copper Corporation, 1929, no. 272, AGN, ELV; *La Defensa*, no. 3 (16 April 1927), pp. 1–2.

23. Peru, *Ley del empleado no. 4916*, pp. 18–21.

24. César Augusto Zevallos v. Cerro de Pasco Copper Corporation, 1929, no. 1691, AGN, ELV.

25. Luis Chirinos Segura, "Conflictos laborales y negociación política: El conflicto bancario de 1964" (Law thesis, Pontificia Universidad Católica del Perú, 1975), p. 171.

26. Peru, Senado, *Diario de los debates: Congreso Extraordinario 1923*, p. 608.

27. Chile, Cámara de Diputados, *Boletín de las sesiones ordinarias en 1922* (Santiago: Imprenta La Nación, 1929), pp. 762–74.

28. David Chaplin, *The Peruvian Industrial Labor Force* (Princeton: Princeton University Press, 1967), pp. 83–85; David G. Becker, *The New Bourgeoisie and the Limits of Dependency: Mining, Class, and Power in "Revolutionary" Peru* (Princeton: Princeton University Press, 1983), pp. 282–83.

29. Law 6871 of 1930 transferred the arbitration tribunals from the executive to the judicial branch. Law 8077 of 1935 made it possible to appeal arbitration rulings through a *recurso de nulidad*. These measures gave employers powerful legal tools they had previously lacked. See S. Martínez G., *Ley del empleado particular*, 2d ed. (Lima: Imprenta "El Carmen" [1984?], pp. 26–29, 36.

30. Richard Edwards, *Contested Terrain: The Transformation of the Workplace in the Twentieth Century* (New York: Basic Books, 1979), chap. 8.

31. Dirk Kruijt and Menno Vellinga, *Labor Relations and Multinational Corporations: The Cerro de Pasco Corporation in Peru, 1902–1974*, trans. Henk Jarring (Assen, The Netherlands: Van Gorcum, 1979), p. 96.

32. Ibid., p. 93, n. 14.

33. *Segunda convención regional de trabajadores mineros y metalúrgicos del Centro, Oroya* (23 December 1945), in Arturo Sabroso Montoya Archive, Lima, Peru, Centro de Documentación, Programa de Ciencias Sociales, Pontificia Universidad Católica del Perú.

34. Martínez, *Ley del empleado particular*, pp. 41–108 passim. See esp. p. 64 for Law 12527 (1956), which gave empleado status to foremen and other manual workers with supervisory duties.

35. Rosa Silvia Arciniega Arce, "Mineros, sindicalismo, y conciencia de clase: Southern Peru Copper Corp., 1968–1981" (Licenciatura thesis, Pontificia Universidad Católica del Perú, 1985), vol. 1.

36. William F. Whyte and Graciela Flores, *La mano de obra de alto nivel en el Perú* (Lima: SENATI, 1964), p. 38.

6

Race, Gender, and Protest in Ecuador

Marc Becker

Ecuador is among the Latin American nations given the least attention by scholars outside the country. Dominated by a small white elite, its economy was characterized by sharp contrasts in the size of landholdings, fierce competition to control scarce good lands, and domination by the United Fruit Company. Native American ethnic groups, themselves engaged in rivalries that had waxed and waned since the Inca conquest of the region, proved difficult to organize.

This selection by Marc Becker raises issues that bore heavily on the life of workers in the 1930s. He highlights cases of women from both the upper-class and popular sectors who worked to organize against the male-dominant political culture of the country. As Becker points out, many of the problems of class, race, and gender were embedded in the question of citizenship and citizens' rights. Although Ecuador was the first country in Latin America to extend suffrage to women (1929), this gesture was meaningless as long as it was not accompanied by a wider set of rights. If successful, a campaign to secure those rights would have given women access to privileges held exclusively by white men: to organize socially, to gain access to a bilingual education, and to bargain for labor. In reading the Becker selection it becomes clear that elite and Indian women in Ecuador were not interested in pursuing bilingual education to undermine Indian culture but rather to provide a vehicle for the rights of labor, women, and Native Americans. The dynamic women from the white and Indian sectors highlighted here overcame separate ethnicities in an effort to create new cultural identities.

On May 28, 1944, women and Indians joined with workers and students in a popular revolt that ousted the government of Ecuadorian president Carlos Arroyo del Río. In the northern highland town of Cayambe, long-time Indian leader Dolores Cacuango led indigenous forces in an attack on the local army barracks. In Quito, women's committees played an important role in large antigovernment street demonstrations. White feminists including Nela Martínez and Luisa Gómez de la Torre were featured speakers in the protests, helped organize a human enclosure around the government palace in Quito, and gained the surrender of the men stationed there. For three days, Martínez served as a minister of government.[1] Ecuador, one author observed, finally "was in the hands of its legitimate owners."[2]

Despite the important roles white and Indian women played in this "Glorious May Revolution," white male political leaders excluded them from the subsequent government that emerged out of this revolt. Significant racial, class, and gender barriers deterred their full participation in society. Ecuador remained a deeply racially divided society that systematically barred the large Indian population from involvement in public affairs. A small elite class with a near monopoly on political and economic power attempted to keep the masses out of active decision-making processes. Furthermore, in a male-dominated society, women were relegated to the private, domestic sphere. All of these hurdles would have to be overcome in order to gain a political voice in the shaping of a society that would respond to their needs and concerns. This process would require that strong challenges be raised against the exclusion of Indians and women from the dominant society's constructions of citizenship rights.

Examining the relationships between white and Indian women in Ecuador highlights the types of alliances subaltern actors developed in their struggle to achieve social changes as well as the nature of the obstacles they needed to overcome in order to realize their goals. Rural, illiterate, Quichua-speaking indigenous women leaders including Dolores Cacuango and Tránsito Amaguaña played an active role in organizing social movements that challenged their exclusion. Urban, educated, Spanish-speaking white women such as Nela Martínez and Luisa Gómez de la Torre joined Indian women in these efforts to expand social opportunities and political power for both Indians and women. There were significant ethnic, class, and cultural gaps between the two groups, but they managed to cross these boundaries in order to struggle together for a common vision of social change. In the process, they influenced each other's notions of the role of class, gender, ethnicity, and citizenship rights in Ecuadorian society.

Citizens and Nationals

Women and Indians faced similar cultural barriers and legal obstacles that denied them access to citizenship rights and prevented their full participation in the political life of the country. This history of exclusion and repression facilitated alliances that crossed race, class, and gender boundaries. From the founding of the country of Ecuador in 1830 to the reforms that reimplemented civilian rule in 1979, every constitution recognized a fundamental distinction between "nationals" and "citizens." Nationals were those who were either born in Ecuador or who gained the status through a process of naturalization. To enjoy citizenship rights, the 1830 constitution required a person to be male, married or older than twenty-two years of age, own property worth at least 300 pesos or be engaged in an independent "useful" profession or industry (domestic servants and day laborers were explicitly excluded), and be able to read and write.[3] Although not explicit about the subject, property and literacy requirements of the constitution excluded Indians from the body politic. With some minor variations (the age requirement varied between eighteen and twenty-one years, the property requirements were eliminated in 1861, the marriage requirement was dropped in 1897), these have been the determining factors for claiming citizenship throughout most of the country's history. As long as these legal hurdles remained, Indians and women could never hope to become fully participating members in society.

The liberal state excluded both Indians and women from political discourse for similar reasons. Despite a liberal tradition that theoretically viewed all Ecuadorians as equal before the law, some people were less equal than others. In the public mind, women were associated with tradition and religion. Politicians extended the vote to women in Ecuador in 1929 (although it was optional, unlike for men, who were obliged to vote), the first country in Latin America to do so. This action was not designed to advance women's rights, but rather to preempt a nascent feminist movement, prevent many women from entering the political arena, and create a bulwark against what was perceived as a growing socialist threat in society.[4] With the cult of *marianismo*, women were treated as second-class citizens and relegated to the domestic sphere. Something that on the surface might appear to be a political opening was, in fact, an elite attempt to tighten their grip over society. Similarly, the rhetoric of legal equality cloaked the reality of a racist situation in which the dominant culture viewed Indians as inherently inferior.

Suffrage, however, comprises only part of the exercise of citizenship rights. In his classic study, T. H. Marshall defined citizenship as encompassing civil, social, and political rights. Civil rights refer to individual liberties, including freedoms of speech and religion. Social rights refer to legal constructions of equality and access to due justice. Political rights including the ability to participate in the exercise of state power, therefore, represent only one aspect of citizenship.[5] Full citizenship requires access to all of these rights. Indians and women (and particularly Indian women who faced a situation of triple discrimination based on race, class, and gender biases) were excluded through a variety of legal and social mechanisms from the exercise of these rights. Civil liberties, including freedom to marry, work, live, and own property, often translated into more significant aspects of citizenship than the occasional right to cast a vote in an election. Recognizing this, elite men were very careful to control the civil rights of women and Indians. By subjugating constructions of female citizenship rights to male control and Indians' rights to white control, women and Indians could be effectively maintained in a marginalized position in society.[6] Even after the expansion of suffrage rights, Indians and women continued to face what Guillermo O'Donnell termed "low-intensity citizenship" with a notable gap between principle and practice.[7]

Eric Foner has pointed out that the phrase "we the people," which opens the U.S. Constitution, reveals a similar, though unstated, division within Benedict Anderson's imagined community. "The people" were the white males who held citizenship rights, while Indians, Africans, women, and others were relegated to an inferior status.[8] Similarly in Ecuador, there was no concept of universally held civil, social, and political rights. The political elite enjoyed "what has been euphemistically termed 'democracy in the Greek sense,' in which effective citizenship is limited to a few men of education and culture, with the others rigidly barred from participation."[9] A small minority of the country's elite—white and *mestizo* educated urban dwellers (varying from about 0.3 percent at the time of Ecuadorian independence to about 3 percent in the 1940s[10])—selected the government that would rule over the rest of the populace. The majority of the country's population—women and Indians—had no say in the regime to which they were subject. An Indian remained "a complete outsider in government and public affairs" and was "treated by the rest of the population like a domestic animal."[11] As Jeff Gould noted in the case of Nicaragua, "to accept the validity of indigenous claims to citizenship and communal rights would be to delegitimize and destabilize local ladino identities and power."[12]

To overcome these barriers and gain the right to full political, social, and economic participation in society, white and Indian women in Ecuador overcame long-standing racial and class barriers and began to organize together around common interests and concerns. This action led to what James MacGregor Burns and Stewart Burns called an activist citizenship that extends beyond the "outer frame" of voting to a concern for political, civil, economic, and social rights. Legal establishments did not grant these rights, but they "are created far more by those who actively shape them and live them in the thick of personal and social struggles."[13] Similarly, Joe Foweraker and Todd Landman concluded that "the essentially *individual* rights of citizenship can only be achieved through different forms of *collective* struggle."[14] In Ecuador, four key women led this collective struggle. In order to understand better the ideological changes that occurred as a result of their efforts, this essay examines their lives and analyzes their roles in three realms: the construction of indigenous community social structures, the formation of political federations, and the creation of bilingual education programs. This history demonstrates what Charles Epp discovered, specifically, that citizenship rights grow "primarily out of pressure from below, not leadership from above."[15]

Dolores Cacuango

Dolores Cacuango is one of the primary symbols of indigenous resistance in Ecuador. She was born in 1881 on the Pesillo hacienda in the canton of Cayambe in northern Ecuador. When she was fifteen years old, as partial payment of her parents' debt to the hacienda's owners, she was sent to the capital city of Quito to work as a servant. Like most indigenous peoples born in the nineteenth century, she had to work from a very young age and never attended school or learned to read or write. This experience raised her awareness of the nature of racial discrimination and class divisions in her society. It led her to dedicate her entire life to a struggle for the rights of her people.

Upon her return to Pesillo, Cacuango began to organize hacienda workers. She rose to a position of leadership in the fight against the hacienda system and participated in the struggle for land rights, to end the payment of *diezmos* (tithes), and to terminate the *huasicama* system that forced Indian girls like her to work in the landlords' houses. A hacienda administrator later complained that "this pernicious woman" helped Indians build houses on hacienda land even though they did not have a formal contract to do so.[16] Although illiterate, she fought tirelessly for schools for indigenous communities and was instrumental in setting up the first Quichua-Spanish bilingual schools in Ecuador. A newspaper article from the 1940s described her at the head of indigenous struggles, the last to retreat, and always ready to suffer for the cause.[17] In 1946 the government of José María Velasco Ibarra threatened to exile her to the Galápagos Islands. The local priest in Cayambe attempted to bribe her so that she would stop leading indigenous revolts, but she continued her work for a more just society.[18]

Cacuango served on the Central Committee of the Ecuadorian Communist Party along with Luisa Gómez de la Torre and Nela Martínez.[19] Founded by Ricardo Paredes in 1926, the Communist Party was the first political party in Ecuador to defend the rights of Indians and women. Jesús Gualavisú, an Indian leader from Cayambe and a colleague of Cacuango's, actively participated in the founding congress of the party, particularly around issues concerning land and indigenous peoples. Through the influence of Gualavisú, Paredes, Gómez de la Torre, and Martínez, Cacuango came to see the party as the best avenue to struggle for her interests as a woman and as an Indian. In 1958 she was imprisoned for leading this party in Cayambe but continued her work after being freed. When she died in 1971, Indians remembered her as a hero who inspired hope for a better future, while landowners were relieved to finally be rid of one of the most memorable "agitators."[20] Her thought was immortalized in a mural that the well-known Ecuadorian artist Oswaldo Guayasamín painted on the wall of the National Congress. The mural (combining her native Quichua with a heavily Quichua-influenced Spanish) says in part:

Ñuca tierra es Cayambe,	My land is Cayambe,
y no me jodan . . . carajúand	don't screw me around . . . dammit
Porque somos libres como el viento	Because we are free like the wind
libres fuimos, libres seremos . . .	we were free, free we will be . . .
Todo manos, todos oídos,	All hands, all hearing,
todo ojos, toda voz . . .	all eyes, all voice. . .[21]

Tránsito Amaguaña

Tránsito Amaguaña was another important indigenous leader who struggled for a more just social order in Ecuador. She was born in 1909 on the Pesillo hacienda into a family that already had a history of political activity.[22] Her mother, Mercedes Alba, led struggles demanding payment for the work women did on the haciendas, and in response the landlord took away the family's small *huasipungo* plot on which they relied for subsistence agriculture. Like Cacuango, from a very young age she was required to work for the hacienda without pay at a variety of jobs such as sweeping, washing dishes, and taking care of livestock. As a result, Amaguaña was able to go to school for only six months. She was married at the age of fourteen, and at fifteen with a baby on her back she joined clandestine political meetings on the hacienda in Cayambe where she met Cacuango.

Amaguaña has been called "a tireless fighter" who "represents the female memory of the history of past struggles."[23] In order to effect the desired profound changes in Ecuador's land tenure system, she helped take indigenous demands directly to the central government located in Quito. People would walk for two days, often barefoot with babies on their backs, for these meetings and protests. In Quito they would spend anywhere from a few days to a month at the Casa del Obrero, a meeting place for peasants, artisans, artists, workers, students, and intellectuals who were interested in causes of social justice. Amaguaña claimed to have made twenty-six trips like this on foot to Quito.[24] In the 1990s she still occasionally went down to Quito from her small house high up in the *páramo* to participate in indigenous gatherings.

Like Cacuango, Amaguaña was also involved in leftist political organizing efforts. Amaguaña traveled to Cuba in 1962 as a representative of indigenous peoples in Ecuador. Later, she traveled to the Soviet Union where bands and parades of schoolchildren received her. Upon her return to Ecuador, the military overthrew the government of Carlos Julio Arosemena. The military persecuted the political left and imprisoned its leaders, including Amaguaña, for four months and four days. In prison, guards would taunt her in order to break her spirit so that she would incriminate other peasant leaders. She never gave in, and upon leaving prison the government wanted her to sign a statement that she would not return to organizing peasants. She refused to sign the statement and instead continued her organizing efforts.[25]

Nela Martínez

Several white, educated women emerged during the 1930s to 1950s who actively supported indigenous organizing efforts. One of these, Nela Martínez Espinosa, a writer and intellectual, was born to an elite landholding family in southern Ecuador in 1912. Her life was marked with an internationalist ideology and a commitment to solidarity "with her people, with humble people, with the workers, Indians, and women."[26] She was an untiring fighter for the rights of women and social justice. Martínez began her political life in 1934 as a member of the Communist Party and later served on its Executive Committee and Central Committee. Deeply involved in politics, she took an active role in current issues. She participated in the 1945 National Assembly as a representative of the working class. She used this position to fight for the rights of women and denounce the sexual discrimination that women faced in the political, cultural, and social realms. She also later led the list of candidates for the Frente Popular coalition for deputy for the province of Pichincha.

Martínez is primarily known for her feminist work. Together with Luisa Gómez de la Torre and other mostly white, upper-class women in Quito, she formed the Alianza Femenina Ecuatoriana (AFE, Ecuadorian Feminist Alliance) in 1939. Its objectives were to contribute to the cause of world peace, provide solidarity to victims of war, and promote the incorporation of women into political movements in opposition to the government. Although its leadership was comprised largely of elite intellectuals, the AFE also had a presence in marginalized neighborhoods in Quito and in other cities throughout the sierra and on the coast.[27] While this would appear to indicate the presence of a paternalistic and condescending intervention from the outside, Martínez made it clear that women's liberation had to come from women themselves, including indigenous women. These movements also could not be isolated from broader struggles for social liberation.[28] This same attitude would influence her work with indigenous groups.

Particularly important is how Martínez's feminism intersected with ethnic issues and the struggles of indigenous peoples. She was one of the founding members of the Ecuadorian Federation of Indians (FEI), which was formed in the aftermath of the May 1944 Revolution, and she used her literary skills to edit the organization's newspaper, *Ñucanchi Allpa*. It is through these cross-cultural interactions that we see the influences that female leaders had on each other in Ecuador. Martínez notes that in the 1920s and 1930s, *Amauta*, a journal edited by Peruvian Marxist José Carlos Mariátegui, arrived in Ecuador. Leftists would read and discuss his writings (both among themselves and with the indigenous activists), and years later Mariátegui's works still maintained a central place in Martínez's private library.[29] Educated urban leftists such as Martínez provided an important conduit to bring important intellectual trends from the outside world to illiterate indigenous leaders such as Cacuango and Amaguaña. In exchange, isolated intellectuals such as Martínez became more critically aware of the true nature of social inequalities that indigenous women faced. Together, white and Indian women struggled for a more just social order.

María Luisa Gómez de la Torre

Like Martínez, María Luisa Gómez de la Torre (commonly known as "Lucha") was an urban, elite leftist leader who became deeply involved in the struggles of indigenous peoples in rural communities in Ecuador. Gómez was born in Quito in 1887, geographically not far from highland Indian communities but culturally worlds removed from them. She worked with Martínez and others on a variety of projects, including the Communist Party, the AFE, and the FEI.[30] Gómez was involved in the founding congress of the Ecuadorian Socialist Party in May 1926. She was an active participant in the Socialist and later Communist parties and served on the Communist Party's Central Committee. She felt at home "among the men, treating them as equals, sharing with them ideas and emotions."[31] Whereas Martínez was known primarily for her feminist work, Gómez was known more for her role as an educator. Gómez was the first woman to teach at the Colegio Mejía, a prestigious all-male school in Quito.[32] She used her skills as a schoolteacher to become deeply involved in early Quichua-Spanish bilingual education projects in Ecuador.

How well accepted were these white women into indigenous communities? Given the deep racial barriers in Ecuadorian society, it would only be reasonable to assume that Indians would view the actions of people such as Gómez with suspicion. If such was indeed the case, years of dedicated labor overcame these hesitations. When Gómez died in November 1976, the Communist Party applauded "her example as a fighter for a more just and humane country." The FEI noted her role "as a fighter for democratic agrarian reform, education, and the rights of the exploited and oppressed indigenous masses."[33] Fifteen years after her death, Gómez's biographer reported that her portrait still hung in indigenous huts among images of saints and other treasured objects.[34]

Women and Indigenous Communities

Because women in Latin America traditionally have played a marginalized role in white-mestizo society, many people assume that indigenous women were marginalized within their own communities. The emergence of strong women leaders in rural indigenous struggles, however, indicates a distinction between the dominant white culture that sought to disenfranchise women, and indigenous societies that embraced and encouraged their contributions. As Cacuango's and Amaguaña's stories indicate, indigenous women organized within their communities as equals with men. For example, in March 1931, 141 Indians walked from Cayambe to Quito to present their demands directly to the government. Of this number, fifty-seven (including Cacuango) were women and about a dozen were children. Barely half were men.[35] Throughout the twentieth century, Indian women took aggressive leadership roles in social protest movements, from mothers confronting young soldiers at roadblocks to later leaders such as Nina Pacari earning a law degree and arguing land rights with the national government.[36]

The 1937 Ley de Organización y Régimen de las Comunas (commonly called the Ley de Comunas), which extended legal recognition to local indigenous communities, gave tacit acknowledgment to the unique nature of gender relations within them. The law explicitly states that both men *and* women from the community were to gather every December to elect leaders for the coming year. Indeed, both men and women participated in these annual meetings and were listed on the membership rolls, although men usually held the top positions in the *comuna*. Placing both men and women on an equal legal footing is perhaps ironic given that in the dominant society, which wrote this law, women did not enjoy such equality. In any case, in the administration of *comunas*, as in other organizations that indigenous peoples formed, women could play a role equal to that of men.[37]

Anthropologist Muriel Crespi, who conducted her field work on the Pesillo hacienda in Cayambe in the 1960s, voiced the possibility that women rose to positions of leadership in peasant syndicates and other radical organizations because they had less to lose than their male counterparts. Under the patriarchal social order on the haciendas, only men could own property and thus face sanction from the existing power structures for their political activities.[38] Although this interpretation is compelling, it fails to explain their actions. As Crespi acknowledges, these women suffered for the ways they defended their communities: military troops abused them, the government imprisoned them, and the landowners evicted their entire families from the haciendas. Crespi also observes that most of these leaders were married, in their thirties or forties, and often had many children and grandchildren. These women were not young, unattached single militants who could act with little thought as to the consequences of their deeds. They had deep roots in their communities. In fact, this may have been a significant factor in forcing the women to action. For centuries they and their ancestors had lived under the oppressive rule of outsiders. The time had come for them to make a significant push to ensure that their descendants would not be condemned to the same fate. They fought for their rights not because they had nothing to lose but because they had everything to gain.

White women and Indian women brought different but complementary skills to their efforts to expand concepts of citizenship. Indian women were accustomed to participating in communal decision-making processes and enjoyed social prestige and authority in their own communities. On the other hand, white women had access to the political and social privileges of living in an urban society, including access to education and knowledge of the broader world. These two groups of women possessed important but distinct skills that converged in the successful formation of political federations and bilingual schools.

The FEI

In addition to their participation in local community organizational efforts, these women also became deeply involved in indigenous-rights federations at the national level. For example, they played key roles in the founding of the FEI, or Ecuadorian Federation of Indians. In particular, Cacuango played a leading role. At the inaugural session of the FEI, she spoke as the representative of the peasant syndicates of Tierra Libre, El Inca, and Yanaguaico from her native Cayambe. Nela Martínez also spoke as a delegate of the Ecuadorian Feminist Alliance.

Even though women played a major role in the founding of this organization, its goals for social reform as laid out in its statutes did not embrace an explicitly women's or feminist agenda. The Federation sought to:

- Gain the economic emancipation of Ecuadorian Indians;
- Raise the Indians' cultural and moral level while conserving whatever is good in their native customs;
- Contribute to national unity;
- Establish links of solidarity with all American Indians.[39]

In general, these goals indicate that the FEI would demand social and economic changes in society, in addition to defending the ethnic interests of the Indians. The goals included ending an old practice whereby women and children were required to work without compensation on haciendas that employed their husbands and fathers. These obligations were considered to be particularly abusive and odious, and terminating them became a key demand of the indigenous federations. This was part of the exploitative social structure that white and Indian women worked together to change. For people like Cacuango and Amaguaña, the only way to improve their lot as poor, illiterate, Indian women was to agitate for changes in a society that systematically restricted their access to broader citizenship rights.

Delegates at the FEI congress elected Cacuango as the secretary general of the new organization. In this capacity, she traveled widely to represent the FEI both within Ecuador and outside the country. This position required her to make many public appearances and speeches as well as meet with representatives of labor unions and the government.[40] Cacuango overcame these challenges to make a dramatic impact on the white, male-dominated, Spanish-speaking political structures in Ecuador. It would be naive to assume that she accomplished this on her own. White women such as Gómez and Martínez played critically important supportive roles in these endeavors. Martínez, in particular, served as Cacuango's personal secretary and accompanied her on trips such as that to the Second Congress of the Confederación de Trabajadores de América Latina (CTAL, Confederation of Latin American Workers) in Cali, Colombia.

The roles of Indian and white women also complemented each other in other political endeavors. As indigenous women, Cacuango and Amaguaña had no hope of making their voices heard in national politics. They could, however, use their connections with white women such as Martínez and Gómez to communicate their concerns. During debates in the 1944 constituent assembly, which drafted the most liberal constitution Ecuador has ever had, members of the Communist Party were the only ones who consistently pressed for universal citizenship and suffrage rights, including extending those rights to women and illiterate peasants, Indians, and urban workers. The Communist Party incorporated both Indians and women (such as Dolores Cacuango) into its upper ranks and even presented women as candidates for office. With their place in the urban world, white women could more easily make their voices heard in seats of power. But in a country that remained predominately rural and Indian, they lacked the mass support that Indian women could provide. Indian and white women created a bridge between these two worlds so that they could work together on issues of common concern. Their success relied on spanning these cultural gaps. They realized their chief successes in the political and educational realms.

Bilingual Education

From the beginnings of liberal rule in 1895, the Ecuadorian government expressed a desire to create special schools to educate Indians and train them to be good citizens. Elites recognized the need for "a special kind of instruction to address the particular conditions and situation" of the "backwards and ignorant" Indian race. They instructed the teachers' training school in Quito to create a section to equip teachers with the necessary special skills to teach Indians.[41] Liberal concern for the education of Indians revolved around a desire to improve their hygiene, train them in new agricultural techniques, and raise their cultural horizons. Underlying this goal, however, was a much more important political project. The liberals saw education as a way to extract Indian children from their traditions and customs, which they saw as holding them back from realizing their full potential. For these Indians to become part of their unified mestizo nation, they would have to suppress their ethnic identity.

The liberals faced opposition to their educational project on two fronts. Hacienda owners saw little need to train a group of people whom they believed to be inherently and innately inferior and suited only to hard manual labor; it was a waste of time. Children should be toiling (for free) on their haciendas rather than learning skills that would only turn them into demanding and pretentious workers. Furthermore, a literate population would be harder to cheat and exploit because the workers could then verify the records that were kept on their indebtedness. In the 1950s, Bishop Leonidas Proaño, who ministered to Indians in the central highland province of Chimborazo, found that large landowners opposed his education programs because "an illiterate Indian is unlikely to protest against the land-tenure system or demand the payment of the legal minimum wage if he does not know that he has any rights."[42]

The liberal educational project also gained little support among the Indians. In 1933 anthropologist Moisés Sáenz observed that "the Ecuadorian Indian does not demonstrate any enthusiasm nor love for schools."[43] Indians had not been consulted in designing the curriculum, and the schools did not respond to their needs or concerns. It is not surprising that education leaders found a rural population apathetic to or even antagonistic toward schooling. Despite repeated attempts to implement a program of universal and rural education, a wide gap remained between this ideal and its reality. The government failed to appropriate the funds and delegate the personnel necessary to make these projects happen.

Despite these problems, the need for schools should not be underestimated. One scholar calculated that in 1934, 80 percent of the Indian workers on haciendas (as compared to 40 percent of the rest of the rural population) were illiterate.[44] Furthermore, Indian actions demonstrate that when they controlled the schools and when these schools responded to their needs, they strongly supported educational endeavors. One of the demands from a strike on the Pesillo hacienda in northern Ecuador in 1931 was for the establishment of a school.[45] Perhaps the Indians demonstrated little love for Ecuadorian schools, but they surely wanted their own.

The first and most successful Spanish-Quichua bilingual schools for Indian children were established in the 1940s on the Pesillo hacienda, where Cacuango and Amaguaña lived. In Latin America, often elite, educated, white urban female reformers who paternalistically sought to improve the lot of those less fortunate than themselves took leadership roles in creating educational opportunities for the lower classes. These Indian schools developed rather differently in Ecuador. The impetus for these schools emerged from within the indigenous communities, with Cacuango and Amaguaña taking the lead in their organizations. Indigenous women joined forces with radical white women such as Martínez and Gómez, who played supportive but critical roles in the formation of the schools.

An unusual situation resulted. Martínez and Gómez were not involved in the schools because they sought to assimilate the Indians into a mestizo culture. Rather, Indian and white women organized around common issues and concerns. Neither group of women could have started these schools on their own. Cacuango and Amaguaña had the authority and prestige in the Indian communities to organize the schools, but they lacked the pedagogical training and skills to draw up a curriculum. Martínez and particularly Gómez de la Torre possessed the knowledge and training to develop bilingual programs, but without local initiative and support for their project they would have failed. Together, white women and Indian women overcame cultural barriers and created a force that challenged the political hegemony of the Ecuadorian state. By teaching indigenous children to read and write, they empowered them to take a more active role in society. Their work forced an expansion in the understanding of citizenship rights and responsibilities.

These schools represented true grassroots efforts, but the Ecuadorian government never officially recognized, sanctioned, or supported them. The goal was to have indigenous teachers instructing children in their own native Quichua language. These teachers included José Tarabata in Pesillo, Neptalí Ulcuango in La Chimba, José Amaguaña (brother of Tránsito Amaguaña) in Moyurco, and Luis Catacuango (son of Dolores Cacuango) in San Pablourco. The Indian-run schools were so successful and posed such a threat to elite hegemony that in the 1950s and 1960s the government attempted to replace them with their own. Unlike the locally run bilingual schools, the Indian workers did not have a high degree of identification with these new schools, and they never were very successful. In the 1980s the government once again attempted to implement rural literacy programs in Cayambe. Local activists, however, confronted these programs with a great deal of mistrust and rejected them as the efforts of a government that represented the interests of the oligarchy. These educational programs were not designed to respond to local interests, but rather imposed an elite agenda. Instead of hiring local people, the government brought in outsiders who did not understand peasant cultures and stirred up divisions and discord.[46]

Tránsito Amaguaña later said that "we did not only struggle for land and better treatment, but we also wanted our children to be educated so that they would learn how to read the laws and keep track of accounts."[47] As noted, it would be harder for landlords to abuse and exploit literate workers. It was critical to the Indians and their urban supporters that control of the schools remain in local hands in order to ensure that they would achieve this purpose. Through this process, education became an empowering tool to improve the role of Indians in society. It provides one of the clearest examples of how women in Ecuador were able to utilize a traditional role of educational reform to agitate for profound structural changes.

Conclusion

T. H. Marshall observed that "citizenship and the capitalist class system have been at war." Capitalism requires and creates social inequalities. If "citizenship is a status bestowed on those who are full members of a community," then capitalism requires a subclass of people who are denied these rights.[48] For those who valued an egalitarian and just society, this meant fighting to overthrow the current capitalist system. As Marshall understood, extending citizenship meant expanding social rights. As white and Indian women discovered in Ecuador, fighting for citizenship became an effective means to push for broader changes in society. This goal still has to be realized as popular movements continue to "struggle to protect and promote values of equality and inclusion" in the face of exclusionary neoliberal models of citizenship.[49]

In commenting on the significance of Nela Martínez's life, Lilya Rodríguez observed that history does not have a gender. Men and women participate equally in historic actions, but it is in the *writing* of history that women disappear into the shadows of male heros. The result is a sexist history that serves the interests of the dominant culture.[50] Similarly, particularly in a situation such as rural Ecuador in the first half of the twentieth century, a history that excludes the actions of poor, noncitizen Indians who comprised the majority of the population also merely serves the interests of the dominant culture. Writing a history that includes these elements is not only a more comprehensive history, but it is also a more accurate one.

The lives of these four women (two indigenous, rural, illiterate, and poor; and the other two white, urban, educated, and elite) intersected at many different points. They participated together in political parties and movements, fought for indigenous rights and bilingual education, and organized themselves into women's groups. All of these factors (their class, ethnicity, and gender) influenced who they were and how they interacted with the larger society. They clearly informed the demands which they advocated. In working side by side in their struggle for common goals, white and Indian women gained mutual respect for each other and developed deep friendships.

All four of these women in Ecuador, along with many others, personally felt the oppression of social inequalities. The quadruple (class, ethnic, gender, citizenship) oppression under which Cacuango and Amaguaña lived, and which Martínez and Gómez directly observed through their work in indigenous communities, was not something that could be easily mitigated through reformist legislation. It was tightly bound up in the nature of society. Simply extending to women the right to vote would not make any difference in Cacuango's and Amaguaña's lives, since no one in their communities could exercise the franchise. For them, the only way to improve their lot appeared to be through a wholesale, radical, and socialist transformation of society. As all four of these women recognized, these changes would have to take place on a variety of levels, including the class, ethnic, and gender structurings of society. It meant struggling for a fundamental redefinition of citizenship rights.

Notes

1. Sergio Enrique Girón, *La revolución de mayo* (Quito: Editorial Atahualpa, 1945), 336, 118.

2. Raquel Rodas, *Nosotras que del amor hicimos . . .* (Quito: Raquel Rodas, 1992), 60.

3. "Constitución de 1830," in Federico E. Trabucco, *Constituciones de la República del Ecuador* (Quito: Universidad Central, Editorial Universitaria, 1975), 35. For a general discussion of citizenship in Ecuador, see Amparo Menéndez-Carrión, "Ciudadanía," *Revista Paraguaya de Sociología* 30:88 (Sept.–Dec. 1993): 81–92.

4. Francesca Miller, "The Suffrage Movement in Latin America," in *Confronting Change, Challenging Tradition: Women in Latin American History*, ed. Gertrude Matyoka Yeager (Wilmington, DE: Scholarly Resources, 1994), 169.

5. T. H. Marshall, *Class, Citizenship, and Social Development: Essays* (Garden City, NY: Doubleday, 1964), 71–72.

6. Donna J. Guy, " 'White Slavery,' Citizenship, and Nationality in Argentina," in *Nationalisms and Sexualities*, ed. Andrew Parker et al. (New York: Routledge, 1992), 202–3.

7. Guillermo O'Donnell, "On the State, Democratization, and Some Conceptual Problems: A Latin American View with Glances at Some Postcommunist Countries," *World Development* 21:8 (1993): 1361.

8. Eric Foner, *The Story of American Freedom* (New York: W.W. Norton, 1998), 38–39.

9. Joseph S. Roucek, "Ecuador in Geopolitics," *Contemporary Review* 205: 1177 (February 1964): 77–78.

10. Rafael Quintero and Erika Silva, *Ecuador: una nación en ciernes*, 3 volumes, Colección Estudios No. 1 (Quito: FLACSO/Abya-Yala, 1991), t. 1, 100; t. 2, 148.

11. Harry A. Franck, *Vagabonding down the Andes: Being the Narrative of a Journey, Chiefly Afoot, From Panama to Buenos Aires* (New York: The Century Co., 1917), 152.

12. Jeffrey L. Gould, *To Die in This Way: Nicaraguan Indians and the Myth of Mestizaje, 1880–1965* (Durham: Duke University Press, 1998), 86.

13. James MacGregor Burns and Stewart Burns, *A People's Charter: The Pursuit of Rights in America* (New York: Knopf, 1991), 462, 13.

14. Joe Foweraker and Todd Landman, *Citizenship Rights and Social Movements: A Comparative and Statistical Analysis* (Oxford: Oxford University Press, 1997), 1.

15. Charles R. Epp, *The Rights Revolution: Lawyers, Activists, and Supreme Courts in Comparative Perspective* (Chicago: University of Chicago Press, 1998), 2.

16. Letter from Juan Francisco Sumárraga to Director, Junta Central de Asistencia Pública, March 21, 1946, in Correspondencia Recibida, Segundo Semestre, Segundo Parte, 1946, 1555, Archivo Nacional de Medicina del Museo Nacional de Medicina "Dr. Eduardo Estrella," Fondo Junta Central de Asistencia Pública, Quito, Ecuador (hereafter JCAP); Letter from C. Anibal Maldonado, Administrador, to Jefe, Departmento de Haciendas, Asistencia Pública, October 10, 1946 (Oficio #27), in Correspondencia Recibida, 1946, JCAP. For basic biographical data on Dolores Cacuango, see Osvaldo Albornoz Peralta, *Dolores Cacuango y las luchas indígenas de Cayambe* (Guayaquil: Editorial Claridad S.A., 1975); and Raquel Rodas, *Crónica de un sueño: las escuelas indígenas de Colores Cacuango: una experiencia de educación bilingüe en Cayambe* (Quito: Proyecto de Educación Bilingue Intercultural, MEC-GTZ, 1989).

17. "Dolores Cacuango," *Antinazi* (Quito) 2:19 (April 17, 1943): 4; facsimile edition in Raymond Mériguet Cousségal, *Antinazismo en Ecuador, años 1941–1944: autobiografía del Movimiento Antinazi de Ecuador (MPAE-MAE)* (Quito: R. Mériguet Coussegal, 1988), 214.

18. Rodas, *Crónica de un sueño*, 63.

19. A photo in Elías Muñoz Vicuña, *Masas, luchas, solidaridad* (Guayaquil: Universidad de Guayaquil, 1985), 91, of a Central Committee meeting in Quito, July 26–28, 1947, shows seventeen people, of which Cacuango is one of three women and the only indigenous person.

20. Muriel Crespi, "Mujeres campesinas como líderes sindicales: la falta de propiedad como calificación para puestos políticos," *Estudios Andinos* 5:1 (1976): 165.

21. "Dolores Cacuango: un orgullo para Cayambe," *La Hora del Norte* (Quito), November 10, 1989.

22. Amaguaña recounts her life's story in interviews published in José Yánez del Pozo, *Yo declaro con franqueza (Cashnami causashcanchic); memoria oral de Pesillo, Cayambe*, 2d ed., revised (Quito: Ediciones Abya-Yala, 1988); Raquel Rodas, *Tránsito Amaguaña: su testimonio*, 3 (Quito: CEDIME, 1987); and Martha Bulnes, *Me levanto y digo, testimonio de tres mujeres quichua* (Quito: Editorial El Conejo, 1990), 31–40.

23. Bulnes, *Me levanto y digo*, 14.

24. Rodas, *Tránsito Amaguaña*, 25.

25. Ibid., 35–37.

26. Lilya Rodríguez, "Acción por el Movimiento de Mujeres," in *Homenaje a Nela Martínez Espinosa* (Quito: Acción por el Movimiento de Mujeres, 1990), 23. This publication is from a homage paid to Martínez on May 29, 1990, in the Salón de la Ciudad in Quito. The following biographical data are extracted from it.

27. Silvia Vega Ugalde, *La Gloriosa: de la revolución del 28 de mayo de 1944 a la contrarrevolución velasquista* (Quito: Editorial El Conejo, 1987), 52, 79–80.

28. Rodríguez, "Acción," 17, 22.

29. Nela Martínez, interview with author, Quito, April 27, 1996.

30. Rodas, *Amor*, 50.

31. Ibid., 46. For examples of her participation, see Partido Socialista Ecuatoriano (PSE), *Labores de la Asamblea Nacional Socialista y Manifiesto del Consejo Central del Partido(16-23-Mayo), Quito, 1926* (Guayaquil: Imp. "El Tiempo," 1926), 28–29, 34, 97.

32. Vega Ugalde, *La Gloriosa*, 79–80.

33. Published newspaper notes (possibly from *El Comercio*) on Gómez's death dated Quito, noviembre 23 de 1976 (FEI), and Quito, noviembre 25 de 1976 (PCE), both located in Mercedes Prieto's personal archive, Quito, Ecuador.

34. Rodas, *Amor*, 9.

35. "141 peones de Cayambe han venido a esta ciudad intempestivamente abandonando sus faenas del campo," *El Comercio*, March 13, 1931; "Ayer fueron apresados 156 indígenas de las haciendas de Cayambe," *El Día*, March 13, 1931; "No se efectuó la audiencia del presidente con los indígenas de Cayambe," *El Día*, March 14, 1931.

36. Marc Becker, "Nina Pacari," in *Notable Twentieth-Century Latin American Women: A Biographical Dictionary*, ed. Cynthia Tompkins and David William Foster (Westport, CT: Greenwood, 2001), 218–22.

37. "Ley de Organización y Régimen de las Comunas" (Decreto no. 142), *Registro Oficial*, No. 558 (August 6, 1937): 1517–19. Also see Marc Becker, "Comunas and Indigenous Protest in Cayambe, Ecuador," *The Americas* 55:4 (April 1999): 531–59.

38. Crespi, "Mujeres campesinas," 167.

39. Federación Ecuatoriana de Indios (FEI), *Estatutos de la Federación de Indios* (Guayaquil: Editorial Claridad, 1945), 3.

40. Crespi, "Mujeres campesinas," 165.

41. "Decreta de 18 agosto de 1895," in Rubio Orbe, comp., *Legislación indigenista del Ecuador* (México: Instituto Indigenista Interamericano, 1954), 63; "Decreta de 12 abril de 1899," in ibid., 67; "Creación de Escuelas Prediales," in ibid., 84; "Creación de escuelas para la raza indígena," in ibid., 68–69.

42. Penny Lernoux, *Cry of the People* (Garden City, NY: Doubleday & Company, 1980), 147.

43. Moisés Sáenz, *Sobre el indio ecuatoriano y su incorporación al medio national* (México: Publicaciones de la Secretaría de Educación Pública, 1933), 145.

44. Udo Oberem, "Contribución a la historia del trabajador rural de América Latina: 'conciertos' y 'huasipungueros' en Ecuador," in *Contribución a la etnohistoria ecuatoriana*, ed. Segundo Moreno Y. and Udo Oberem (Otavalo, Ecuador: Instituto Otavaleño de Antropología, 1981), 323.

45. "Pliego de peticiones que los sindicatos 'El Inca' y 'Tierra Libre' situados en la parroquia Olmedo, presentan a los arrendatarios de las haciendas donde trabajan," *El Día*, January 6, 1931.

46. Manuel Escobar, "La FEI . . . el indio de poncho colorado," *Cuadernos de Nueva* (Quito) 7 (June 1983): 49.

47. Rodas, *Tránsito Amaguaña*, 30. Also see Rodas, *Amor*; Rodas, *Crónica de un sueño*; and Consuelo Yánez Cossío, *La educación indígena en el Ecuador:*

historia de la educación y el pensamiento pedagógico ecuatorianos, 5 (Quito: Imprenta Abya-Yala, 1996), 28.

48. Marshall, *Class, Citizenship*, 84.

49. Cathy Blacklock and Jane Jenson, "Citizenship: Latin American Perspectives," *Social Politics* 5:2 (Summer 1998): 128.

50. Rodríguez, "Acción," 16.

7

Races and Cultures in the Venezuelan Oil Fields

Miguel Tinker-Salas

Miguel Tinker-Salas takes us in the interwar period to a Latin American country where cultures crossed borders and race played a complex role in society. Race and racism rest upon stereotypes of several groups, Afro-Caribbeans and Asians as well as creole Venezuelans and North Americans. As this selection illustrates, the North American oil companies were in a position as industrial producers to write the rules regarding the complicated social hierarchies that prevailed. They did so through the oil-worker wage system. A form of discrimination familiar to those who have examined the U.S.-dominated banana industry in Central America, Ecuador, and the Caribbean islands and the occupation economy in the Panama Canal Zone, parallel wage scales reinforced existing racial and national hostilities in places where good-paying jobs were scarce. Yet despite the difficult tensions fomented by the oil companies as well as by the Venezuelan government and the press, the workers saw through socially divisive tactics. They managed in the end to support one another. Perhaps, as Tinker-Salas suggests here, it was the oil camp culture that bound them together. No doubt, the high pay also encouraged the oilworkers to see themselves as a special group.

O n December 14, 1922, after many failed attempts, the Barroso well, near the town of La Rosa on the outskirts of Cabimas in Venezuela, erupted and sent oil streaming over two hundred feet into the air to capture the attention of the nation and the world. The events at Cabimas capped a process of oil exploration begun almost a decade earlier by Dutch and British corporations. Trade journals and Venezuelan and U.S. newspapers publicized the news, which sparked interest among dozens of foreign oil companies. The *New York Times* declared the well at La Rosa the most productive in the world.[1] Oil triggered the internal migration of thousands of rural Venezuelan laborers from surrounding states and represented the most significant movement of people since the wars of independence in the early nineteenth century. In these oil camps, Venezuelans from Zulia and the nearby states of Trujillo, Tachira, Mérida, Falcón, Lara, and Nueva Esparta converged, clashed, and, in the end, forged a new identity.

News of the oil bonanza also attracted Americans, and hundreds of *musiúes*, as Venezuelans called foreigners, soon inundated Maracaibo and the nearby lake shore districts. The oil boom seduced American roustabouts, roughnecks, and riggers who arrived daily at the port city of Maracaibo, hoping to strike it rich. As one American émigré put it, "if you wanted to be in the oil industry, Venezuela was the place to be."[2]

Besides Americans, oil also attracted a patchwork of other immigrants from throughout the Caribbean and beyond. The colonial relations maintained by the British and Dutch in the Caribbean inspired most of this migration. Oil companies such as Caribbean Petroleum, Venezuelan Oil Concessions (VOC), Lago Petroleum, and Standard Oil Company of Venezuela (SOCV) used Trinidad and Curaçao as staging areas for their operations, hiring local labor to work in Venezuela. They also used Curaçao and Aruba as sites for refineries where they processed Venezuelan oil. Consequently, people from the Caribbean, especially Trinidad, Grenada, and Curaçao, as well as from Mexico, Asia, and the Middle East flocked to Venezuela for a share in the newfound wealth. This dramatic movement of people represented a social and racial cauldron, where beneath the surface a host of tensions began to boil. This process took place under the watchful eye of complacent Venezuelan government officials and American and British bosses who, at times, demonstrated a callous disregard for the contradictions that the massive relocation of people generated.

Historical Antecedents

Prior to the oil boom, Trinidadians and Venezuelans, from the states of Sucre and Monagas, shared a long history. The Spanish colonial experience facilitated commercial and social exchanges between the regions that continued after the British occupation.[3] During the colonial period, the towns that dotted the Gulf of Paria engaged in trade with Trinidad. From the muddy banks of the San Juan River, cotton, cacao, and cattle were shipped to the British colony.[4] Trinidadian and Venezuelan fishermen plied the waters of the Gulf of Paria in search of daily catches. Removed from Caracas by great distances, and with no viable overland road system, Port of Spain, the capital of Trinidad, represented an important economic and social nexus for eastern Venezuelans. At times, Trinidad and Curaçao served as safe havens for Venezuelan political exiles seeking to avoid persecution. Many aspiring Venezuelan families also sent their children to school in Port of Spain for a British education. Marriage and family linked many Afro-Venezuelans to the social life of the island.

Anthropologist Angelina Pollak Eltz found that older residents at Güiria in the state of Sucre still conserved Trinidadian customs and traditions.[5]

West Indian Men

Trinidadians represented the largest group of West Indians in Venezuela. Increased foreign migration to their island, competition for employment, and depressed wages provided the impetus for many to seek work in Venezuela and throughout the Caribbean.[6] As Venezuelan migrants flocked to the oil fields, foreign companies found it necessary to explain their preference for hiring West Indian labor. They offered several contradictory arguments for employing West Indian or other non-Venezuelan labor. The most commonly used echoed old Spanish and British colonial justifications for the introduction of African slaves or indentured workers to cane fields. These arguments included the supposed "unskilled nature" of the Venezuelan labor force, their purported "feeble physical" condition, and insufficient numbers.[7] These objections had a familiar ring and reflected decades-old stereotypes about "indolent" Latin American laborers, unable to work in the searing tropical climate.

Contrary to foreign stereotypes, most Venezuelans proved adept at their designated duties: stripping away dense tropical growth, draining swamps, felling trees, transporting supplies, digging trenches, constructing roads, or erecting oil derricks and other structures. According to one American observer, when given the opportunity, Venezuelans performed all but the most technically skilled operations. In an unusual expression of candor, one American *petrolero* concluded that "the companies won't teach the natives all the tricks of the trade. They're afraid if the natives get to know it all these countries down here will kick the Americans and the English out and run the fields themselves."[8]

Thus, at many levels, the oil companies' rationale regarding "indolent" Venezuelan labor proved duplicitous and disingenuous. When Standard Oil Company of New Jersey contemplated building a refinery in Aruba, it described the conditions of Afro-Caribbean workers in the same stereotypical manner in which it had previously characterized Venezuelans. Their internal memos lamented the Afro-Arubans' lack of skills, their insufficient numbers, and their supposedly "malnourished state."[9] In reality, neither Afro-Caribbeans nor Venezuelans had any significant experience in the oil industry. Both groups were obliged to acquire new skills and adapt to new production methods and labor relations.

In researching these contradictory assertions, an examination of internal oil company documents uncovers other reasons for hiring Afro-Caribbean labor, or what one Standard Oil official called "British Negroes." According to Standard Oil, the Afro-Caribbean has "many excellent characteristics.

He is thrifty, home loving, and industrious, and has an excellent tempera-
ment, with few of the Latin characteristics, such as excitability, irrespon-
sibility, etc. The young ones have a greater sense of responsibility and are
more regular in their attendance on the job."[10] Evidently, such cultural
and social attributes, real or imagined, played a significant role in the oil
company's decision to hire Afro-Caribbean labor, especially from Brit-
ish- and Dutch-held colonies. Beyond these characteristics, the ability of
West Indians to speak English and their experience with the British colonial administration and educational system increased their social value in
the eyes of the oil companies. Moreover, previous relations with Europeans raised the expectation that West Indians would accommodate to the
demands of their new employers and would be less likely to join Venezuelan labor unions.[11] Intense competition marked the formative period of
the oil industry in which most companies typically operated twenty-four
hours per day. This expansion in operations necessitated an abundant
supply of labor. In order to minimize costs and maximize profits, the foreign companies sought large numbers of workers regardless of their
nationality.

In addition to laborers, the oil companies also hired skilled West Indians and Asians with previous experience as accountants, typists, book-
keepers, or general secretarial staff. Cecil Aleong, for example, a Chinese
immigrant from Trinidad, worked twenty-nine years as a bookkeeper for
Creole Petroleum and its precursors at Lagunillas, La Salina, and finally
Maracaibo, before retiring in the late 1950s.[12] Given their fluency in English, limited Spanish skills, and minimal ties to the Venezuelan community, many companies assumed that West Indians could be entrusted not
to divulge private internal matters. The companies appeared especially
sensitive to any public disclosure of the oil industry's racially stratified
salary scale.[13] This concern surfaced again years later when they finally
hired Venezuelan office staff.[14]

Besides clerical positions, oil companies such as Lago, Gulf, Standard Oil, and Caribbean employed Afro-Caribbeans in skilled crafts as
electricians, mechanics, carpenters, sheet metal workers, and mariners or
as drivers or in materials delivery. A good example is a Trinidadian named
Eduardo Elcock, who arrived in Venezuela in 1921 and after several years
found employment in the oil industry. He worked throughout the country,
serving as a de facto nurse in oil camps that lacked formal medical services. His ability to prescribe home remedies for common illnesses earned
Elcock the nickname *el brujo* (witch doctor) among his fellow workers.[15]
Another Trinidadian, Stephen Joseph, who immigrated to Venezuela in
1927, worked his entire life in the materials department of Creole Petroleum alongside a compatriot, Theophilus Wickham Jones, in the metal
shop.[16] Gordon Wildman arrived from Port of Spain in 1929 without speaking a word of Spanish and obtained employment with Lago Petroleum

first as a telephone operator in Lagunillas, then in the electrical department, and finally as a dispatcher in the materials warehouse.[17] Besides Trinidadians, other Afro-Caribbean workers followed the same pattern. Joseph Modest arrived from Grenada in 1924 and found employment with Standard Oil at Las Palmas, later making the transition to Creole Petroleum.[18] Morain O. C. Bruno, also a native of Grenada, moved to Venezuela in 1925 and worked in the metals department at La Salina for most of his career.[19] Other Grenadians such as William James Linton soon followed and also worked for several decades with Creole Petroleum before retiring.[20]

West Indian Women

Beyond the oil fields, many American families hired either Venezuelan or, in some cases, English-speaking Trinidadian women for domestic labor. As one American woman who lived in eastern Venezuela candidly admitted, the "lazy Americans went to Trinidad to get help so they would not have to speak or learn Spanish."[21] Similarly, some Americans in Cuba preferred English-speaking Jamaicans instead of Cuban women to work in their homes.[22] The American perceptions of local women reflected the stereotypical view of the Venezuelan oil laborers. One publication directed at American women described Venezuelan maids as "an *alpargata* (sandals) shod gal just in from the Andes or the *llanos*, she'll have two hands but you will have to explain to her just about everything she'll do with them."[23] A Venezuelan government commission found that "many of the British, Dutch, and Americans who desired English-speaking help (maids) employed Trinidadian women for whom the company initially provided separate bungalows."[24] Trinidadian Gladys Joseph served as a cook and housekeeper for five single Europeans who lived at the Socorro staff houses in the Caribbean Petroleum camp. When she left their employ, the men wrote her a glowing letter of recommendation. Georgina Millete, from Grenada, worked in the house of Charles Rider for three years before seeking employment elsewhere.[25]

The West Indian housekeeper became a common sight entering and leaving the oil camps. Ironically, the humble domestic, either West Indian or Venezuelan, was one of the few non-Americans or non-Europeans who could enter the inner sanctum of a foreign senior staff camp. In the words of one American, "native cooks and nursemaids, for the American colony are seen slap-slap-slapping down the sun baked road in their woven sandals, minus shape or heel."[26] In the early 1930s in eastern Venezuela, Standard Oil Company actually tested all "family servants for Kahn and amebic dysentery."[27] To assist new arrivals in selecting "suitable *muchachas*" (maids), several American women organized a registry.[28] More formal publications, such as Mary George's *A Is for Abrazo*, served as a social primer for newcomers.[29] Creole Petroleum and the other oil companies also published guides.

Life for the Trinidadian women proved just as arduous as it did for their male counterparts. American staff homes usually did not offer maids separate quarters. Most lived in the makeshift communities that arose outside the barbed-wire fences that surrounded the American camps. Working in what one American observer described as a "country club suburb" and residing in subsistence conditions were poignant reminders of their subordinate social position.[30] Single Trinidadian women left their immediate family and friends behind and established new lives in Venezuela. These immigrant women inspired relatives to make this journey. Besides housekeepers, some Trinidadian women ventured into other areas of work. In eastern Venezuela they toiled in laundries, served as cooks, and in some cases actually operated brothels. In Caripito, Doña Lola, as she was fondly known, ran one of the town's best-known bordellos.

Chinese

The Chinese who had previously migrated to the Caribbean, especially to British colonies such as Trinidad, joined the migration stream to Venezuela. Once on the islands, many had served as conduits for other family members from Mainland China, Taiwan, and Hong Kong. The father of Angel Kingland arrived in Trinidad from Taiwan in the early 1920s where he married Juana Reyes, a young Venezuelan woman from Yaguaraparo in the state of Sucre. When the opportunity arose, George (Jorge) Kingland contracted with Standard Oil and began to work as a cook in Pedernales in the Amacuro Delta region of Venezuela. Kingland utilized his knowledge of English to advance. He moved from the Pedernales camp and eventually settled in El Tigre and the area of San Tome, where he obtained employment in the American staff dining hall. Initially, Juana, who had learned English in Trinidad, acted as the family translator. She facilitated communications between her English-speaking husband, their children, and the larger community. The family had twenty-two children. Although Jorge's social circle included some Venezuelans, he still regularly socialized with fellow Chinese.[31]

Other Chinese followed a similar route in their journey to Venezuela. The great majority of Asians who worked for the oil companies found themselves relegated to mess hall kitchens as cooks and bakers or to the laundry facilities. Chan Fai, for example, was "1st cook" for Caribbean Petroleum at the San Lorenzo mess hall on the Lake Maracaibo shore.[32] John Fui and Jaime Chen also worked with Fai in the San Lorenzo mess hall.[33] At the Creole Petroleum camp in Tía Juana, Eddie Sie Hong, a baker, gained quite a reputation among the staff residents who lined up outside his kitchen every day to await fresh bread.[34]

Those Chinese who were not employed by the foreign companies turned their energies to the new consumer markets that flourished in the oil towns. By 1929, Ramón Ho operated as a successful merchant in Cabimas. After two years he requested permission from Zulia's governor, Vicencio Pérez Soto, to expand and bring his sons and brothers from Havana and Canton to assist in his business. To support his claim, Ho presented a letter from the local *jefe civil* (municipal boss) of Cabimas that attested to his good conduct.[35]

The economic census for Zulia, Monagas, Anzoátegui, and other oil-producing states reveals Chinese involved in varied forms of commercial activity. In Lagunillas, in the state of Zulia, for example, Andres Fan Fung operated a grocery store, Emilio Yo owned the Half Moon tailor shop, the Chin family ran a laundry, and San Lee claimed to have the best restaurant in the district.[36] In Caripito, in the eastern state of Monagas, the Hung family managed a bakery and a grocery store, and sold gasoline and lubricants.[37] This pattern of ownership could be found throughout the small oil towns that dotted western and eastern Venezuela. Although Asians established a foothold as merchants, they confronted stiff competition from other groups. Besides the Chinese, Italians, Spaniards, and Lebanese also opened retail businesses in rural oil towns. In fact, immigrants from the Middle East gradually dominated certain areas of commercial retail activity within the oil towns. A Venezuelan government commission studying the camps in the late 1950s reported that in the state of Anzoátegui "all small commerce with an average capital of 6,000 bolivares is almost totally in the hands of the Lebanese."[38]

The Mexican Connection

Besides Afro-Caribbeans and Asians, oil companies with operations in Mexico, such as Pantepec and Pan American, also brought to Venezuela skilled Mexican employees to serve as translators or to perform other administrative duties. Before his untimely death in 1930, Bernardo Calero, a Mexican citizen, worked as a translator in the Maracaibo land and legal department of Lago Petroleum. A 1928 letter from the Secretaría General del Estado de Zulia reported that Pan American, Pantepec Oil, and Lago Petroleum had recently recruited increased numbers of former Mexican oilworkers. Judging from payroll records, however, the number of Mexicans employed by these companies never equalled the number of West Indians.[39]

The presence of Mexicans in Venezuela became a highly charged and politicized issue. Government circulars warned local *jefes civiles* to monitor the activities of the Mexicans closely since they were citizens "of an enemy country of Venezuela where communism has sunk roots and is expanding."[40] On the heels of the Mexican Revolution, Mexican political leaders publicly criticized Venezuelan dictator Juan Vicente Gómez, who ruled from 1908 to 1935. José Vasconcelos, Mexican minister of education in the government of Alvaro Obregón, branded Gómez as the "Porfirio Díaz of Venezuela." Obregón also lent moral and financial support to Venezuelan exiles attempting to overthrow Gómez.[41] The relocation of dozens of Americans and British companies to the new Venezuelan oil fields frustrated Mexican officials and probably also fueled the attacks on Gómez.[42] Confronted by these criticisms, Gómez directed Venezuelan agents to shadow Vasconcelos when he traveled abroad and report on his speeches. Pedro Arcaya, one-time Venezuelan ambassador to the United States, reported on Vasconcelos's visit to Washington and branded his pronouncements as "socialist, almost anarchist or even Bolshevik."[43]

Throughout the 1920s, relations between Mexico City and Caracas remained tense. In 1923, Gómez formally severed relations.[44] The U.S. media took advantage of the rupture to criticize Obregón's inability to manage Mexico's affairs.[45] Even after the formal break, accusations continued to fly between both sides. Government-sponsored publications promoting the advantages of Venezuela pointed out that "Maracaibo is 240 miles nearer to New York than is Tampico, Mexico."[46] The Venezuelan government denied a Mexican opera company and several magazine distributors entrance into the country, labeling their activities as "nondesirable."[47] Contending that Mexicans functioned as "Bolshevik agents" in 1928, Gómez ordered their expulsion from Venezuela and prohibited any future migration.[48] Yet, despite the acrimony between both governments, many Venezuelan workers admired some Mexicans who did not appear intimidated by the actions of their American bosses.[49] During the 1940s and 1950s, Mexican films also proved popular among Venezuelan oilworkers.[50] Concerned officials at the American embassy feared competition and the political content of Mexican cinema.[51]

Life in the Oil Camps

Overrun by outsiders, the handful of towns—La Rosa, Tía Juana, La Salina, and Cabimas—that had existed prior to the oil era underwent dramatic changes. The population of Cabimas and Lagunillas de Agua soared in a very short period of time. In 1920, Cabimas recorded a population of 1,940; by 1936 it increased to 21,753, and by 1940 it had skyrocketed to 33,328.[52] Similar development occurred in the nearby district of Lagunillas. In the capital of the district, the precolonial town of Lagunillas de Agua, people lived in houses elevated on stilts over the lake itself. The 1920 population of 982 climbed to 13,922 by 1936, and by 1941 it had reached 19,391. To accommodate the large influx of Venezuelans and foreigners implied the complete reorganization of these towns. In the words of one observer, "choked with whites, yellows, and blacks, Cabimas became a hodgepodge of races and ambitions, a Babel of tongues. It became a fantastic, tropical Klondike with all the attendant maladies that once hit Alaska and also California."[53] According to one American *petrolero*, Maracaibo and many of the new oil towns acquired an air of "insanity . . . a mad carnival."[54] Jesús Prieto Soto, an early labor activist and journalist, described Cabimas as a "chaotic amalgam of humanity."[55] The development of the oil industry and the infusion of thousands of foreigners permanently transformed the Venezuelan social and cultural landscape. Fear of reprisals from the Gómez regime initially muted criticism of these dramatic changes.

Inevitably, this stunning growth spawned various social and recreational opportunities. Bars, gambling establishments, and a host of bordellos soon appeared all along the lakeshore. On paydays, Venezuelan, West Indian, and American oilworkers frequented these places, creating crowds that flowed out into the streets. The celluloid images of Tom Mix, William Hart, and other Hollywood stars flickered on open-air movie screens sponsored by the oil companies.[56] As one early American observer remembered, "when day faded into dusk, the conglomeration of hot, sweaty humanity was swelled by hundreds of professional girls, procurers, gamblers and foreigners all hell bent on a boisterous and happy evening."[57]

The physical appearance of the oil towns reflected their impromptu character. Open-air accommodations, amounting to no more than a few poles and tin metal roofs, sprung up all over town to give newcomers somewhere to hang their hammocks and store their belongings. Street vendors prepared food on mobile carts to feed the mostly male workers.[58] Those who already had employment erected quarters wherever they could obtain land, thus forming a labyrinth of houses that actually obstructed the movement of automobiles.

At many levels, regionalism and nationality determined where and how many newcomers congregated. The mosaic of barrios bore the name of home states, nations, or some other regional-specific identifier. Seeking a greater sense of security in this improvised society, migrants clung to their customs, traditions, and cultural symbols. Neighborhoods named Corito, after Coro, the state capital of Falcón, dotted the eastern lakeshore.[59] Margariteños built shrines to the Virgen del Valle, patroness of their island. Zulianos and Andinos also gathered in distinctive neighborhoods and socialized with members of their *patria chica*. Mutual aid societies and social clubs such as the Unión Mutua Falconiana provided a meeting place for people from the same state.

People from Trinidad, Grenada, and Curaçao, who constituted the largest Afro-Caribbean community, similarly settled in their own ethnic enclaves. In Cabimas one neighborhood was named Curazaito.[60] In these barrios, Caribbean immigrants re-created customs and traditions from their island homes. On weekends, cricket teams played a game alien to most

Venezuelans except in its vague resemblance to baseball. Cricket spread and eventually teams formed in all the oil camps throughout the lake region. Leagues that pitted West Indians from Lagunillas, Cabimas, and other areas soon followed. In the evenings the sounds of steel drums and Caribbean tunes filled the night air. On Sundays, Methodist ministers, some of whom had traveled from Trinidad, preached to the faithful.

After the oil companies built camps for their employees, they paid particular attention to providing recreational outlets for their workers. By the 1930s, informal sports among West Indians or Venezuelans had been formally organized by Caribbean, Lago, VOC, and the other oil companies. In 1941 the Campo Rojo cricket team of Lagunillas defeated all its rivals in Zulia and was crowned "Lake Maracaibo champions." Creole Petroleum donated the trophy and the individual medals, and its public relations department reported the victory in their local bulletins and national magazines.[61] Some oil companies such as Creole retained full-time athletic directors who sought to strengthen morale and increase company loyalty through sports. Critics of this practice contended that such programs sought to create the ultimate "company man or woman."[62]

Ties to the Homeland

West Indians, in particular Trinidadians and Grenadians, maintained close ties to their homelands. Vacations afforded them the opportunities for regular visits, and a frequent stream of immigrants kept the population informed of events in their island nations. The constant movement of West Indians fostered an exchange of cultures between Venezuela and the Caribbean. Many Trinidadians in Port of Spain incorporated Venezuelan *aguinaldos* and foods such as *hallacas* into their Christmas festivities.[63] A Caracas newspaper reported that Christmas in Trinidad included the "traditional Anglo-Saxon customs with a touch of Venezuelan flavor."[64] For their part, Venezuelans incorporated West Indian condiments into their foods. Goat meat prepared in a spicy curry sauce became a favorite of Venezuelan workers on the desert peninsula of Paraguana in the state of Falcón.

Although residing in Venezuela, many West Indians preferred that their children be educated in their homeland. Cecil Aleong had worked twenty-nine years in the Creole accounting office, yet he still sent his daughter to study in Trinidad.[65] His compatriot William James also had two children in school in Port of Spain.[66] The desire for their children to obtain a British education did not preclude West Indians from establishing deep and at times permanent roots in Venezuela. Many single West Indian men married Venezuelan women and raised their children as Venezuelans. Others returned to the islands to seek spouses. When they retired, those with Venezuelan families remained in the country. Augustus

Wharwood, a native of Grenada who had emigrated in 1929, referred to Venezuela as his second country.[67] Horatio Baptiste, also from Grenada, married María Lourdes and had four Venezuelan children. He retired after almost three decades of working in the oil industry and stayed in Venezuela.[68] Moreover, the Venezuelan Ministry of the Interior reported that West Indians, especially Trinidadians, had the highest rate of naturalization among all immigrants.[69] For example, John Dickson, a Trinidadian by birth, married Elvina Inciarte, a Venezuelan woman. The couple had six children and Dickson became a naturalized citizen.[70]

Straddling the Middle

West Indians and Chinese employed in staff or skilled positions found themselves in contradictory circumstances. Many held significantly different positions from most Venezuelans and represented an intermediary stratum between the local laborer and the American or European boss.[71] The presence of foreign laborers further complicated the already difficult process of union organizing. Moreover, as historian Judith Ewell points out, "many Venezuelans found the West Indians as arrogant in their attitudes as the white American and English bosses."[72] This social distance quickly became a source of tension between some West Indians and Venezuelans. Not surprisingly, the inability of Afro-Caribbeans and Chinese to communicate in Spanish and their positions within the companies' social-racial structure drove a wedge between some West Indians and Venezuelan laborers. Since Trinidadians tended to address locals as "my friends," Venezuelans began to describe all West Indians as *mainfrens*. The term had several connotations; according to historian Charles Bergquist, it "sarcastically" scorned conformist West Indians, yet under different social circumstances it also reflected a level of familiarity and even camaraderie.[73] Inevitably, all persons of Asian background became identified as *chinos* regardless of their real ancestry. Similarly, all Middle Easterners were labeled *turcos*.

Beyond cultural and social tensions with Venezuelans, the American-dominated oil camps reproduced the virulent racism present in the United States. The corrosive nature of American-style segregation permeated labor relations and employment practices and deeply influenced the nature of social life in most oil camps. Initially, these attitudes sanctioned segregated restrooms, drinking fountains, mess halls, and social clubs, officially separating "white Americans" from employees of color. In Maracaibo, at one company administrative office, a sign read "Toilette unicamente para Americanos" (Toilet only for Americans).[74] Caribbean, VOC, Gulf, Lago, and Standard also constructed separate and comfortable living facilities for their American staff and inferior housing for Venezuelan and other employees. Consequently, many Americans lived in restricted, well-kept camps that shielded them from the Venezuelan or West Indian population. Foreign enclaves with such names as Hollywood, Victory, and Star Hill represented self-contained units where North Americans attempted to replicate their status in the United States. Moreover, West Indians, Asians, and Venezuelans continually confronted strict color barriers that marked their daily existence and drew clear lines between them and their American supervisors.

Language differences limited communication between the foreign bosses and the West Indian and Venezuelan laborers. According to journalist G. Bracho Montiel, American "drillers gave orders in a mixed language, half English and half Spanish, with extravagant corruptions that formed their own slang."[75] Oil camp "Spanglish" created such linguistic adaptations as *pagerol* (payroll), *overol* (overalls), *socates* (sockets), *swiches* (switches), *tipiando* (typing), *gut bai* (goodbye), *guachiman* (watchman), and a whole host of other terms. Accustomed to social distinctions, some Americans expected to be addressed as "Mister" by the local labor force. Many Venezuelans complied, yet the term acquired a double meaning: besides a formal salutation, it also became a way of mocking offensive American behavior. The newspaper *Petróleo*, for example, often used the term "Mister" or *mistersito* to describe bigoted American supervisors.[76] English speakers also underwent adaptations, although their use of language often had pejorative connotations indicative of the power relations between Venezuelan workers and foreign bosses. Venezuelans particularly resented the term *muchacho* (boy), frequently used by foreigners to describe all Venezuelan adults. Writer Miguel Otero Silva, in his classic novel *Oficina N. 1*, argued that Venezuelans remained *muchachos* in the eyes of the Americans.[77]

Social, racial, and national distinctions found expression in the wage and salaries paid workers and employees. Companies such as Caribbean, Lago, and Standard maintained separate payrolls for their American, West Indian, and Venezuelan employees.[78] They utilized a monthly dollar salary for their American employees and a monthly bolívar payroll for the handful of semiskilled Venezuelans. Some Mexicans, unlike Venezuelans, who had worked with Americans in their home country, received payment in dollars.[79] Standard Oil also retained a monthly Trinidadian payroll to compensate West Indians. The majority of the Venezuelans employed by the company found themselves relegated to the daily bolívar roll. Beyond different pay classifications, the salary structures reflected an inequitable social-racial hierarchy that dictated the nature of interpersonal relations in the oil camps.[80]

The contentious intermediary position of the West Indians in this social/racial hierarchy was represented in early Venezuelan novels that depict conditions in the oil fields.[81] *Mene* by Ramón Díaz Sánchez and *Guachimanes* by Bracho Montiel provide sympathetic portrayals of the ostracized Trinidadians, without family and friends, enduring racism because of the color of their skin. Díaz Sánchez's novel narrated the story of one Trinidadian man, Enguerran Narcisus Philibert, who, stricken by stomach ailments, mistakenly used a "whites only" restroom. After being reprimanded by the American boss, he lost his job and was placed on the infamous blacklist that many companies kept to exclude previously discharged employees, potential labor agitators, or leftists. Denied employment in all the fields along the eastern lakeshore, and refusing to return to Trinidad in disgrace, he took his own life by jumping into the oily waters of Lake Maracaibo.[82] Incidents of Chinese confronting similar conditions and resorting to suicide, though less frequent, still occurred.[83]

The Numbers Game

The actual number of West Indians or Chinese employed by the oil companies proved difficult to ascertain. Companies submitted regular reports to the Ministerio de Fomento that, among other things, indicated the number of foreigners they employed. Yet, these communications loosely categorized employees as *extranjeros* (foreigners) and Venezolanos, without distinguishing their nationality. Prior to the discovery at La Rosa, a 1922 notice from Caribbean Petroleum, a major subsidiary of Shell, simply indicated that in the month of October it employed 243 foreigners and 1,033 Venezuelans.[84] Likewise, a 1939 Lago Petroleum document indicated a generic classification of 268 foreigners and 3,119 Venezuelans.[85]

Luis F. Calvani, a critic of the foreign oil companies, sharply condemned their reporting practices, alleging that these concealed the actual conditions that Venezuelans confronted. According to Calvani, Caribbean's 1926 report indicating 3,337 Venezuelans and 1,233 foreigners and Gulf Oil's claim of employing 3,323 Venezuelans and 742 foreigners intentionally obscured the status of the local workers. It gave the impression that together both companies employed 6,660 Venezuelans. Calvani asserted that of the "6,600 Venezuelans that appear as employees only 2 percent, at most, are actually in staff positions, while 98 percent serve as simple laborers who receive a daily wage."

Placing West Indians under the general category of "British Citizens" also biased company reports and prevented an adequate count. This practice also skewed some early Venezuelan censuses that recorded them in the same manner. Payroll records, where available, provide greater insights into the number of West Indians, Venezuelans, and other foreigners employed by any particular company. Internal documents from Standard Oil Company of Venezuela (SOCV) shed some light on the actual number of West Indians employed. In January 1933, for example, SOCV had 2,427 people on its payroll. Of that number, Venezuelans represented 1,924 (79 percent); British West Indians, 248 (10.2 percent); Americans, 141

(5.8 percent); and Chinese, 18 (0.7 percent). The remaining employees included other Latin Americans, a smattering of Germans, Spaniards, British, Poles, Italians, and French. By 1940 the numbers had changed significantly. In January of that year Standard employed 4,906 workers, including 4,406 (89.8 percent) Venezuelans, 397 (8 percent) Americans, 25 (0.5 percent) British West Indians, and only 7 Chinese (0.1 percent).[87] Again the remaining employees represented people from throughout Europe and Latin America.

SOCV Employee Reports, 1933 and 1940

	January 1933	January 1940
Venezuelans	1,924 (79%)	4,406 (89%)
British West Indians	248 (10.2%)	25 (0.5%)
Americans	141 (5.8%)	397 (8%)
Chinese	18 (0.7%)	7 (0.1%)
Others	96 (4.3%)	71 (1.5%)
Total	**2,427 (100%)**	**4,906 (100%)**

In the early phase of oil production, dozens of companies operated in Venezuela. Standard's employment practices do not represent the entire industry. Some companies maintained higher or lower percentages of West Indian and Chinese employees. Yet the SOCV numbers indicate that West Indians had a significant presence in the initial phase of the oil industry followed by a gradual and steady decline throughout the decade of the 1930s. This tendency reflects the growing pressure on the part of the Venezuelan labor movement and the government to raise the local employment rate. The figures also underscore the increasing role that Americans played in the management of the day-to-day operations of the company.[88]

Labor organizers and a host of social critics insisted that oil company policies exacerbated tensions between Venezuelan, Afro-Caribbean, and Asian workers.[89] During the late 1920s, when some companies reduced their labor force, they kept foreigners and dismissed Venezuelans who performed similar tasks. Once again, the companies argued that Chinese and West Indians possessed "greater skills" than Venezuelans. In 1927, Lago Petroleum discharged several dozen Venezuelan *sirvientes* (servants) at Cabimas and Lagunillas while retaining their Chinese counterparts. Lago insisted it kept the Chinese laborers since they were "specialists" in their fields and felt no obligation to provide severance pay to the Venezuelans.[90] The same month, when Venezuelan Oil Concessions (VOC) removed twenty-one "servants, including cooks, kitchen helpers, and dishwashers," it contradicted Lago's assertions. VOC contended that they "had only used the services of Chinese as cooks or kitchen helpers and other inferior positions and never in important posts."[91]

Despite being pitted against each other, Venezuelans and West Indians confronted similar discriminatory conditions of employment, and occasionally examples of labor solidarity surfaced. Joseph Nesfield, described by VOC officials as an *antillano de color*, signed petitions circulated by Venezuelan workers protesting their dismissal.[92] Workers sent complaints to Zulia state officials and forwarded petitions to President Juan Vicente Gómez, who then ordered an investigation into the matter.[93] Other Trinidadians also joined the incipient labor movement with their Venezuelan counterparts. Francisco Sotillo, for example, became an important organizer for the Sociedad de Auxilio Mutuo de Obreros, founded in 1933 under the direction of Rodolfo Quintero.[94]

Opportunistic politicians exploited racial and cultural differences between Afro-Caribbean, Asian, and local labor. The nascent middle class pressured the government for access to the staff positions held by some West Indians. Although Venezuela had openly promoted immigration to increase its population, it had always viewed blacks and Asians with suspicion. The federal constitution and numerous proclamations from the Ministry of the Interior specifically prohibited the immigration of "blacks and Asians to national territory." Pedro Arcaya, who served as minister of the interior in 1930, reported that "under the pretext of labor shortages, (the oil companies) seek to flood our communities and above all the oil-producing region with inadmissible individuals brought from the Antilles, thereby increasing the number of our ethnic groups and complicating our population question."[95] While professing that Venezuela remained open to all immigrants, Arcaya underscored the ideal that newcomers must represent a race that "increases our physical, intellectual, and moral standing." He added: "numerical increase without selection retards progress."[96] Arcaya reported to Gómez that his office exercised constant vigilance to ensure that "blacks and Asians would not enter the national territory." Some scholars asserted that Venezuelan policy was not overtly racist, but rather reflected broader social and cultural concerns.[97]

Race and culture in this context, however, appeared largely indistinguishable. Despite popular representations that defined the nation's racial heritage as *café con leche* (coffee with milk), the reality was that the Venezuelan elite had historically expressed a disdain for people of color.[98] Intellectuals such as Alberto Adriani warned of the dangers of "colored immigration" and cited the need to "whiten Venezuela."[99] These racial beliefs pervaded cultural attitudes and found expression throughout Venezuelan society, government policy, and popular literature. While reporting on the progress of Maracaibo's aqueduct, engineer Pedro José Rojas addressed the issue of West Indians in the lake region. Dismissing the issue of race, Rojas complained about purported West Indian "religious prejudices and depraved private customs . . . where in the Antilles they form cults and commit mysterious crimes. In Cuba they sacrifice young and robust whites to save the lives of old, wretched, and ailing blacks."[100] Alleging that already, young white children had begun to disappear in Maracaibo, Rojas encouraged authorities to take action. His view resonated with others who thought West Indians represented an indistinguishable black mass prepared to absorb Venezuelan society. Beyond concerns about West Indians, these arguments reflected historic apprehensions about the sizable Afro-Venezuelan population and their influence on the country's culture.

As in other areas of Latin America, Asians did not escape the increasingly antiforeign sentiment and polarized racial climate in Venezuela. Politicians and newspapers assiduously noted the increased role of Chinese in commerce. Maracaibo's daily, *Panorama*, berated the gains they had made since their arrival in the country. It reported that "the evolution or metamorphosis of these silent yellow men known as Chinese appeared notable. Previously, the children of the Celestial Republic had been defined only as laundrymen . . . now they have abandoned their irons and have installed themselves behind counters and bars as if they were in Peking."[101] This criticism resurfaced wherever Chinese managed to make inroads in commerce and competition intensified for the growing consumer market.

Conditions for foreigners (non-American or non-British) worsened, and in 1929 the government officially ordered the expulsion of all Afro-Caribbeans and Chinese. It warned about the racial dangers posed by the presence of too many blacks and Asians in Venezuela. The *London Times* reported: "The President of Venezuela has decided forthwith to prohibit coloured immigration into Venezuela, even when immigrants are provided with passports. Coloured foreigners already domiciled in the country are obliged to carry a certificate from local authorities. The decision will have a serious effect on the regular flow of West Indian immigrants to the Venezuelan oil fields."[102]

Several factors influenced the government's decisions on this issue. As the boom era of petroleum exploration concluded, most companies curtailed their labor force, thus increasing competition for employment. The Gómez administration had received numerous complaints from Venezuelan workers, and the nascent middle class remained gravely concerned about the role of foreigners in the oil industry.[103] Since 1925, labor had been flexing its muscle and several strikes had erupted throughout the oil camps that dotted Lake Maracaibo.[104] Rather than address labor's demands for wages and improved conditions, the government sought expedient political solutions. With the expulsion of the Afro-Caribbean and Asian population the government hoped to defuse the mounting pressure it confronted from workers and other groups.

In practical terms, the government edict forced the West Indians and Chinese to request certificates of employment and good conduct from oil company officials and local *jefes civiles* in order to travel or seek a job. State officials requested that Lago Petroleum and other companies gather information about "undesirable aliens" in their employ.[105] In practice, even before the presidential proclamation, West Indians and Chinese had already begun to comply by requesting such documents. The state historical archives in Zulia contained hundreds of these petitions. Joseph Sylvan, for example, sought and received a certificate of good conduct from the *jefe civil* of Lagunillas in July 1929.[106] Chan Fai carried credentials provided by Caribbean Petroleum attesting to his honesty and good character.[107] A. Thompson, a native of Trinidad, retained a letter indicating that Caribbean Petroleum employed him as a typist.[108] To avoid confusion, whenever Caribbean Petroleum hired white Dutch or British employees living in Curaçao or Trinidad, they also provided authentication that indicated that these individuals belonged to the "white race and possessed Dutch or British citizenship."[109]

Neither the need to carry certificates nor the prohibition against immigration deterred West Indians. The application of presidential mandates by state and local governments varied considerably. Moreover, many officials did not consider West Indians as immigrants but rather temporary laborers who would return to their homeland once their employment ceased. Motivated either by monetary gain or pressured by the oil companies, government officials continued to approve requests by West Indians seeking work. In June 1929, Luis Lampp, a Trinidadian employed as a carpenter, requested and received permission from Governor Pérez Soto to have a friend join him in Maracaibo.[110]

The enactment of the new repressive regulations continued to fuel anti-West Indian sentiment. A headline in *Panorama* in August 1936 proclaimed "El Peligro Negro" (The Black Threat). The unnamed author of the article lamented the number of "Antilles blacks who daily obtained (Venezuelan) citizenship as if it was a bond issued at a stock market." If the government did not put an end to this practice, the author believed, Venezuelan identity (*venezolanidad*) would soon be extinguished.[111] Not all Venezuelans supported the government's actions against West Indians. The leftist paper *Petróleo* railed against this scapegoating and rebuked *Panorama*'s headlines insisting that the "danger was not black, the danger was white." According to *Petróleo*, Venezuelans did not fear Afro-Caribbean or Chinese workers, but rather the "white imperialist *musiúes* that exploit native workers and workers from throughout the world. . . . Imperialism and its national allies are our principal enemy."[112]

Many Venezuelans also rebuked the public campaign against the West Indians, even while demanding that oil companies should hire more locals in staff positions. Nonetheless, when confronted by ill treatment, workers expressed their dissatisfaction. In May 1936 over 2,000 laborers staged public demonstrations to protest against mistreatment by a West

Indian and a Mexican supervisor.[113] The protest reflected the deep-seated resentment building among Venezuelan workers against abuses by foreign bosses. Yet Venezuelans also took action to defend foreigners who they believed had been harassed by the oil companies. When Lago Petroleum attempted to replace a Trinidadian supervisor in the transportation department with a Venezuelan, laborers protested and defended the West Indian. In January 1947 the *Maracaibo Herald* reported that laborers at Mene Grande also demanded the reinstatement of Vern Goldstein, an American boilermaker, asserting that he belonged to their union.[114] According to one newspaper, Venezuelans cared more about the treatment they received than about making "racial distinctions between Chinese, Japanese," or West Indians.[115]

Conclusion

Beyond economic consequences, oil transformed the Venezuelan cultural and political landscape. The conditions of work in the oil industry brought Venezuelans from different regions into contact with each other. As thousands of these people congregated in the oil camps and interacted with one another, a distinct national identity gradually emerged. The oil camp created a new social environment for workers who previously had functioned within a local frame of reference rooted largely in provincial regional experiences. As they stepped out of their previous frame of reference, they also grappled with the contradictions of a national industry in which international interests played a predominant role. Regional distinctions, although important, took a back seat to the common political and social demands affecting all Venezuelans. Moreover, opposition to the privileges afforded foreigners united Venezuelans from various social classes and provided new common ground for political action.

Work in the oil fields between 1920 and 1940 reflected a complex racial division of labor, where Americans, Dutch, and British monopolized most managerial positions. In some cases, foreigners carried out the actual drilling operations and directed a large Venezuelan force employed predominately as day laborers. West Indians held secretarial or administrative positions, while others held higher-paying skilled occupations. Asians found themselves relegated to relatively menial positions or sought new opportunities in commerce. West Indians and Chinese played a significant, if unheralded, role in the development of the early oil industry in Venezuela. Their presence underscores the role that transnational corporations play in dislocating population groups and spawning immigration throughout the Third World. Confronted by a near-total foreign monopoly over their principal natural resource, many Venezuelans indiscriminately lashed out against the West Indians. Oil company policy only served to exacerbate these conditions. Yet, despite company actions, government scapegoating, and distinct language and cultural differences, Trinidadians, Curaçaolenes, Grenadians, Chinese, and Venezuelans developed bonds that endure to this day.

Notes

1. "Biggest Oil Well Yet," *New York Times*, March 18, 1923.
2. A. Shero, interview with author, Creole Annuitants Reunion, May 1999.
3. María D. González Ripoll Navarro, *Trinidad: la otra llave de América* (Caracas: Cuadernos Lagoven, 1992).
4. José Alberto Figueroa, "Historia Pre-Petrolera de Caripito, Una Contribución a su estudio" (Tesis de Maestría, Universidad Santa María, 1988), 79.
5. Angelina Pollak Eltz, *La negritud en Venezuela* (Caracas: Cuadernos Lagoven, 1991), 85.
6. See Charles Gordon, "Effects of Underdevelopment on Migration from Trinidad and Tobago to the U.S." (Ph.D. diss., Howard University, 1984), 17–18. See also Gordon K. Lewis, *The Growth of the Modern West Indies* (New York: Modern Reader, 1968), 201; Eric Williams, *From Columbus to Castro* (New York: Vintage, 1970), 348.
7. Susan Berglund, "Las bases sociales y económicas de las leyes de inmigración venezolanas, 1831–1935," *Boletín de la Academia Nacional de la Historia* 260 (Oct.–Dic. 1982): 953.
8. Jonathan Leonard, *Men of Maracaibo* (New York: G. P. Putnam and Sons, 1933), 215.
9. Standard Oil Company of New Jersey, agenda for Spring Conference, "Training of Native Employees for Skilled and Semi-skilled Positions," Seaview Golf Club, Absecon, New Jersey, 1937.
10. Ibid.
11. Judith Ewell, *Venezuela and the United States: From Monroe's Hemisphere to Petroleum's Empire* (Athens: University of Georgia Press, 1996), 135.
12. *Nosotros*, Octubre de 1956.
13. See *Petróleo*, 29 de abril, 1936, Letter signed by directors of Caribbean, Lago, and Gulf.
14. *Petróleo*, 30 de mayo, 1936.
15. Amuay, *25 años en la historia de una refinería* (Caracas: Creole Petroleum Corporation, 1975), 25; *Nosotros*, septiembre de 1955.
16. *Nosotros*, octubre de 1957.
17. *Nosotros*, abril de 1954.
18. *Nosotros*, marzo de 1949.
19. *Nosotros*, octubre de 1957.
20. Ibid.
21. Myriane Marret (Woolen camp resident), interview with author, May 28, 1999.
22. See Una Lawrence, *Cuba for Christ* (Atlanta: Southern Baptist Convention, 1926), 100.
23. Mary George, *A Is for Abrazo* (Caracas: VAAUW, 1961), 44.
24. Archivo Histórico de Miraflores (hereafter AHM), Caja E39:15.2, Comisión de la Oficina Central de Coordinación y Planificación, 7 de octubre, 1959.
25. Archivo Histórico del Estado de Zulia (hereafter AHZ), 1929, Tomo 16, Legajo 16 y 18, 1929: 5 de junio, 1929; 12 de julio, 1929, Recommendations.

26. Anne Rainey Langley, "I Kept House in a Jungle," *National Geographic* (February 1939): 97.

27. Standard Oil Company of Venezuela, January1932, "Manager's Review," H.E. Linan, Acting Manager.

28. *Caracas Journal*, January 10, 1949.

29. George, *A Is for Abrazo.*

30. Henry J. Allen, *Venezuela, A Democracy* (New York: Doubleday, 1941), 245.

31. Angel Kingland, interview with author, June 21, 1997.

32. AHZ, 1929, Tomo 11, Legajo 30: 9 de septiembre, 1929, Caribbean a Secretario de Estado.

33. AHZ, 1927, Tomo 11, Legajo 30: 17 de septiembre, 1929, Cartas de recomendación, Caribbean, San Lorenzo.

34. Isabel Story, camp resident, interview with author, Caracas, November 11, 1997.

35. AHZ, 1929, Tomo 16, Legajo 16–18, 1929: Cabimas, jefe civil, 11 de junio, 1929, 13 de junio, 1929 (names are given as they appear in the original document).

36. See *El Condor*, Lagunillas, 10 de diciembre, 1933; *El Escudo*, Lagunillas, 5 de julio, 1929. Also *Suplemento de la Guia Industrial y Comercial, 1943* (Caracas: Lit. y Tip. Vargas, 1944), 57.

37. Ibid., 243–53.

38. AHM, Caja E39, 15.2: Comisión de la Oficina Central de Coordinación y Planificación, 7 de octubre, 1959.

39. Lago Petroleum Corporation, "Report of Operations," and Standard Oil Company, "Report of Operations," several years, 1930–1940.

40. AHZ, 1928, Tomo 3, Legajo 2: 13 de septiembre, 1928, A la Secretaría General del Estado de Zulia.

41. Thomas Rourke, *Gómez, Tyrant of the Andes* (New York: William Morrow, 1941), 239.

42. For the shift between Mexico and Venezuela see Jonathan C. Brown, "Why Foreign. Oil Companies Shifted Their Production from Mexico to Venezuela," *American Historical Review* 90 (April 1985): 380.

43. AHM, #442-C, 27 de diciembre, 1922: Pedro Arcaya to Gómez.

44. "La Ruptura con México," *Paz y Trabajo*, 3 de noviembre, 1923.

45. See "Mexico Arraigned in Diplomats' Snarl," *New York Times*, October 6, 1923; "Mexico and Venezuela," *Washington Post*, November 20, 1923.

46. Aurelio de Vivanco y Villegas, *Venezuela al día. Venezuela Up to Date* (Caracas: Imprenta Bolívar, 1928 [Bilingual Edition]), 1033.

47. "La Ruptura con México."

48. AHZ, 1928, Tomo 3, Legajo 2: 13 de diciembre, 1928, Prohibición a la entrada de mexicanos a Venezuela por ser nacionales de un país enemigo a Venezuela.

49. Edgar Campos, interview with author, Maracaibo, October 1997.

50. José Antonio Sarache and José Omar Colmenares, interviews with author, Mérida, respectively, July 13, 1991, October 1997. Sarache worked at Cabimas and Colmenares at Mene Grande.

51. Caracas, Venezuelan Motion Picture Report, Maurice Bernbaum, United States National Archives, *Consular Trade Reports*, 1943–1950, M238, Reel 137, July 14, 1943.

52. Antonio J. Briceño Parilli, *Las migraciones internas y los municipios petroleros* (Caracas: Corporación Venezolana de Fomento, 1947), 34.

53. John Lavin, *A Halo for Gómez* (New York: Pageant Press, 1954), 304.

54. Ibid., 303.

55. Jesús Prieto Soto, *El Chorro, Gracia o maldición* (Maracaibo: Universidad de Zulia, 1962), 105.

56. *El Bronce*, Lagunillas, 20 de agosto, 1932. The newspaper lamented the bad quality and content of the foreign films.

57. Lavin, *Halo for Gómez*, 305.

58. J. A. Colina Nava, *Sucesos históricos sobre Cabimas v Lagunillas hasta 1938* (Maracaibo: Tipografía Cervantes, 1965), 12. Also see Prieto Soto, *El Chorro*, 105.

59. "Corito," *El Taladro*, 9 de junio, 1934.

60. *Diario de Occidente*, 2 de agosto, 1951. Also see Ramón Diaz Sánchez, *Mene* (Buenos Aires: Editorial Universitaria, 1966), 96.

61. *El Farol*, junio de 1942. The team included Rufus Raymond, G. Pinder, S. Joseph, Gordon Wildman, Ulrich Massiah, Claudio William, Alfredo Murray, Errol Charles, Juan Dixon, Ulrich Attale, and Mauricio John.

62. Rodolfo Quintero, *La cultura del petróleo* (Caracas: Universidad Central de Venezuela, 1985), 51. Quintero refers to the creation of the "hombre Shell" and the "hombre Creole" as prototypes of this process.

63. *Hallacas* resemble tamales wrapped in banana leaves. *Aguinaldos* are holiday tunes.

64. *El Diario de Caracas*, 30 de diciembre, 1992.

65. *Nosotros*, octubre de 1956.

66. Ibid.

67. *Nosotros*, enero de 1961.

68. *Nosotros*, diciembre de 1954.

69. See *Petróleo*, 7 de octubre, 1936. Company policy may have contributed to the increased naturalization, since after 1936 it required many West Indians to become Venezuelan citizens in order to retain their jobs.

70. *Nosotros*, octubre de 1957.

71. Quintero, *La cultura del petróleo*, 36.

72. Ewell, *Venezuela and the United States*, 135.

73. Charles Bergquist, *Labor in Latin America: Comparative Essays on Chile, Argentina, Venezuela, and Colombia* (Stanford: Stanford University Press, 1986), 218. Also see Díaz Sánchez, *Mene*, 95; Quintero, *La cultura del petróleo*, 38.

74. Luis F. Calvani, *Nuestro máximo problema* (Caracas: Editorial Grafolit, 1940), 24.

75. G. Bracho Montiel, *Guachimanes: Doce aguafuertes para ilustrar la novela del petróleo* (Santiago: Francisco Javier, 1954), 15.

76. "Otro mister indeseable," *Petróleo*, 27 de febrero, 1937.

77. Miguel Otero Silva, *Oficina N. 1* (Buenos Aires: Editorial Losada, 1961); also George, *A Is for Abrazo*, 33.

78. See *Petróleo*, 29 de abril, 1936.

79. Lago Petroleum Corporation, "Report of Operations," and Standard Oil Company, "Report of Operations," several years, 1930–1940.

80. Standard Oil Company of Venezuela, "Statement of Payrolls, February 1933," in *Petroleum Engineering Report, January–June 1933*. Also see Standard Oil Company of Venezuela, *Petroleum Engineering Report* (January 1941), 4.

81. Otero Silva, *Oficina N. 1*.

82. Díaz Sánchez, *Mene*, 98–104.

83. "Un chino se ahorca," *El Taladro*, Cabimas, 2 de junio, 1934

84. Ministerio de Fomento, *Memoria* (Caracas: Tip. Cosmos, 1923), 19 de abril, 1923.

85. Lago Petroleum Corporation, "Monthly Operating Report, January 1939."

86. Calvani, *Problema*, 27.

87. Standard Oil Company of Venezuela, *Monthly Operating Report*, January–June 1933, February 1940.

88. After the Great Depression, the actual number of Americans employed in the oil industry declined.

89. *Petróleo*, 7 de octubre, 1936.

90. AHZ, 1927, Tomo 4, Legajo 28, 2 de mayo, 1927, Lago a V. P. Soto.

91. AHZ, 1927, Tomo 4, Legajo 28, 3 de mayo, 1927, VOC: G. Witteven a Secretario de Gobierno.

92. Ibid.

93. AHZ, 1927, Tomo 4, Legajo 28, 5 de mayo, 1927: Obreros despedidos a J. V. Gómez.

94. Paul Nehru Tennassee, *Venezuela, los obreros petroleros y la lucha por la democracia* (Caracas: Editorial Popular, 1979), 153.

95. Pedro Arcaya, *Memoria. Ministro de Relaciones Interiores* (Caracas: Lito del Comercio, 1930), xv.

96. Ibid., xv, xvi.

97. Berglund, "Las bases sociales," 954.

98. See Winthrop Wright, *Café con Leche: Race, Class, and National Image in Venezuela* (Austin: University of Texas Press, 1990); Marvin Lewis, *Ethnicity and Identity in Contemporary Afro-Venezuelan Literature* (Columbia: University of Missouri Press, 1992).

99. Ermila Troconis de Veracoechea, *El proceso de la inmigración en Venezuela* (Caracas: Academia Nacional de Historia, 1986), 217.

100. AHM, 16 -1:7-2, 23 de abril, 1926, Ing. Civil Pedro José Rojas to Gómez, "Report Maracaibo Aqueduct."

101. "Chinos," *Panorama*, 13 de enero, 1931.

102. "Coloured Immigration to Venezuela," *London Times*, November 2, 1929.

103. AHZ, 1927, Tomo 4, Legajo 28, 5 de mayo, 1927: Obreros despedidos a J. V. Gómez.

104. Tennassee, *Venezuela*, 135.

105. Lago Petroleum, *Report of Operations*, Land and Legal Department, January 1930.

106. AHZ, Tomo 16, Legajo 16 y 18, 1929: jefe civil, Lagunillas, 10 de julio, 1929.

107. AHZ, Tomo 11, Legajo 30, 9 de septiembre, 1929: Caribbean to Secretarío de Estado.

108. AHZ, Tomo 16, Legajo 16 y 18, 1929: Caribbean, 28 de marzo, 1929.

109. AHZ, Tomo 1, Legajo 4, 1930: Caribbean Petroleum, 17 de noviembre, 1930.

110. AHZ, Tomo 16, Legajo 16 y 18, 1929, 12 de junio, 1929: Luis Lampp a Soto, Pres. Zulia.

111. "El Peligro Negro," *Panorama*, 27 de agosto, 1936.

112. *Petróleo*, 29 de agosto, 1936.

113. Ibid.

114. *Maracaibo Herald*, 18 de enero, 1947.

115. *Petróleo*, 16 de mayo, 1936.

8

Women and the Right to (Needle)Work in Puerto Rico

María del Carmen Baerga

In large part because of Puerto Rico's special status as a commonwealth of the United States—neither state nor colony—its workers have faced many difficulties when they demanded their rights. They sought to gain them in an organized way throughout the twentieth century. It would be easy to slough off the failure to organize Puerto Rican workers by arguing that it has been due to the opposition of the American businesses located there, the U.S. government, and its stepchild, the Commonwealth government. But María del Carmen Baerga refuses to accept that tired canard. In this selection she looks carefully at the conditions of labor on the island to try to assess the failure of the movement. One factor that interests her above others is the cultural meaning of gender. In earlier selections in this volume, gender was a divisive issue in twentieth-century working-class life. Here, rather than addressing it as a community or class issue, Baerga examines the gendered perceptions of different sectors of the garment industry by labor organizers themselves. Hers is an effort to understand how conditions within the working class undermined the successful organization of the female needleworkers in the years before World War II. What is revealing is the agonized position of women on both sides of the organizing issue, and how each group defined themselves as workers.

The collective action of the needleworkers is a topic that has received little attention in Puerto Rican historiography. Most of the research on the needlework industry[1] treats the theme only tangentially, since the focus has been upon the productive structure of the industry and the prevailing working conditions.[2] Other studies concern the participation of women in the labor movement.[3] These studies use union membership and participation in strikes as indicators of women's collective action. Since needleworkers were most often not union members and did not take part widely in strikes, these authors conclude that women were not frequently involved in collective action. They argue that women working at home could not easily share their experiences with other workers in their same situation, thus hindering the development of the necessary class consciousness that would have promoted their involvement in the organized labor movement.

These traditional approaches to the study of women's collective action have failed to consider that different production processes and variations in the household division of labor may produce different kinds of collective action, among them unionization and strikes. Since proletarianization was not an entirely homogeneous process in Puerto Rico, there is no reason to believe that resistance and collective action took only one form—the organized labor movement. Indeed, Louise Tilly has argued that both the organization of production and the household division of labor are fundamental factors in the shaping of different manifestations of collective action.[4] However, none of these factors—the organization of production, the household division of labor, or unionization—was a gender-neutral process. Therefore, to understand the possibilities and patterns of collective action among needleworkers in Puerto Rico, it is necessary to consider how the organization of the needlework industry resulted in the formation of workers with different interests who therefore responded to the call for unionization in different ways. In addition, gender hierarchies were clearly evident in the organization of the unions, which often turned a deaf ear to the particular interests of the female homeworkers.

Indeed, the needleworkers were not homogeneous members of the working class, which was itself divided by differences in the labor process, domestic responsibilities, life cycle, region (urban vs. rural), and, of course, gender. These differences were crucial for the articulation of their particular interests and resulted in very divergent struggles at times. On the one hand, the factory needleworkers joined the union—the Free Federation of Labor—and united in their struggles with the organized male workers. They were all interested principally in higher wages and better working conditions. On the other hand, homeworkers were often at odds with the organized labor movement, which advocated the abolition of homework. The homeworkers engaged in a struggle for the right to work at home, even while confronting the lowest wages and the poorest working conditions. The union offered little to the homeworkers and did not reflect their interests. It was for this reason, and not any lack of class-consciousness, that the homeworkers did not respond to—and even frequently opposed—the efforts of both female factory workers and skilled male workers to organize them.

Unionization of the Needleworkers: Factory Workers
Respond to the Complexities of Daily Life

Notwithstanding sparse bursts of strike activity in a few embroidery factories, there is little evidence in the historical record of collective action undertaken by needleworkers prior to 1930. In 1919 the Puerto Rican Department of Labor reported that up to that moment no protests had taken place in the needlework factories.[5] Likewise, in 1928 the department reported that the workers "continued in complete disorganization," without initiating the "redeeming task" of unionization.[6] This picture began to change drastically during the early 1930s, when the Free Federation of Labor began for the first time to seriously attempt to organize the needleworkers.[7]

The Free Federation of Labor considered collective actions in the ideological and material realm as the principal tool for the advancement of the working class. However, the struggles for social or protective legislation were seen as appropriate to remedy only those problems of the "working masses" that resulted from their disorganization and weakness. This distinction was established by Santiago Iglesias Pantín in a congress of the Free Federation: "For ten years we workers have asked the legislature of Puerto Rico for that which this body can concede and for that which cannot be obtained in any other way given the conditions of the working masses of Puerto Rico. The organized workers have not sought in the legislature or the government those remedies that they can apply and fulfill presently through their own initiatives and activities."[8]

According to Iglesias Pantín, the Federation's founder, workers had resorted to the legislature or the government only in those particular cases in which they could not secure their objectives through their own means, for example, through collective bargaining. In other words, protective legislation was pushed in those cases in which the workers themselves could not successfully carry out their struggle.

A similar view was expressed by Samuel Gompers, the president of the American Federation of Labor, during a trip to Puerto Rico in 1914. In discussing minimum wage for all working people, a piece of legislation that the Free Federation of Labor had advocated since its foundation, the local labor leaders asked Gompers's assistance in elucidating the matter. His opposition was categorical:

> Among the declarations for which my assistance was urged was one demanding for the Porto Rican legislature the enactment of a law providing for a minimum wage for all working people. In my address there I attacked the soundness and the wisdom of such a demand. . . . I stated that a minimum wage for governmental employees was justified, as in that case the government was the employer, but workers in private employment must depend upon the intelligence, the energy, and the solidarity of the organization of wage-workers. Progress is a matter of manhood, character, persistence, and determination for a better standard of life and higher ideals. After the conclusion of the interpretation of my answer, the resolution was dropped from the demands of the Porto Rican Federation.[9]

According to Gompers, real men advanced the cause of labor by relying on their organizational capabilities and their class solidarities. To expect relief from the legislature or the government was considered a sign of weakness and lack of manhood.

Interestingly enough, even though the Free Federation dropped the demand for the establishment of a general minimum wage in 1914, as Samuel Gompers had argued they should, it did not do so in the particular case of women. In 1919 the Free Federation succeeded in its effort to set a minimum wage for women although the law was quickly challenged in the courts by the employers. In fact, for years the union challenged various court decisions that reversed the 1919 minimum wage law for women.[10]

The Free Federation of Labor always pursued a policy of protective legislation for those whom they considered ignorant and unorganizable, such as young women, women from the countryside, and peasants, or those who they thought should not be in the work force, such as children, the elderly, women with children, and the infirm. Among the pieces of protective legislation that the Free Federation consistently advocated through the years were the creation of safe and comfortable houses in working-class neighborhoods; the creation of farms, with technical instruction and the provision of animals, tools, seeds, and credit for landless peasants; a state-sponsored insurance system for workers and their families against work-related accidents and deaths; a law to provide safe scaffolds and platforms for workers; and the regulation of the employment of women and children.[11] Other measures were strongly advocated in the 1930s, such as the regulation and eventual elimination of industrial homework, pensions for widowed mothers with small children, and pensions for the elderly.[12] As can be seen, most of these measures were directed to women, children, the incapacitated and their dependents, and the elderly.

Notwithstanding multiple petitions from the rank and file to organize women, the Free Federation of Labor never devoted the necessary resources to addressing these claims. With the exception of the tobacco strippers in the 1910s and the needleworkers in the 1930s, there were few organizational efforts geared toward women workers on the part of the Free Federation. In the case of the tobacco strippers, their organization was the result of the threat felt by the cigar makers who feared the intrusion of women into a male-defined trade. This stance was clearly expressed in 1913, during a cigar makers' union congress: "Women and children are employed by the manufacturers in Puerto Rico in the processing and preparation of the materials used in the making of handmade cigars, in conflict with the best interests of the adult male workers, professionals of their trade, and contrary to the most delicate impulses of sentiment and respect for humanity."[13]

Faced with an imminent danger, the cigar makers deployed the weapon of organization to control the entrance of women into "their" industry:

"Since it is impossible to impede completely the access of women into the industry, we should adopt easy and practical solutions in order to organize them in all the centers where they are working, and to impede, as far as possible, the growth in the number of women in the cigar industry in Puerto Rico."[14]

In the case of the needleworkers, organization stemmed also from the interests of male workers in general, who sought to increase their bargaining power through the elimination of industrial homework and the subsequent retirement of women from the ranks of the wage labor force. While in the 1910s the concern of the organized workers had to do more with the entrance of women into male-dominated industries such as tobacco, the subsequent loss of control of the trade and diminished bargaining power, the situation in the 1930s was different. The precarious state of the economy had depressed the conditions of work for all laborers on the island. The problem was not so much how to limit the access of new recruits from different backgrounds to certain industries or occupations, but how to control the overabundance of workers in general. By the 1930s, employment in the skilled trades had greatly declined, and workers found more opportunities in unskilled occupations associated with sugar production and needlework. Both the general standard of living and the low wages in the different occupations were linked to high seasonal unemployment, especially among men. Thus, the organized workers' movement proposed a reduction in the number of people willing to work for wages, together with other social and economic measures, as a means to reconstruct the island's economy. For them, the best way to reduce male unemployment was to limit the employment of women and children through their organization in unions affiliated with the Free Federation of Labor.

This argument was embodied in a resolution presented in the 1934 labor congress sponsored by the Free Federation. The resolution argued that the rise in the employment of women meant that men were "being displaced in all occupations" and that the greater employment of women reflected the "employers' selfishness" because it reduced wages and allowed working conditions "that would be difficult to impose upon men." Because no important effort had been made to organize women, the resolution proposed that the Thirteenth Congress of the Free Federation of Labor resolve to begin a systematic campaign of organization among all employed women.[15]

Similarly, protective legislation was used to control unemployment among male workers. For example, the commission for the investigation of the consequences of unemployment on the island, presided over by labor leader and socialist representative Rafael Alonso Torres,[16] identified as one of the main causes of unemployment on the island the "employment of women and children in competition with the head of the family, who should pay for the urgent needs of the household."[17]

One of the subjects under study by the commission was precisely the issue of protective legislation for women and children. After reviewing some of the laws regarding women and children that had been under discussion in the legislature throughout the years, the commission concluded that "since the regulations are not strict, more that 200,000 women and children in the last fifteen years have replaced, without wanting to, many male heads of family in the field of industrial activities."[18]

Indeed, a critical analysis of the type of legislation that the Free Federation of Labor advocated for women and children throughout the years reveals a tendency toward securing the position of male workers in the work force. The legislation put forth was not only protective but also restrictive. It attempted to limit the types of occupations in which women and children could engage, while it sought to prohibit wage work for children and nocturnal work, overtime, and work during pregnancy for women.[19] Even though the labor movement emphasized the need for protective legislation for the well-being of the unorganized, for all intents and purposes protective legislation was a strategy to control the entrance and participation of these groups in the work force.

The extension of the National Industrial Recovery Act of 1933 to the island provided a great incentive for the organization of the needleworkers on the part of the Free Federation of Labor. This law provided for the formation of governing boards—composed of representatives of labor, business, and government—to develop codes of fair competition to guide and regulate business activity in the different industries.[20] The drafting of the codes gave the opportunity to the Free Federation to pursue the two aspects that concerned them the most regarding the needlework industry on the island: the establishment of a minimum wage and the elimination of industrial homework. In addition, it gave the Free Federation the opportunity to pursue these issues at the governmental level, an arena that they considered appropriate to deal with the "problems" of the "disorganized" segments of the working class.

The efforts exerted by the Free Federation of Labor to organize needleworkers yielded considerable fruits. By 1931, the First Needleworkers Union (Unión Número Uno de Trabajadoras de la Aguja) was founded in San Juan.[21] It was composed mainly of women in the factory owned by J. A. E. Rodríguez in Santurce.[22] This union was the result of the work of perhaps the most important labor leader among the factory needleworkers, Teresa Angleró.

Angleró took it upon herself to organize the needleworkers around the island. She began with the women in the big factories in the San Juan area. As noted, the first to organize were the workers at J. A. E. Rodríguez, where more than 500 women labored.[23] After that, the workers in the establishments devoted to the production of men's clothing, such as Miranda Hermanos, Catalán, González y Cia., M. Rodríguez y Cia., as well as those from big needlework companies, such as Morris Storyk, began the task of organizing.

On September 4, 1932, amid the celebrations of Labor Day on the island, the women convoked their First Insular Conference of Needleworkers (Primera Conferencia Insular de las Trabajadoras de la Aguja).[24] More than 200 delegates from various towns attended. The resolutions presented at the conference illustrate the concerns of the needleworkers in factories and explained their overwhelming response to the call for organization. The women who participated in the conference were all factory workers, and the most vocal ones were machine workers. As such, they were concerned with the competition that industrial homework presented for them. They passed their first resolution in support of a law prohibiting sewing in homes.

Plain sewing, as opposed to embroidery, became more generalized in the industry in the 1930s. Changes in the type of garments produced on the island made the industry more dependent on machine sewing.[25] Any plain sewing done at home, whether by hand or machine, competed directly with the work executed by the factory women, particularly with those employed in the bigger establishments. This point was clearly articulated by Teresa Angleró during the hearings held by the National Recovery Administration in 1934:

> Then with the outside workers [that is, homeworkers] we have great competition in all lines, in silk underwear, children's dresses and everywhere, and the competition is not only among contractors but it is also among the workers. The workers from inside the factory are having the competition of outside workers in all lines of work, and if we are in favor and are trying to take the home workers into the factory we cannot accept a minimum so low for the outside workers that it will destroy our plans and all our business.[26]

The conference also advocated the regulation of industrial homework, presumably for those who did embroidery. The low wages paid to the homeworkers exerted a downward pressure in the industry as a whole. Although everyone on the island knew that it was impossible to abolish homework at once, its regulation was thought to be a more realistic path toward its eventual elimination. By controlling wages and conditions of work through regulation, industrial homework would lose its attraction for the employers. These demands set the tone for the multiple struggles carried out by the factory workers in the 1930s, particularly during 1933 and 1934.

The First Insular Conference of Needleworkers of 1932 appointed an Insular Committee, presided over by Teresa Angleró, to lead the task of organizing the industry. According to the Free Federation of Labor, 75 percent of all workers in needlework factories were unionized by 1934.[27] This was no small accomplishment, taking into consideration that three years earlier there were no needleworkers unions on the island. In this environment of agitation and excitement, it is no small wonder that conflicts within the factories mushroomed.

Strikes and controversies erupted in various shops and factories around the island beginning in 1932. In May there was a strike in the town of Coamo, which involved 900 workers. During that same year the Mediation and Conciliation Office of the Department of Labor intervened in conflicts in San Juan, Arecibo, Sabana Grande, and Santa Isabel.[28] Most of these confrontations were related to salary increases, dismissed workers, and working conditions in general. Although there were instances— for example, the strike in Coamo—when a great number of workers was involved, most of the conflicts that took place in 1932 involved between fifteen and sixty workers. However, this picture began to change in 1933.

During that year, tensions in the industry reached a high point due, on the one hand, to the campaign of labor agitation orchestrated by the Free Federation of Labor and, on the other hand, to the beginning of negotiation of the codes of fair competition for the industry. On top of all this, many contractors, fearing the establishment of minimum wages, began to press the women to perform a greater quantity of work for the same or even lower wages and began to send more work to homeworkers.

Out of the thirty-three incidents reported by the Mediation and Conciliation Office of the Department of Labor between 1932 and 1934, twenty took place in 1933. Among the 1933 conflicts, eight took place in San Juan, two in Arecibo, two in Mayagüez, two in Ponce, two in Aguadilla, one in Adjuntas, one in Utuado, one in Yauco, and one in Lares. The profusion of conflicts in the San Juan area is explained by the fact that the factories there were the biggest and had the highest average number of workers per factory. In addition, the first recognized needleworkers unions were formed in these establishments.

The annual reports of the Department of Labor show that most of the strikes took place in the bigger establishments where a great deal of machine work was performed.[29] This was definitely the case in ready-made men's clothing, in which most of the work was done on industrial machines with a rather detailed division of labor. It was also the case at Morris Storyk, Esteva Vidal, Carlos Rosich, and Saab y Cia., known for their detailed division of labor, the generalized use of machinery, and the large size of their factories. The only exception was the Lande and Miskend firm, which depended heavily on handwork but which also reported considerable labor disputes during this period. This company, specializing in the production of silk underwear, could not send pieces to homeworkers because the fine fabric that they used could not be washed or reworked without losing its luster.[30] Thus, the needleworkers who were able to carry out collective action most successfully against their employers were those who worked in big factories with a detailed division of labor and industrial machinery. Due to the way the production process was organized, these women could not be replaced easily by homeworkers.

Home Needleworkers and Their Defense of Wage Work

Although it might seem at first sight that factory and industrial home-workers had more in common than not, in practice they never were able to forge a common bond. The issue that separated them was precisely the issue of industrial homework. Since the beginnings of the organizational drive, both the Free Federation of Labor and the Needleworkers Union talked about the need to organize the homeworkers. The leadership of the organized workers toured the whole island in an effort to reach all the women in the industry. While the response of the factory needleworkers was considerable, the reception of the homeworkers to the call of unionization was rather cold.

The most frequent explanation for the homeworkers' lack of interest in unionization is that sewing at home prevented them from sharing experiences with other workers in the same condition, thus hindering the development of a class consciousness.[31] However, the situation of the homeworkers was much more complex than that.

To begin with, women workers in general did not trust unions. The Free Federation of Labor was a masculine social space, created to advance the interests of the dominant segment of the working class, the so-called aristocracy of labor.[32] Organized male workers perceived the entrance of women and children into the wage labor force as a threat to their aspired privileged position, since they were seen as low-wage competition. The struggle of women workers during the first four decades of the twentieth century, in contrast, was centered around the issue of the right to work for a wage. These women perceived the attempts of the organized male workers to become gatekeepers of the labor market as a peril to their already precarious position in the labor force.

Felicia Boria, the director of the Bureau of Women and Children in Industry of the Puerto Rican Department of Labor, raised this point in a newspaper article. She stated: "The majority of the women that work still have a certain apathy and look jealously at the collective contracts, fearing the loss of their jobs, remembering the needs of their families, or because they do not have sufficient experience in the problems of collective organization."[33]

Women workers were skeptical of collective bargaining because their best interests were rarely taken into consideration. Furthermore, most of the claims of the organized men regarding women workers were couched in terms of "protective" legislation, which in practice meant "restrictive." Felicia Boria also brought up this point in the same article. She argued: "Another erroneous idea is a legacy of the Middle Ages. It is the repressive notion of chivalry that implies that a woman needs the protection of the man. But the result has been quite the opposite. A dual social and economic system with regard to wages, and the absence of real chivalry on the part of men, have been the more obvious consequences of that legacy. That same tradition has meant the unscrupulous exploitation by men of the vital energies of womanhood."[34]

In this very interesting commentary, the director of the Bureau of Women and Children in Industry questioned the traditional view of women as being in need of protection and criticized the exploitation of their capacity to conceive and bear children. In practice, the idea of the need to protect women was used to keep them in a subordinate position in the labor force. In this sense, the women's cold reception to the calls for unionization was not related precisely to the lack of class consciousness. The home needleworkers did not join the unions, but this did not mean that they did not have a deep understanding of their particular situation and that they did not struggle collectively to improve their conditions of life and work.

The homeworkers' difficulty in articulating a collective voice makes reconstructing their stances and struggles a challenge. This issue is an important one, because both commentators of the period and current social historians have interpreted the "absence" of homeworkers in the public debates regarding the garment industry during the 1920s and 1930s as lack of participation. This does not mean that they did not articulate their positions and the struggle to be heard. In fact, in the course of this investigation, many documents were found in the form of letters and telegrams sent to the local press, government authorities, and even the president of the United States, in which the homeworkers from different towns stated their positions as a group regarding the issue of industrial homework. However, these expressions were not formally considered in the public debates taking place at the time. In other words, they were not "heard."

Homeworkers did, in fact, voice their positions in public gatherings. For example, a group of needleworkers from Mayagüez asked to speak at a public hearing celebrated in San Juan by the National Industrial Recovery Administration regarding the codes of fair competition for the needlework industry. During the hearing they stated the position of the group that they represented regarding industrial homework. This position differed from the one voiced by the representatives of organized labor in the same hearing. For example, Carlota Goyco, a homeworker from the district of Rosario on the western part of the island, defended their right to work at home in the following terms:

> I come in representation of the workers of the district of Rosario, to inform you that it is impossible for us to come to the factories—we have to work in our homes. We live in a rural district that unfortunately has no means of communication. To come from here to Mayaguez [*sic*]

we have to go on foot, and when sick in a hammock. We do not come to do harm to anybody. I merely come to explain that we cannot live without work in the home. Let us see, I am a country woman who has a little house—I cannot sell it to go to Mayaguez. Those who have a little plot of ground would have to sell it or abandon it in order to go to Mayaguez, and those who have agricultural work would have to leave it, and then the agriculture would fail. . . . We need help—even though we live in the mountains, we are Puerto Ricans just as you are and we need to work just as you do. Therefore, I am utterly opposed to the abolition of home work. It is an absolute necessity. The country women need it and there must be justice for all. I am a poor widow.[35]

Carlota felt strongly enough about this issue to go beyond Mayagüez all the way to San Juan, the capital, to defend her right to work for a wage. In all likelihood these workers were assisted during their journey by their employers, who also defended homework, but this fact should not have made the experience any less intimidating for them. Speaking out was not an easy task, since for most of them it was their first public speaking experience. Again, Carlota Goyco expressed this concern very clearly when she noted "This little district of Rosario is the last place in the world [*sic*]—I think very few here have ever heard of it, so I am completely rustic, and do not pretend to know how to speak in public. I merely come to defend the workers in our district."

And their concerns were not unfounded. Once she finished, the president of the Machine Workers' Union from Mayagüez, a man named Felipe Rivera, challenged the homeworkers. Rivera questioned the claim of the speakers to represent the homeworkers from Mayagüez. "Inasmuch as these women have just spoken on behalf of the home workers, I desire to ask what number of workers they claim to represent who work in the home?"[36] His question, which was followed by a round of applause from the organized workers present on the floor, prompted the intervention of the legal adviser of the National Industrial Recovery Administration. The legal adviser reminded Rivera of the rules of the hearings that stated that under no circumstances would those of opposing views be allowed to cross-examine witnesses, since it was not a judicial process. Rivera went on to make a counter statement, in which he claimed to represent the needleworkers from Mayagüez and set out to expose the evils of homework. The record shows no response from the home needleworkers to Rivera's overwhelming challenge.

Furthermore, the hearing went on as if the homeworkers had not even spoken. The organized workers who spoke later did not make any reference to the homeworkers' statements, although they directed their remarks to the subject of homework. The next day, when Pascuala Figueroa, the president of the Needleworkers Union from Mayagüez, was called to testify, she used part of her turn to read a statement from the homeworkers of Cabo Rojo asking for the elimination of homework. The statement ended with the following remark: "If the employer cannot raise our salaries, we prefer the industry to disappear for it is impossible to live under present conditions on the wages we are getting now." The statement was signed, "Needleworkers Union of Cabo Rojo, by Pascuala Figueroa, President, Needleworkers Union of Mayagüez."[37] This statement, in all probability, was read to counteract the effect of the earlier testimony by the homeworkers. Yet, at no time, with the exception of Felipe Rivera's direct challenge, did the factory workers acknowledge the presence of the homeworkers or their testimony.

Teresa Angleró was also challenged in another of the hearings of the National Industrial Recovery Administration, but the outcome of this case was different. While the homeworkers could only attend the public hearing celebrated in San Juan, Angleró attended all the other private meetings held by the administration in Puerto Rico and in the United States. Her participation as labor representative was possible thanks to the North American labor leader Rose Schneiderman. In her multiple interventions, she always stated very clearly that she was there in her capacity as representative of all the needleworkers in the country. On one occasion this claim was challenged by Víctor Domenech, a prominent contractor.

MR. DOMENECH: Mr. Deputy, I would like to ask Mrs. Anglero [*sic*] a question.
DEPUTY LONG: Proceed.
MR. DOMENECH: Mrs. Anglero, are the home workers organized?
MRS. ANGLERO: Many of them, but I do not know if all [of them are]. There are too many for me to tell.
MR. DOMENECH: For the home workers? You represent them?
MRS. ANGLERO: I am representing them.
MR. DOMENECH: Do you say that they have a representative, these home workers?
MRS. ANGLERO: Certainly. I represent them myself.
MR. DOMENECH: The home workers?
MRS. ANGLERO: The home workers and the shop workers.
MR. DOMENECH: I want to go on the record that never, to my knowledge, has there ever been a meeting exclusively of home workers in Puerto Rico, exclusively of home workers, and I know what I am talking about. I live there and I have seen all of these meetings of home workers of Puerto Rico and they have never had a proper representation. These meetings that have been taken care of, they have been taken care of by filling them up with workers from the factories of Puerto Rico. But, I know for a fact that if a conscientious canvass was made of the home workers of Puerto Rico there would be an immense majority against the abolition of home work.[38]

Like the homeworkers discussed earlier, Angleró did not respond to Domenech's forceful challenge of her claim to represent the homeworkers. However, a few pages later, North American labor leader Jacob Potofsky of the Amalgamated Clothing Workers responded to the challenge in equally forceful terms:

> As Mr. Domenech, who represents the employers' interests here, undertakes to speak for the home workers, I find myself at that point in some confusion. I do not understand why Mr. Domenech, who represents the employers, should undertake here to speak for these home workers. . . . What is this that he is coming to? What is the basis of his knowledge? Why, Mr. Domenech may be a very expert manufacturer. But, I deny his claim to talk for the workers, the home workers, or otherwise for the home workers of Puerto Rico. We have authorized representatives for them here, and they alone should be permitted to speak for them. (Applause.)[39]

Interestingly enough, Potofsky not only contested the legitimacy of Domenech to speak for the homeworkers, but he also denied him the right to do so. Instead, he bestowed that authority on himself, Rose Schneiderman, and Teresa Angleró, who attended the hearing as labor representatives. This time it was Domenech who kept quiet in the face of such a display of authority from Potofsky, who, though a worker, also happened to be a man and a North American. Both examples show very clearly that in addition to class relations, gender and ethnic relations were an integral part of the labor struggles of the time.

There is no doubt that the success of the factory needleworkers at articulating a public voice was related to their alliance with the organized male workers and the North American labor movement. Indeed, those needleworkers unions affiliated with the Free Federation of Labor achieved access to the social spaces that this organization had conquered—for example, the local press or the economic and political arena—which they used to convey their perspectives and carry out struggles. Similarly, the relationship of the factory needleworkers to some important women labor leaders from the United States, such as Rose Schneiderman and Rose Pesotta, also granted the local workers public recognition. The visits from these North American women were amply covered by the local press, as were the two local factory needleworkers who received a grant from the International Ladies' Garment Workers' Union (ILGWU) to continue advanced studies in economics, social sciences, and labor organization at the union's college.[40]

The failure of the homeworkers to articulate a public voice was related to the fact that their particular interests prevented them from forging alliances with the organized male and female workers. In this sense, they never achieved the status of social actors in the struggles taking place at the time. Instead, other social actors, such as the factory workers, the

Free Federation of Labor, and even the contractors claimed for themselves the authority to speak for the homeworkers.

In abstract terms, the principal goal of the homeworkers was the same as the factory workers as well as all the working women of the first decades of the twentieth century on the island. Working women wanted to be granted the status of full citizens with the recognized right to work for a wage.[41] Wage work was seen, in turn, as a vehicle to strengthen their position as citizens and to improve working and living conditions for themselves and their families. However, the conditions for the development of collective struggles to attain this goal were not the same for all working women of the period. The particular position of the factory needleworkers in the labor process granted them some relative bargaining power that allowed them to conduct struggles at the point of production in ways traditionally recognized as signs of defiant collective action. The situation of the homeworkers, however, was different. The informal process of skill acquisition that characterized the industry transformed huge segments of the population of the island into potential candidates for its work force.[42] In such a context, collective action in the form of strikes or protests directed at the employers on the part of the homeworkers was condemned to failure.

However, the homeworkers were not blind to the terrible conditions in which they lived and worked and they did resist abuses in the industry. For example, a committee of home needleworkers from Ponce went to Senator Moisés Echevarría to complain about the unfairness of a set of new rules imposed in the John K. Knust factory. The senator passed the case on to the Department of Labor fearing a more serious conflict, since the workers were indignant.[43]

Homeworkers resisted in less obvious ways, such as refusing to accept very complicated pieces that demanded a long period of time to complete or pieces that paid extremely low wages. Instead, they favored pieces that could be finished in short periods of time.[44] One of the few options that the homeworkers had to increase their earning power was to work more hours in order to be able to finish more needlework.[45]

Nevertheless, the single most important issue that concerned the home needleworkers and that mobilized them was the possible elimination of industrial homework. Every time that this kind of work came under fire, the homeworkers swung into action. Most of the time these mobilizations took the form of written protests and manifestoes directed at government officials. For example, in 1931, Rafael Alonso Torres introduced a project in the legislature to ban industrial homework. In response, a group of homeworkers from Cabo Rojo sent telegrams to the governor and the presidents of the Puerto Rican Senate and the House of Representatives, urging them to veto Alonso Torres's project. These women claimed that more than 1,000 people in their town supported them.[46] Other homeworkers from the town of Mayagüez also joined them in their protest.[47]

In the debates on homework prompted by the National Industrial Recovery Act of 1933 and the Fair Labor Standards Act of 1938, the homeworkers used other vehicles, such as taking part in public hearings, forming committees, and staging public protests to communicate their position on the matter. For example, the homeworkers from Lares met in assembly on November 13, 1938, to discuss the Fair Labor Standards Act. During the assembly, which was attended by more than 600 homeworkers, a resolution was adopted asking the President and the Congress of the United States to amend the law with respect to the elimination of industrial homework.[48] On November 19, 1938, a group of about 2,000 women from Lares paraded in that city and staged a protest against the Fair Labor Standards Act in front of City Hall. Among other demands, they asked for wage work.[49]

Why were the homeworkers so attached to this kind of organization of production? How can one explain their defense of industrial homework? After all, the arguments of organized labor regarding the bad conditions of work in the homes rang true. Why, then, did these women support it? The testimony of Antonia Villaflores in the National Industrial Recovery Administration's public hearing can shed light on these questions. Let us allow a homeworker herself to explain at length in her own voice, so often "unheard," what industrial homework meant to her in the particular context in which she lived:

> Our fellow workers from San Juan seem to be a little bit apprehensive regarding us workers from Mayagüez, thinking that we are trying to make obstacles. We merely desire to come here to state that we will be very severely affected if the home work is taken away from us. We have no prejudice against machine workers, but we understand the work in San Juan is almost exclusively machine work, whereas we depend entirely on handwork, of which the greater part is done in homes. The factories in Mayagüez are not large enough so that everybody can work in them, as might be the wish of the Coordinator and the employers. As this is really impossible, at least until things get better, and later on we might see all the needleworkers united, with good wages, because it is to be expected that the employers will help. I hope you in San Juan will be convinced that we have nothing against you, but that on the contrary we feel that we should all unite, but we want to urge that our work in homes should not be taken away from us, for it would be difficult to get other work. I do not mean that if the work goes we will starve to death because up to the present we have always been able to live, but at the present moment, due to the situation as regards work, we are in a difficult position and it would be still more difficult if this work were taken away from us. I have ten children and the absolute necessity of taking care of them and of educating them. They have to go to school and they have to be fed and clothed. If I had them at home and I had to go out to

work I could not attend to them and we would be destitute, with some here and some there, and in the same position are all the good mothers who want to take care of their own children. If it were necessary to go to the factory, not half of us would be in a position to do so. As a matter of fact, this home work is not done exclusively as a livelihood, but as an assistance and if we lose it, each mother would miss it, for it is a help for their children and for the husband. Moreover, the children, who have time free from school, and on Saturdays, can help, and every bit they can do is a help for themselves, because you all know that children in school need many things that their mothers cannot give them; if they have an opportunity to do some work it is a help. So don't think we are against you workers in San Juan—it is a mistake if you think we are. I want you to feel cordial towards us, and we do towards you, for we are all Puerto Ricans. That is all I have to say.[50]

As Antonia's testimony shows, there were important differences between the needleworkers that created tensions among them. It is interesting that in her speech she expressed a desire for the unity of all needleworkers, while at the same time she stressed the divergent interests of the homeworkers.

There were definite divergences in the way in which the homeworkers and the factory workers were incorporated into the labor process. As discussed earlier, the workers from San Juan were employed in big factories, with industrial machines and a rather detailed division of labor. The tasks performed by the homeworkers, although they very frequently involved some machine work, were considered "handwork." They usually performed more than one operation and also executed a great deal of handwork in addition to any machine work.

As Antonia Villaflores pointed out in her testimony, there were not enough factories to accommodate all the homeworkers. Furthermore, even if there were, the women would probably be unable to work there, since roads were in bad condition and there was no easy way to commute to the towns, as stated by Carlota Goyco in her earlier testimony. Besides the obstacles posed by distance and poor communication and transportation between urban and rural areas, there were also other issues, such as the availability and cost of housing and the lack of access to garden plots in the towns. Whereas housing in the urban areas was scarce and more expensive, many country people constructed their homes on lots that were rent free or nearly so. Furthermore, access to a small garden or having a few chickens or other domestic animals allowed them to supplement the very low wage earnings of the members of the household. Many of the males in the needleworkers' households were agricultural workers.[51] These families combined the incomes from agriculture, needlework, and other sources of cash and in-kind income in order to survive precariously. Moreover, needlework was an important source of cash income and, without any doubt, the most important source during the agricultural dead season.

Finally, there was the issue of domestic responsibilities. Factory needleworkers exhibited an age and civil-status composition among its work force akin to that generally associated with female workers in labor-intensive productive processes outside the home in industrial capitalism. In general terms, this work force has been depicted in the literature as younger, single women.[52] Likewise, most of the needlework union members were girls and women under age 35.[53]

The average home needleworker, in contrast, was married (either legally or consensually) and in the middle of her reproductive years.[54] This period is associated with child bearing and heavy domestic responsibilities. The domestic environment of the needleworker was rather complicated. Families tended to be large with a high number of children. Homeworker Antonia Villaflores, for example, had ten. For her, a "good mother" was one who took care of her children.

Arguments based upon motherhood were used very frequently by the needleworkers in their defense of industrial homework. Almost every letter, telegram, or resolution drafted by homeworkers alluded to their condition as mothers. Phrases such as "don't take away the bread from our children," "take pity on mothers of families," or "the thousands of Puerto Rican mothers who make a living doing needlework in their homes throughout the island . . . request that you do not approve the elimination of homework" appeared often in the discourse developed by the homeworkers.[55]

Factory workers, on the other hand, rarely used motherhood to defend their right to work. They usually couched their arguments in terms of the equality and justice that they deserved as wage workers. Gloria Rivera, treasurer of the Needleworkers Union No. 2, expressed her views in the following way: "As I said before, we do not want women who do homework to be kept out of work, but we want them to be paid just and reasonable wages so that they can live decently. Their necessities are the same as ours."[56]

For these factory workers, decent wages for both home and factory workers was a matter of principle; they had equal needs that should be covered by a just wage. Even when addressing the issue of motherhood, factory workers approached it in a different way from homeworkers. This point is illustrated by the testimony of Catalina Otero, secretary of Needleworkers Union No. 2 of San Juan and a machine worker in the Morris Storyk factory. "For example, in my case, I have eight children and I have to work for them alone at my home. It is not possible for me to educate and clothe them with only $8.00 weekly, pay rent and buy food, and I cannot bring them up properly and nourish them well. . . . I believe that a worker should be well fed and our children also, because we are human beings, we need food and demand a decent living and at the same time some recreation."[57]

Otero did not confront her familial responsibilities in maternal terms but as the head of the household. In this case, she alone provided for her children, and the low wages of the industry did not permit her to be a good provider. Furthermore, both she and her children deserved a decent life because, above everything, they were "human beings." These divergent discourses no doubt reflected the differences in life cycle and in positions within the household division of labor among the workers. But, more important, they also reflected the social struggle that was taking place regarding the dominant definitions of the concept of work and worker.

The entrance of women into the sphere of wage work was seen with apprehension even by the most advanced segments of the male working class. The idea that women and children represented "competition" to the male workers was based upon the notion that they were alien to the factory. In other words, they belonged elsewhere. In this sense, the struggle of working women concentrated, among other factors, on demonstrating their equality vis-à-vis men, as members of the working class in need of a just wage.

In the case of industrial homework this struggle was even more complicated. Many did not conceive of industrial homework as wage work and, as a consequence, did not consider homeworkers to be wage workers. This was the vision of the dominant classes on the island, for whom the participation of women in the needlework industry was not wage work because, supposedly, their subsistence and that of their families did not depend on their earnings.[58] Likewise, organized male workers did not perceive industrial homeworkers as common wage workers but rather as mothers. For example, one of the principal reasons that labor leader Sandalio E. Alonso presented against industrial homework was that it resulted in the "degeneration of the race." Women working under precarious conditions could only give birth to sickly infants.[59]

The underlying assumption was that mothers did not belong in the work force but in the home taking care of their children. In the event that they did not have a husband or son to take care of them, these women should be protected by the state. The identification of industrial homework with women's work and in conflict with motherhood was so great that many of the petitions for the regulation and eventual elimination of homework also asked relief from the government for the displaced women.

Homeworkers did not want relief from the government, they wanted wage work. Moreover, they wanted to be considered as legitimate wage workers despite their condition as mothers and wives. In the context of Puerto Rico in the 1930s, the only alternative that guaranteed women access to a wage was industrial homework. This point is expressed clearly in the previously quoted testimony of homeworker Antonia Villaflores and is worth repeating. She asserted: "but we want to urge that our work in the homes should not be taken away from us, for it would be difficult to get other work. I do not mean that if the work goes we will starve to death because up to the present we have always been able to live, but at the present moment, due to the situation as regards work, we are in a difficult position and it would be still more difficult if this work were taken away from us." Interestingly enough, Antonia, although a mother and a wife in need of wage work, did not present herself as a victim. Industrial homework was very important to her, but if eliminated she was confident that she could do something else in order to provide for herself and her family. This confidence was admirable in the face of so few opportunities for women workers.

Although the study of the working-class household economy in the 1930s has shown that the needlework earnings represented much more than "a help" to the children and the husbands, indeed for many families needlework wages were the only cash income.[60] There was the general belief, even among the homeworkers themselves, that their earnings were complementary to the supposedly principal earnings of the male head of the household. Yet this was no reason, in the views of the homeworkers, to eliminate this source of income. Once again, homeworker Antonia Villaflores's testimony addressed the issue: "As a matter of fact, this home work is not done exclusively as a livelihood, but as an assistance and if we lose it, each mother would miss it, for it is a help for their children and for the husband."

The struggle of women to achieve the right to work for a wage as workers who had other responsibilities as mothers and wives, who perhaps belonged to households where there were other wage earners, or who perhaps lived in remote rural areas, took the form of a general defense of industrial homework. Although they aspired to a wage that would constitute reasonable compensation for their efforts, they were willing to accept the kind of retribution that would secure the continuous operation of the industry on the island and thus protect their access to wage work in a society that resisted the incorporation of women into the labor force.[61] This point was clearly expressed by a group of unemployed needleworkers: "We declare that we cannot permit that our work be paid with ridiculous wages that do not compensate our effort, but we equally declare that we cannot demand that they pay us the wages stipulated by law, because these wages cannot sustain the life of the industry."[62]

This posture placed the home needleworkers at odds with the factory workers. For them, the existence of a large group of women who were willing to work for lower wages threatened the position they had forged for themselves as factory workers and as wage earners. In this sense, working women not only competed with male workers but also competed among themselves. Furthermore, women, both factory and home needleworkers, were struggling for the right to work, but their struggles took different forms due to their particular contexts and conditions. The same goal placed them in conflicting camps due to their different social position.

This complex situation was summarized by Rose Schneiderman when she was advocating the elimination of industrial homework. She put it in the following terms: "We may find that the inside workers will have the code [fair competition] but the home workers will have the work."[63] The struggle was over what constituted legitimate wage work and who would have access to it. In defending their job conditions, factory workers attacked industrial homework as an unsuitable form of wage work. In doing so, they developed a discourse that alienated the homeworkers, who were more concerned with getting wage work even under poor conditions.

For example, Teresa Angleró equated homework with "slavery," although she admitted that most homeworkers were in favor of it. "It is, however, not to be wondered at that many of these workers pronounce themselves in favor of home work, as it is a well-known fact that the slaves of all nations have always had to be set free by those at liberty to clamor for human freedom. And even after they were given their freedom, these former slaves would remain doubtful and still ponder what else to do with their lives."[64]

In her opinion, it was the duty of "the workers who had some preparation" to demand the abolition of this kind of slavery.[65] In doing so, Angleró, as a representative of the union, denied the homeworkers the capacity to understand their particular situation and the ability to do anything for themselves. It should surprise no one that the homeworkers resisted the call for unionization.

Conclusion

The present work has demonstrated the heterogeneity of the working class in early-twentieth-century Puerto Rico. The process of proletarianization produced profound differences within the working class according to the labor process, the household division of labor, life cycle, geographical region (urban and rural), and gender. These elements were crucial in the configuration of different working and living conditions, which often positioned disparate segments of the working class in competition with one another. In particular, the urban, skilled, male workers organized themselves to confront the threat of low wages and unemployment. These organized men often saw the ever-growing group of working women as a threat since they were swamping the ranks of those in need of a wage. The organized workers' movement utilized the dominant gender notions that claimed wage work as a male prerogative in order to achieve a privileged position in the world of labor. The principal strategy to reach this goal was protective legislation as a mechanism to lessen the effects of the competition presented by an ever-growing number of women in the wage labor force.

Among the female needleworkers, the struggle for the right to work took two different paths. On the one hand, for the needleworkers in the big factories in urban areas, the fight for the right to work took the form of an offensive against industrial homework and a struggle for the establishment of a minimum wage for all the workers in the industry. On the other hand, the struggle for the right to work led the homeworkers from the rural areas to defend industrial homework, their only means of earning a wage given their relative geographic isolation and their substantial domestic responsibilities. The divergent stances of the factory and home needleworkers reflected these differences in life cycle, household division of labor, and location within the work process. The needleworkers were only apparently a homogeneous group—female wage workers. However, their different social and productive situations ascribed different meanings to the experience of womanhood and wage work. This analysis questions any exclusive focus on gender identities and attempts to surpass the explanatory limits of the category of "woman."

Finally, the analysis of the struggles of the needleworkers allows for the understanding of other dimensions of the processes of social change. During the first decades of the twentieth century, working women in Puerto Rico succeeded in transforming the dominant notions of wage work and worker that depicted them as alien to the sphere of labor. Thus, they also succeeded in challenging and transforming the dominant gender notions that did not consider wage work as feminine. In the case of the needleworkers, their struggle disputed the relegation of women to temporary or secondary membership in the work force. Over the years, women, including those married with children, joined the labor force to stay. Wage work became part of their identity and way of life. It is no coincidence that when the industrialization program on the island started in the 1940s and 1950s, a very large group of women were mobilized as part of the work force. Today, very few people in Puerto Rico would doubt for a moment that married women with children have the same right as men to work for a wage.

Notes

1. In Puerto Rico the term "needlework industry" generally refers to the industry that developed in the country in the early twentieth century fueled by North American investments. By the 1930s it had become the principal employer of women on the island. Even though it is often said that the needleworkers in Puerto Rico specialized in embroidery and openwork exclusively, they also produced men's and children's clothing as well as women's shirts and dresses. Some of these pieces required embroidery, others did not. The industry on the island

exhibited many of the features that have historically characterized the clothing industries in capitalist societies, that is, low wages, poor working conditions, piece rates, industrial homework, and low unionization rates.

2. Luisa Hernández Angueira, "Auge y decadencia de la industria de la aguja en Puerto Rico, 1914–1940" (Ph.D. diss., Universidad Nacional Autónoma de México, 1983); Lydia M. González, *Una puntada en el tiempo: La industria de la aguja en Puerto Rico, 1900–1929* (Santo Domingo: CEREP/CIPAF, 1990).

3. Yamila Azize, *La mujer en la lucha: Historia del feminismo en Puerto Rico, 1890–1930* (Río Piedras: Editorial Cultural, 1985); Blanca Silvestrini, "La mujer puertorriqueña y el movimiento obrero en la década de 1930," in Edna Acosta Belén, ed., *La mujer en la sociedad puertorriqueña* (Río Piedras: Ediciones Huracán, 1980).

4. Louise A. Tilly, "Paths of Proletarianization: Organization of Production, Sexual Division of Labor, and Women's Collective Action," in Eleanor Leacock and Helen Safa, eds., *Women's Work* (South Hadley, MA: Bergin and Garvey, 1986), 38.

5. Puerto Rico, Negociado del Trabajo, *Informe anual* (San Juan: Negociado de Materiales, Imprenta y Transporte, 1919), 13.

6. Puerto Rico, Negociado del Trabajo, *Informe anual* (San Juan: Negociado de Materiales, Imprenta y Transporte, 1928), 13.

7. The Federación Libre de Trabajadores de Puerto Rico (Free Federation of Labor of Puerto Rico) was founded in 1899 under the unquestioned leadership of Santiago Iglesias Pantín, a Spanish immigrant. Following in the tradition of the skilled workers in Europe and the United States, it adopted the organization by crafts typically used by the so-called aristocracy of labor. Although the great majority of the wage workers in Puerto Rico was unskilled, mostly rural agricultural workers, the leadership of the union was composed of skilled laborers such as cigar makers. By the 1930s, the Free Federation was the principal union in the country and cooperated closely with the American Federation of Labor, with which it was affiliated from 1901 onward. Rafael Alonso Torres, *Cuarenta años de lucha proletaria* (San Juan: Imprenta Baldrich, 1939).

8. Federación Libre de Trabajadores, *Procedimientos del Sexto Congreso Obrero de la Federación Libre de los Trabajadores de Puerto Rico* (San Juan: Tipografía Murillo, 1910), 11.

9. Samuel Gompers, "Porto Rico: Her Present Condition and Fears for the Future," Record Group 350, Records of the Bureau of Insular Affairs Relating to Puerto Rico (1898–1934), Files 975-36 to 69, Box 5, Entry 5, United States National Archives, Washington, DC (hereafter USNA).

10. Puerto Rico, Departamento del Trabajo, *Informe anual* (San Juan: Negociado de Materiales, Imprenta y Transporte, 1936), 17; Juan S. Bravo, *Leyes y organismos para la protección de la mujer en la industria* (San Juan: Departamento de Trabajo, 1944).

11. Alonso Torres, *Cuarenta años de lucha*, 211–12; Sandalio E. Alonso, "Conversando con las uniones de oficios y sus líderes," *El Mundo*, June 6, 1934.

12. Alonso Torres, *Cuarenta años de lucha*, 267; "La Federación Libre luchará porque se establezcan en la isla pensiones para ancianos," *El Mundo*, September 30, 1934; " 'Favorecemos el Proyecto de Alonso,' dice Prudencio R. Martínez," *Unión Obrera*, March 2, 1933; "El proyecto para pensionar a viudas insolventes," *El Mundo*, August 5, 1933.

13. Federación Libre de Trabajadores, *Actuaciones de la Segunda y Tercera Asambleas Regulares de las Uniones de Tabaqueros de Puerto Rico* (San Juan: Porto Rico Progress Publishing Co., 1914), 80.

14. Ibid., 49.

15. "Se nombró un comité para impulsar la organización de la mujer obrera," *El Mundo*, October 7, 1934.

16. "Lo que informa el Departamento del Trabajo sobre la Comisión Legislativa Investigadora del Desempleo," *El Mundo*, February 22, 1933.

17. Asamblea Legislativa, *Tercer informe de la Comisión para investigar el malestar y desasosiego industrial y agrícola que origina el desempleo en Puerto Rico* (San Juan, 1932), 125.

18. Ibid., 251.

19. " 'La legislación social que está pendiente es la misma que se ha estado forzando desde el año 1898,' dice Sandalio E. Alonso," *El Mundo*, March 12, 1933.

20. Eileen Boris, *Home To Work: Motherhood and the Politics of Industrial Homework in the United States* (New York: Cambridge University Press, 1994), 202.

21. Rose Pesotta, *Bread upon the Waters*, 2d ed. (New York: Dodd, Mead and Company, 1945), 109.

22. "El trofeo de la Unión Obrera Central de San Juan ha sido adjudicado a la firma de J.A.E. Rodríguez Inc.," *El Mundo*, September 9, 1932.

23. Ibid.

24. The following discussion on the First Insular Conference of Needleworkers is based on the information contained in an extract of the verbatim record released by the Free Federation of Labor and published in "Se formó un comité insular de organización en la asamblea de trabajadoras de aguja celebrada el Domingo," *El Mundo*, September 9, 1932.

25. Cámara de Comercio de Puerto Rico, "Puerto Rico: 1933 Year-Book," *Boletín de la Cámara de Comercio de Puerto Rico* 10 (September 1934): 157–58.

26. "Adjourned Hearing from Washington on Porto Rican Needlework Industry Code (Number 2)," April 7, 1934, 80, Records of the National Industrial Recovery Administration [hereafter NIRA], Record Group 9, Box 39, Entry 1944, USNA.

27. Silvestrini, "La mujer puertorriqueña y el movimiento obrero," 85.

28. Puerto Rico Department of Labor, *Annual Report* (San Juan: Bureau of Supplies, Printing, and Transportation, 1933), 60; Puerto Rico Department of Labor, *Annual Report* (San Juan: Bureau of Supplies, Printing, and Transportation, 1935), 72–73.

29. Puerto Rico, Departamento del Trabajo, *Informe anual* (San Juan: Negociado de Materiales, Imprenta y Transporte, 1933), 55; P.R. Department of Labor, *Annual Report* (1933), 53–56, 60; P.R. Department of Labor, *Annual Report* (1935), 57–61, 72–73.

30. "Memorandum on Homework in Puerto Rico," 20, Records of the Homework Committee, Puerto Rico, NIRA, Record Group 9, Box 8389.

31. González, *Una puntada en el tiempo*; Hernández Angueira, "Auge y decadencia," 94.

32. María del Carmen Baerga, "¡Á la organización, á uniros como un solo hombre....!: La Federación Libre de Trabajadores y el mundo masculino del trabajo," *Op. Cit.* 11 (1999): 221–54.

33. Felicia Boria, "El salario de la mujer," *El Mundo*, September 24, 1934.

34. Ibid.

35. "Hearing on Code of Fair Practice and Competition for Puerto Rico, February 28, March 1, 1934, San Juan, Puerto Rico," 150; NIRA, Record Group 9, Box 38, Entry 44.

36. Ibid.

37. Ibid., 213–14.

38. "Hearing on Cotton Garment Industry and the Needlework Industry in Puerto Rico, Modification Proposal, March 28, 1934," Patio Room of Carlton Hotel, Washington, DC, 138–39; NIRA, Record Group 9, Box 38, Entry 44.

39. Ibid., 143–44.

40. "Para intervenir en la redacción de los códigos llegó ayer a Puerto Rico la señorita Rose Schneiderman," *El Mundo*, January 23, 1934; "Homenaje a la Srta. Schneiderman," *El Mundo*, March 22, 1934; "La señorita Rosa Pezzota [*sic*] fué presentada a las trabajadoras de la aguja," *El Mundo*, July 23, 1934; "La Unión Internacional de Trabajadoras de la aguja envía a la Srta. Rosa Pesotta.–Hará labor de organización," *El Mundo*, July 17, 1934; "Llegó ayer el presidente de la Unión Internacional de Trabajadoras de la Aguja, Sr. Charles Zimmerman," *El Mundo*, September 20, 1934; "La Federación Libre agasaja a Charles Zimmerman y a Rosa Pesotta," *El Mundo*, September 24, 1934; "Becas a dos señoritas para realizar estudios sociales," *El Mundo*, September 23, 1934; "Fueron asignadas y las becas de la Internacional de Trabajadoras de la Aguja," *El Mundo*, September 24, 1934.

41. The right to vote was an important part of this quest. However, this theme goes beyond the scope of this work. For a thorough analysis of the matter see María de F. Barceló-Miller, *La lucha por el sufragio femenino en Puerto Rico, 1896–1935* (San Juan: Ediciones Huracán/Centro de Investigaciones Sociales, U.P.R., 1997).

42. María del Carmen Baerga, "Trabajo diestro sin trabajadoras diestras: La (des)calificación en la industria de la aguja en Puerto Rico, 1914–1940," *La Ventana: Revista de Estudios del Género de la Universidad de Guadalajara* 9 (1999): 158–89.

43. "El Senador Echevarría protesta ciertas reglas dictadas por un taller de Ponce," *El Mundo*, September 11, 1933; "Un telegrama," *Unión Obrera*, September 12, 1933.

44. "Hearing on the Cotton Garment Industry and the Needlework Industry in Puerto Rico, Modification Proposal, Night Session, March 29, 1934," page 528, NIRA, Record Group 9, Box 7118 .

45. María del Carmen Baerga-Santini, "Exclusion and Resistance: Household, Gender, and Work in the Needlework Industry in Puerto Rico, 1914–1940" (Ann Arbor, MI: University Microform Inc., 1997), 147–60.

46. "Porque no se prohíba el trabajo a domicilio abogan varias obreras del pueblo de Cabo Rojo," *El Mundo*, March 25, 1931.

47. See, for example, "En contra del proyecto que prohíbe la realización de trabajo a domicilio," *El Mundo*, March 26, 1931.

48. "Resolution of the Needleworkers Assembly of Lares, Puerto Rico, November 13, 1938, Lares, Puerto Rico," Record Group 126, Records of the Office of the Territories [hereafter Territories], File 9-8-74, Box 882, USNA. See "Appendix Three" for the complete text of the resolution.

49. José Benet to Hon. Harold E. Ickes, Secretary of the Interior, Washington, DC, February 3, 1939, Record Group 126, Territories, File 9-8-74, Box 882.

50. "Hearing on Code of Fair Practice and Competition for Puerto Rico, February 28 and March 1, 1934, San Juan, Puerto Rico," 147–48, NIRA, Record Group 9, Box 38, Entry 44.

51. Caroline Manning, "The Employment of Women in Puerto Rico," *Bulletin of the Bureau of Women* 18 (1934): 16.

52. June Nash, "The Impact of the Changing International Division of Labor on Different Sectors of the Labor Force," in *Women, Men, and the International Division of Labor*, ed. June Nash and María Patricia Fernández Kelly (Albany: SUNY Press, 1983)

53. Pesotta, *Bread upon the Waters*, 116.

54. "Test Survey of Homeworkers in Puerto Rico," San Juan, P.R., October 4, 1935, NIRA, Record Group 9, Box 63; "Ortiz-Hayes Survey of Homeworkers in the Needlework Industry," San Juan, P.R., September 9, 1935, NIRA, Record Group 9, Box 65; "Reverse Needlework Survey," San Juan, Puerto Rico, NIRA, Record Group 9, Box 67.

55. Telegrams in favor of industrial homework, "Hearing on Code of Fair Practice and Competition for Puerto Rico, February 28 and March 1, 1934," San Juan, Puerto Rico, 270–272, NIRA, Record Group 9, Box 38, Entry 44.

56. Ibid., 198–99.

57. Otero, a factory worker, stated that she had to "work for them alone in my home." By this she meant that she was the only wage earner in the household, not that she worked at home. Ibid., 201.

58. See, for example, José C. Benet, "Los errores en cuanto el trabajo a domicilio en la industria de la aguja a mano," *El Mundo*, January 20, 1934.

59. Sandalio E. Alonso, "Trabajo a domicilio en Puerto Rico y en los Estados de la Unión Americana," *Unión Obrera*, February 14, 1933.

60. María del Carmen Baerga, "From Colony to Colony: Household Transformations in Puerto Rico," in *Creating and Transforming Households*, coords. Immanuel Wallerstein and Joan Smith (Cambridge: Cambridge University Press, 1992).

61. See for example "Contra la supresión del trabajo a domicilio," *El Mundo*, March 16, 1934, "Statement by a Group of Needleworkers from San Sebastián," Territories, Record Group 126, File 9-8-74, Box 882.

62. "Manifesto by a Group of Unemployed Needleworkers from Aguadilla," no date; Territories, Record Group 126, File 9-8-74, box 882.

63. "Hearing on Cotton Garment Industry, March 28, 1934," 131.

64. "Hearing on Code of Fair Practice, February 28 and March 1, 1934," 85.

65. Ibid., 224.

9

Colombian Bananas, Peasants, and Wage Workers

Catherine LeGrand

One of the more riveting aspects of this engaging selection by Catherine LeGrand is the attention it gives to a rural working class that persisted in the midst of an urban-oriented working class in the twentieth century. LeGrand highlights the activities of the rural wage-workers. By doing so, she offers a reminder of a number of points critical for understanding the condition of Latin American workers throughout the century. For one, the evidence shows that industrialization emerged not only in the towns and cities but in the countryside as well. To make matters more complicated, the two processes occurred at the same time. LeGrand's study also illustrates the continuing obstacles faced by workers as they tried to improve their conditions and struggled for power. They ran into all sorts of problems in the search for support from other sectors of society. By looking at the banana plantations of the United Fruit Company in the Santa Marta region of the Caribbean coast of Colombia, LeGrand shows how a banana-exporting corporation sought to manipulate workers and peasants in order to keep them from uniting to oppose its tactics, especially in the critical decades between the 1930s and 1960s. As has been the case in other essays, workers in their efforts to overcome differences between them encountered obstacles that were personal as well as social.

Introduction

The region surrounding the Caribbean port of Santa Marta in Colombia is a hot plain, fed by seven rivers that flow out of the Sierra Nevada mountains to the east. During the nineteenth century, a few prominent families with mercantile interests inhabited the town. Many of these families owned rural estates as well, but in the 1850s the estates lay virtually abandoned; neither the labour nor the markets existed to sustain ranching or agriculture on a large scale. Interspersed with and largely indistinguishable from the great estates were vast expanses of public lands (*terrenos baldíos*) to which no one claimed ownership.[1] A few Indians fished and grew subsistence crops there, and a few widely dispersed hamlets of mixed Indian, black, and mulatto squatters raised foodcrops for their own consumption. Occasionally squatter familes trekked to town to sell their surpluses. As late as 1875, the Santa Marta region was a sparsely populated economic backwater. Boundaries between private properties and public lands remained undefined, the land itself had little commercial value, and what rural production there was fed local markets.[2]

All of this was to change around 1900 with the advent of the Boston-based United Fruit Company.[3] Over the next three decades, the production of bananas for international markets under United Fruit Company auspices came to dominate all aspects of local life. The Company built the wharves, railroad lines, and irrigation canals that permitted Colombia for the first time to grow bananas for world markets. It planted banana groves covering thousands of hectares and also provided credit to members of the local dominant classes who formed hundreds of additional banana plantations under contract to the Company. Exports of bananas from Santa Marta climbed rapidly from 250,000 bunches in 1901 to five million bunches in 1915 and thence vertiginously to ten million bunches in 1929 [*White*, 1978: 123]. In that year the banana production of Santa Marta made Colombia the third largest international supplier of bananas, surpassed only by Jamaica and Honduras.

Thereafter the expansion of the export economy gave way to a gradual and sporadic contraction: the boom period, as is typical of neocolonial export economies, was followed by a bust. For a variety of reasons including the development of new production areas and shifting market conditions, Colombian bananas no longer held their competitive edge. Cutbacks in banana production in the Depression years were succeeded by a partial recovery and yet another recession during World War II. Finally, in the 1960s, the United Fruit Company pulled out of Santa Marta altogether and banana production virtually died out.

This essay explores the impact of the rise and decline of the banana export economy on the rural population of Santa Marta, centring on the issue of social conflict. United Fruit Company banana enclaves in the Caribbean and Central America have long been associated with the formation of a rural proletariat. Not only were rural wage-labourers particularly concentrated there, but the banana enclaves also became early focal points of labour organisation and protest. Most previous studies of protests against the United Fruit Company focus upon the strikes of wage-labourers for better working conditions,[4] overlooking the variety and complexity of rural protests directed against the Company. This is because they neglect one important element: the presence of a peasantry in the banana regions and its participation in shaping the forms of protest that emerged.

To make sense of the ways in which tensions between the rural population and the Company came to be expressed in Santa Marta, three major factors must be considered: first, structural tensions between the peasant economy and the export sector; second, the relationship between peasants and wage-labourers; and third, the effects of international market cycles on local conditions. From this case study it will then be possible to draw some broader conclusions concerning capitalist transformation of the countryside, class formation, and agrarian protest.

Effects of Export Expansion on the Rural Population

The United Fruit Company needed labour to build railroads and irrigation canals; to clear land, plant banana trees, and harvest the fruit; and to load the ships. Frustrated in its efforts to import workers from the Caribbean islands, the Company faced a problem of labour scarcity during the years of commercial expansion from 1900 through 1929.[5] The Company's willingness to pay wages 75 to 100 percent higher than those in other parts of rural Colombia directly expressed its need to attract a labour force.

News of the economic opportunities to be had in Santa Marta appears to have spread rapidly. Throughout the early decades of the twentieth century, streams of migrants converged on the region from other parts of the Colombian coast and, to a lesser extent, from the interior. Some were military conscripts who, brought into the region during the last and bloodiest of the nineteenth-century civil wars, decided to stay on once the fighting ended. Others were Indians from the Sierra Nevada and the Guajira, and still others *mestizo* peasants from the interior highlands where the decline of artisanal activity and the fragmentation of landholding had led to deepening poverty. The United Fruit Company itself is said to have sent labour contractors to the interior to recruit such people. Yet other migrants were individuals of rural origin who previously had worked for wages, either in railroad construction or in one or another of the foreign-owned enterprises that sprang up along the Caribbean coast in the late nineteenth and early twentieth centuries.[6]

Through immigration, the population of the banana zone swelled several times over to an estimated 90,000 people in 1928 [*Cortés Vargas*, 1979: 80]. Some of the migrants congregated around the port and the county seats where commerce thrived and where there was work to be had in the railroad stations or on the docks. Most, however, remained in the rural areas. Large numbers hired on with the United Fruit Company as wage-labourers on the banana plantations. As the banana economy expanded, the number of wage workers employed in the export sector—dock, railroad, and plantation workers—increased apace from 5,000 in 1910 to over 25,000 in 1925 [*White*, 1978: 42–43]. Somewhat more than half of these people worked directly for the United Fruit Company, while the others were employed by members of the local dominant classes on land they either owned or rented from the Company. Thus, the growth of the banana economy gave rise to a new group that had not previously existed in the Santa Marta region—a landless rural proletariat.

Many of the rural proletarians of Santa Marta did not work permanently on any one estate. Some, it would seem, did stay put for long periods of time. Others, however, tended to move from plantation to plantation, working one week on a Company plantation and the next week for one or another of the Colombian planters.[7] Such movements reflected the fluctuating demand for labour inherent in the banana economy. The fruit itself was not cut every day, and packers and longshoremen were needed only when the banana ships were in port. Bananas, moreover, do not ripen at a constant rate throughout the year: the major harvests in Santa Marta lasted from October to January with smaller harvests from February through May [*White*, 1978: 51]. Some banana workers not only moved among several different employers within the banana zone but also took part in interregional migrations. According to a letter from the Company manager written in 1928, it was not unusual for banana workers to take off for the sugar or cotton harvests further west along the Caribbean coast or to hire on for a time in the Barrancabermeja petroleum works several hundred miles to the south [*Colombia*, 1929b: 17–18].

This relatively mobile character of the rural proletariat is one element to be borne in mind. The other is the form of work organisation on the banana plantations. Both the United Fruit Company and national planters relied on piecework to produce bananas. The United Fruit Company itself structured this piecework through a labour contracting system. Typically, the Company hired a group of workers through a labour contractor to do a specific task, be it clearing new land for banana groves, weeding, harvesting, or construction. When the task was done, the Company paid the contractor, who in turn distributed the pay among the work group. Members of work gangs generally were paid in scrip redeemable at Company stores supplied with goods by the banana boats on their return voyages. The Company maintained that the piecework contract system was the only way to make efficient use of a mobile labour force; its critics argued that the Company had adopted this system to circumvent Colombian labour laws. And, in truth, workers hired through the contract system never figured in the list of United Fruit Company employees, although most lived in barracks on the plantations [*Colombia*, 1929b: 17–18; *Urrutia*, 1969: 102; *Cortés Vargas*, 1979: 32–34].

If some of the migrants attracted to the banana zone became rural proletarians, other newcomers were not so eager to work for wages. They chose instead to join the squatter population on the public lands that dotted the area. Whereas in the years before bananas, to be a squatter meant to be a poor subsistence producer, the development of commercial agriculture created new economic opportunities for the peasant population. The squatters themselves did not raise bananas: to do so required a contract with the United Fruit Company, and the Company did not care to deal with small producers. But the population growth that accompanied the growth of commercial agriculture generated an increasing demand for foodstuffs within the Santa Marta region, and transport improvements made it possible for the squatters to respond to that demand. The development of the banana economy thus fostered the growth of a peasant economy complementary to the export sector.

In the years after 1890, the number of independent peasant cultivators involved in petty commodity production increased dramatically through in-migration. This settlement movement responded both to economic incentives and to Colombian legislation encouraging peasants to homestead the national domain. Called *colonos*, the squatters staked small claims on public lands that, because of their distance from the rail lines, lack of irrigation, or poor soils, had not yet been incorporated into the banana plantations.[8] Most *colono* families cleared some ten to 30 hectares of land on which they built thatched huts of wattle and daub and planted a variety of crops, including sweet manioc (*yuca*), maize, plantains, rice, sugar cane, cacao, and tobacco. These squatters are designated peasants here, meaning small rural cultivators who rely on family labour to produce what they consume, as well as a surplus for commercial markets.

Most of the squatters of Santa Marta lived on individual freeholds scattered throughout the countryside. This pattern of dispersed settlement is characteristic of rural Colombia where the closed corporate peasant communities typical of Mexico and Peru are the exception [*Smith*, 1967: 257–86]. Not infrequently, however, *colono* families came together to form small villages. The old squatter hamlets that antedated the banana economy grew in size in the early twentieth century through the influx of migrant families. The continuing expansion of the peasant population also gave birth to a succession of new villages that took on marketing, religious, and administrative functions. Most of the new settlements (variously referred to as *caserios*, *aldeas*, or *poblaciones*) took form when a group of squatters in a certain area decided to create a town. True to their Spanish cultural heritage, they did this by tracing out a central plaza, erecting a Catholic chapel, and setting a market day. With the passage of time, the new villages took on greater complexity: traders, shopkeepers, and self-taught lawyers (*tinterillos*) appeared on the scene. Later, if enough money could be collected, the developing community would hire a school teacher and, finally, a police inspector would be sent to keep order [*Henriquez*, 1939].

A process of internal differentiation of the rural population certainly was under way, but the evidence is sketchy and the mechanisms unclear. We do know that *colono* families often tried to establish *de facto* control over as much land as they could with the intention of selling rights to later arrivals or of moving into pastoral activities, which were generally the province of the larger landholders. At the same time, some members of the local dominant classes also asserted claims to public lands: a census of land claims taken by a government commission in the mid-1920s found that a number of prominent individuals and small land companies had established rights to several hundred hectares of public lands each [*ANCB* Vol. 60 f.125]. These were generally banana planters or cattlemen who had consolidated their claims by buying out the original peasant settlers or pressuring them off the land. There seems also to have been a middle group of shopkeepers, lawyers, and artisans based in the villages, some of whom asserted claims to public lands which they worked with a few hired labourers. Subjected at times to the same pressures as the small *colonos*, members of this group sometimes sided with the peasants in conflicts with the United Fruit Company, providing them with a larger vision of their problems and with occasional leadership.[9]

While the process of internal differentiation of the *colono* group is not entirely clear, the economic contribution of the peasants of the zone is fairly obvious. The United Fruit Company commissaries could by no means supply the whole banana zone with foodstuffs. Hence the peasant squatters, who grew many of the foodstuffs, made it possible to support the burgeoning population and, in a larger sense, to sustain the banana economy. The fact that the *colonos* sent surpluses as far as the port of Baranquilla, some 75 miles to the west, attests to their productivity [*Colombia*, 1935: 18–19]. Beyond the provision of foodstuffs, *colonos* filled a second economic role vital to the functioning of the export economy: they provided the banana plantations with a cheap supply of reserve labour. Members of *colono* families often hired on to the plantations for a wage when the banana harvest was plentiful or when new land had to be cleared for production [*Torres Giraldo*, 1974: 66]. The piecework system favoured by the United Fruit Company facilitated the incorporation of peasants into the plantation labour force on a part-time basis. The work gangs contracted by the United Fruit Company not infrequently included members of peasant squatter families as well as landless labourers.

Thus, the birth of the banana economy, which gave rise to a rural proletariat, also stimulated the growth of an independent, market-oriented peasantry. On the surface, the relationship between the export economy and the peasant economy was a symbiotic one: the peasants fed the banana workers and occasionally worked the plantations themselves; at the same time, the growth of the banana economy gave the peasants greater scope for commercial activity. Nevertheless, the relationship between the peasants and the export sector was not without friction. From the beginning there was constant tension between the United Fruit Company and the peasants, a tension expressed in competition over land, labour, and water.

Tensions between the Peasant Economy and the Export Economy

The most important tension between the Company and the peasants centred on control of the land. The process by which the United Fruit Company established property rights to the territory it planted in bananas explains this opposition. The arrival of the United Fruit Company stimulated an upward surge in property values and a dramatic quickening of the land market. The result was a flurry of real estate activity: many of the local dominant classes ransacked family trunks for old property titles, while others applied for public land grants from the government or simply fabricated new property claims. Such speculative activity paid off in profitable sales to the Company itself or to other Colombians anxious to form their own plantations of "green gold." Through the purchase of such titles, the United Fruit Company gradually consolidated private holdings totalling 60,000 hectares in the area around Santa Marta. Meanwhile, Colombian planters under contract to the Company formed more than 350 smaller banana plantations and cattle ranches covering at least another 20,000 hectares. Thus, the spread of the banana economy brought in its wake a massive privatisation of public lands.[10]

Many of the new property claims had no legal basis whatsoever, while others, based on grants dating from the colonial period, had extended their boundaries over time, illicitly incorporating large areas of public lands. In regions apt for banana production, the United Fruit Company continued in the first decades of the twentieth century to enlarge its holdings through constant encroachments onto public lands. The use of metes and bounds surveys, and the venality of local mayors, notaries, and surveyors considerably facilitated such manoeuvres. By the 1920s, the property issue had become a hopeless morass of conflicting claims: the Colombian government maintained that there were still some 90,000 hectares of public lands in the banana zone, while the United Fruit Company and Colombian planters insisted all was private property.[11] What is certain is that no precise boundaries had ever existed between private properties and public lands and that much of the territory suddenly claimed to be private after 1900 was reputed locally to be public domain and was already occupied by peasant cultivators.

This rapid privatisation of public lands implied the expropriation of hundreds and probably thousands of peasant squatters. As the construction of new railroad lines and irrigation canals constantly brought new land within the radius of the banana economy, the United Fruit Company came into direct confrontation with peasant cultivators already living there. Typically at this point a Company agent informed a group of *colonos* that the land they had settled was private property and that if they did not abandon their fields at once, they would be evicted. Some, faced with the prospect of losing all, sold out at a reduced price. With those who refused, the Company used force: in cooperation with local authorities, it evicted the peasants, turned livestock into their crops, burned their huts to the ground, and jailed their spokesmen.

The first of these forced expropriations to be recorded dates from 1907. Thereafter the accelerating expansion of the banana plantations intensified the pressure on peasant lands. Such pressures reached a peak during the boom years of the 1920s when the area planted in bananas around Santa Marta doubled in size. During this period, the peasants of the zone were constantly agitated by conflicting property claims. Between 1920 and 1929 peasant groups alerted the Colombian government to more than 35 encroachments of this sort, some of which threatened as many as 100 peasant families.[12] Certainly many more incidents passed unreported.

The major part of the United Fruit Company's properties always remained undeveloped. Of the 60,000 hectares the Company claimed at the height of its influence, only 16,000 hectares were ever planted in bananas and another several thousand hectares were devoted to pastures for livestock [*Colombia*, 1930]. Similar practices in United Fruit Company enclaves in other countries have been explained by the Company's concern to keep out competitors and by the struggle with banana blight, which required shifting cultivation and the continual opening of new land. In Colombia the intrusion of rival banana companies was a real possibility, but disease did not become a problem until the late 1930s. Given that the United Fruit Company typically operated in regions of abundant public lands, an additional factor motivating the Company to monopolise great areas may well have been the desire to restrict the availability of free land to the rural population, thus reinforcing the wage-labourer alternative.

Faced with the problem of securing plantation workers, it appears likely that the United Fruit Company evicted *colonos* not only because it wanted land, but also because it wanted labourers. Obviously the Company did not publicise this as a policy, but the peasant population accurately sized up the situation. A group of *colonos*, threatened with eviction, complained bitterly to the Ministry of Agriculture in 1919: "They harass us only because we refuse to be mercenary labourers for the Company" (*Solo lo asen* [sic] *por rabia de que no somos mercenarios trabajadores de la empresa*) [*ANCB* Vol. 44 f.434].

The fate of those *colonos* who lost their land remains obscure. Some may have moved a few miles inland to merge with other *colono* groups and clear new fields. Many others, lacking the resources to begin again, certainly joined the rural proletariat on the banana plantations. Thus, not only did some *colonos* work part-time in the banana groves, but others, dispossessed of their land, were transformed into full-time wage-labourers.

Even those who managed to stay on the land were not invulnerable to the expanding banana economy. Because of the confusion of property rights in the Santa Marta zone, the remaining peasants knew they could face incursions at any time. The expansion of the banana economy, more-over, disrupted their productive activities in other ways. The canals the United Fruit Company built to water the banana groves literally circum-scribed some peasant communities, cutting them off from access to local markets. Furthermore, in rerouting rivers for irrigation, the Company ex-acerbated problems of drought on unirrigated land during the dry season and problems of flooding in the rainy season. Several *colono* settlements were completely washed out by Company canals [*Colombia*, 1935: 17–19]. And peasants in the zone were convinced that the Company purpose-fully flooded certain areas in order to force them off the land.[13]

The United Fruit's company store policy also deprived peasants of market possibilities. As already mentioned, the Company frequently paid its employees in scrip that could only be redeemed at its own commissar-ies. Stocked with foodstuffs imported on the banana ships' return voy-ages, the Company stores generally undersold local producers. The aim was to keep food prices low so as to keep wages down. By providing such a service, however, the United Fruit Company restricted potential mar-kets for peasant crops and antagonised local merchants as well.

Thus, at the same time the presence of the United Fruit Company stimulated the emergence of a vigorous peasant sector, the expanding banana economy and corporate practices undercut that development. Thou-sands of peasants lost their land to the banana plantations and were con-verted into wage-labourers, while those who survived as peasants found their access to water and markets restricted and their land claims subject to dispute.

Relations between Peasants and Wage-Labourers

The process of historical development that generated peasant grievances also produced a particularly close and fluid relationship between the peasants and the wage-labourers of Santa Marta. This phenomenon, which has been noted in the Caribbean sugar islands [*Mintz*, 1973], also characterised the Colombian banana zone. The reasons lie in the specific historical process of property and class formation that occurred with export growth in the Santa Marta region. Both peasants and wage-labourers were recent mi-grants into the area. Some peasants were wage-labourers who had gath-ered enough savings to start up a claim, while some of the wage-labourers were former peasants who had been dispossessed of their fields. Still oth-ers took on both roles simultaneously.

Admittedly, the grievances held against the Company by each group were different in kind. The peasants' interests lay primarily in secure land titles. The abolition of Company stores and nationalisation of the irriga-tion canals also would have bettered their lot by providing access to new markets and productive resources.[14] In contrast, wage-labourers sought to improve their working conditions by demanding collective work contracts, higher salaries, social security, and improved housing and medical care. These differing concerns were rooted in the organisation of production that divided wage-labourers on the great banana estates from smallholding peasants on public lands.

Many of the rural people of Santa Marta, however, refused to define themselves as either peasants or wage-labourers. Rather, seeking to maximise security and income, they adopted strategies that, over time, encompassed both roles. According to labour organiser Ignacio Torres Giraldo [1974: 66], banana field workers often expressed the desire to establish themselves permanently in the region by becoming cultivators of public lands. And, when laid off by the Company, workers frequently took refuge with *colono* families. In an area of high food prices and grinding inflation, the *colono* alternative represented not only the security of subsistence, but also an opportunity for economic advancement. At the same time many *colono* families sent relatives to work for the United Fruit Company specifically in order to claim the benefits allotted Company workers. Such benefits included agricultural tools, reduced train fares, and, perhaps most importantly, admittance to Company hospitals. In the Santa Marta region where anaemia and dysentery were widespread, access to health care was important indeed.[15] A strategy that combined the roles of peasant and wage-labourer made good sense. Thus, beyond the objective circumstances of their lives, a certain correspondence existed in aspirations between the peasants and wage-labourers of Santa Marta.

This fluid, overlapping relationship between peasants and wage-labourers created the basis for the mutual comprehension and support that came to be expressed through their protest movements. The precise forms of rural protest that evolved over time reflected the cycles of export expansion and contraction.

Forms of Protest during the Period of Export Expansion

During the period of commercial expansion, the first protests to be directed against the United Fruit Company came from many small nuclei of *colonos* who put up a fight against the encroachments of banana planters. Peasant families threatened with expropriation in the years 1900–1930 directed scores of petitions to national authorities in Bogotá describing their plight and requesting protection.[16] In contrast to many Latin American countries, Colombia had homestead laws that protected settlers of public lands, and it was to these laws that the *colonos* appealed.[17] Even when evicted, many *colonos* refused to recognise the legality of such actions, and some even tried to defend themselves in court. So, in the early years of the banana economy, one major form of social protest centred on the peasants' legal struggle to defend their land claims.

Peasant attempts to use the legal process in their own defence were generally unsuccessful. The national government at this time exercised little influence over local authorities, who generally complied with the interests of the United Fruit Company and the dominant classes of Santa Marta. Nevertheless, *colono* resistance had important long-term effects: it served to imprint on the public consciousness the idea that the banana plantations were really public lands usurped violently and illegally. *Colono* leaders—usually the more educated and prosperous cultivators of public lands, lawyers, or local banana producers with their own grievances against the Company—took a particularly active role in spreading the word [*ANCB*, Vol. 44,f.435bis].

At first, *colono* resistance to the loss of land was spontaneous and localised in nature. In the 1920s, however, such resistance assumed more organised forms. This change was in part a response to the ever greater pressures on the peasant population growing out of the rapid expansion of the banana economy in those years. But more than this, it reflected new social and political developments affecting the country as a whole. In the 1920s, Colombia, like many other Latin American nations, witnessed the birth of organised labour and the appearance of the working classes on the political scene. During the 1920s, Colombian labour movements were particularly strong in the United States-controlled petroleum enclave at Barrancabermeja and in the United Fruit Company banana zone.[18]

The first in the banana zone to organise were the dock and railroad workers who participated in the initial strike against the United Fruit Company in 1918. This strike was promoted by some local banana planters and merchants disgruntled with the Company's export monopoly. In the early 1920s a few local worker societies made their appearance, and, following an abortive strike in 1924, the United Fruit Company itself sponsored the formation of a small workers' association, the Sociedad Unión, often called the Yellow Union (Sociedad Amarilla) because of its Company connections.

The rural population of the banana zone only really began to organise after 1924 through the influence of a few Spanish and Italian anarchosyndicalist immigrants. In December 1926 the first independent union to involve the rural population was formed—the Unión Sindical de Trabajadores de Magdalena (USTM). Early in 1927 the leadership of this group passed to the newly formed Revolutionary Socialist Party (PSR), which had emerged out of the National Workers Congress held in Bogotá the previous year and which was to play a leading role in the Colombian labour movement throughout the 1920s.[19]

It is often assumed that proletarians—whether urban or rural—will be at the forefront of labour organisation, while peasants, more traditional and conservative, lag behind. For this reason, the contrasting process of rural organisation in the Colombian banana zone in the 1920s is of particular interest. According to Ignacio Torres Giraldo [1974: 66], a PSR activist, labour organisation actually began with the *colonos* who, because of their antagonism to the United Fruit Company, were particularly receptive to the initiatives of outside organisers. The peasants, through their close ties with plantation labour, were largely responsible for the unionisation of the wage workers.

The formation of unions of wage-labourers and of peasant leagues (*ligas de colonos*) proceeded concurrently. The composition of the many local organisations that proliferated after 1925 varied. Some included only wage-labourers, others comprised *colonos*, while still others grouped together *colonos*, plantation workers, and banana packers and loaders. The USTM functioned as the umbrella organisation to which most local groups sent representatives.

In the late 1920s, a second form of rural protest emerged in the banana region—the strike of plantation labourers for better working conditions. Although the USTM supported the petitions of *colonos* menaced with dispossession, its primary efforts went into planning a general strike against the United Fruit Company. These plans came to fruition in the great strike of November 1928, the first work stoppage to mobilise the rural population on a massive scale. The strike erupted at a time dissatisfaction in the zone was at its height: the national government, Colombian banana planters, local merchants, peasants and wage-labourers, all were in conflict with the United Fruit Company, but for different and sometimes contradictory reasons. No doubt this "breakdown of authority" gave the rural labourers an incentive to act, but the workers acted independently. More than 30,000 people participated in the strike, paralysing the United Fruit Company's operations in Colombia for more than three weeks.[20]

The peasants of the banana zone fully supported the plantation workers in their confrontation with the United Fruit Company. The General League of *Colonos*, which grouped together all of the local *colono* organisations, signed the petition of demands, as did six local syndicates with *colonos* among their members. In practical terms, the *colonos'* contribution lay in their refusal to work the banana fields for the duration of the strike and their provision of foodstuffs to landless workers.

According to Charles Kepner, social historian of the United Fruit Company, the strike was in part a "peasant revolt" [1936: 199]. Yet, the strikers' demands were those of plantation workers: they focused on salary raises, the enforcement of Colombian labour laws, and improvements in housing and medical care. The petition presented to the Company by the USTM made no mention of the land problem and, indeed, none of the demands, except possibly that calling for the abolition of Company stores, would have benefited the peasants as peasants [*Colombia*, 1929a: 179–82]. An observation made by the General Manager of the United Fruit

Company throws some light on the thorny question of peasant action at this time. The aim of the Company's contract workers in supporting the strike, he maintained, was to win the benefits accorded full-time employees [*Colombia*, 1929b: 17–19]. As we have seen, many of these contract workers were in fact *colonos*. Thus, at this time, the proletarian side of peasant concerns came to the fore.

Despite the strength of its numbers, the strike ended in tragedy. The merchants of the area, who at first had supported the strike, later turned in fear against it. Meanwhile, the national government sent a military force to reestablish order. As vividly portrayed in the Nobel Prize-winning novel *One Hundred Years of Solitude*, Colombian soldiers massacred hundreds of banana workers who had assembled for a peaceful march on the port of Santa Marta on the night of 8 December 1928 [*García Márquez*, 1970]. The massacre broke the strike, and in the following months the army took control of the banana zone and many strike leaders were imprisoned.[21]

During the period of commercial expansion, then, rural protest against the United Fruit Company took two characteristic forms—the strike of wage workers, supported by peasant groups, for better working conditions; and peasant resistance against the loss of their land. These forms of conflict reflected the economic conditions that prevailed in the 1920s and particularly the expansion of export agriculture that promoted the conversion of peasant lands into banana plantations and the transformation of *colonos* into part- or full-time wage-labourers. What stands out in this period is, first, the primacy of wage workers' concerns, and second, the close collaboration between the two major rural groups.

Forms of Protest during the Period of Export Contraction

When, after 1929, the banana economy went into recession, the close relationship between peasants and wage-labourers allowed for the emergence of yet a third form of agrarian protest—land invasions. Following a period of rapid expansion, the contraction of the banana economy was to have profound repercussions on life in the zone. The contraction began with several damaging windstorms that swept the area in 1928, 1929, and 1930, followed by the onslaught of the world Depression. The problems, however, reached even deeper than the contraction of world markets. With hindsight, it is clear that banana production in Colombia was becoming increasingly uneconomic for the United Fruit Company. The Colombian fruit was too small and transport costs too high, while conflicts with labour, the Colombian government, and national planters further threatened profits. Facing competition from other marketing companies and banana firms, the Company sought new, more productive areas and found them in Honduras, which in the succeeding decades was to become the quintessential "Banana Republic" [*White*, 1978: 34–40].

In response to its problems in Colombia, the United Fruit Company began in 1930 to cut back production around Santa Marta. Between 1929 and 1934, the Company reduced the acreage it cultivated in bananas by 75 percent. At the same time, it restricted the use of export facilities and advances of credit to national producers, thereby causing many Colombians to abandon their plantations as well. As a result, several thousand plantation workers lost their jobs.[22]

At this juncture, the unemployed, some of whom had been peasants in earlier years, turned their sights towards the land. Thus in the early years of the Depression the *colono* movement, born of a defensive reaction against the expanding banana plantations, took to the offensive. Land, rather than wages, became the primary focus of rural protest. During the summer and fall of 1930, thousands of unemployed wage workers, calling themselves *colonos*, moved onto idle United Fruit Company properties, cleared small fields, and planted food crops. Some 10,000 hectares, formerly controlled by the Company, were repatriated by *colonos* between 1930 and 1935. Once they had occupied the land, the new cultivators sent petitions to the national government asserting that the land had been illegally incorporated into private properties, that it was in reality public domain (*baldío*), and that they, as settlers, had a right to it. And so, under adverse economic circumstances, the peasant to wage-labourer transition reversed itself. Many of the large estates built up over the preceding decades were broken down as the banana sector receded and a peasantry began to reconstitute itself in the commercial core of the zone.[23]

The response of the United Fruit Company to the "invasion" of its properties was ambivalent. On one hand, the peasant occupations served its interests by keeping the unemployed in the Santa Marta region at no cost to the Company. Later, if the banana economy took an upturn, they might be reincorporated into the plantation labour force. On the other hand, the Company was disturbed to have its property claims challenged, especially because the Colombian government by now took a hard line against usurpers of public lands.[24] Given these preoccupations, the Company demanded that the new *colonos* sign tenancy contracts in which they agreed to recognise its titles. If the *colonos* refused, the Company initiated eviction proceedings against them. A variant approach involved renting sections occupied by peasant squatters to well-to-do Colombian nationals on the condition that they deal with the *colono* problem, either by clearing the peasants off the land or by forcing them to acknowledge the Company's rightful ownership [*Colombia*, 1935: 18, 35].

Despite the United Fruit Company's efforts to manipulate the situation to its own advantage, the *colonos* remained recalcitrant. They refused to recognise the Company's property rights and repeatedly reoccupied the parcels from which they were ejected. Conflicts over land between alleged proprietors and *colonos* (both new and old) were legion

throughout the Santa Marta region in the 1930s. *Colono* leagues appealed
to justice in defending peasants on public lands against forcible dispossession, while the United Fruit Company and Colombian planters claimed
legitimate resistance against squatters invading private properties.[25]

From this time on, public land movements challenging the tenuous
property rights of the banana planters became a major theme in rural protests directed against the United Fruit Company. While reformist politicians and unions called on the government to review the Company's
property titles and donate public lands to peasant cultivators, the Colombian Communist Party (formed out of the PSR in 1930) urged the unemployed to invade Company properties.[26] Plantation labourers, in the
ongoing strikes of this period, identified themselves closely and explicitly with peasant concerns. The first strike of plantation workers after
1928, that of 1934, was organised from a *colono* village and included
among its leadership a semi-proletarianised *colono* who worked part-time
as a banana cutter. The list of demands recalled that of 1928—the minimum wage, the eight-hour day, hospitals, schools, sanitary housing—but
with one major difference. In 1934 and in subsequent strikes against the
Company, banana workers explicitly demanded that the *colonos* of the
zone be left to farm their claims undisturbed [*Torres Giraldo*, 1978: 1150–
58].

In fact, the United Fruit Company never recovered the territory it lost
to peasant squatters in the 1930s. The reason, however, has less to do with
the influence of the workers than with the fact that the Colombian banana
economy never fully regained the expansionist dynamic of the 1920s. Problems with blight, soil exhaustion, labour, and an increasingly intervention-
ist national government caused the Company to concentrate its efforts in
other countries. A partial upswing in banana production in the late 1930s was
succeeded by another recession in the early 1940s when wartime conditions
led the Company to suspend all banana exports from Colombia for five
years. After World War II, the United Fruit Company lost its monopoly in
the Santa Marta region and withdrew from production, selling or renting
much of the land it claimed to Colombian banana planters. The decision
of the United Fruit Company no longer to involve itself directly in production undermined the unity of the labour movement. The unions fragmented, their membership dwindled, and the living standards of the
plantation workers declined. Throughout this final period, the Company
retained control of marketing, credit, and disease control in most of the
Santa Marta area until, in the early 1960s, it pulled out of Colombia
altogether.[27]

The departure of the United Fruit Company spelled the demise of the
banana economy. It plunged the Santa Marta region once again into economic crisis. The local dominant classes returned to extensive cattle ranching which could employ but a fraction of the people in the zone. Thousands

of wage-labourers found themselves without work. Some abandoned the region altogether, seeking opportunity elsewhere. Others remained, drifters and vagrants, in the poverty-stricken towns of the old banana region.

Still others turned to the land. As had first occurred in the early 1930s and again in the early 1940s, large numbers of wage workers laid off from the plantations moved into unimproved areas of the banana zone as peasant cultivators. They called themselves *colonos* of public lands. In the early 1960s, more than 1,200 new *colonos* occupied 8,000 hectares of territory, giving rise to often violent disputes over land rights between the peasants and landlords of the region. When in 1961 the Colombian Agrarian Reform Institute (INCORA) sent a team to investigate what it believed to be a potentially explosive social problem, it found that the property situation was as chaotic as it always had been. And, returning to the scene of the *colono* movements of the 1930s, INCORA discovered some 7,000 hectares of territory still claimed by the United Fruit Company occupied by 300 squatter families, many of whom said they had been there for 30 years [*Quiñonez and Jaramillo*, 1962; *Padilla and Llanos*, 1964].

In response to this situation, INCORA determined to intervene in the Santa Marta region to facilitate peasant acquisition of land titles and to establish cooperatives. An American anthropologist who lived in the area in the early 1970s reported that squatter invasions of cattle ranches were still a common occurrence. Wage-labourers on the cattle ranches, former banana workers themselves, often supported the peasant invaders, hoping that through the intervention of national authorities they too might win legal rights to the land [*Partridge*, 1979: 503–5]. Thus, the fluid relationship between peasants and wage-labourers forged in the days of the banana economy continued in subsequent years to shape the course of rural protest.

Theoretical Implications

This saga of peasants, wage-labourers, and export agriculture in the Colombian banana zone sheds light on several issues of broader concern. First, Marxist theorists tend to argue that the transformation of peasants into wage-labourers is an inevitable concomitant of capitalist penetration into rural areas. Certainly it is true that wage-labourers form a much larger part of the rural work-force in Latin America today than they did in 1900. But, as so much recent work has shown, a unilinear perspective advances much too simple an interpretation of the Latin American reality [*Bartra*, 1974; *de Janvry*, 1981]. The Santa Marta case sheds some additional light on the subject. The study of Santa Marta suggests that the introduction of commercial agriculture into frontier regions may actually stimulate the emergence of a complementary peasant economy. Generally settlers of public lands, such people provide foodstuffs for regional markets and particularly for the growing population engaged in export production.[28]

During the period of export growth, the Colombian banana economy tended in classic fashion to absorb the nascent peasant sector by appropriating the land and labour of the *colonos*. This process gave rise to a large wage-labour pool and to an intermediate sector of semi-proletarianised peasants who served the United Fruit Company's fluctuating labour needs. Here, and later in periods of economic recession, capital was able to make use of a variety of labour relations and to move strategically among them.

The experience of Santa Marta also shows that the transition from a peasant economy towards wage-labour relations is not irreversible. Indeed, the boom-bust rhythms of the export economies have profoundly affected the evolution of productive roles in Latin American agriculture. In any given region, the contraction of commercial agriculture, together with the initiative of the rural people themselves, may well contribute to the regeneration of a peasant economy that appeared headed for dissolution.

A second point concerns the study of rural protest movements. Recently, students of Latin America have realised that neither the peasantry nor rural unrest can be discussed in generic terms. Rather, one of the major tasks we face is that of tracing the influence of economic developments on the internal differentiation of the rural population and of investigating the relations of production specific to each group. This has important implications for the study of rural protest, for the interests, behaviour, and outlook of a tenant farmer with labour obligations may differ significantly from that of a small proprietor or a day worker or a sharecropper. Following this line of thought, several scholars have attempted to develop typologies that link the various forms of agricultural enterprise and class relations to specific types of rural class conflict. An early and influential example of this approach is that of Arthur Stinchcombe [1961]. Such a perspective also characterises the work of Hamza Alavi [1965], Jeffrey Paige [1975], and, to an extent, Eric Wolf [1969], though they come to differing conclusions.

The focus on productive organisation leads most observers to draw a sharp distinction between peasants and rural proletarians. Peasants, by definition, have access to land; proletarians do not. This observation has given rise to an assumption widespread in the Latin American literature that peasants will agitate for land, whereas landless rural wage workers resemble their urban counterparts in their concern with wage issues and contract disputes. Sidney Mintz expressed this distinction most clearly in his early work:

> A rural proletariat working in a modern plantation inevitably becomes culturally and behaviourally distinct from the peasantry. Its members neither have nor (eventually) want land. Their special economic and

social circumstances lead them in another direction. They prefer standardised wage minimums, maximum work weeks, adequate medical and educational services, increased buying power, and similar benefits and protections. In these ways, they differ . . . from the peasantry—who are often conservative, suspicious, frugal, traditionalistic. . . . Peasants who, by a swift process of plantation development, have been transformed into rural proletarians, are no longer the same people. [*Mintz*, 1964: xxxvii]

The new research that focuses on productive organisation represents a step forward in our understanding of rural unrest. The Santa Marta material, however, suggests an additional dimension to this formulation. We need to admit the possibility not only that peasants are often transformed into wage-labourers through the expansion of capitalist agriculture, but also that wage-labourers may purposefully transform themselves back into peasants. Just as there is no inexorable progression from peasant to wage-labourer, neither is there a progression from "peasant mentality" to "proletarian mentality." The same labourers who, in a period of commercial expansion and labour scarcity, will agitate for higher wages, may instead demand land under less favourable circumstances. As we have seen, the *colono* movement in the Colombian banana zone in the early 1930s was not really a peasant movement at all, but rather a migration of unemployed wage-labourers back to the soil. Thus, wage-labourers may well make land the focus of their protests when it is in their interest and capacity to do so. And rural people may purposefully adopt new social roles at specific historical junctures in order to improve their economic situation.

In stressing that rural Latin Americans often move among several different productive roles—including various combinations of peasant and proletarian—in a single lifetime, this study builds upon work by Sidney Mintz [1973, 1974] and Anthony Leeds [1977]. The particular contribution of this paper lies in the connection drawn between such transformations and rural protest movements. Certainly, external pressures may force peasants to move into new roles, but rural people may also initiate such shifts. Just as some rural protests are defensive, aiming to prevent change, the goal of others may be to bring about an active transformation. Exactly which roles are thought desirable depends on the structural conditions prevailing in a society at a given time. In the 1930s, the people of Santa Marta found the security of peasant life preferable to the uncertainty of wage work. In Venezuela in the 1950s, the situation was reversed: small coffee producers were willing and eager to move into more permanent and lucrative positions as wage workers [*Roseberry*, 1978].

A final point concerns the ideology of agrarian protest. To understand the discontent of rural people and why and how they come to express it, it is important to consider not only productive organisation, but also property relations and the laws governing such relations. The problem with most typologies attempting to link class structure to agrarian protest movements is that they assume property relations are fixed. They neglect the historical process of class formation by which labour is separated from the means of production through the creation of private property. These formative stages are of crucial importance. Indeed, it may be these times of transition that most inform popular consciousness and shape rural protest strategies. In the Santa Marta banana zone, the creation of private property that divided peasant from wage-labourer also united them—in protest against it.

The creation of private property is inextricably bound up with the law that designates who shall own and on what terms. Recently there has been a tendency in Latin American agrarian history to minimise the importance of legal forms, to regard them as irrelevant if not misleading for those concerned with local social processes. This tendency is particularly marked in the comparative slavery literature, although it also runs through current writing on highland Indian areas.[29]

The Colombian case material challenges this perspective by providing an example of the potential contribution of law—in its violation—to rural protest ideology. The *colono* form of agrarian protest reflected both the historical process of land concentration that had taken place within the banana zone and the specific content of Colombian public land legislation. As mentioned above, this legislation did support peasant cultivators of public lands. The Santa Marta *colono* movement appealed to peasants and wage-labourers because it drew on their common conviction that the formation of the banana plantations had occurred through the illegal privatisation of public lands. The rural populace believed that Colombian law had been violated, that the United Fruit Company was in the wrong, and that peasants had a legal right to squat on those lands. This acute sense of injustice fuelled both the resistance of peasants against expropriation during times of export growth and the squatter occupations of United Fruit Company properties during periods of export contraction.

In conclusion, static class analysis is not enough to explain the genesis, forms, and ideology of rural protest movements. It is essential to consider the historical process of class formation and the influence of economic cycles and evolving legal-institutional forms upon it. Rural social consciousness does not just reflect the organisation of production at a specific point in time. In Santa Marta, at least, it is a product of the transformations that are an integral part of rural life. It is an expression of historical memory that cuts across occupational bounds and that gives rural people, both peasants and proletarians, a set of shared convictions and forms of action on which they may or may not choose to act at any given point in time.

Notes

1. Public land in Latin America is territory to which the state holds right of domain. It is equivalent to public land in the United States or Crown land in Canada.

2. On conditions in the Santa Marta region prior to the advent of the United Fruit Company, see Uribe Uribe [1908], Nichols [1973], Botero and Guzmán Barney [1977], and Partridge [1979].

3. In the late 1870s and 1880s, several English, French, and American investors purchased large tracts of land around Santa Marta and began to experiment with producing tobacco, cacao, sugar cane, and, finally, bananas for export. Among these operations was the Colombian Land Company in which Minor Keith, soon-to-be founder of the United Fruit Company, was a major shareholder. With the incorporation of the United Fruit Company in 1899, the properties of the Colombian Land Company passed under its control. See Botero and Guzmán Barney [1977: 313–36].

4. See, for example, Kepner [1936]; May and Plaza [1958: 200–205]; Urrutia [1969: 99–108]; and Casey Gaspar [1979: 118–24].

5. The efforts of the United Fruit Company to import Jamaican labourers into Colombia were blocked by the Departmental Assembly around 1908 for, it has been suggested, racist motives [*Fonnegra*, 1980: 17].

6. See Uribe Uribe [1908: 102]; Zambrano et al. [1974: n.p.]; White [1978: 43–51]; and Fonnegra [1980: 15–18].

7. For descriptions of work patterns, see Luna Cardenas [1960] and Partridge [1979: 495–96].

8. In Colombia, the term *colono* generally refers to a cultivator of public lands.

9. On the role played by middle- and large-scale cultivators of public lands in Colombian land conflicts, see LeGrand [1980: 244–55].

10. See Botero and Guzmán Barney [1977: 337–55, 377–86]. In the late 1920s, the United Fruit Company produced approximately 40 percent and Colombian planters 60 percent of the bananas shipped out of Santa Marta. Unfortunately, available statistics do not allow us to determine the total amount of land held by the Colombian planters apart from that devoted to banana groves.

11. The records of the Public Land Commission (Comisión de Baldíos) appointed by the Colombian government to defend public property in the banana zone provide insight into the methods of land accumulation employed by the United Fruit Company and Colombian planters in the period 1924–1931. See ANCB volumes 52, 56, 60, 61, and 66.

12. These cases of peasant expropriation are described in detail in the Colombian Public Land Archives [ANCB]. See LeGrand [1980: 335] for exact references. Most of these confrontations. it would seem. occurred along the path of the Company railroad, which pushed further and further into the interior during the early decades of the twentieth century. The construction of new rail lines and the formation of private property went hand in hand. Eventually all land within 30 miles of the railroad was incorporated into the banana plantations.

13. Government officials working with the Public Land Commission in the banana zone also believed that the United Fruit Company was capable of such action [See *ANCB* Vol. 60 f.147].

14. Both of these issues were openly debated in the banana zone in the 1920s. Local merchants were particularly vocal in advocating the abolition of Company stores, while a group of native banana planters urged the Colombian government to nationalise Company canals so as to provide for a more equitable distribution

of water in the zone. See Gilhodes [1967] and White [1978: 53–72] for analyses of tensions between the United Fruit Company and local planters and merchants.

15. According to Partridge [1975: 151], the United Fruit Company deducted 2 percent from its workers' salaries to cover health services. For data on the number and type of illnesses treated in Company hospitals, see Colombia [1922: 27].

16. These petitions are to be found in the Colombian Public Land Archives. See LeGrand [1980: 335] for exact references.

17. These were Laws 61 of 1874 and 48 of 1882. For a history of Colombian public land legislation, see LeGrand [1980: 36–74].

18. For the history of labour movements in Colombia, see Urrutia [1969] and Pécaut [1973].

19. On early labour organisation in the banana zone, see White [1978: 73–85]; Fonnegra [1980: 59–70]; and ANCB [Vol. 65, fs.346, 380 and 462; Vol. 60, f.169bis; and Vol. 72, f.293].

20. Most studies of the Colombian banana zone centre on the strike of 1928, which was not, as novelist Gabriel García Márquez [1970] suggests, immediately forgotten. Rather, the strike and its repression contributed to the fall of the Conservative government in 1930 and the rise of the great populist politician Jorge Eliécer Gaitán to prominence. Despite growing interest in this strike, the definitive study has yet to be written. Useful material is to be found in Colombia [1929a]; Kepner [1936]; Cortés Vargas [1979]; Castrillón [1974]; Gaitán [n.d.]; Urrutia [1969: 99–108]; White [1978: 85–122]; and Fonnegra [1980: 77–187].

21. The number of deaths in the banana massacre has yet to be determined. Estimates range from 13 to 3,000 [*Partridge*, 1979: 496]. The U.S. ambassador in Colombia at the time admitted that as many as 1,000 people may have been killed [*DS/NA RG59*:821.6156/129]. The role played in the strike by the merchants of Santa Marta remains to be investigated. Interestingly, of the 31 strike leaders jailed, ten were merchants. Five female house servants (*domésticas*), four day-labourers, three printers, two cultivators (*agricultores*), a carpenter, a mechanic, and a tailor also received prison sentences [Cortés Vargas, 1979: 167–68].

22. On the economic crisis in the banana zone, see Padilla and Llanos [1964: 2–4]; AHOH [box 1, folder 23, fs. 182–3; box 2, folder 37, f.8; and box 3, folder 76, "Informe del Inspector de Policía al Gobernador de Magdalena"]; and DS/NA RG59 [821.50/20, 821.77/650, 821.6156/119, 821.6156/132, 821.6156/143, 821.6156/152, and 821.6156/216].

23. See Colombia [1935: 35]; Padilla and Llanos [1964: 3–6]; and ANCB [Vol. 60, fs.167–9 and 201; Vol. 72, fs.66, 293, and 343].

24. LeGrand [1980: 290–306]. At this time the Colombian government was engaged in a dispute with the United Fruit Company over the control of the Santa Marta railroad and the irrigation canals and was encouraging the formation of a national banana cooperative to compete with the foreign monopoly. The United, therefore, had no reason to assume that the Colombian government would necessarily favour its interests. For information on relations between the Colombian government and the United Fruit Company, see Randall [1977: 128–45].

25. See *El Estado*, 2 July 1930 and 12 November 1930; *El Bolshevique*, 8 December 1934; *Tierra*, 24 September 1938 and 12 December 1938; Colombia [1935: 17–19]; Colombia [1939: 11–13]; and DS/NA RG59 [821.5041/14].

26. See *El Estado*, 9 October 1930; AHOH [box 2, folder 35, "Informe de la Zona Bananera al Ministerio de Gobierno," and box 2, folder 37, f.8]; DS/NA RG59 [821.00B/35]; and Gilhodes [1967: 313].

27. For the history of the United Fruit Company in Colombia after 1935, see Gilhodes [1967]; Colombia [1957]; INCORA-ILACO [1967]; and SAGROCOL [1967].

28. Donald Sawyer [1979] also makes this point in his study of peasants on the Amazonian frontier of Brazil.

29. See, for example, Orlove and Custred's otherwise admirable book [1980], which denies altogether the importance of property relations in studying Andean social history.

References

Archives

AHOH—Academia Colombiana de Historia, Archivo del Presidente Enrique Olaya Herrera, Bogotá.
ANCB—Archivo Nacional de Colombia, Ministerio de Industrias, Correspondencia de Baldíos, Bogotá, 78 vols.
DS/NA RG59—General Records of the U.S. Department of State, Record Group 59, National Archives, Washington, DC.

Government Publications and Secondary Sources

Alavi, Hamza, 1965, "Peasants and Revolution," in Ralph Milliband and John Saville (eds.), *The Socialist Register*, London: The Merlin Press.
Bartra, Roger, 1974, *Estructura agraria y clases sociales en México*, Mexico City: Ediciones Era.
Botero, Fernando, and Alvaro Guzmán Barney, 1977, "El enclave agrícola en la zona bananera de Santa Marta," *Cuadernos Colombianos*, 11: 313–37.
Casey Gaspar, Jeffrey, 1979, *Limón, 1880–1940: Un estudio de la industria bananera en Costa Rica*, San José: Editorial Costa Rica.
Castrillón, Alberto, 1974, *120 días bajo el terror militar*, 2nd ed., Bogotá: Editorial Tupac-Amaru. Originally published 1929.
Colombia, 1922, Departmento de Magdalena, *Informe del Gobernador de Magdalena a la Asamblea Departamental y del Secretario de Gobierno al Gobernador*, Santa Marta: Imprenta Departamental.
_____, 1929a, Ministerio de Industrias, "Informe rendida por el Sr. Jefe de la Oficina General de Trabajo y el abogado de la misma sobre el movimiento obrero occurrido en el departamento del Magdalena," in *Memoria del Ministerio de Industrias al Congreso Nacional*, Bogotá: Imprenta Nacional.
_____, 1929b, *Exposición motivada que presenta el gobierno a las cámaras legislativas acerca de la turbación del orden público en una provincia del departamento de Magdalena a fines del año pasado*, Bogotá: Imprenta Nacional.
_____, 1930, "Informe de la comisión nombrada para estudiar el conflicto surgido entre la United Fruit Company y la Cooperativa Bananera Colombiana," published in *El Tiempo* (Bogotá), 15 November 1930.
_____, 1935, *Informes que rindió a la honorable Cámara de Representantes la comisión designada para visitar la zona bananera del Magdalena*, Bogotá: Imprenta Nacional.

_____, 1939, Departamento de Magdalena, *Informe del Gobernador del Departamento a la Asamblea Departamental*, Santa Marta: Imprenta Departamental.

_____, 1957, Contraloría General de la República, "Monograffa económica del Magdalena y de la industria del banano," *Economía Colombiana*, Vol. 12, No. 35, 611–29.

Cortés Vargas, Carlos, 1979, *Los sucesos de las bananeras*, 2nd ed., Bogotá: Editorial Desarrollo. Originally published 1929.

de Janvry, Alain, 1981, *The Agrarian Question and Reformism in Latin America*, Baltimore: Johns Hopkins University Press.

Fonnegra, Gabriel, 1980, *Bananeras: testimonio vivo de una epopeya*, Bogotá: Tercer Mundo.

Gaitán, Jorge Eliécer, n.d., *1928: la masacre en las bananeras: documentos–testimonios*, Medellín: Ediciones Pepe.

García Márquez, Gabriel, 1970, *One Hundred Years of Solitude*, trans. Gregory Rabassa, New York: Harper and Row.

Gilhodes, Pierre, 1967, "La Colombie et l'United Fruit Company," *Revue Française de Science Politique*, Vol. 17, No. 11, 307–17.

Henriquez, Demetrio Daniel, 1939, *Monografía completa de la zona bananera*, Santa Marta: Tipografía el Progreso.

INCORA-ILACO (Instituto Colombiano de la Reforma Agraria), 1967, *Estado actual y perspectivas agro-económicas de la zona bananera de Santa Marta y del area de influencia en el departamento de Magdalena*, Bogotá: INCORA.

Kepner, Charles, 1936, *Social Aspects of the Banana Industry*, New York: Columbia University Press.

Leeds, Anthony, 1977, "Mythos and Pathos: Some Unpleasantries on Peasantries," in Rhoda Halperin and James Dow (eds.), *Peasant Livelihood: Studies in Economic Anthropology and Cultural Ecology*, New York: St. Martin's Press, 227–56.

LeGrand, Catherine, 1980, "From Public Lands into Private Properties: Landholding and Rural Conflict in Colombia, 1870–1936," Ph.D. dissertation, Stanford University.

Luna Cardenas, Alberto, 1960, *Un año y otros días con el General Benjamin Herrera en las bananeras de Aracataca*, Medellín: Editorial Bedout.

May, Stacey, and Galo Plaza, 1958, *The United Fruit Company in Latin America*, Washington: National Planning Association.

Mintz, Sidney, 1964, "Foreword" in Ramiro Guerra y Sánchez, *Sugar and Society in the Caribbean*, New Haven: Yale University Press.

_____, 1973, "A Note on the Definition of Peasantries," *The Journal of Peasant Studies*, Vol. 1, No. 1, 91–106.

_____, 1974, "The Rural Proletariat and the Problem of Rural Proletarian Consciousness," *The Journal of Peasant Studies*, Vol. 1, No. 3, 291–325.

Nichols, Theodore, 1973, *Tres puertos de Colombia*, Bogotá: Banco Popular.

Orlove, Benjamin, and Glynn Custred (eds.), 1980, *Land and Power in Latin America*, New York: Holmes Meier.

Padilla B., Pedro M., and Alberto O. Llanos, 1964, "Proyecto Magdalena 4: zona bananera," Bogotá: Instituto Colombiano de la Reforma Agraria (mimeo).

Paige, Jeffrey, 1975, *Agrarian Revolution: Social Movements and Export Agriculture in the Underdeveloped World*, New York: The Free Press.

Partridge, William L., 1975, "Cannabis and Cultural Groups in a Colombian Municipio," in Vera Rubin (ed.), *Cannabis and Culture*, The Hague: Mouton Publishers, 147–72.

_____, 1979, "Banana Country in the Wake of United Fruit: Social and Economic Linkages," *American Ethnologist*, Vol. 6, No. 3, 491–509.

Pécaut, Daniel, 1973, *Política y sindicalismo en Colombia*, Bogotá: Editorial La Carreta.

Quiñonez, Jorge, and Gustavo Z. Jaramillo, 1962, "Informe sobre la zona bananera del Magdalena," Bogotá: Instituto Colombiano de la Reforma Agraria (mimeo).

Randall, Stephen, 1977, *The Diplomacy of Modernization: Colombian-American Relations, 1920–1940*, Toronto: University of Toronto Press.

Roseberry, William, 1978, "Peasants as Proletarians," *Critique of Anthropology*, Vol. 3, No. 11, 3–18.

SAGROCOL, 1967, "Desarrollo agropecuario del Proyecto Magdalena 4: zona bananera," Bogotá: Instituto Colombiano de la Reforma Agraria (mimeo).

Sawyer, Donald, 1979, "Peasants and Capitalism on an Amazon Frontier," Ph.D. dissertation, Harvard University.

Smith, T. Lynn, 1967, *Colombia: Social Structure and the Process of Development*, Gainesville: University of Florida Press.

Stinchcombe, Arthur, 1961, "Agricultural Enterprise and Rural Class Relations," *American Journal of Sociology*, Vol. 67, No. 2, 165–76.

Torres Giraldo, Ignacio, 1974, *Los incomformes: historia de la rebeldía de las masas en Colombia*, Vol. 4, Bogotá: Editorial Margen Izquierda.

_____, 1978, *Los inconformes: historia de la rebeldía de las masas en Colombia*, Vol. 5, Bogotá: Editorial Latina.

Uribe Uribe, Rafael, 1908, *El banano: conferencia dictada ante la Sociedad de Agricultores de Colombia*, San José, Costa Rica: Imprenta Avelino Alsina.

Urrutia, Miguel, 1969, *The Development of the Colombian Labor Movement*, New Haven: Yale University Press.

White, Judith, 1978, *Historia de una ignominia: La United Fruit Co. en Colombia*, Bogotá: Editorial Presencia.

Wolf, Eric R., 1969, *Peasant Wars of the Twentieth Century*, New York: Harper & Row.

Zambrano, Fabio, et al., 1974, "Colombia: desarrollo agrícola, 1900–1930," Tesis de Grado, Universidad Tadeo Lozano, Bogotá.

Newspapers

El Bolshevique (Bogotá)
El Estado (Santa Marta)
Tierra (Bogotá)

10

Labor Control in the Declining Mexican Revolution

Norman Caulfield

As Norman Caulfield explains in the book from which this selection is drawn, the revolutionary governments of Mexico took on an enormous task when they guaranteed the rights of labor in the Constitution of 1917. A complex relationship arose in which organized workers derived a certain satisfaction from the government's promise to provide for their welfare. Yet they soon realized that such guarantees did not come without a price. In repeated instances over the decades following the Revolution, the cost was seen in government efforts to control labor activities. Particularly, governments wished to control the timing and circumstances of strikes without, however, taking control of that process. In the paradoxical view of the Revolutionary governments, it was important that labor be dependent on them for its independence. Growing labor discontent became a potential embarrassment to a regime that based much of its claim to rule on the support of the workers. The emergence of the charro, a local nationalist (and anti-Communist) union leader loyal to the Revolution, was vital to the government's program of economic and social development in Mexico. Caulfield analyzes the difficulties in getting charro candidates elected to leadership positions. In the selection included here, he focuses on a famous 1959 wildcat strike by railway workers. The strike was an outcome of a combination of circumstances: pressures arising from U.S. investment, federal development programs in the initial stages of the Cold War, and the government's use of charros to keep workers in line.

The state's efforts to enlist the support of organized labor for a national development policy of industrialization reached a climax during the early years of the Cold War. The Mexican development project converged with U.S. business and government desires for new markets and outlets for capital investment. Because the industrialization program required continued capital flow from the U.S. to reinvest profits and establish joint ventures with American companies, leaders from both countries realized that profits and returns depended on social stability, which to a great extent rested upon the ability of the Mexican trade-union bureaucracy to manage rank-and-file discontent.[1] As U.S. investment poured into Mexico, government leaders embraced and employed the anti-communist politics of the Cold War to consolidate charro rule and rid the trade unions of independent elements that opposed state development policy.

American union leaders cooperated with U.S. government officials in opposing economic nationalism in all of its forms, and in the process shaped the development and direction of the Mexican labor movement. Working through ORIT [Organización Regional Interamericano de Trabajadores] and the U.S. embassy, American trade-unionists provided cooperating Mexican labor leaders with logistical and financial support in their battle against forces within the movement that resisted charrismo.[2] The AFL's [American Federation of Labor's] activities in Mexico were part of a larger effort by U.S. officials to bolster centrist, pro-capitalist unions at a global level.[3]

The American policy focused particularly on gathering information on the Mexican labor movement by inviting labor leaders to the U.S. Through these contacts, U.S. officials designed a strategy to provide crucial technical and financial assistance to Mexican labor leaders who increasingly embraced the anti-communism of the Cold War. U.S. State Department personnel relied heavily on AFL leader George Meany as a point man for selling their policy objectives to Mexican labor leaders. Meany and other U.S. trade union leaders played instrumental roles in escalating anti-communist rhetoric by alleging that Mexican unions had been infiltrated by communists and agents of Russia. Meany explained that the AFL goal in Latin America was "to create friendship and support for the U.S. in opposition to the Communists who sought the same support and friendship of Russia."[4]

The communists and agents Meany had referred to were elements within the Mexican labor movement that opposed placing economic growth before the rights of workers and improvement in their living standards. Although the Mexican economy grew and foreign investment increased, inflation continued to eat away at wages. New labor federations and factions within unions emerged to defend the workers' right to strike and earn a decent living. Although these new labor groups generally supported Mexico's drive to industrialize, they welcomed foreign investment only if it contributed to the authentic progress of Mexico. Upholding working-class nationalism and the gains made by workers during the Revolution, these labor groups were the first line of defense against state attempts to impose development policy through charro leadership. The struggle between autonomists and charro forces reached a climax during the teachers' rebellion and the railroad workers' strike of 1958–1959, both of which the government successfully suppressed.

The Americans and the CTM's Struggle for Hegemony

The government-CTM [Confederación de Trabajadores Mexicanos] campaign to manage rank-and-file discontent and tie organized labor to state development policy evolved into a two-track strategy. First, the CTM attempted to "raid" smaller independent unions that opposed the state's industrialization program. The second strategy entailed the removal of "autonomists" and "independents" from key leadership positions at both local and national levels in the major industrial unions. Both of these strategies involved the direct participation of ORIT, U.S. trade unions and the American government. The internationalization of the conflict strengthened the hand of the state and their trade-union allies as they forced the opposition to engage in ideological debate rather than welding unity around the fight for higher wages and union autonomy. Armed with American dollars and anti-communist ideology, the CTM attempted to absorb and to transform smaller unions that resisted charrismo and state development policy.

In an effort to defend smaller unions against CTM encroachment, the Confederación Unica and remnants of older federations merged to form the Confederación Revolucionaria de Obreros y Campesinos (CROC). Representing around 100,000 workers, the CROC suffered from personality conflicts and ideological differences.[5] Leaders subordinated the fight for wage increases to quarrelling over international affiliation. While railroad union leader Luis Gómez Z. promoted affiliation with the leftist CTAL [Confederación de Trabajadores de América Latina] and opposed Enrique Rangel, a former anarchosyndicalist who argued for joining ORIT, other CROC leaders opted for an alliance with the Agrupación de Trabajadores Latino Americanos Sindicalistas (ATLAS). ATLAS attempted to unite all Latin American workers' organizations under the aegis of the Argentine government and its president, Juan Domingo Perón, who successfully had placed the labor movement in that country under tight state control.[6] While Rangel rejected affiliation with ATLAS because it was a government-controlled federation, Gómez Z. argued that joining ORIT was no different, because it would also lead to state control of the Mexican labor movement. At the same time, however, Gómez Z. defended Perón's economic nationalism by comparing it with Mexico's situation. He added that the U.S. opposed ATLAS and the CTAL because both represented a challenge to American economic hegemony in Latin America.[7]

While the CROC remained non-affiliated to an international labor federation, the ideological bickering weakened its resolve to combat the CTM's raiding of smaller unions. In early 1954 the CROC further discredited itself when the CTM threatened a general strike during the government's devaluation of the peso. Instead of joining the CTM in opposing the devaluation plan, the CROC attempted to curry government favor. The strategy backfired as the CTM signed a "pact of friendship" and "bloc of unity" with the CROM [Confederación Regional de Obreros Mexicanos], the CGT [Confederación General de Trabajadores], and the charro union leadership of the miners, railroad, electrical and Federation of State Workers (FSTSE). While negotiating meager wage hikes for their members, the participants received official labor status from the ruling PRI in exchange for pledging to fight communist and subversive activities within their respective locals.[8] The financial assistance provided by ORIT facilitated the unity and played an even more important role in the CTM's campaign to absorb smaller unions.[9] The help provided by ORIT was particularly timely because the Mexican government had curtailed subsidies to the CTM and all "friendly" labor organizations. Fidel Velázquez personally requested assistance from the CIO's Latin American representative, Ernst Schwarz, who assured him that ORIT's resources would be available for CTM operations in the absence of Mexican government funding.[10]

The financial pledge was an integral part of ORIT's strategy in aiding the CTM in the removal of communists and independents from Mexico's industrial unions. A key component of ORIT funding involved the printing and distribution of literature and propaganda critical of radical unionism. Initially, the CTM-ORIT propaganda offensive targeted the traditionally militant miners' union, in which communists and independents held a number of high posts. The campaign began after a 1953 Mexico visit by Paul Reed, the United Mine Workers' international representative. With ORIT money and the support of Serafino Romualdi, the AFL's point man on Latin American labor relations, Reed hoped to convince the miners' national leadership to join the CTM and take measures to rid their local unions of communists. Although Reed's lack of spoken Spanish and knowledge about Mexico's labor movement contributed to his failure to convince the miners to join the CTM, he did manage to negotiate an agreement between the American government's United States Information Service (USIS) and the miners' union.[11]

Through the agreement, the USIS distributed films and forty projectors for use in miners' locals throughout Mexico. The content of the films represented the best in Cold War propaganda as they pointed out the dangers of communism, extolled the virtues of business unionism and emphasized labor-government cooperation. The USIS also printed and distributed free pamphlets to union locals throughout Mexico and donated fifty books to a new labor library in San Luis Potosí.[12] As miners' locals were flooded with USIS propaganda, Reed proposed the formation of a Latin American miners' federation that would function under ORIT authority. The long-range strategy to tie the miners' union to ORIT also included financing the campaigns of charro and anti-communist candidates in local union elections.[13]

The USIS and ORIT dollars elected a substantial number of anti-communist union officials, some of whom captured posts at the national level. As a means to consolidate charro power, ORIT funded a speaking tour of the elected officials to other union locals to convince the membership of the necessity of removing the communist threat from the miners' union. With the cooperation of the mining companies, the charros succeeded in obtaining the dismissal of about twenty-four active Communist Party members as well as independents and communist sympathizers.[14]

Although effective, the charro tactics failed to eliminate all independents and communists in many mining locals, especially in Coahuila and Chihuahua. In those states, leaders allied with [Vicente] Lombardo Toledano and the CTAL to counter ORIT dollars by offering the national union $1,500 in disaster relief for the families victimized by a disaster at the Dolores Mine in Michoacán during April 1954. They also invited the miners' union on a paid trip to the leftist-leaning World Federation of Trade Unions (WFTU) Congress in Vienna, Austria. Attempting to counter growing anti-communist sentiment, Lombardo stressed that the invitation entailed no ideological commitment.[15]

With more funds at their disposal, ORIT overcame Lombardo's shrewd maneuvering. Through the use of the Mexico City newspaper, *Noticiario Obrero Interamericano*, ORIT denounced Lombardo and all anti-charro elements within the miners' union as communist agents in the service of the Soviet Union. Complementing the propaganda offensive, Paul Reed enticed the miners' leadership with American dollars to pay for additional staff and services. With ORIT dollars, mining locals enhanced their prestige and visibility on a national level. Commanding more resources, ORIT and Reed convinced the miners' national leadership to reject Lombardo's invitation. In effect, Reed and ORIT had bought the miners' union leadership and helped to entrench the charro administration of Filiberto Rabalcava.[16]

The CTM and ORIT also worked to influence the leadership of the federal workers' union. Once again, financial resources were a central feature of ORIT strategy. Federal workers' union leaders affiliated with the American Cultural Institute in the United States Embassy. Through the institute, they received instruction in English and collaborated in the development of a new course in industrial relations at the National University of Mexico.[17] The American embassy also awarded promising union leaders USIS Leader Grants to travel to Washington and receive further training.

The Leader Grants were an outgrowth of the Mutual Security Act, which empowered President Harry Truman's "Point Four" programs initiated in 1949 and designed to fight communism in developing countries through U.S. economic expansion. Sections 516 and 528 of the Mutual Security Act called on the United States to encourage the development of "free labor" union movements. In practice this involved identifying pro-U.S., anti-communist trade-unionists to send to the United States for training. The grants were part of a broader strategy to assist in the struggle against communist and independent unionists, a category that included national-ists, socialists and intransigent rank and file. As part of the program, pub-lic employees' union Presidents Abelardo de la Torre and Florencia Maya received extensive labor relations training through the study of labor sta-tistics, collective bargaining, safety inspection and wage and cost-of-living indexes.[18] Besides providing training the USIS grants allowed Mexican trade-union leaders to establish cordial and working relation-ships with U.S. public employee unions like the postal workers.[19] Other grant recipients followed and stayed in the United States for six months, in which, after three weeks of intensive English, they studied labor eco-nomics, statistics and American history. Grantees spent their final weeks observing operations of unions and visiting work sites.[20]

When labor leaders returned from training, ORIT financed travel and lectures for them throughout Mexico. With ORIT and USIS dollars, Mexi-can labor leaders published dozens of books, articles and pamphlets that extolled the virtues of AFL-style unionism and partnership between gov-ernment, industry and organized labor. One result of the propaganda was the founding of an association of labor leader grant recipients, called the Círculo Samuel Gompers.[21] Instrumental in starting the group was former anarchist and trade-union leader Rosendo Salazar, who with USIS and ORIT money, published a biography of Samuel Gompers. The USIS dis-tributed the Gompers biography to union locals throughout Mexico free of charge.[22]

The ORIT financing also helped Círculo Samuel Gompers members publish newspapers for smaller unions in remote areas of Mexico. This contributed to the CTM's efforts to incorporate these unions into its ranks, all of which had been struggling financially. Key to the CTM's success was the ORIT and U.S. industrial unions' financing of the construction of a new office building and headquarters. Besides providing ample space for the CTM national directorate and all of its affiliates, the structure also housed ORIT's executive operations. The building provided a symbol of strength for the CTM and served to legitimize its policies. It also facili-tated the CTM's absorption of smaller unions that struggled to provide logistical and staff support for their membership. ORIT funding enabled these organizations to affirm their existence; in the process they strength-ened the CTM's position within the Mexican labor movement against the forces that opposed charrismo.[23]

In the immediate years ahead, government officials and charro leaders put their extensive training into practice when they settled close to 40,000 labor disputes, most of which provided for minuscule wage increases.[24] To enforce the new contracts, the CTM and charro union leaders formed the Bloque de Unidad Obrera—Workers' Unity Bloc (BUO)—whose sole purpose was to legitimize agreements drawn up by industry, charro-controlled unions and the government. Although these maneuvers limited the expression of workers' demands, they were not able to repress rank-and-file militancy and convert unions into passive instruments of the state.

Rank-and-File Rebellion and the Charro Counterattack

The overwhelming financial backing of American labor unions to charro leaders failed to quell discontent. Rank and file continued to protest wage freezes, no-strike pledges and attempts to discipline them in the workplace. As workers' incomes stagnated and the distribution of wealth skewed upward, rank-and-file union members joined insurgent movements within the established trade unions and federations in opposition to charro leaders. Although some insurgent leaders were communists, socialists and ideologues, the majority merely sought the democratization and autonomy of their unions as a means to achieve higher wages and better working conditions. They viewed these goals as tantamount to defending the rights guaranteed to workers in the 1917 Constitution.

An insurgent movement among communication workers began on February 6, 1958, when 7,000 telegraph workers walked off the job in protest of the secretary of communications and public works violation of contract work rules. The secretary had transferred what he called thirty-seven communist agitators to posts outside Mexico City. Strikers called for a fifty percent pay increase and defied government and charro demands for a return to work by cutting off the Federal District's internal telephone services. The strike gained momentum when nearly 500 international telephone operators struck, severing communications with dozens of countries. On February 15, 1960, Radio Chapultepec employees and hundreds of telegraph workers who operated direct lines in banks and aviation companies began walking picket lines. As postal workers threatened to join their ranks, charros desperately sought a solution to the conflict.[25]

In conjunction with the charro leadership of the Federation of State Workers' union, the secretary of communications revoked the transfer order and petitioned the government for a modest wage increase, infuriating the charro leadership. Instead of negotiating, the charros denounced the secretary's concession to communist agitators and insisted that no negotiations take place until the strikers returned to work. The strikers responded by sharply criticizing the union leadership for not representing genuine worker sentiment. The government, trying to avoid making martyrs of the strikers during an election year, timidly watched as charro leaders attempted to defuse the situation during a February 16, 1958, Mexico City meeting.[26]

The meeting witnessed strikers shouting down Federation of State Workers' union General Secretary Abelardo de la Torre as he attempted to speak and to offer them a meager seven percent wage increase. Strike leaders stood on chairs and denounced the union's leadership as traitors. The speakers repudiated the leadership's authority and declared that only they should represent the membership in negotiations with the government. As the walkout progressed, strikers clandestinely received financial support from other unions. The expression of solidarity ultimately led to the formation of a new union—Alianza. Immediately the press and the charro leadership orchestrated a propaganda campaign to discredit the Alianza by calling it unpatriotic and communistic. The Cold War rhetoric eventually produced cracks in the Alianza's leadership and pressure mounted for a negotiated settlement. The strikers finally accepted the original offer of a seven percent wage increase under the name of the Alianza, not the charro-led union.[27]

The communications workers' rebellion gave railroad and petroleum workers new faith. Stymied by charro manipulation of parliamentary procedures, railroad rank and filers followed former union heads Valentín Campa and Luis Gómez Z. in an attempted forceful takeover of six local union headquarters. The insurgents targeted a group of charro leaders called "October 14," which was led by Fidel Velázquez's cousin, Ricardo Velázquez Vázquez. After barricading themselves inside the local union halls for several hours, police and federal soldiers used tear gas and night-sticks to dislodge them. The authorities' actions ensured the continuation of charro leadership.[28]

In the petroleum workers' union, charro leaders conspired with the secretary of labor to hold a secret-ballot referendum that would nullify previous elections where independents and communists had won a majority of the national union posts. With government complicity, the charro slate of candidates stuffed ballot boxes and lost ballots, as well as other frauds, to win the election.[29] The results demoralized the independent forces and led to more labor-management agreements that limited union autonomy and held down wages. Working-class living standards continued to deteriorate.

While the real wages of federal employees had fallen fifty percent between 1938 and 1952, teachers' salaries suffered a worse fate. Urban primary school teachers, especially the 15,582 of Mexico City, experienced acute inflationary pressures.[30] In 1956, after suffering attacks from charros and failing to win wage increases, members of the National Education Workers' Union (SNTE) decided to organize an independent faction much like the CTM depuradas of the 1940s. Under the leadership of Othón Salazar, a former member of a communist youth organization, teachers formed the Comité de Lucha y Democratización.

Based in the Federal District, the Comité de Lucha attempted to regain control of its local unions from the charro leaders. When the national union refused to conduct elections and called for the dissolution of the rank-and-file committee, the insurgents held their own convention. With over 15,000 Mexico City teachers in attendance, they elected Othón Salazar as general secretary. The committee asserted that the national union leadership had betrayed the Mexican Revolution, and accordingly, had changed its name in late 1957 to the Teachers' Revolutionary Movement (MRM). The Revolutionary Movement hoped to attract nationalistic elements within the PRI by backing Adolfo López Mateos, the ruling party's official candidate for the presidency in 1958. The Revolutionary Movement leaders based their strategy on advice given to them by Lombardo Toledano, head of the People's Party (PP), and Dionisio Encino, general secretary of the Communist party. Lombardo and Encino suggested that the rank and file work through the established political system and not challenge the charros directly.[31]

While supporting López Mateos, the Revolutionary Movement called for a forty percent wage increase and retirement after forty years' service. It attempted to present the demands during an April 12, 1958, demonstration in Mexico City where police greeted them with tear gas, clubs and pistols. The repression prompted the Revolutionary Movement's leadership to call for a strike of Mexico City kindergartens and primary schools. Teachers responded and shut down the schools for several weeks, generating a propaganda offensive by the national teachers' union charros and Unity Bloc leader Jesús Yuren, a Leader Grant recipient and Círculo Samuel Gompers member, accusing Salazar and the Revolutionary Movement of being part of a "plan of an international character," bent on destroying national worker unity and creating a climate of anarchy.[32] Despite the attacks, the strike continued and received support from parents, students and other unions, such as the electricians and railroad workers. The unity expressed by rank and filers prohibited the charros from recruiting strikebreakers, and thus forced the government to grant a substantial enough pay increase to end the strike.

The charro bureaucracy still refused to recognize Salazar and others, however, as the legitimate heads of the Mexico City locals. On September 6, 1958, the Revolutionary Movement organized a demonstration at the Monument of the Revolution and called for the recognition of the union's democratically elected officials. Police attacked the demonstrators and arrested 208 persons, including Salazar, whom authorities charged with conspiring to "dissolve" the state. The seriousness of the charges reflected the Mexican and U.S. government's concern over the growth of the anti-charro movement. U.S. officials working in Mexico expressed concern about the growing discontent among Mexico's lower classes and the communist influence within trade unions. They specifically identified Othón Salazar and railroad worker Demetrio Vallejo as communist agitators and as threats to Mexico's stability.[33]

Although the concern about a communist threat was probably exaggerated, the rank-and-file challenge to the charro system was genuine. Telegraph workers already had left the communications workers' union and had joined teachers in their efforts to form a committee that advocated labor union democracy and autonomy. A month prior to Salazar's arrest, petroleum workers belonging to Locals #34 and #35 staged a hunger strike in the PEMEX building to pressure the secretary of labor to recognize anti-charro leaders Carlos Castillo and Ignacio Hernández Alcala as presidents of their respective unions. As with the teachers, police used tear gas and clubs to remove the workers from the PEMEX facility.

The repression strengthened the resolve of the anti-charro forces, and, as a consequence, the government began negotiations and promised to release all of the arrested teachers, except strike leaders, provided that the work stoppages ended immediately. In another tactical move, the Labor Department exerted pressure on the national teachers' union leadership to hold new elections. The Revolutionary Movement insurgents easily won the fairly held elections. On December 4, 1958, three days after López Mateos became president, the government released Salazar and other union officials and recognized the anti-charro officials in the petroleum workers' union. The rank-and-file victories encouraged workers in other unions to demand democratization as the path to better working conditions and a decent wage.

The Great Rebellion of 1959

Despite almost a decade of widespread repression against rebellious elements in the railroad workers' union—which included a reign of terror by paramilitary groups—rank-and-file members organized local committees to agitate for immediate wage increases. On May 2, 1958, they gathered their forces at the union's national headquarters to pressure the charro leadership.[34] The dissidents were part of a group called *pro-aumento salarios* (for salary increases). Historically railroad workers had resisted government tutelage and fought tenaciously against wage discrimination. During the Porfiriato they had struggled against the American management's practices of discrimination against Mexican nationals. They had resisted joining the CROM and demanded self-management during the Cárdenas era. Railroad workers now called for an immediate monthly pay increase of 350 pesos at the government-controlled Mexican National Railway. Their leaders, Demetrio Vallejo and Roberto Gómez Godínez from Local #13 in Matías Romero, Oaxaca, came under attack from charro Samuel Ortega Hernández, the railroad union's general secretary. Ortega Hernández denounced them as "communist agitators" and demanded that the commission they headed cease its activities. While Vallejo dismissed Ortega's comments and continued to challenge his authority, the Mexican Communist Party (PCM) central committee sided with the charro bureaucrats and called for a wage increase of only 250 pesos a month.[35]

When the director of the Mexican National Railway asked for sixty days to study the situation, rumors spread that the state-run enterprise was only prepared to offer the railroad workers sixty pesos per month, 140 less than the charro local executive boards had asked for. In Matías Romero, Vallejo reported to Local #13 members the events from Mexico City, despite the local general secretary's attempts to stop the meeting. Local #13 members responded by electing a new executive committee and voted to support the 350-pesos-a-month demand. Although not officially recognized, the local executive board convened a special meeting on June 11, 1958, to discuss the wage issue. The membership gave the company ten days to meet their demands or face a series of work slowdowns. Known as the "Plan of the Southeast," the demand for 350 pesos became the cry of rank and filers in Southern Mexico after Vallejo and Local #13 members had organized dissidents in other locals.[36]

In an attempt to defuse the situation, Ortega Hernández agreed to meet with a group of representatives from six Southern Mexico locals on June 25, 1958. A day later, when the general secretary refused to support the proposed wage increase, workers went on strike. After two consecutive days of two-hour, system-wide shutdowns, the company asked to negotiate with Vallejo's commission instead of the national union leadership. On the strike's third day, oil workers, teachers and students joined the railroaders in street demonstrations. The show of solidarity forced the government to compromise. Despite Vallejo's reservations, railroad workers accepted an increase of 215 pesos, a raise three times greater than originally proposed by the company and more than the union executive committee had demanded.[37]

Spurred on by their victory, the commission forces rallied on July 12, 1958, at the General Union Convention and elected Demetrio Vallejo as their new general secretary. The overthrow of the charros stunned the secretary of labor and the national company. They reacted by refusing to recognize the new leadership. The unionists immediately gave both the company and the secretary of labor an ultimatum: either accept the election results or face another series of work stoppages. Government attempts to negotiate the impending walkouts failed when the secretario de gobernación insisted that the charro leaders return to power. As the shut-down commenced, strikers received support from electrical workers' union leader Agustín Sánchez Delint and representatives of the teachers' union.[38]

An alarmed government ordered the army and the police to seize the railroad workers' union halls. Authorities arrested over 100 strikers and used tear gas to break up daily street demonstrations, which included participants from several other unions. The government combined the use of repression with offers of bonus pay and salary increases. State officials hoped to convince enough strikers to abandon the picket lines and begin operating some of the trains. In Monterrey and San Luis Potosí, where the company tried to run the trains, the strikers' wives physically blocked operations.[39] When efforts to run the trains failed, the government announced that strikers would no longer receive pay. Other unions, such as the telegraph workers, responded by holding one-hour sympathy strikes. When authorities countered by arresting a strike leader, the walkout spread until the army occupied telegraph offices with battalions of infantry and communications personnel. Even as telegraph workers slowly drifted back to their jobs, the show of solidarity forced the government to compromise.[40]

On August 5 the Ministry of Labor announced that an agreement had been reached. It called for an end to the strike and a government promise to allow new elections within fifteen days. In addition, the government withdrew all troops from railroad stations and union halls, released all prisoners with no reprisals, and awarded strikers back pay. Without charro interference, the Vallejo slate of candidates won a landslide victory.[41]

As the 120,000-member railroad workers' union fell to anti-charro forces, the emboldened rank and file began carrying out acts of revenge against supervisory personnel and workers who had remained loyal to the company. In Monterrey, Vallejo supporters seized divisional headquarters and severely beat the superintendent. They also physically abused several of his assistants and union members who had refused to strike. The rank and file's actions left the Monterrey division of the Mexican National Railway without management personnel for more than a week. As attacks against supervisors and charros escalated, the government ordered the 7th Military District to police the railway and provide protection for employees.[42]

After settling scores with old union bureaucrats and management personnel, the new union executive committee drew up an economic analysis of the Mexican National Railway that called for the complete restructuring of the state-owned enterprise. Presented by Demetrio Vallejo to President López Mateos, it called the railroad a "tool of foreign interests" and demanded that the company raise rates and terminate the subsidies given to American-owned mining and metal companies. The report concluded that the proposed changes would make the railroad more profitable and, thereby, enable the business to provide higher wages and better working conditions for employees. The union's critique of the company reflected the enduring working-class nationalism, which traditionally had opposed subordinating labor's interests to the demands of U.S. corporations. The nationalistic overtones in the executive committee's report directly challenged the government's economic plan of continued industrialization through foreign investment.

When the government refused to consider the proposed company reorganization, union leadership rallied its members around the plan in the upcoming contract negotiations with the Mexican National Railway. The plan served as a springboard to develop a strategy to secure higher wages and improved working conditions on smaller lines, which routinely violated contractual terms with their employees. The union set a target date of February 25, 1959, for a general railroad strike if company officials refused to meet the demands for a 16.66 percent raise over the previous 215 pesos, medical attention and medicine for workers' families and new workers' housing or daily rent subsidies paid for by the company.[43] The CTM reacted by initiating a propaganda campaign against the union's leadership, denouncing it as communistic and unpatriotic. The Unity Bloc joined the campaign by accusing the union of "planning acts of sabotage that would lead to the communist leadership's goals of changing the public order."[44]

In spite of the labor bureaucracy's attempts to discredit their demands, Vallejo initiated the strike as planned on February 25, 1959. Immediately, the Ministry of Labor declared the strike illegal. While the union sought injunctions to continue the strike, the government placed police and soldiers in most train terminals. Meanwhile, Vallejo worked through the union's council to try to reach an agreement with President López Mateos. Finally, the government and the union came to terms. The agreement granted workers a 16.66 percent pay increase and promised to rectify previous violations of the contract. The union's willingness to negotiate and remove the red-and-black strike flags stemmed in part from Vallejo's eagerness to respond to the orchestrated propaganda campaign against the strikers. Vallejo insisted throughout the conflict that rather than trying to disrupt and destroy the existing social order as critics claimed, the union intended to work through the system and exercise the workers' constitutional right to strike.[45]

Despite the legality of the union leadership's actions, the entrenched labor bureaucracy continued the verbal assault. Fidel Velázquez charged Vallejo and his followers with "wanting to create a climate of agitation for the benefit of their communist theories."[46] Railroaders working on private lines, however, chose to listen to Vallejo and the union. The recently negotiated victory and Vallejo's defense of Article 123 prompted employees of the Ferrocarril Mexicano to demand wage hikes as well. Workers employed by the Ferrocarriles Unidos de Yucatán and the

Ferrocarril del Pacífico followed suit and set late March strike deadlines. Militancy spread to the telegraph workers as they carried out a series of two-hour strikes and pressed for an election to oust their charro leaders. Both the railroad and telegraph companies refused to negotiate for higher wages because they claimed running contracts did not expire until July 1960.[47]

While workers on the private lines remained militant, Vallejo and the union leadership intervened and set March 25 as a uniform deadline for the walkout. Despite the fact that the strike deadline appeared to increase the bargaining leverage of the private line workers, the companies refused to meet the union's demand for a thirty-five peso daily wage increase. Even as the government prepared army units to intervene, the strike involving 14,000 workers began on schedule. Immediately, the government declared the strike "non-existent" and ordered troops to occupy the rail yards.

The strike affected the Mexican public because it shut down rail traffic at the peak of Holy Week, a traditional time for travel. The strike's effectiveness increased when workers on other lines conducted thirty-minute sympathy strikes. The railroaders received further support when longshoremen in Veracruz walked off their jobs and joined other workers in street demonstrations. Vallejo countered government and charro claims that the strike was "unpatriotic" by consistently stating that the railroad workers were only exercising their constitutional right. He used legal channels to contest the state's ruling and even pledged to determine the sentiment of the rank and file by conducting an election that would decide whether to resume work if the government's position did not change.[48]

The strike held together when Vallejo and the union attained a seventy-two-hour injunction from the court that challenged the government's "non-existent" ruling. The court's action froze the strike's legal status and delayed the possible mass dismissal of employees. Mexican National Railroad workers seized the opportunity by staging one-hour sympathy strikes in Torreón, Durango, Aguascalientes and Tampico. The sympathy strikers even threatened to expand the time of the shutdowns from one to two hours. The government reacted by threatening to initiate mass firings. Union leaders in four Federal District locals responded to the threats by promising a system-wide walkout if the dismissals took place.[49]

On March 28, the government and the private rail companies began mass firings. Strikers on the Mexicano lines also faced dismissal, despite the protection they received from the injunction against the government. Simultaneously, the government began recruiting replacements and rejected Vallejo's offer to renew negotiations. On the Nogales-Guadalajara and Mexico City-Veracruz lines, troops occupied the trains and protected replacement workers and supervisors. While some lines operated at a limited capacity, the workers on the National Railways continued to halt most of the nation's rail traffic. Soon, however, the repression began to take its toll. While the army protected an increasing number of replacement workers, sympathy strikes by Veracruz longshoremen and other unions failed to materialize.[50]

Meanwhile, police made sweeping arrests throughout the country; in Mexico City they jailed the principal leaders, including Vallejo. Initially, the arrests involved about 450 strikers. Authorities charged them with inciting disorder and sedition. Subsequent apprehensions resulted in the jailing of over 1,500 strikers. In Guadalajara alone, authorities incarcerated several hundred strikers. With the militants in jail, the government moved to create a new charro leadership. The morning after Vallejo's arrest, the charros selected a group of workers to convene a meeting and designate a four-man national representative committee as a provisional directorate of the union. The relatively unknown directorate repudiated Vallejo and his tactics and issued a statement that urged the union members to return to their jobs as "good" Mexicans.[51]

The majority of railroad workers ignored the call. Railway operations continued to run only at twenty percent capacity nationwide. Conflict also erupted between pro-Vallejo forces and charro supporters. On April 1 in Monterrey, Vallejo supporters attempted to meet inside the railway union building that police and pro-government unionists had occupied. A pitched battle followed and finally a crowd of about 3,000 strikers moved to the electrical workers' union headquarters where an overwhelming majority voted to reject the government-sponsored bosses. They also vowed to continue the strike until the railroad administration recognized Vallejo's authority and complied with the previous agreement. Finally, as a condition for their return to work, they demanded the release of all jailed union members.[52]

The strikers' bold actions—sabotage and mass street demonstrations—temporarily stopped the government's back-to-work movement. During one protest in Mexico City, police arrested forty Vallejo supporters as they attempted to block the entrance to railroad shops and prevent replacements from working. In Torreón and Durango, strikers destroyed bridges and burned freight cars. The government reacted to the escalating militancy by threatening to cancel the seniority rights of strikers who did not report back to work by April 2.[53]

The ultimatum was effective: key railroad employees such as engineers and mechanics returned to their jobs. By April 3, an estimated sixty percent of Mexico City's National Railway workers as well as those on other lines had returned to work. As the strike ended, the government-sponsored charros announced that they would conduct negotiations with all companies for the reinstatement of fired workers and the restoration of seniority rights. A delegation of pro-government Tampico union members even solicited support from the American consulate for financial aid to reconstruct its local under anti-communist, anti-Vallejo leadership.[54] Even sympathetic elements in other unions joined the anti-Vallejo chorus. Sánchez Delint, leftist leader of the electrical workers' union, condemned the Vallejo-led strike as illegal. He added that his union wholeheartedly supported the government and repudiated tactics that would be "detrimental to the economic needs of the government."[55]

As former allies deserted Vallejo and his followers, repression against the strike movement escalated. During the first two weeks of April the government made mass arrests of union leaders and jailed them incommunicado. In the Nogales Division authorities arrested fifteen key union leaders along with sixty strikers accused of disrupting rail communications in the local terminal. The CTM placed full-page bulletins in the nation's major newspapers that denounced the strike as communist inspired and supported the actions taken by the government. The Mexican press went as far as blaming the Soviets for the strike and called for the immediate expulsion of its diplomatic delegation. The only exception to the press onslaught against the strikers was an editorial in *El Noreste*, which defended the railroad workers' constitutional right to strike.[56]

As the press escalated its attacks against Vallejo, the government formally indicted him on charges of "social dissolution." The charges included acts of sabotage, subverting national institutions, committing provocative acts to disturb the public peace, paralyzing the nation's communications system, endangering the economy by impeding the movement of merchandise and creating shortages of supplies, coercing and interfering with public policy and making threats against constituted authority.

Vallejo answered the charges by insisting that he strictly adhered to the provisions of the Federal Labor Code throughout the negotiations and the strike. He also claimed that he tried to prevent illegal walkouts but was unable to because the strikes represented the "will of the rank and file." Vallejo complained that the government's actions were unjust and that they were only carried out to prevent the existence of trade unions independent of the state.[57] The charges against Vallejo did indeed indicate that the government intended to sweep the union of militants and independents. Authorities declared only two minor union officials of the sixty-five arrested eligible for release on bail. In Vallejo's case, the charge of attempting "social dissolution" made him ineligible.

Despite the charges brought against Vallejo, which resulted in his fifteen-year incarceration, the state's efforts to restore the charro system in the railroad workers' union encountered problems. Even after the government selectively cut the number of regular employees by 5,000 to eliminate "undesirable" elements, the charro leadership failed to consolidate its authority and rebel factions loyal to Vallejo continued to emerge.[58] Pro-Vallejo sentiment remained strong among union members in Oaxaca, Tapachula, and in Tonala, Chiapas, as well as in Guadalajara and

Monterrey, where workers continued to call for the "Defense of the Collective Agreement." In Monterrey on June 21, 1959, 500 Vallejo supporters seized Local #19's hall and held an assembly to denounce the national union leadership and the Monterrey charros. The government reacted immediately, ordering troops to seize the building and remove the rebels. As radical workers in Saltillo, Torreón and Nuevo Laredo followed the example of Monterrey union members, the army occupied union headquarters and rail installations. The rebel workers responded by holding solidarity demonstrations to celebrate the first anniversary of the Vallejo-led June 25, 1958, strike.[59]

Finally, the government used widespread layoffs and more arrests in an attempt to reinforce the charro leaders. Meanwhile, the new charro leaders, Alfredo A. Fabela and Francisco Calderón, accused Vallejo and his administration of robbing the union's treasury of ten million pesos. They claimed that Vallejo had disbursed the majority of money to dissident factions in other unions. In order to tie the union closer to the state and consolidate the government's authority over its activities, Fabela and Calderón secured a thirty million-peso loan from the national treasury.[60] Repression, company retrenchment and the actions of the new charro leaders assured state power in a union that had long advocated autonomy and resisted government meddling in its internal affairs. More importantly, the failure of the railroad workers' challenge to the charro system facilitated governmental ability to impose charro control in other unions and tighten its grip over organized labor.

The 1959 railroad strike represented organized labor's greatest challenge to state authority since the 1916 Casa general strike. Like Vallejo's fifteen-year prison sentence, the severity of that challenge explains the harsh punishment given to the strikers' leadership. But it also demonstrated that charro effectiveness in containing labor unrest would have to become more flexible and responsive to the rank and file. As a result, both the CTM and the government pursued more conciliatory policies toward labor demands after the 1959 conflict. Nonetheless, government control of the movement through political links and violence against intransigent, militant and independent trade-union activists remained the cornerstone of state policy.

Crucial to the development of this strategy during the 1950s was the U.S. labor movement's participation in consolidating the Mexican charro system. American labor officials exercised their traditional role, which dated to the revolutionary period, as liaisons for American corporations and the United States government. During the era of the Cold War, when the U.S. labor movement fell in line with the American government's anticommunist foreign policy, the help that American unionists gave the Mexican government and the CTM bureaucrats was crucial. Using ORIT resources and dollars, the CTM and the Mexican government eradicated militant and independent forces in organizations that opposed state policy. As economic ties between the U.S. and Mexico increased and industrialization accelerated, a disciplined labor movement void of militant and independent elements became essential. Mexico's role in the post-war international division of labor—that of providing raw materials and inexpensive labor markets for more economically advanced countries like the United States—depended upon the entrenchment of the charro system.

Although the 1950s witnessed the advancement and entrenchment of the charro system, unionized workers still demanded a decent wage, better working conditions and the right to strike. As the Mexican economy grew, peaceful industrial relations depended upon the state's open manipulation of trade-union officials and the use of brute force against intransigent rank and file. Legitimizing charrismo required organized labor's total ideological allegiance to a state that increasingly favored capital, both foreign and domestic. As capital enhanced its position against labor in the decades that followed, the contradictions that surfaced between the working class and the state during the 1950s emerged once again.

Notes

1. For discussion on the growing relationship between the Mexican state, industrialists and American capitalists see James D. Cockroft, *Mexico: Class Formation, Capital Accumulation and the State* (New York: Monthly Review Press, 1983), 178. *Latin American Weekly Report*, 16 November 1979, reported that between 1945 and 1979 Latin America received roughly twenty percent of all U.S. investment in the Third World and added that the highest return on investments came from Mexico, which averaged nineteen percent.

2. Norman Caulfield, "Mexican State Development Policy and Labor Internationalism, 1945–1958," *International Review of Social History* 42 (1997): 45–66.

3. Cited in Hobart A. Spalding, Jr., "Unions Look South," in *NACLA Report on the Americas* 22 (May/June 1988): 15.

4. United States National Archives (USNA), State Department (SD) Records, RG 59, 820.06/3-2353, memorandum of J. T. Fishburn, State Department labor advisor, to John Moors Cabot, 23 March 1953.

5. USNA, SD Records, RG 59, 812.062/5-952, R. Smith Simpson to the Secretary of State, 9 May 1952.

6. Ibid., 812.06/9-1153, Stephansky to the Secretary of State, 11 September 1953.

7. Ibid.

8. Ibid.

9. Ibid., Stephansky to the Secretary of State, 17 March 1954.

10. Ibid.

11. Ibid.

12. Ibid.

13. Ibid.

14. Ibid.

15. Ibid., 812.06/10-1454, Stephansky's Semi-Annual Labor Report to the Secretary of State, 14 October 1954.

16. Ibid.

17. Ibid., 812.06/3-1754, Stephansky to the Secretary of State, 17 March 1954.

18. Ibid., 812.06/11-2652, Report from Windsor Stroup, American Labor Officer in the U.S. Embassy in Mexico, to the Secretary of State, 26 November 1957.

19. Ibid.

20. Caulfield, "Mexican State Development Policy," 61.

21. USNA, SD Records, RG 59, 812.06/11-2657, Stroup to the Secretary of State, 26 November 1957.

22. Ibid. Ironically Salazar had opposed Gompers and the AFL's activities during the early 1920s when he was an important intellectual leader of the anarchosyndicalist CGT. As early as 1926, however, he began working with Morones and the CROM. The title of his Gompers biography is *Samuel Gompers: presencia de un líder* (Mexico: Servicio Informativo y Cultural de los Estados Unidos [USIS], 1957).

23. USNA, SD Records, RG 59, 812.06/6-657, Stephansky to the Secretary of State, 6 June 1957.

24. Ibid., 812.06/3-2057, Stephansky's 1956 Annual Labor Report, 20 March 1957.

25. Ibid., 812.0621/3-1258, A. Kramer, labor attaché of the American Embassy, to the Secretary of State, 12 March 1958.

26. Ibid. A. Kramer, labor attaché of the American Embassy, reported that Mexican government officials were concerned that forceful intervention in the strike might produce martyrs for the strikers, something the ruling party did not want during an election year.

27. Ibid.

28. Ibid.

29. Ibid., 812.06/3-1754, Stephansky to the Secretary of State, 17 March 1954.

30. Aurora Loyo Brambila, *El movimiento magisterial de 1958 en México*, 2nd ed. (Mexico: Ediciones Era, 1980), 29.

31. Gerardo Peláez, *Historia del sindicato nacional de trabajadores del la educación* (Mexico: Ediciones de Cultura Popular, 1984), 91.

32. Loyo Brambila, *El movimiento*, 46–49.

33. USNA, SD Records, Central Files, 712/8-2985, 712.00/8-2958, telegram from the U.S. Embassy in Mexico City to the Department of State, 29 August 1958.

34. José Luis Reyna and Raúl Trejo Delarbe, *De Adolfo Rúiz Cortines a Adolfo López Mateos, 1957–1964*, vol. 12 of *La clase obrera en la historia de México*, Pablo González Casanova, ed. (Mexico: Siglo Veintiuno Editores, 1981), 79–81.

35. Demetrio Vallejo, *Las luchas ferrocarrileras que conmovieron a México*, 4th ed. (Mexico: Editorial Hombre Nuevo, 1975), 5–6. Also see Arnoldo Martínez Verdugo, ed., *Historia del comunismo en México* (Mexico: Grijalbo, 1985), 248–49.

36. Vallejo, *Las luchas*, 18.

37. Ibid., 20.

38. Ibid., 26, 27.

39. Ibid.

40. Antonio Alonso, *El movimiento ferrocarrilero en México: 1958–59*, 3rd ed. (Mexico: Ediciones Era, 1979), 130.

41. Ibid., 133.

42. USNA, SD Records, RG 59, 812.062/9-1158, John F. Killea, American Consul General of Monterrey, to the Secretary of State, 11 September 1958.

43. Ibid., 143; Vallejo, *Las luchas*, 39.

44. Cited in Alonso, *El movimiento*, 143.

45. Ibid., 144–45.

46. Ibid., 147.

47. USNA, SD Records, RG 59, 812. 062/3-759, labor attaché Kramer's telegram to the Secretary of State, 7 March 1959. Also see USNA, SD Records, RG 59, 812.062/3-1059, telegram from Gray to the Secretary of State, 19 March 1959.

48. Ibid., 812.062/3-2659, telegram from Gray to the Secretary of State, 26 March 1959.

49. Ibid., 812.062/3-2759, telegram from the American Embassy in Mexico City to the Secretary of State, 27 March 1959.

50. Ibid., 812,062/3-3059, telegram from Gray to the Secretary of State, 30 March 1959.

51. Ibid.

52. Ibid., 812.062/4-159, Gray to the Secretary of State, 2 April 1959.

53. Ibid.

54. Ibid., 812.062/4-359, Gray to the Secretary of State, 3 April 1959.

55. Ibid.

56. Ibid., 812.062/4-1459, Terrence Leonhardy, American Consul at Nogales, to the Secretary of State, 14 April 1959.

57. Vallejo, *Las luchas*, 56.

58. USNA, SD Records, RG 59, 812.062/7-1059, U.S. Embassy assistant labor officer David Simcox to the Secretary of State, 10 July 1959.

59. Ibid.

60. Ibid., 812.06/8-2459, David Simcox, assistant labor officer of the American Embassy, and A. Kramer, American Embassy labor attaché in Mexico City, to the Secretary of State, 24 August 1959.

11

The Human Details and Argentine Militancy

Rachel May

By the mid-1970s it was commonplace that workers throughout Latin America faced a number of responsibilities and complications in their lives. Depending on the location—Colombia, Argentina, Mexico, Peru, the Dominican Republic, or Chile—labor militancy, once a phrase that characterized activism in the workplace, now could include a regimen of work, participation in labor-organizing activities, raising children, and political action. The latter especially had become difficult and danger- ous. In part the risks of political action were a product of the wide impact of the Cuban revolution of 1959. Without question the Cuban success en- couraged radical political organizations throughout the region to think that they too might be able to stand up to a modern regime that excluded the workers and the poor. But the Cuban success was only an example, not a cause, of the turn to labor politics.* Radical workers throughout the region had to assess their own conditions and determine if the tensions were sufficient to sustain a popular, militant confrontation with the re- pressive state. In many instances the answer to that question was slow in coming, if at all. But in a few cases—Brazil, Argentina, and Chile, par- ticularly—the workers and their allies among students and other middle- class sectors answered with a "yes." Thus began an era of tragic confrontation between workers, their allies, and the state in those three countries. In this selection, Rachel May discusses some of the political organizing and maneuvering that took hold in Argentina in the 1970s, at a time when the state's efforts to repress all forms of militancy reached levels of violence theretofore unknown. The militants of whom May speaks redefined labor issues as human issues. Strictly labor questions had be- come questions for the entire society.

---

*A far more sweeping analysis of government-labor movement relations in twentieth-century Latin America is offered by Ruth Berins Collier and David Collier, *Shaping the Political Arena: Critical Junctures, the Labor Movement, and Regime Dynamics in Latin America* (Princeton: Princeton University Press, 1991).

The requirements of political "militancy" as defined in the context of Argentina in the 1960s and 1970s demanded enormous personal sacrifice. Indeed, most militants suffered imprisonment, torture, and death. But the structures of Argentine militancy in this period—as well as the structure of state terror—also exacted subtler costs in the form of human *detalles*, the elements of the human experience that give texture and meaning to life. It is in these details of human experience that we find the deeper motivations for social activism, and ironically these meaningful details were often the first sacrifice that Argentine militants made.

This essay studies the personal, social, and political motivations for political militancy and the human details that defined the lives of Argentine militants between 1966 and 1978. The essay also addresses the effects on those motivations and personal *detalles* of the evolution of the two major militant organizations in Argentina (the Ejército Revolucionario del Pueblo, or ERP, and the Montoneros) as well as the effects of the evolution of state-sponsored terror.

I began to think of this connection between *detalles* and social conscience in a synchronous sort of way. In 1998, I was sitting in a rented room in the San Telmo neighborhood of Buenos Aires. I had recently arrived there with my then four-year-old son. Our laundry was spread out on one of the beds, and my son was "wrestling" with an invisible "nuclear man" on the other bed. I sat at a small card table in the corner reading the book, *Mujeres guerrilleras*, by Marta Diana. She told about having recently arrived in Buenos Aires from Córdoba with her four-year-old son, Esteban, and getting settled in a small, new apartment.[1] In 1972, she wrote, "I was making the bed, mentally organizing all the tasks I needed to complete while Esteban occupied himself acting out an 'intergalactic struggle.' I gathered up the laundry without paying any attention to the news flash that appeared on the television, and I started toward the washing machine when the name 'Susana Lesgart' caught my attention and I turned back to the television."[2]

Marta Diana then describes the experience of hearing about the death of her childhood friend's older sister, a "militant." This blow eventually led her to an understanding of her own friend's militancy and eventually, some twenty years later, on a search to find out what had happened to her friend, Adriana. "I stayed for a long time, sitting on the bed, holding my clothes against my chest. I suppose that in the shock of the news, my clothes became my lifeline, a reminder of the reality that only a few minutes before had been my only real world."[3] The book, *Mujeres guerrilleras*, is the fruit of her search for Adriana as well as for an understanding of what motivated Adriana and other women militants.

The parallels between Marta Diana's life (her preoccupation with day care and preschool, laundry, keeping food and milk in the refrigerator, neighbors, family, work, intellectual life, and social conscience) and mine were somehow startling to me. I imagined Diana in a room very much like mine, with her Esteban performing the same "moves" that my son, Nicolás, performed. I imagined her neighbors wondering the same sorts of things about her that my neighbors inevitably wondered about me. As I continued my research into Argentine women militants (which I later expanded to include men), I found myself making the same parallels between my subjects—the details of their daily experiences—and my own life in Buenos Aires. Somehow these parallels transcended the obvious commonality of space and geography. The parallels were, in fact, more universal than that.

All of the literature on the Argentine militancy focuses on the time and the experience of these people as a great human tragedy. Mostly the period is treated as a closed and fixed episode in Argentine history. There is practically no mention of any continuity between this period and the present. There is no sense of how this "episode" influenced what came afterward. This gap represents a striking dissimilarity with most Latin American historiography, particularly with that which explicitly concerns social movements or questions of injustice, exploitation, and violence. Even on a much more general level, Latin American historiography is unusually preoccupied with how history has influenced the present. The assumption that this period is over and that it essentially was a tragedy of enormous proportions shapes the paradigm that defines this literature in a peculiar way. The overriding question that is either explicit or implied is "why?" Why did it turn out the way it did? Was it a strategic mistake of the militants themselves? Is it just evidence of the efficiency of state terror? Was it just the times that they lived in? But there is rarely, if ever, any questioning of the assumption that the experience was totally and completely tragic, with no redeeming positive outcome, or that what happened has any kind of connection to, or lesson about, the contemporary social and political reality of Argentina. Indeed, I posed the question (of how the experience of Argentina in the 1960s and 1970s might be relevant to the current situation) to a broad range of Argentines, both former militants and others, and not one had any sense that the country's tragic events had any meaning in contemporary society—not even any mention of *nunca más*, nothing.

A sort of natural dichotomy emerges in which scholars and other writers (journalists and former militants who have written memoirs) adopt either a critical stance toward the militants—they made errors, or the militancy itself was seriously misguided—or a defensive apologist position —they did what they had to do, the times or the circumstances conditioned their choices, and they were simply destined to fulfill this tragic narrative.

Militancy

Argentine guerrillas—former members of the ERP and former Montoneros—rarely refer to themselves as "guerrillas" but rather as *militantes*. This peculiar terminology is common to Argentine Spanish in general. As a rule, "guerrilla" is more specifically identified with violence and terrorism, and *militancia* with a high level of commitment. "Militancy" in the rest of Latin America is usually less neutral than "guerrilla," although it does always imply being part of a collective project. Nevertheless, the first or most common definition for *militar* is "to serve in a war or profess the 'military arts.' "

Pablo Pozzi claims that the origin of the common use of the words "militant" and "militancy" as synonymous for "commitment" is in Argentine trade unionism of the 1920s. And "militant" signified, even then, a high degree of commitment to the movement. According to Pozzi, the term is still used in trade unions today and in other social movements, although I found it to be usually associated by average Argentines with the experience of ERPistas and Montoneros.[4] The unusual use of this word is somewhat ironic for non-Argentine researchers. It is common for former ERPistas and Montoneros to claim that they "were not guerrillas, but rather they were militants." When this claim is made, it is usually an effort to distance the speaker from the use of arms: "I was not a guerrilla, I was a militant . . . I was never armed." Also for non-Argentine scholars, "militant" has more of a connotation of violence than does "guerrilla," which is generally a more neutral term.

María José Moyano's critical study of the Argentine militancy argues that after 1973, the armed struggle became highly militarized.[5] She defines militarism as "a vast array of customs, interests, prestige, actions, and thought associated with armies and wars and yet transcending true military purposes."[6] "Militancy" is used by Moyano as a synonym for dogmatism and an irrational commitment to violence. She refers to her subjects as "combatants" or "guerrillas" because she claims that she wants to avoid pejorative terms, although she argues that the combatants were rarely "guerrillas."[7] She fails to mention that "guerrilla" is the more pejorative term in Argentina and that "militant" has a completely different meaning to her subjects. Moreover, she never says that the terminology is reversed in Argentina, nor does she mention (although it is impossible given her research that she was unaware of the fact) that to argue in Argentina that the ERPistas and the Montoneros became "militant" after 1973 would be a simple tautology.

The two major "militant" organizations in Argentina were the ERP and the Peronist Montoneros. There were many other splinter groups and small, short-lived movements, but the ERP and the Montoneros had longevity, numbers, a clearly defined hierarchy, and significance. There were three attempts at launching a Cuban-style rural guerrilla movement in Argentina after 1959. None of these attempts at rural insurgency ever commanded a very wide following or posed a serious threat. The political dynamic of Argentina changed significantly after 1966 with the first military dictatorship of General Juan Carlos Onganía (the Onganiato). After the coup, *los muchachos* were granted much broader legitimacy and support.

The PRT-ERP

In late 1963, Mario Roberto ("Roby") Santucho was a young, dark-skinned Marxist intellectual who had been in Cuba during the Bay of Pigs invasion. He was one of the founders and the leader of the Frente Revolucionario Indoamericano Popular (FRIP). A political party based at the University of Tucumán (Santucho's alma mater), the FRIP did extensive organizing among the sugar workers of Tucumán, arguably among the poorest and most exploited sectors of Argentine society. The ideology of the FRIP was influenced by Cuban Marxism—nationalist, anti-imperialist, with a dimension of ethnic politics thrown in. The FRIP joined forces with a small Trotskyist group called the Palabra Obrera. The union became official at the First Party Congress held in 1965, and the name was changed to the Partido Revolucionario de Trabajadores (PRT). In 1968, at the Fourth Party Congress, the PRT split in two. Santucho led the much larger *combatiente* (combatant) faction, which leaned toward armed struggle. And in 1970, at the Fifth Party Congress, the PRT launched the Ejército Revolucionario Popular (ERP) as the armed faction of the Partido. From 1970 to 1978 the PRT-ERP, usually referred to simply as the ERP, were one of the two largest guerrilla insurgent "militant" groups in Argentina. The ERP was led by the charismatic Roby Santucho until his death in 1976.[8]

The Montoneros

The Peronist Montoneros had their origins in four separate factions: a group of Catholic Action members from Santa Fé, a group of university students from Córdoba, a group of union activists and university students from Buenos Aires, and another group of students from Buenos Aires who were all alumni of the prestigious public high school, Colegio Nacional Buenos Aires. The first public act of the Montoneros was on May 29, 1970—Army Day as well as the first anniversary of the pivotal massacre of demonstrators in Córdoba, known as the Cordobazo. The Montoneros kidnapped, "tried" in a revolutionary court, and killed former president General Pedro Eugenio Aramburú. A few months later on July 1, 1970, they seized the town of La Calera, Córdoba. The Montoneros merged in 1972 with another Peronist group whose origins were in radical Christian democracy, the Descamisados. In 1976, after a long period of brutal repression by the military, the Montonero leaders went into exile, and in 1979, after a disastrous offensive, their chief, Horacio Mendizábal, was killed. This setback was effectively the end of the Montoneros.[9]

The period of active insurgency is often broken down into three separate phases: first, 1966–1973, opposition to the Onganía dictatorship; second, 1973–1976, the rule of the Peróns; and third, *el proceso*. There is some disagreement about the numbers that these organizations commanded. Most agree that they reached their height in 1974 when there may have been as many as 5,000 *militantes*, some of whom did not carry arms.[10]

Motivations for Militancy

Most apologists for the Argentine militancy as well as former militants themselves explain their motivations as having been conditioned by "the times." This argument is, in fact, the underlying "thesis" of the most significant oral history project to date on the Argentine militancy, the two-volume *La Voluntad* by Eduardo Anguita and Martín Caparrós. It is also a point that Anguita strenuously emphasized in my own discussion with him.[11] The idea that "the times" profoundly conditioned decisions was actually voiced by every former militant I spoke to. There were numerous references made to the Cuban Revolution, Che Guevara, Vietnam, Paris 1968, the Prague Spring, the election of Salvador Allende, the Tlatelolco massacre, the civil rights movement in the United States, the "counter-cultural revolution," the Onganiato, and the return of Juan Perón. Former militants still seem amazed, even bewildered at the historical context in which they came of age. There was a sense that they could never adequately express to me, a thirty-something political scientist from the United States (I was born in 1965), "what it was like." This shortcoming was as much a function of my age as it was of my nationality. That is, despite frequent mentions of the international context, there is a feeling among Argentine militants and others of their generation that what happened in their country was a uniquely Argentine phenomenon. Eduardo Anguita said that it was not possible to understand the social conscience of Argentine militants outside of the very particular context of the national reality.[12]

Also significantly, most former militants explain their militancy in terms of their desire for social justice. They describe their despair over the misery they witnessed in the shantytowns of urban Argentina and the rural provinces: "We could never just accept the injustices we witnessed." Thousands of high school and university students worked in the villages and among the poor. They were disturbed by the reality of Argentine poverty. They were moved by the details of the existence of the poor—the lack of food, of clean water, of decent housing, of leisure time. One informant told the story of her work in a village. A wall had collapsed and crushed several small houses. The rubble, which included the bodies of those who were killed, had to be cleaned up. She was part of a Peronist youth brigade that had volunteered. The villagers had prepared a meal for the volunteers and the resident workers to share, and they all sat down to eat together. The middle-class volunteer was reluctant to eat while there were still bodies lost in the rubble. She recalled thinking, "this is their life. This is normal."[13]

The vast majority of militants were students who read Marx, Lenin, and their compatriot, Che Guevara. They had a fairly sophisticated and complex understanding of the theory of revolution and class struggle. And although they talk about their intellectual commitment to the ideology they ascribed to, they also talk about these little experiences and their empathy for the poor. They describe an almost visceral desire for social justice that they often recount in terms of "little experiences," or *detalles*.

Many also point to a particular relationship or set of relationships that motivated them. Many women were typically introduced into the militancy by romantic partners. Indeed, some couples "militated" together and found that committing themselves to revolution was a very powerful experience that often seemed to become mingled with the feelings of love they had for each other. This sentiment is particularly true of those whose partners were martyred. In addition, it is very common for former militants to describe the period of their militancy as the greatest time in their lives. The sense of solidarity and love they had for one another was as powerful as the belief that they were on the brink of radically changing the world for the better. So there is an ironic sort of memory operating for many of these people—their experience was an almost unspeakable tragedy but also the most wonderful thing that had ever happened to them.

There was an overwhelming tone of "humanness" that gave the militants a sense of meaning—something that seems far more profound than typical descriptions of "social conscience." Roby Santucho's "humanness" is frequently mentioned. His relationship to Ana María Villareal was regarded by their *compañeros* and the rank and file of the ERP as a genuine "love match." Somehow the depth of their love became very important within the ERP. The ERP maintained strict requirements about monogamy between *compañeros* (although it generally opposed "marriage" for ideological reasons), and probably more than half of the *militantes* of the ERP were "coupled." Roby and María de Santucho's separation (they were married) represented a morale problem for the entire organization. After the death of María and the "remarriage" of Roby, something was lost from the organization—not because of María's charisma (like Evita Perón), but rather because of the dynamics of their relationship.

The emphasis on "humanness" seems somehow a way of finding meaning in so much death and tragedy. For example, "I left Argentina as an 'organic militant,' and I returned as a militant of life."[14] "I did not want death, and I desperately sought out life for the little shipwrecked crew that we were."[15] "I left [for exile] with a cemetery inside myself where I had buried my losses, and I referred to it obsessively to question why I was alive and they weren't."[16]

On a more abstract level, some were motivated by religious sentiment. And for Peronists, the desire to bring back Juan Perón and to oppose the suppression of Peronism figured into their motivation.

Detalles Humanos

Marta Diana asks everyone of her subjects about Adriana Lesgart ("Patricia" was her *nom de guerre* in the Montoneros), her childhood companion. Her first interview, in 1992, was with a former Montonera whom she refers to simply as "S." When Diana asks her about Adriana, this is what she remembered:

> When I left the country, I arrived in Madrid and from there I was looking for some way to hook up with Patricia. She was still based in Paris, so I went there to wait for her. She did something that was very typical of her . . . she had a concern and a kind of thoughtfulness that was very rare among our compañeros. She remembered my children. She was always very human . . . she was a very good compañera in "human things". . . at that time my children wanted to have "Kickers" boots. They were in fashion, and they weren't available in Buenos Aires. She arrived in Paris, after a trip to Belgium, and she came with a pair of these boots for each of my girls. This detail—to remember a pair of shoes—in that moment, it is something that really defines her well. She was always attentive to the personal things [*detalles*] of her compañeras.[17]

It was this particular description of Adriana that made me first think about *detalles*. I began to notice that all of the subjects whose "testimonies" are reproduced in the oral histories focus on little personal details like this—in their descriptions of their own experiences as well as of each other. This is particularly true when they talk about their *compañeros* who were killed, like Adriana, who disappeared in 1979. In addition, the Spanish term *detalles* means more than "details"; it also refers to a trait of courtesy, friendliness, or affection; that is, it specifically refers to the emotional "human" connection between people. Why is it that memory focuses on these details? Why is it that these details, these moments, seem to define these people and this painful period?

The focus on details and "humanness" is partly a function of the nature of memory. Because of the essentially tragic nature of the Argentine experience, these little moments of humanity—these visceral memories of love, solidarity, faith, and purpose—provide meaning to the former *militantes* and even to members of that generation of Argentines in general. So many of their details revolve around their children—this is true of both men and women—not only because pregnancy, childbirth, and raising children, especially in this situation of "public clandestinity," were incredibly consuming but also because their children were little oases of life among all the death.

The particular dogmatism of the Marxist-Leninist ideology of the times also caused many militants to essentially deny the *detalles* of their identities during the period of militancy. That is, they felt compelled to abandon their "bourgeois identities," which in many cases meant abandoning family, values (religious and secular), intellectual pursuits, art, music, creature comforts, and even simple *gustos* or preferences. It was too bourgeois to play soccer or the piano. Any sort of admission of weakness—loneliness, discomfort, fear—was a sign of their lack of commitment. Eventually, just being alive made many militants feel that they had failed to live up to their commitments. These people expressed some confusion about themselves both during and after their periods of militancy. Although they willingly abandoned their middle-class identities, there was often a sense that their adopted working-class personas were somewhat disingenuous, no matter how humble their living arrangements were or how dangerous their lives had become. Powerful memories of human details were not "allowed," to some extent—and when they did emerge, they were like little rebellions, little reminders of life.

The particular kind of clandestinity that was required of Argentine militants also heightened the loss of "details." These militants, for the most part, lived in cities in regular apartments. They often held regular jobs and kept up appearances with regular people. Because their only real contacts came with other members of their cells, they led lives of secrecy and deception. This life was isolating and even tortuous at times. As the violence against them escalated, they became even more isolated as their organizations became more clandestine and many militants went into exile. Again, somehow the little details of normalcy are more intense and important under these circumstances. Their children's day care, love and desire, sex, food, jokes, songs—these are the sorts of things that made their lives meaningful. They became symbols of life.

One of the most powerful critiques of militant strategy—the insistence on dogmatic Marxist-Leninist analysis, on revolutionary military victory over capitalism—is that it did make them "militant" in the traditional sense of the word. And their organizations probably lost sight of the human details that motivated the members in the beginning. One former militant said: "I believe that one of the reasons [for the tragedy] is that the people, *el pueblo*, whom the revolutionaries have eternally tried to 'wake up' . . . had their own dreams . . . smaller, more intimate, more immediate than our grand revolutionary dreams."[18]

Luis Mattini sees the contradiction between the Marxist-Leninist analysis and the reality of the masses as somehow tied to this question of identity that plagued the militant vanguard:

> The sincere and profound search of Marxism-Leninism was always permanently hindered by the lack of a genuine social conscience. We took on a borrowed class consciousness . . . an identity that did not really belong to us.
>
> To adopt a priori a political ideological identity was not something the PRT-ERP invented for itself. It has been and still is the norm for most of the left. Overcoming this error is a necessary condition for the recovery of the ground lost by the left.[19]

Mattini is correct in generalizing this phenomenon with the Latin American left overall. There is, beyond Marxist dogmatism, an even more general and fundamental tension between social conscience and *detalles* (not individualism). It seems to be precisely the task of post-Cold War popular movements to acknowledge and even exploit this tension rather than to simply eliminate all the *detalles*.

Argentina is an important case study of the destructive potential of sacrificing *detalles*. Why is the contradiction so much more pronounced and so intensely damaging in Argentina? (Much worse than in Guatemala, for example.) Partly it is explained in the particular type of clandestinity that was required by urban guerrilla warfare. Partly it is explained in the middle-class, highly educated, and largely female makeup of the Montoneros and the ERP. But much of the explanation lies in the specific kind of state terror that plagued Argentina.

Jaime Malamud-Goti claims that the Argentine military used terror to "disarticulate" any kind of social mobilization that existed or might exist. Malamud convincingly argues that state terror in Argentina was a very effective form of "disarticulating power." Disappearance, torture, targeted and calculated murder, and "public secrets" served its purpose well. Certainly, isolation and the contradictions between the vanguard and *el pueblo* took their toll on solidarity within the militancy. The almost desperate focus on military strategy increases in direct proportion to the escalation of state-sponsored violence.[20]

Most of the young people who became real militants in Argentina are dead. They sacrificed their very lives for their idealism. The vast majority of those who survived only did so because they were imprisoned at a fairly early stage in the conflict. They spent a good part of their youth in prison, where they were tortured, or they lived in exile, which was its own peculiar kind of incarceration. Their sacrifices are real and obvious. But there were other, less obvious losses as well. They lost a part of their identity that is difficult to regain, and this part is found in the details.

Notes

1. Marta Diana, *Mujeres guerrilleras: La militancia de los setenta en el testimonio de sus protagonistas femininas* (Buenos Aires: Planeta, 1996), 12.

2. Ibid., 13.

3. Ibid.

4. Pablo Pozzi, interview with author, Buenos Aires, August 1998.

5. María José Moyano, *Argentina's Lost Patrol: Armed Struggle, 1969–1979* (New Haven: Yale University Press, 1995), 5.

6. Ibid., 6.

7. I assume that this claim is based upon the idea that guerrillas are combatants who engage in traditional guerrilla warfare in a rural arena, in the mode of Ernesto "Che" Guevara.

8. There is a very detailed history of the ERP written by Mario Roberto Santucho's brother, Julio Santucho: *Los últimos guevaristas: surgimiento y eclipse del Ejército Revolucionario del Pueblo* (Buenos Aires: Puntosur, 1988). For the history of the origins of the ERP, see 113–69. There is also a biography of Roby Santucho that functions as a fairly detailed history of and explanation for the ERP: Maria Seoane, *Todo o nada* (Buenos Aires: Planeta, 1991).

9. There are fewer studies of the Montoneros. One is the study by former Montonero militant Ernesto Juaretche: *Violencia y política en los 70: No dejés que te la cuentan* (Buenos Aires: Ediciones del Pensamiento Nacional, 1997). There is also an excellent collection of documents compiled by Roberto Baschetti: *Documentos, 1973–1976: De Campora a la ruptura*, Vol. 1. Some of the various collections of oral testimony also include testimony from former Montoneros, such as Eduardo Anguita and Martín Caparrós, *La voluntad: Una historia de la militancia revolucionaria en la Argentina*, Vols.1, 2 (Buenos Aires: Grupo Editorial Norma, 1997, 1998). A third volume that will cover the post-1976 period was expected in 1999. *La voluntad* is fairly heavy on the ERP and fairly light on the Montoneros. Marta Diana's *Mujeres guerrilleras*, in contrast, is focused more heavily on former Montoneros.

10. Moyano, *Argentina's Lost Patrol*, 2.

11. Anguita and Caparrós, *La voluntad*; Eduardo Anguita, interview with author, Buenos Aires, August 12, 1998.

12. Eduardo Anguita, interview with author, Buenos Aires, August 12, 1998.

13. Unnamed subject, interview with author, Buenos Aires, August 3, 1998.

14. Diana, *Mujeres Guerrilleras*, 43.

15. Ibid., 37.

16. Ibid., 124.

17. Ibid., 18–19.

18. Luis Mattini, *Hombres y mujeres del PRT-ERP: La pasión militante* (Buenos Aires: Editorial Contrapunto, 1990), 20.

19. Ibid.,.20 fn.

20. Jaime Malamud-Goti, *Game without End: The Politics of State Terror* (Norman: University of Oklahoma Press, 1996).

12

Copper Workers and Popular Protest in Chile

Thomas Miller Klubock

The scene in Chile for workers went through extraordinary changes between the 1960s and the 1990s. Before 1973 workers in many industries— primary as well as secondary, urban as well as rural—found solidarity with the urban and rural poor along with the urban middle sectors. As this solidarity grew in strength it helped to bring Salvador Allende to power in spite of enormous opposition from entrenched traditional elites, the U.S. government, and other forces. After 1973 the situation reversed and the workers found themselves isolated from one another and from their traditional base of allies and supporters by the repressive Pinochet regime. Reading Tom Klubock's analysis of the situation, we see that it took the workers about a decade to recover from the blows leveled against them by Augusto Pinochet's neoliberal policies.

As Klubock demonstrates in this selection, the copper miners were not ideologically or organizationally rigid during the era of state terror. They needed new forms of organization, and they also needed to reach out more to their natural compatriots, the urban poor, who themselves had suffered mightily in those years. In the end, the miners sought to redefine the meaning of class and to include within the ambit of workers those groups who pursued the interests of women, the poor, and nonmining sectors, especially service and informal workers. Klubock drew his example from the El Teniente copper mine, formerly owned by the Kennecott Copper Company and one of the most famous in the country, and the nearby city of Rancagua. The spread of miner-led democracy in Chile evidently began clandestinely. By 1983, however, nationwide protests in support of the miners began to occur, and soon workplace movements were joined by neighborhood efforts in which women, themselves part of a broad, poorly paid workforce, were heavily involved. The copper miners found that their movement had shifted from the camps to the urban neighborhoods and was engaging similar labor sectors in nationwide protests against neoliberal repression.

In April of 1983, the Chilean copper miners' confederation (the Confederación de Trabajadores de Cobre, or CTC), representing 26,000 copper workers, called for a general strike in Chile's copper mines and for a
day of national protest against the military regime of Augusto Pinochet.
More than 8,000 workers in El Teniente, the world's largest underground
copper mine, paralyzed production for twenty-four hours in an illegal
wildcat strike while tens of thousands of workers and urban poor people
(*pobladores*) went out in the streets to demand a return to democracy and
to protest the military regime's repressive labor policies and neoliberal
economic policies. The CTC declaration and the strike in the El Teniente
mine placed the miners in the leadership of opposition to Pinochet and at
the head of the reinvigorated national labor movement.[1]

In spite of the copper miners' central role in the resurgence of civilian opposition to the military regime, they have been largely ignored in
the literature on the transition to democracy in Chile. While historians
and social scientists have described the important role played by unions
and workers in modern industrial sectors in Brazil and Argentina during
the 1970s and 1980s, no corresponding analysis of Chile's industrial workers and unions under the Pinochet regime has emerged. Social scientists
and historians have focused on the mobilizations of the unemployed, the
poor, and members of the informal sector in movements based in working-
class urban neighborhoods and shantytowns.[2] Recent research has shown
that urban industrial workers did organize an independent and militant
union movement between 1980 and 1982 in Chile.[3] Less attention has
been paid to the connections between the struggles of industrial workers
during these years, traditions of left-wing political militancy and labor
activism that existed before the 1973 coup that overthrew the socialist
government of Salvador Allende, and the wave of popular protests that
began in 1983.

The case of the copper miners helps to amend the analytical distinction between the organization of industrial workers in factories and mines
and the movements of the urban poor in a number of ways. First, the miners' continued resistance to the military dictatorship in workplace-based
strikes and protests between 1977 and 1982 demonstrates that the revival
of union activity between 1980 and 1982 in Chile, at least in the mining
sector, was tied to the resilience of pre-1973 forms of labor struggle and
political activism in the Communist, Socialist, and Christian Democratic
parties. Second, while a number of writers have regarded this period of
plant-level activism as separate from the period of popular protest in poor
urban neighborhoods, in the case of the copper mines the labor movement of the 1980–1982 period played a major role in the popular protests
and in the formation of a new national labor federation, the Central Unitaria
de los Trabajadores (CUT). Unions and the clandestine networks of the

opposition political parties organized protests and provided an institutional space and voice, no matter how restricted, for a national demand for a return to democracy and an end to the deprivations of the regime's harsh economic restructuring.

Third, the role of the El Teniente miners in strikes and protests between 1977 and 1986 shows that structural economic changes introduced by the dictatorship and the climate of institutionalized state terror made necessary new forms of labor activism and new forms of working-class identity. The combination of community-based mobilizations in urban spaces with traditional forms of union organization and political militancy in the copper mines makes the frequently drawn division between industrial workers and the urban poor in Latin America less stark and suggests that, at least in some cases, traditional forms of workplace organization and left-wing political activism played a role in the elaboration of new forms of neighborhood and community-based mobilization in Chile. Authoritarian rule and the introduction of radical free-market economic policies undermined the traditional strength of miners' unions, fragmented their tightly knit communities, and dismantled the corporatist system of labor relations that had guaranteed miners a number of social and economic securities. Structural changes in the economy made the division between industrial workers and the urban poor increasingly thin. In the context of severe repression and extremely high rates of urban unemployment, miners had to fashion political protest outside of the workplace. They had to redefine the meanings of class and community to include new social actors—the unemployed, women, and members of the service and informal economies—in national struggles for democratization and an end to the neoliberal economic model.

Copper Miners in Chile before 1973

Before the 1973 coup, the El Teniente copper miners' unions and the CTC, representing workers in Chile's largest copper mines, had enjoyed a privileged position in terms of government support and recognition. Because earnings from taxes on copper exports composed the bulk of Chile's foreign revenues beginning in the 1930s (reaching close to ninety percent by 1971), miners occupied a strategic role in the national economy and their unions employed a great deal of leverage within the prevailing system of state-administered labor relations. Copper workers' unions were able to press the state to intervene in labor conflicts in order to establish labor peace and high levels of production in the mines, and were thus able to wrest substantial gains in wage levels and benefits from the North American companies that owned the mines. In addition, miners were able to identify their strikes and demands with Chile's national interests and with efforts to exert Chilean control over the foreign-owned mines, and could thus call on national support in their conflicts with the foreign companies.[4]

Workers in the Kennecott Copper Company's El Teniente mine were also able to take advantage of the company's need for a stable and skilled labor force and its capacity to pay high wages relative to other sectors of the economy. In response to traditions of labor mobility and working-class agitation that hampered production in the mine from 1904 to 1919, the U.S. company began to offer high wages and social welfare benefits during the 1920s in order to secure a reliable and trained labor force. Kennecott's Chilean subsidiary, the Braden Copper Company, used high wages, production bonuses, and welfare benefits to induce workers to stay on the job in the mine, and to marry and form families in the camps. The company paid a monthly cost-of-living raise and a family allowance that gave married workers with children special bonuses. The company also built schools for workers and their children and provided cultural and social activities for the mining community. In addition, in the almost-annual strikes between 1938 and 1973 the miners won the right to health care, job security, and pensions along with periodic wage hikes and improvements in work conditions. The mining company offered male workers the possibility of approximating a middle-class lifestyle by maintaining their families on a single "family wage" that was significantly higher than wages in other industrial sectors.

Despite high wages and the company's social welfare system, miners nurtured a combative workplace culture of opposition to company authority. Work in teams (*cuadrillas*) created tight bonds of solidarity among miners who shared a common interest in meeting production quotas in order to earn bonuses. In addition, the constant danger of accidents in the mine drew workers within the teams together and established ties based on their mutual reliance for survival. Like miners around the world, El Teniente's copper miners elaborated an intensely masculinized work identity based on their capacity for hard and dangerous physical labor. Miners expressed this sense of manliness in a defiant and challenging attitude toward foremen and North American supervisors.

The miners' ties of solidarity were reinforced by tight links between the mining community and the mine. Until the late 1960s most El Teniente copper miners lived in isolated camps high up in the Andes. In these camps, the miners and their families forged a resilient community and class identity that lent strength to their struggles with the company. Their shared experiences in mining camps dominated by a single company fostered a sense of collective antagonism toward a common enemy. Recreation, education, the cost of living, housing, and health care were controlled by the company and were linked to miners' wages and work in the mine. Miners' wives participated in strikes, walking picket lines and organizing women's and cost-of-living committees. As housewives, their responsibility for their families' well-being brought them into conflict with the company.

The political culture of the mining community came to be defined around the axes of the male wage earner and union activist and the female housewife, who participated in local committees organized around the concerns of the domestic sphere: consumption and the reproduction of the family. When women participated in miners' labor struggles and community movements they did so as housewives. Their mobilizations never challenged the sexual division of labor in the mining camps that consigned women to the household and that defined wage labor and politics as masculine. In this sense, the miners' class and community identities were built on the foundations of male-headed nuclear families in which women were subordinated to men's sexual and economic control.

After 1938, the El Teniente mining community was integrated into a state-directed corporatist system of labor relations. With support from the state the miners were able to elect independent union leaders and to build resilient unions led by militants of the Communist party (PC) and Socialist party (PS). Communist party activists helped to organize miners' independent union movements during the 1930s and both leftist parties provided crucial support to the miners' organizations during strikes and collective negotiations between the North American copper companies, the unions, and the state. PS and PC senators and deputies frequently made speeches in congress defending the copper miners against Kennecott, echoed the miners' call for nationalization of the mines, and heralded the miners' strikes as part of a broader socialist and nationalist project to win back what Salvador Allende called "*el sueldo de Chile*" (Chile's livelihood). Thus, despite their relatively privileged wages and benefits owing to their location in the national economy, copper miners comprised one of the most combative sectors of the Chilean working class and developed a political culture structured by radical nationalism and strong ties to the Left.

Military Repression and the Neoliberal Economic Model

As for industrial workers throughout Chile, the seventeen years of authoritarian rule in Chile wrought radical changes in the lives of the El Teniente copper miners and their families. After the 1973 coup hundreds of leftist activists were fired and many others were arrested and tortured. Members of El Teniente's administration appointed by Salvador Allende's socialist Unidad Popular (UP) government (1970–1973) and prominent militants of the UP parties and union leaders were killed; many others were sent to detention camps and then into exile. While union structures in El Teniente remained nominally intact, the military exercised a firm control over union leaders, and activity within the unions remained dormant until 1980. As in other sectors of the economy, union elections were prohibited, union leaders were appointed by the regime, and collective bargaining was suspended.

A 1973 strike against the UP government by El Teniente's white-collar workers and Christian Democratic party (PDC) union leaders, supported by the Chilean Right and the U.S. Central Intelligence Agency, had earned the miners a certain level of approval in the eyes of Chile's new military rulers. Therefore, repression in the mine was not as harsh as in Santiago's militant industrial belts (*cordones industriales*) and urban factories, which had been nationalized after workers' takeovers (*tomas*). The PDC had made inroads into white-collar mine employees' unions during the late 1960s, challenging the traditional hegemony of the Communist and Socialist parties, which retained their base in the large blue-collar workers' unions.[5] The importance of copper production to the economy and the national symbolic and institutional weight of the copper miners' unions also impeded the implementation of more repressive measures in the mines. The regime hoped to use sympathetic PDC union leaders in the copper industry, as well as copper's singular importance to the national economy, to create the appearance of labor support for military rule and national unity. During the first years following the military coup, the Pinochet regime also experimented briefly with nationalist and corporatist labor programs and policies under the direction of some members of the military, particularly the minister of labor, General Nicanor Díaz Estrada.[6]

The regime drew on the support of Guillermo Medina, a leader of El Teniente's white-collar office workers' union, the Sindicato Profesional Rancagua, in order to claim the backing of organized labor and the copper workers for the dictatorship. Medina acted as an "independent" union leader, with ties neither to the left-wing parties that dominated El Teniente's blue-collar unions nor to the Christian Democratic leaders whose base of support lay in the smaller white-collar workers' unions. He had played a central role in the 1973 strike against the UP and, following the coup, was the only labor leader to be appointed to the regime's "Council of State." Throughout the period of Pinochet's rule, Medina met frequently with Pinochet, his ministers, and the military officers placed in charge of the national copper company to discuss issues related to workers' demands in the copper sector. In addition, Medina was employed by the military regime as an unofficial spokesman for organized labor during discussions of national labor policy.

By 1974–1975, the regime had begun to consolidate its rule and to plan a long-term project for the complete transformation of the nation's political and socioeconomic structures according to the "radical" neoliberalism of *los Chicago boys*, a group of economists trained in the United States. The regime began to direct its repressive apparatus even at

Christian Democratic union leaders, who were trying to organize a limited amount of autonomous union activity and to enter into collective negotiations with the state-run copper company, the Corporación del Cobre (CODELCO). After 1975, PDC political leaders and labor leaders who had supported the coup and who had hoped to carve out some space for unions under military rule while building Christian-Democratic control of the labor movement now felt the brush of repression, and many were arrested and sent into exile. Only union leaders loyal to the Pinochet regime, like Medina, maintained their positions in the miners' organizations.

As oral histories testify, the decade following the military coup was defined by intense repression and a generalized climate of terror. Miners no longer attended union assemblies, met in groups, or talked openly with one another. One worker recalls, for example, that "participation was braked because when someone spoke in the union, when they noted that he was making a demand for something, he fell detained the next day."[7] Another miner remembers that until 1980 unions had to request police permission to hold assemblies and that police were sent to watch over union meetings.[8] At work, supervisors and foremen ruled with an authoritarian discipline that earned them the reputation of being worse than North American bosses and the epithet *gringos chilenos*. Supervisors (often appointed from the ranks of the military) and mine foremen frequently violated job classifications and forced workers to do extra jobs and work overtime without pay. As one miner said,

> The situation deteriorated as to work conditions. Abuses by *jefes*, lack of respect for the workers and threats. The *jefes* drive us hard, as they say. They swear at us and treat us with arrogance: "If you don't do this job you're fired." And go complain to the union. They don't respect the classifications. The *jefe* says, "you have to do this job," and you have to do it . . . they punish you for every slip-up and order you to do hard jobs.[9]

Union leaders were chosen by CODELCO, and were widely perceived to be the agents of the dictatorship. The union had to receive permission from the police to hold assemblies, and miners reported that spies denounced workers who talked politics or spoke at union meetings to the company administration and police. They only went to the union hall to take out loans, visit the dental clinic, or receive benefits like worker's compensation.

The miners' once-tight bonds of workplace solidarity began to erode in this climate of fear and repression. As one miner remembers, "I would say that everyone sought refuge, they kept quiet . . . often the workers didn't even greet one another out of fear. You saw it everywhere. You were walking and sometimes you bumped into someone who crossed the street to avoid contact, conversation, or greeting."[10] Another remembered that "you couldn't give your opinion; it was an atmosphere in which you couldn't work peacefully, where you couldn't talk to anyone; everyone was mistrustful."[11]

The military repression of organized labor and the Left was exacerbated in El Teniente, as in other working-class communities in Chile, by the regime's economic policies, which reduced job security, wages, and benefits for most workers. As prices for copper declined steadily on the world market during the 1970s and 1980s, the military regime attempted to reduce production costs by lowering workers' wages, limiting their benefits, reducing employment, and subcontracting many of the jobs not directly related to production. Through the use of subcontractors the new administration began to privatize many above-ground "support" functions, and even some activities directly related to production inside the mine. New construction and expansion projects were given to private firms, thus diminishing the significance of El Teniente's organized workers. By 1986, just over half the total workers employed by El Teniente (8,250) worked for nearly 200 private contractors. These firms paid workers half the wages earned by miners employed by the national copper company, provided no benefits, and offered little job security. Workers' efforts to unionize these small companies were easily thwarted.[12] Before 1973, children of El Teniente workers could depend on a steady job in the mines. Most miners had been born and raised in the mining camps, and a career as a miner and a healthy pension were viewed as rights guaranteed by the paternalist labor system established by Kennecott during the 1920s. By the early 1980s, neither the miners nor their children had a secure future in El Teniente since subcontractors were able to take advantage of an ever-increasing pool of urban unemployed.

The introduction of sophisticated new machinery by the firm after 1980 also rendered the copper miners' livelihoods more precarious. While most of the work involved in building tunnels and extracting ore before 1980 was labor-intensive (drilling, placing charges, shoveling ore into cars), new machines transformed the nature of work in the mines and reduced the company's labor requirements. As one miner remembers,

> where the miner drilled and then blasted—a lot of that was done with physical force like with the shovel, today they have huge mechanical shovels—before you needed a bottle of oxygen, of gas . . . you had to carry it on your shoulder, today this is transported by a vehicle; today they are trying out machines that do everything the miner used to do . . . the machine drills into the hill, deposits the explosive . . . that means a reduction in personnel.[13]

Mechanization and the reduction of the work force within the mine also disrupted the organization of miners' work teams and eroded workplace solidarity.

During the 1970s and early 1980s, the use of new mining technology led to increased production and lower production costs. Combined with a reduced labor force, these resulted in record earnings for the state-run national copper company, CODELCO, despite the steadily dropping price of copper on the world market. In 1982, for example, the price of copper dropped from seventy-three to sixty-two cents per pound on the world market, yet the company still earned fifty percent more than in 1981. In 1974, CODELCO employed 32,849 workers; in 1981, 27,900; by 1982, the figure had fallen to 26,387. In addition, the cost per worker declined by sixteen percent between 1981 and 1982 alone, due to the intensification of work, salary reductions, and mechanization. Between 1982 and 1983, copper miners' real wages fell six percent. Combined with stagnating real wages, the use of new machinery in the copper mines led to a decline in the cost of production of 27.6 percent.[14]

CODELCO also cut costs by reducing workers' benefits. El Teniente workers no longer had access to free medical attention and health care from the company, a benefit they had won from Kennecott in the 1920s— and a basic necessity in an industry where work-related injuries and illnesses proliferated. By the late 1970s, El Teniente miners had to pay fifty percent, and for some procedures up to ninety percent, of their medical costs. As union leaders noted, workers who suffered accidents on the job often fell deeply into debt in order to pay for medical treatment. To pay for health care, workers took out loans from the company or went to "officialist" union leaders for help in acquiring credit from the company or from banks. Miners also noted a radical deterioration in the quality of the medical care they received. As their newspaper put it in 1985,

> It's a demonstrable fact that with the creation of the FUSAT [El Teniente's health maintenance organization], the provision of health care to the workers and their family members has suffered a considerable deterioration of quality and quantity. This is demonstrated by the hundreds of demands and debts that pressure the workers.[15]

In an industry where work accidents were frequent and silicosis was rampant, private health organizations frequently refused to classify workers' injuries and illnesses as job-related. In 1983, one union leader noted that "our most serious problem right now is medical attention. Many people have had work accidents and they haven't received good care."[16]

The privatization of Chile's social security system in 1980 also eroded the miners' economic situation. While Kennecott (and then the state under the Unidad Popular government) had provided pensions, now workers had to contribute funds from their wages to private financial groups. Some miners who had little experience with finance lost their pensions, which had been held in precarious investment firms that went out of business during the economic recession that began in 1982. The privatization of social security and health care left workers vulnerable to the whims of the market and many deeply indebted.[17]

Before 1973, copper workers lived in housing provided by the company in the mine's camps or in housing subsidized by the state and the company in Rancagua, the city below El Teniente. After the military coup, workers had to take on financial responsibility for their homes, adding rents and mortgages to their ever-increasing debt burdens. By the mid-1970s, most El Teniente workers lived in housing developments in Rancagua built according to plans elaborated in 1966 by Kennecott and the Christian Democratic government of Eduardo Frei (1964–1970). Following the nationalization of the copper mines in 1971 by the UP coalition, the state assumed all of the costs for supplying miners' housing in Rancagua. However, after 1973 the military regime made rents and mortgages in working-class housing projects for miners the workers' responsibility.[18]

The regime's 1979 Labor Plan also took away many of the economic gains that the El Teniente miners had won from Kennecott over the years, and which had also been guaranteed by the state. Along with the privatization of health care and social security, the Labor Plan constituted one of the regime's major "modernizations" in its efforts to restructure the Chilean economy and society according to the dictates of neoliberalism. For the ideologues of the military regime, the institutionalization of the economic model required the introduction of a new labor relations system that allowed for the "free play" of the market by profoundly weakening the position of organized labor.[19]

The Labor Plan established a number of laws that severely limited workers' organizations. First, unions could only be organized in individual companies. Industry-wide federations like the copper miners' CTC, which had won legal status after a general strike in the 1960s, were given no legal standing and could not represent workers in collective bargaining. In addition, the law made it possible for an unlimited number of unions with twenty-five or more members and comprising at least ten percent of the labor force to exist within an individual company. This paved the way for the establishment of "yellow" company unions and resulted in divisions among workers during collective bargaining and strikes. The possibility of company-wide or industry-wide negotiations, which had lent the miners tremendous leverage during strikes between the 1940s and the 1960s, was eliminated.[20]

In addition, workers' right to strike was severely curtailed. Many workers in "industries whose paralyzation would damage the supply of goods to the population, the economy, or national security" could not go on strike. In addition, employers were given the right to hire replacement workers during strikes. After sixty days on strike, workers were required either to return to work and accept the conditions offered by the employer or to leave the company. Thus, the introduction of the Labor Plan eroded the once-strong position of miners' unions and transformed their relation to the state. The CTC had no remaining legal status and could not represent workers in collective bargaining. In El Teniente, unions became atomized by work section and the strike became an unreliable and restricted tool.[21]

Community, Consumerism, and Working-Class Culture

The military regime's intense repression and neoliberal economic policies not only eviscerated El Teniente's leftist political traditions, institutions, and militant workplace culture—they also radically transformed the nature of unionism, community, and gender relations among miners and their families. Oral histories reveal the general disintegration of the miners' community and culture that occurred during the parallel moves to a neoliberal economy and to the city below the mine, Rancagua. The dismantling of the material securities that miners had enjoyed since the 1940s and that had kept them and their families committed to life and work in the mining camps was exacerbated by the cultural transformations wrought by the twin pressures of repression and the market economy. El Teniente miners traveled one to two hours by bus from Rancagua every morning to reach the mine, leading to a significant separation of workplace and community. In the mining camps and the workers' barracks the culture and experiences of the mine had infiltrated all areas of everyday life, while the miners' neighborhoods and communities in the city were integrated into the larger urban environment. There, miners and their families were exposed to a broad spectrum of cultural activities and influences. Housing was urban and privately owned, and the city provided a variety of forms of recreation, theater, music, cinema, newspapers, and magazines. Miners' children attended public schools. Miners and their families watched television for the first time, went to movies, and participated in the vibrant cultural life of urban society.

Workers and union leaders were alert to the cultural transformations that occurred as the mining communities were broken up:

> Life in Rancagua is totally different; in the camps we were marginalized from many things, marginalized from culture, from recreation, from sports, marginalized from everything . . . there was one theater, but we were obliged to see the movie that was shown there—but in the city there are four or five theaters and you choose; before we didn't even have television.[22]

With the Left silenced and repressed, the news, politics, and entertainment [that] workers absorbed were generated by the dictatorship or imported from abroad and received through official and approved newspapers and television. As one miner noted, "the problem was that the workers received only what the dictatorship said, nothing else, since there was no opposition or freedom of expression. So all the propaganda, on the radio, TV, [and in the] newspapers was the dictatorship's; every day you saw the same thing."[23] The barracks, which had been the central space in the camps where miners' families came together, were replaced by individual homes and apartments. Workers now lived dispersed around the city in different neighborhoods. One woman described, for example, how she no longer saw her friends and neighbors or spent time at the miners' union hall, which had operated as a community center in the camps:

> I still see my neighbors and friends, but now we don't do the things we used to do, and life has separated us here [in the city] politically; we've become distant from one another, because in the camp above we didn't notice our differences: We all went to the union, but here, no. For many the husband goes to the union, but many women no longer go.[24]

Similarly, a miner described how "above [in the mining camps], the workers lived in more of a community. There was more unity; the unions were stronger because everything was right there; the camp, life in the camp, it's different below [in the city]."[25]

Stimulated by economic policies that encouraged the import of cheap foreign manufactured goods, consumerism also played a role in transforming the culture of the mining community. By the late 1970s Rancagua's stores were flooded with consumer items that the miners, with their relatively high wages, could afford to buy on credit—and many miners fell quickly into debt. The new culture of consumption, promoted by the neoliberal economy and the proliferation of media like cinema and television, transformed workers' relationship to the union and the company. The mine administration and the union often operated as credit agencies; workers began to look to union leaders who, through their contacts, could arrange loans. Officialist union leaders with ties to the company, like Guillermo Medina, organized a base of support around their ability to get individual workers credit and advances from the company. With the privatization of health care, union leaders also became important in providing sick workers and their families money and loans to pay medical expenses.

The system of loans in El Teniente eroded miners' traditions of militancy and combativeness and encouraged individualism. Opposition activists and miners noted that workers only went to the union hall to solicit loans from union leaders appointed by the dictatorship. Union activists lamented the growth of consumerism among miners and the ways in which miners began to see the union as a source of credit and material benefits, rather than as an instrument of struggle.[26] One CTC report described, for example, how the dictatorship

> imposed an economic system on Chileans, given by the Chicago School, of free market, with which they imposed on Chile consumerism that poisoned us with autos, color TVs, sophisticated electronics equipment. Economic groups made money with banks, finance groups, and mutual

funds that flourished like mushrooms in support of this sinister and shady system.[27]

Similarly, according to a group of opposition union leaders, the dictatorship brought "consumerism . . . electrodomestics, stereos, color TVs, all these things . . . finance groups were created, the guys began to take out loans, so they had more and more economic problems every day because they owed so much."[28] According to another opposition union leader,

> they tried to make the workers stop going to the union, to change their consciousness, so that they didn't worry about shared problems . . . and they showed the workers a bunch of things and the workers were tempted, they bought things that they couldn't afford with credit, by quotas. For the government and for the company, the indebted worker is a worker who is not going to have any possibility of struggling for his things, for his wage.[29]

With the liberalization of the economy, workers increasingly approached issues crucial to their well-being as individuals. Where before health care, housing, and pensions had been the subject of collective community movements in the camps in struggles with the mining company and the state, now each worker contended on his own to adjust to the realities of the neoliberal economy, which was precisely the goal of the regime's "modernizations." Union leaders often found that their jobs consisted mainly of helping workers deal with the many bureaucratic procedures required by banks, pension funds, health care firms, and loan agencies. The atomization of the miners' community was reinforced by the move to the city, by the miners' forced entrance into the privatized market economy, and by the consumer culture fostered by *los Chicago boys*.

The Reorganization of an Independent Labor Movement

Despite the regime's intense repression and the spread of a culture of individualism and materialism, the El Teniente miners mounted a series of challenges to the authority of the company and state during the late 1970s. Traditions of labor activism and political militancy in the leftist PS and PC, as well as the PDC, established the basis for clandestine organizing in the mine and in miners' neighborhoods and helped mine workers resist the destruction of their community. In 1977, following the regime's rejection of efforts by PDC union leaders to negotiate a new contract, miners boycotted the mess halls to symbolically protest working conditions and the dismissal of independent union leaders. That same year over twenty percent of the El Teniente work force engaged in a wildcat strike. In 1978, miners engaged in another wildcat work stoppage in the mine, again resulting in a wave of dismissals.

Workers organized these movements at soccer matches, over lunch in the mess hall, on the buses going up to work, and in the mine's changing room, where word of stoppages and clandestine pamphlets and leaflets were distributed. In general, these movements were organized by workers outside the company-controlled union. As one worker remembered,

> The movement was formed out of sight of the union leadership, because at that time the workers didn't trust the union leaders, because they hadn't been elected by the workers . . . [it] was organized by the workers in the cage, in the train. They threw clandestine pamphlets. . . . The leaders began to make demands before the trains left, because there's a strategic point where all the workers put on their work clothes, they change clothes and get on the train, when the time came to get on the train and they were conversing and the train would leave and they wouldn't go up to the mine.[30]

Following the 1977 wildcat strike, over eighty miners, including leftist activists involved in leading the stoppage, were fired; four Christian Democratic union leaders were arrested, and two were sent into internal exile. These repressive actions brought militants of the PDC, PC, and PS together for the first time.[31] In El Teniente, militants from the PDC, PS, and PC came together to organize grassroots opposition to the officialist leadership of the unions. Nationally, anticommunist union leaders (many from the PDC) who had attempted to forge a new labor relation system through negotiations with the regime had formed in 1975 a new organization, the Group of Ten, that staked out a more independent and critical stance toward the military government. In 1977, the Group of Ten adopted an increasingly militant oppositional stance and sent a public letter, signed by 852 union leaders, criticizing the regime's labor policy and calling for democratization. In 1978, Socialist, Communist, and PDC union activists, many from the Group of Ten, formed a more militant labor organization more clearly opposed to the regime: the Coordinadora Nacional Sindical (CNS).[32]

The implementation of the new labor relations system in 1979 provided Chilean workers some space for organization. Union elections and collective bargaining were legalized under the new Labor Plan and, despite the restrictions on union activity, workers took advantage of this new institutional space to build independent unions and to remove union leaders appointed by the regime. El Teniente workers began to establish legal internal "commissions" to examine the corruption and mismanagement of officialist union leaders. As one miner recalled, the Labor Plan and union elections gave rise to a new workers' movement that sought to win back control of the El Teniente unions. "Inside the mine the workers began to circulate a list to censure the union leaders. A ton of workers signed this list and they presented it to the authorities and three or four days later the workers who were presenting the demands were fired." In the Caletones foundry, "workers formed a revisory commission, established by law, and this commission was accused of political activity and everyone was fired."[33]

The revisory commissions, formed to expose the corruption of officialist union leaders, provided the basis for a new union movement in the copper mine. When union elections were held for the first time between 1979 and 1982, opposition leaders, mostly from the Communist, Socialist, and Christian Democratic parties, took control of the unions and the CTC. At the national level, the regime-appointed head of the CTC was replaced in 1982 by an elected union leader from El Teniente, Emilio Torres. Guillermo Medina was removed from his position at the head of an umbrella organization representing the El Teniente unions and replaced with Eugenio López, a worker who had been active in the movements of the late 1970s. Both Torres and López were militants of the PDC. Militants of the Communist party were also elected to the CTC's national leadership, including Manuel Rodríguez, newly elected president of the El Teniente foundry workers' union (the Sindicato Industrial Caletones).

The workers who helped organize the first strikes and opposition movements within the El Teniente union had profiles as activists and militants of the PDC, PS, and PC. They were known by other workers as combative and articulate. To lead the new movements, they drew on the authority conferred upon them by the miners' history of struggle. As one worker recalled,

> I think at this time there was a terrific participation of the El Teniente old-timers . . . the old-timers were the most enthusiastic . . . they guided the young kids, gave the young kids incentive. . . . It's that the old guys came with a combative mentality . . . and they arrived with only their spirit for fighting . . . it was the old-timers who gave it spirit.[34]

An opposition union leader also recalled that

> the old worker, the worker with many years in the company, is conscious and trusts leftist union leaders . . . the young workers don't have much militancy, they haven't struggled, they haven't suffered what the old ones have suffered, the persecutions, they haven't suffered the great strikes of this mine which had distinguished itself by having many strikes, long strikes . . . it hasn't cost the young workers what it cost the old workers . . . there were great struggles, great strikes to win what we have now and they don't understand this.[35]

Often these older workers were the children of miners, had grown up in the mining camps, and had begun work in El Teniente during the 1960s or early 1970s. They had had close contact with the mine's traditions of labor activism but had been too young to suffer dismissal and repression after the 1973 coup. Workers who spoke out against the regime and organized protests had the experience of militancy in political parties and often had the support of these parties. In this sense, their election and the protests they led depended upon their base within the outlawed leftist parties and the PDC. One PS activist remembers, for example, the election of a Socialist union leader in 1981: "He was a man who had been taken out of clandestinity, because I'll tell you that he had worked clandestinely . . . we all worked clandestinely for his candidacy and I was detained precisely because they knew that I was one of those who supported him."[36] Before the 1973 coup this union leader had been a Socialist provincial delegate for the CUT. Political militancy won workers recognition and trust from other workers. Workers tended to vote for militants of the leftist parties and the PDC who worked actively and, at times, openly against the dictatorship. Thus one Communist union leader elected in 1981 recalled that

> the workers knew me since before '73 because I was a candidate before '73—if I had been elected that time before '73 I would have been fired . . . everyone knew my way of thinking . . . this is because the workers in this union are very old . . . with many years working . . . this is how they knew me for my militancy in the Communist party.[37]

The generation of democratically elected union leaders who led the strike and protests of 1983 emerged from the clandestine networks of the opposition parties. Many had had both political and union experience before the 1973 coup. Militants of the Communist, Socialist, and Christian Democratic parties held underground meetings outside the mine at soccer matches, on buses, in taxis, or walking in small groups on the street. They distributed pamphlets and organized stoppages, slowdowns, and *viandazos* [mess hall boycotts]. Often, the opposition leaders elected after 1980 emerged with the support of these clandestine networks. As one leftist union activist remembered,

> Communists and Socialists were elected . . . there was an underground clandestine [organization] . . . leaders who worked clandestinely . . . speaking on the buses up to the mine—small groups in the strike committee: That was the "school" . . . you could speak at work and had the opportunity to talk on the bus—in the train—in the cafeteria, that's how the new leaders became known.[38]

Another miner recalled that

> people began to organize I would say clandestinely, because in the first place we knew who we were, those who were on the Left knew who we were, so we began to act with a lot of fear, but we began to create an organization, the parties began to organize themselves as we went along meeting and we began to lose fear and we went along talking to one another and holding clandestine meetings. . . . Here I would say that politically we worked together, with Christian Democrats, with Radicals, with Socialists, with Communists.[39]

With the unions under the control of the regime, the opposition parties provided an important resource for organizing. The wildcat strikes of 1970 and 1978 "were directed by the popular parties, they were the initiators of the struggle . . . because the union leaders were still those that the dictatorship had imposed," according to one labor activist.[40] These leftist networks organized small acts of protest. He recalled that

> one year we went clandestinely to the cemetery number two here in Rancagua the fourth of September, the historic day when they held elections in Chile, so we said "the four at eleven in two"; no one knew where it was and we put a floral arrangement as homage to Allende and we made speeches and sang the Marseillaise . . . we were a few brave ones, thirty people, and the youth wrote graffiti in the cemetery—it was very quick. Very committed people . . . we held meetings in cars. Walking along, a group of leaders would hold a meeting, or we would hold meetings in a restaurant seated having a soda, very camouflaged meetings.[41]

The success of the opposition movement between 1977 and 1982 in wresting control of the El Teniente unions from "officialist" leaders did not, however, translate into successful strikes and collective bargaining. Like workers in other industries who organized independent and militant unions between 1979 and 1982, workers in the copper mines found their position in collective bargaining and strikes severely restricted by the regime's labor code. Two years of collective bargaining and strikes in urban industries and the copper mines ended with few favorable results for workers. Nationally, workers won some wage increases, but these did little to make up for increases in the cost of living and the radical decline of real wages since 1973. Overall, by 1979 real wages had dropped by an average of 10.7 percent since 1969, while in the mining sector they had fallen 22.2 percent. The average wage increase of 7.2 percent (9.5 percent in the mining sector) during the first year of collective bargaining (1979–1980) did little to remedy workers' declining standard of living. During the second year of collective bargaining (1980–1981), average wage hikes decreased to between three and four percent of workers' real wages.[42]

For the first time since the coup, workers could strike legally. However, the Labor Plan rendered the strike a limited tool at best, and most strikes ended in defeat before the fifty-nine-day limit it imposed. During the first two years of collective bargaining there were 102 strikes in Chile involving 44,955 workers. While unions requested an average of 23.1 percent in wage increases, employers offered only 4.4 percent. On the average, strikes resulted in an average raise for workers of 6.1 percent over the two years.[43] Unions were weakened by the regime's repression, by their lack of activity since the coup, and by the isolated plant-by-plant process of collective negotiations, which blocked industry-wide or coordinated strikes and support strikes. The wages lost to workers during strikes (the Labor Plan prohibited payment for days on strike) outweighed the minimal increases they could win through negotiations with employers.

In general, in the most important strikes, workers were forced to return to work with little gain as the fifty-nine-day strike limit arrived. In a strike of 1,478 workers at the PANAL textile plant, for example, workers returned to work after fifty-seven days with only a nominal wage increase. The union had petitioned for a twenty-five percent raise above the cost of living but was forced to accept the company's offer of 1.5 percent. Following the strike, the company proceeded to fire forty-seven workers who had been active in leading the strike.[44]

In El Teniente in 1981, 8,230 workers struck for forty-eight days, having demanded a ten percent wage increase and having rejected the company offer of two percent. The strike ended when the miners' unions agreed to the company offer. In 1982, in response to an increasingly devastating economic recession, a new labor law eliminated automatic cost-of-living raises for all workers, one of the copper workers' most cherished conquests. The reality of the new labor legislation was made clear to El Teniente miners when, after fifty-nine days on strike, 1,700 workers in the Caletones foundry who had petitioned for a ten percent raise were forced to return to work and accept their previous contract—gaining no raise at all—which meant the loss of the long-established automatic cost-of-living raise. In addition, the foundry workers, like all workers in El Teniente, lost their right both to company-paid medical care and production bonuses, which had been part of collective contracts since the 1940s.[45]

The reanimation of El Teniente's unions coincided with a general rebuilding of the Chilean labor movement during the period following the institutionalization of the military regime's Labor Plan. As in other industries, the mine workers found that traditional forms of workplace-based labor action like collective bargaining and the strike were ineffective. While mine workers' unions had enjoyed a privileged position in relation to the state due to the strategic location of copper in the national economy, the two-year period of collective bargaining made clear that workers in the mining sector had lost their leverage when confronted with an authoritarian regime intent on dismantling corporatist structures, restricting union activity, and reorganizing the economy according to the dictates of free-market economics.

Economic Crisis and Popular Protest, 1983–1986

In 1982, the military regime's economic model entered a period of prolonged crisis that lasted until 1986. The lowering of import barriers, liberalization of trade, and deregulation of the financial sector under Pinochet had opened Chile to the world market in unprecedented ways. The imposition of the neoliberal model made Chile an attractive market for credit from multilateral lending institutions and foreign investors, while the privatization and deregulation of the economy allowed a few major financial groups to take control of many of the nation's central economic activities and to engage in profitable speculation. Chile's balance of trade deteriorated as domestic producers were driven out of business by a flood of imports. During world recession, with rising interest rates, increasing oil prices, and a decline in copper prices during the early 1980s, the fragility of Chile's "economic miracle" was made clear. By 1983, many financial groups, heavily overfinanced, tottered on the edge of collapse. Banks were pushed to the brink of ruin, and bankruptcies proliferated. Chile's foreign debt rose exponentially, economic growth plummeted, and unemployment grew to over thirty percent, with ten percent of the labor force employed in minimal government programs.

The economic crisis of the early 1980s sparked a period of political unrest in Chile that verged on civil war. The CTC's call for a day of protest on May 11, 1983, was one of the first broad challenges to the dictatorship's repressive policies and economic model and re-created an independent national labor movement. As one publication put it, "the day of national protest represented without any doubt the most significant political event that the Military Government has had to confront."[46] In one of the first national public critiques of the regime's economic policies and political repression, the CTC's announcement stated that "our problem is not one law more or less . . . but a complete economic, social, cultural, and political system that has us smothered and bound. The moment has come to stand up and say ENOUGH."[47] The CTC's call for a national protest received an unexpectedly widespread response, as workers took to the streets in their neighborhoods banging empty pots, blowing horns, burning tires, and erecting barricades.

The CTC's call for a national protest reflected the failures of the independent opposition labor movement to wrest gains from employers during collective bargaining between 1980 and 1982 as a result of the restrictions imposed by the regime's Labor Plan. In the context of the militarization of the copper mines and the weakness of traditional means of organized pressure like the strike, the CTC perceived nation-wide protests to be the only viable form of opposition to the regime. Instead of a movement located at the workplace, the CTC envisioned a national alliance with other workers and opposition sectors, including students, the Catholic Church, the middle class, and the human rights movement, as the best response to regime repression. The protest, rather than the strike, would serve workers better since the Labor Code's restrictions made striking a no-win situation and since the CTC perceived workers' problems to go beyond individual firms to the entire political and economic system.

The copper miners defined the strike and protest of May 1983 as part of a general critique of the regime's free market economic policies. In congresses in 1982 and 1983, the CTC released lengthy analyses of the Labor Plan and the model of *los Chicago boys*, which they linked to the regime's policies of political repression. The 1982 CTC congress issued a detailed examination of workers' many losses under the Labor Plan and concluded that "the Labor Plan . . . permits the strengthening, accumulation, and concentration of economic power in Chile. And today this economic power imposes its decisions and has the power to obligate us to work in the conditions it decides, assuring the functioning of the economic model." The CTC declaration emphasized that a national movement to oppose the economic system of the dictatorship was necessary because traditional forms of workplace-based action were unfeasible:

> During each collective negotiation union leaders have found that they have been able to gain little or nothing. . . they have come to realize that companies present their own petitions to the unions, protected by the criminal laws of the Labor Plan, which permit every kind of excess on the part of the companies and place every kind of limitation on the workers.[48]

The CTC also provided an analysis of the regime's economic program and explained how neoliberalism had led to the economic crisis of the 1980s. The CTC argued that the existence of the model allowed "an enormous concentration of economic power" and depended upon "maintaining workers disorganized, restricted, and crushed by regressive labor legislation." In addition, the report assailed the regime's plans to confront the economic crisis by slashing workers' wages, eliminating cost-of-living raises, and inviting foreign investment in a privatized copper industry against the will "of all Chileans who once said yes to the nationalization of copper." The CTC issued a rigorous critique of the regime's efforts to deplete the copper industry's resources and then, with the mines in crisis, sell them off to foreign investors. As the producers of Chile's major resource, copper miners had led the struggle for nationalization of the copper mines in 1971. Now, the CTC argued, they had the "moral authority" to represent the demands of all of Chile for democracy and an end to the neoliberal experiment.[49] In strikes against the North American copper companies miners had spoken for the national interests of all of Chile. The copper miners now claimed in a reconfigured nationalism to represent the interests of all Chileans in democracy, human rights, and an end to economic restructuring.

Following the May 11 protest and the El Teniente strike, copper miners helped organize a new national labor organization, the National Workers' Command (CNT), and then the Unified Workers' Central (CUT). Christian Democrat Rodolfo Seguel, the CTC's president from 1983 to 1984 and an El Teniente worker, became president of the CNT. For the next three years, despite continued repression in which opposition union leaders suffered dismissal and arrest, the miners continued to mobilize in protests. Every month protests were held in Rancagua as well as in Santiago and other major urban centers, and the CTC became a focal point for the reorganization of the labor movement. For the second national protest in June 1983, the CTC declared an illegal industry-wide strike. In El Teniente, between eighty-five and ninety-five percent of the work force participated in the stoppage. In response, the regime arrested leaders from the CTC and El Teniente and over 600 workers from three mines were fired. El Teniente's major union, the blue-collar mine workers' Sindicato Industrial Sewell y Mina, with over 4,000 members, set up a soup kitchen for the families of fired workers with the help of neighborhood committees and organizations from the city, including the central marketplace and the taxi drivers' union.

Until 1986, the miners continued to march in demonstrations and protests and to hold hunger strikes to denounce the regime's hard-line response to popular opposition. In October of 1984, for example, the El Teniente miners organized a march from Rancagua to Santiago to demand the rehiring of union leaders and workers fired following the June 1983 strike and to call for democratization. Protesters, including women and children from miners' families, were dragged onto police buses and beaten. Many of the marchers took refuge in Rancagua's church. Despite this repression, workers held a mass assembly in the union hall in Rancagua and reorganized the "march" to Santiago in taxis, buses, and by train. When the miners finally arrived in Santiago at a demonstration organized by the Santiago Popular Youth Organizations, they were applauded enthusiastically by the 45,000 protesters, representing an important alliance between the labor movement in the copper mines and the popular protests in Santiago's working-class neighborhoods.[50]

The copper miners were well situated to lead labor and civilian protest against the dictatorship. Unlike workers in other industries, they had managed to maintain their union structures intact. They did not face the massive unemployment of urban areas beset by deindustrialization, and their wages and benefits still placed them in a favorable position compared to workers in other sectors of the economy. Indeed, the miners' relatively high wages and secure jobs allowed them to participate in the new consumer economy like no other industrial workers. This led many miners to fall heavily into debt; when the economy crashed in 1982, the copper workers began to experience the catastrophic effects of their precarious position in the market economy. The miners' earlier integration into that economy thus led, contradictorily, to their growing discontent and disenchantment with the regime's economic model. The promises of neoliberalism embodied in the cars, stereos, and houses made available to miners on cheap credit and pay advances vanished, replaced by the spectres of unemployment, debt, wage cuts, and the loss of benefits. Economic restructuring had begun to erode the many material benefits and securities copper workers had won over the years. Both their relatively secure position and the threats to this same security placed the copper miners in a unique position to organize opposition to the regime.

Following the failures of collective bargaining and strikes between 1980 and 1982, El Teniente miners began to look for new forms of protest. As one miner noted, "the guys were tired of losing and losing their conquests without daring to raise their voices, permanently threatened with unemployment and by the private contractors."[51] As another miner said, "over time the worker saw that his conquests were being erased—the most important conquests, the production bonus, bonuses for [work-related] sicknesses. We lost the cost-of-living raise and hospital benefits."[52] In addition, while El Teniente miners had their jobs, many saw family members fall into unemployment. As one miner noted, "we aren't asking anything for ourselves. You realize what the situation is like in your family. Because you have brothers, brothers-in-law, fathers . . . who are unemployed. We are asking for work, freedom and democracy."[53] As the Chilean economy fell into deep recession and unemployment rates reached more than thirty percent, miners began to suffer the same day-to-day struggles of their jobless neighbors and relatives. Miners thus increasingly came to inhabit urban spaces in which they constructed new forms of identity linked to the struggles of the poor and unemployed.

In Rancagua and El Teniente, long-standing labor traditions, union activism, and the clandestine activities of the leftist parties and the PDC played a major role in the organization of protest and opposition. Unlike urban industrial areas, where work forces had been purged of political activists, ties between the unions and opposition political parties remained strong in the mining community. When the protests began after 1983, the copper miners' unions, now under opposition control, organized and directed the mobilizations, along with the PC, PS, and PDC. One worker remembers that "it began with copper, with the copper workers' leaders, those who directed the protests and leaders from the neighborhoods where the families of the copper workers lived, this is where the protests of the *cacerolazos* [pot bangers] began."[54] Opposition parties, including the PDC and PC, and national and provincial labor organizations held meetings in the miners' union hall. In 1984, for example, opposition parties and the provincial "workers' command" of the CNT held a mass assembly there before initiating a protest in Rancagua. The same worker recalled that

> the unions said that they were going to do a *caceroleo* protest at "such and such time," and that news was spread throughout all Rancagua in hours . . . everyone conversed; it was a great thing because when you took a collective taxi, the bus, or wherever, and everyone talked, and whoever didn't know listened to the person that was in front or the person behind—"at this time there's going to be a *cacerolazo*."[55]

Despite the central role of the miners' unions and the opposition parties in mobilizations in Rancagua, however, the protests were not traditional miners' strikes. Rather, they constituted nationwide movements for democracy based in neighborhoods and communities. In Rancagua, El Teniente miners played a central role in organizing the protests, but they were joined by working-class people from all over the city. Every month the residents of Rancagua's *poblaciones* (poor urban neighborhoods), many of them from miners' families, would bang empty pots, burn tires in the streets, blow auto horns, and do battle with the police.[56] Many of the participants in the movements were women and students. Student organizations and neighborhood networks were central in organizing the protests and disseminating information. The city's taxi and bus drivers, for example, played a major role in passing along information about planned protests, demonstrations, and marches. The May 11 strike and the miners' mobilizations sparked a new form of political protest that included the union and work-related struggles but that was located outside the mine as part of a broader struggle for democracy.

The neighborhood became a central space for mobilization and organization because of the many unemployed and fired miners and because of the authoritarian conditions within the mine. Neighborhood committees began to form *ollas comunes* (soup kitchens) to help feed Rancagua's unemployed and the many miners fired because of their participation in opposition politics and labor protests. Leftist activists, groups affiliated with the Catholic Church, youth organizations, and human rights organizations played a role in these protests against dictatorship and the disasters of the regime's economic model.

As in the rest of Chile's poor urban neighborhoods, women played a crucial role in these community organizations and began to assume a new political position in the movements for democracy. Asserting their rights as mothers to fend for their families, they organized soup kitchens and women's committees and participated actively in the monthly protests. The miners' union organized a permanent common kitchen in the union hall where fired workers and their families could receive three meals a day. Miners' wives formed women's committees that organized medical care, clothing, and food for miners' families. As one woman said,

> before I was a housewife and nothing else. I had never even gone to the *centros de madres* (state-sponsored mothers' centers). But the day came when there was nothing to put in the pot. And the only possibility for eating, above all for the little kids, is through the organization with others who are also affected, looking for community support.[57]

Women's participation in the movements for democracy during the 1980s differed significantly from their mobilization in strike movements before 1973. As miners' wages deteriorated and they lost their benefits, and as many fell into unemployment, women increasingly found jobs in Rancagua's service sector or in the informal market. Miners' wages could no longer support their families, and suspended or unemployed miners had to depend on their wives' wages to keep the family going. Unlike in the mining camps, women had greater opportunities for work in the city, and by the early 1980s some miners' wives were securing jobs as saleswomen and secretaries. Others began their own businesses or opened small stalls in the thriving informal economy of Rancagua's streets. In addition, women from miners' families—like working-class women in Santiago—formed knitting groups and sold sweaters and blankets to make extra money for their families. The economic crisis of the early 1980s, the deterioration of miners' wages and benefits, and growing unemployment due in part to the mass dismissals after the 1983 strike propelled many women into both the formal and informal labor markets.

When women participated in neighborhood kitchens and in protests of the 1980s they mobilized around their rights and responsibilities as mothers and wives as they had before in the mining enclave. However, in the context of the new neoliberal economy they no longer organized only to support their husbands, sons, and fathers. Their wages and informal economic activities were central to their families' survival. Women achieved a certain economic independence for the first time as men's positions as heads of households were eroded by the twin pressures of the market economy and the regime's repression. In community movements in the city and in the broader struggle against the dictatorship, women's political participation took on new meaning. They began to experience both economic and political autonomy for the first time in neighborhood-based economic activities and in movements for democracy.

One woman, the wife of a foundry worker who later worked clandestinely as a Communist party militant, remembers that after the 1983 strike women organized community kitchens to feed unemployed and fired miners and their families:

> First came those who were doing the hunger strike, women, and we began to organize a soup kitchen . . . we had the support of the community, especially the people from the marketplace . . . every day the wives of the people who were on strike came; we formed a women's committee, and we began to have cultural activities in order to make money because there were many basic needs . . . the *compañeros* in Rancagua gave a lot of support, and we became a homogenous group, men with women; it was a very rich experience—the *compañeras* of the workers gave classes to the children . . . it was a very exciting thing where you saw the active participation of women.[58]

Participation in the *ollas comunes* also led to women's politicization. As the same woman recalls,

> for the first time I saw women elbow-to-elbow with their *compañeros* . . . it was there that I saw that women had to have a political-social education . . . because no political party . . . cares about us, none! This

is when we got the *compañeras* out into the street to fight—here at the door of the union, fifty women marched through the streets; the repression didn't hold off because we were women, there were beatings, and I tell you, you have to be afraid of a group of women fighting, especially in this region—the girls were very timid at first but they went out into the street and were transformed.[59]

In the mining camps women's support activities during strikes had been subordinated to the general strategies, tactics, and leadership of the miners' union. Now women's involvement in community organizing in miners' neighborhoods and in the broader movement for democracy created new challenges to traditional gender roles in social movements, as well as within the household. The foundry worker's wife described, for example, how her participation in clandestine organizing and the community kitchen led her to criticize men's dominance of the organizations and inequalities between men and women at home:

> Many times in meetings around here I argued with the men: "How can you expect women's support if you keep them marginalized?" . . . I told them: "For you, women are supposed to be at home. They bring up your kids, wash your clothes, and at night open their legs"—that is to say, they look at you like an object that has to be in the house, the house functions, the bed functions, and you outside function as men, function as leaders, function as militants [of parties]. . . I was always needling them.[60]

Women, through their work and through their participation in the protests, began to challenge male workers' authority within the household for the first time. The regime's economic model had the unintentional effect of increasing female employment in the informal market and service sector and thus transforming family relations and gender roles, despite its official rhetoric of traditional Catholic "family values." In addition, the increased economic burden on women in mining households drove them to protest the regime's economic policies and authoritarian rule.

The copper miners' movements during the 1980s thus brought together traditional forms of labor organization and political militancy around workplace-related issues with new forms of popular protest and mobilization. Rather than two disparate spheres of political resistance to authoritarian rule, the miners' strikes, marches, and demonstrations combined workplace-based forms of organization, clandestine left-wing networks, and neighborhood-based movements that included workers' families, students, taxi drivers, the unemployed, and members of the urban informal sector. The dislocation of miners' traditional communities and their integration into city life made the combination of these forms of struggle necessary. Miners could no longer depend on the strength of the unified and homogeneous community of the mining camps. Similarly, the dismantling of the labor systems in the mines, the increasingly precarious nature of their employment, and the regime's repressive labor policies led miners to look to new forms of mobilization and alliances with other urban working-class groups, often unemployed or intermittently employed family members and neighbors. Symptomatic of this combination of long-standing traditions of labor organization and political militancy with new forms of urban-based mobilization was the new and expanded role of women both in miners' household economies and the protests of the 1980s.

Organized Labor, New Social Movements, and Political Protest

The role of traditions of labor activism and political militancy in the copper mines in organizing a resurgent national labor movement and in mobilizing popular protest against the Chilean military regime throws into question the emphasis in "new social movement" theory on political protest in urban neighborhoods rather than the workplace; on issues of consumption and services rather than production and labor; and on conflicts between social movements aimed at the state rather than capital in Latin America.[61] In the El Teniente mining community, work-related demands were intrinsically linked to protests over issues of consumption of services and goods and state policy because of the overarching effects of the regime's economic restructuring and political repression. Declining real wages and onerous work conditions could be linked directly to free market economics, privatization, and institutionalized state terror. For the miners, their battle was not just over working conditions and wages but over an entire political and economic system that had transformed their lifestyles, patterns of consumption, and the organization of their households and community.

The case of the copper miners also demonstrates that organizing within unions around work-related issues formed the basis for the mobilization of miners' communities in broader forms of social protest against human rights abuses and economic oppression. Unions provided political and institutional space for the organization of national protest movements and became a major vehicle for articulating demands for democratization and an end to the regime's neoliberal economic model. In addition, as Cathy Schneider has shown for shantytown protest in Santiago, the resuscitation of an independent labor movement at El Teniente and its organization of political protest were based on the activities and clandestine networks of the opposition political parties. Schneider found that the shantytowns organized by the PC before 1973 had the highest levels of participation in the protest movements; likewise, at El Teniente the Communist, Socialist, and Christian Democratic parties, which had enjoyed solid bases of support before 1973, played a role in the resurgent union movement.[62] Activists from these parties helped to win back the miners' unions from regime-appointed union leaders and to initiate the formation of an independent labor federation at the national level.

Finally, while the copper miners' strikes and protest movements demonstrate the importance of traditions of labor activism and the clandestine organization of the opposition political parties in the copper mines, they also reveal the shifting nature of class identity in working-class communities in Chile. The social and economic dislocations produced by the regime's economic policies and the repression of the labor movement made new kinds of mobilization necessary. Workers now lived in communities and households with friends, neighbors, and relatives who filled the ranks of the under- and unemployed. The traditional structure of the male-headed household was eroded as mine workers' wives and daughters sought work in the city's service and informal economies and as the formerly cohesive mining community was fractured by the stress of rising unemployment, declining wages, and political repression. The urban uprisings throughout Chile between 1983 and 1986 reflected this transformed social landscape. To be successful, a labor movement had to be a working-class movement that sought to overcome the obstacles of restrictive labor legislation, brutal police repression, atomized work relations in factories and mines, a spreading consumer culture, and economic dislocation; and it had to do so by elaborating new forms of protest that included poor and working-class women, workers in the unorganized informal and service sectors, and the urban poor—as well as factory workers and miners. The copper miners' federation recognized the limits of workplace-based collective action and the need for a national movement that went outside mines and factories to oppose not just an employer, but an economic model that had thrown Chile's working class into the maelstrom of the free market, and a regime that countered opposition with severe repression.

Notes

1. Confederación de Trabajadores del Cobre, Memoria, Congreso Ordinario, Punta de Traica, 1983 (copy in author's possession).

2. Cathy Schneider, for example, has offered an important critique of the "new social movement" perspective, arguing that in urban squatter settlements protests were generated out of the underground survival of neighborhood networks of leftist activists. However, Schneider also takes the subject of the popular protests of the 1980s to be the urban poor, rather than workers or miners. See Cathy Schneider, *Shantytown Protest in Pinochet's Chile* (Philadelphia, 1995).

3. See Joel Stillerman, " 'Dando la Pelea Hasta el Final': Metal Workers' Resistance in Authoritarian Chile, 1976–1983," paper presented at the Thirteenth Annual Latin American Labor History Conference, Duke University, 1996. Other important works on the union movement under the military regime include: Guillermo Campero and José A. Valenzuela, *El Movimiento Sindical en el Régimen Militar Chileno, 1973–1981* (Santiago, 1984); Manuel Barrera, Helia Henriquez,

and Teresita Selamé, *Sindicatos y Estado en el Chile actual* (Santiago, 1985); Jaime Ruiz-Tagle P., *El Sindicalismo Chileno después del Plan Laboral* (Santiago, 1985); Manuel Barrera and Gonzalo Falabella, *Sindicatos bajo Régimenes Militares: Argentina, Brasil, Chile* (Santiago, 1990); Manuel Barrera and J. Samuel Valenzuela, "The Development of Labor Movement Opposition to the Military Regime," in *Dictatorship and Oppositions: Military Rule in Chile*, ed. J. Samuel Valenzuela and Arturo Valenzuela (Baltimore, 1986); Alan Angell, "Unions and Workers in Chile during the 1980s," in *The Struggle for Democracy in Chile, 1982–1990*, ed. Paul W. Drake and Iván Jaksic (Lincoln, 1991).

4. For a history of copper miners before 1973 see Thomas Miller Klubock, *Contested Communities: Class, Gender, and Politics in Chile's El Teniente Copper Mine, 1904–1948* (Durham, 1998).

5. See Sergio Bitar and Crisostomo Pizarro, *La Caída de Allende y la Huelga de El Teniente* (Santiago, 1986). The Chilean labor code divided blue-collar workers (*obreros*), who engaged in mostly manual labor, from white-collar workers (*empleados*), who worked in offices and performed work of a more technical nature. *Empleado* and *obrero* unions often negotiated separate contracts and had access to different benefits and wage structures. In El Teniente, the PDC controlled most of the mine's small *empleado* unions during the late 1960s and during Allende's government, while the PS and PC continued to dominate the *obrero* unions. The 1973 strike was largely the result of the activities of PDC activists and the *empleado* unions that opposed the UP. During the strike, the *obrero* unions mostly continued to work and to express their support for the UP.

6. The nationalist Díaz was replaced in 1976 by Sergio Fernández, who then became minister of the interior in 1978 and one of the most outspoken and radical ideologues of the Pinochet regime, particularly as a champion of neoliberal economic policies.

7. Interview, member of the Sindicato Industrial Caletones El Teniente, Rancagua, July 1991.

8. Interview, former El Teniente union leader and labor activist, Rancagua, March 2, 1992.

9. *Informe del Cobre*, December 1983.

10. Interview, former El Teniente union leader and labor activist, Rancagua, March 2, 1992.

11. Interview, member of the Sindicato Industrial Caletones El Teniente, Rancagua, July 1991.

12. For a discussion of private contractors in the copper industry see Confederación de Trabajadores del Cobre, Congreso Ordinario, Memoria, July 26–28, 1982. Also see Confederación de Trabajadores del Cobre, Congreso Ordinario, Memoria, March 6–8, 1987 (in author's possession); and *Voz del Minero*, December 1985.

13. Interview, former union leader, Sindicato Industrial Sewell y Mina, Rancagua, November 25, 1992.

14. *Informe del Cobre*, June 1983.

15. *Voz del Minero*, October 1985; see also *Voz del Minero*, June 1984, June 1988.

16. *Informe del Cobre*, June 1983.

17. *La Voz del Minero*, October 1985; interview, member of the Sindicato Industrial Caletones, Rancagua, July 1991.

18. Interview, union leader, Sindicato Industrial Rancagua, Rancagua, March 18, 1991.

19. For an analysis of the Labor Plan see *Análisis*, July 1979.

20. Ruiz-Tagle, *El Sindicalismo Chileno.*

21. Ibid.

22. Interview, member of the Sindicato Industrial Caletones, Rancagua, July 1991.

23. Ibid.

24. Interview, Rancagua, June 12, 1992 (with assistance from Paola Fernández).

25. Interview, union leader, Sindicato Industrial Sewell y Mina, Rancagua, November 25, 1991.

26. Interview, union leader, Sindicato Industrial Rancagua, Rancagua, March 18, 1991.

27. "Memoria," Confederación de Trabajadores del Cobre, Congreso Ordinario, Santiago, January 1984 (copy in author's possession).

28. Interview, member of the Sindicato Industrial Caletones, Rancagua, July 1991.

29. Interview, union leader, Sindicato Industrial Coya y Pangal, Rancagua, March 26, 1991.

30. Interview, former El Teniente union leader and labor activist, Rancagua, March 2, 1992. The "cage" is the massive elevator that transports miners to tunnels inside the mine.

31. For accounts of the strike see *El Rancagüino*, November 4–12 and November 24, 1977. Also see *El Mercurio*, November 4–8, 1977.

32. For histories of these organizations see Barrera and Valenzuela, "The Development of Labor Movement Opposition"; Angell, "Unions and Workers in Chile during the 1980s"; and Campero and Valenzuela, *El Movimiento Sindical en el Régimen Militar Chileno, 1973–1981.*

33. Interview, union leader, Sindicato Industrial Rancagua, Rancagua, March 18, 1991.

34. Ibid.

35. Interview, union leader, Sindicato Industrial Coya y Pangal, Rancagua, March 26, 1991.

36. Interview, former El Teniente union leader and labor activist, Rancagua, March 2, 1992.

37. Interview, union leader, Sindicato Industrial Coya y Pangal, Rancagua, March 26, 1991.

38. Interview, workers of the Sindicato Industrial Caletones, Rancagua, July 1991.

39. Interview, former El Teniente union leader and labor activist, Rancagua, March 2, 1992.

40. Ibid.

41. Ibid.

42. Vicaría de Pastoral Obrera, Arzobispado de Santiago, Informe de Trabajo No. 7, 1981, "Balance de Dos Años de Negociación Colectiva." Also see *Páginas Sindicales* for these years. In addition, see Ruiz-Tagle, *El Sindicalismo Chileno después del Plan Laboral,* and Barrera, Henriquez, and Selamé, *Sindicatos y Estado en el Chile actual.*

43. Vicaría de Pastoral Obrera, "Balance de Dos Años."

44. *Páginas Sindicales*, January 1981.

45. *Informe del Cobre*, January 1983.

46. *Informe del Cobre*, June 1983.

47. Ibid.

48. Confederación de Trabajadores del Cobre, Congreso Extraordinario, Antofogasta, 1982; Congreso Ordinario, Punta de Tralca, July 26–28, 1982; Congreso Ordinario, Santiago, January 9, 1984 (copy in author's possession).

49. Confederación de Trabajadores del Cobre, Congreso Ordinario, Punta de Tralca, 1983 (copy in author's possession).

50. *La Voz del Minero*, November 1983, April 1984, June 1984, October 1984.

51. *Informe del Cobre*, December 1983.

52. Interview, member of the Sindicato Industrial Caletones El Teniente, Rancagua, July 1991.

53. *Informe del Cobre*, December 1983.

54. Interview, union leader, Sindicato Industrial Rancagua, Rancagua, March 18, 1991.

55. Ibid.

56. For descriptions of the protests see *La Voz del Minero*, 1983–1985.

57. *Informe del Cobre*, December 1983.

58. Interview, Rancagua, April 4, 1992 (with the assistance of Paola Fernández).

59. Ibid.

60. Ibid.

61. For an important theoretical discussion of the role of urban social movements in Latin America based on struggles over the consumption of basic services rather than issues of production in poor neighborhoods, see Manuel Castells, *The City and the Grass-Roots* (Berkeley, 1983). For a discussion of new social movements and Marxist theory see Ernesto Laclau and Chantal Mouffe, *Hegemony and Socialist Strategy: Towards a Radical Democratic Politics* (London, 1985), and Arturo Escobar and Sonia Alvarez, eds., *The Making of Social Movements in Latin America: Identity, Strategy, and Democracy* (Boulder, 1992). For the case of Chile, see Gabriel Salazar, *Violencia Política Popular en "Las Grandes Alamedas": Santiago de Chile, 1947–1987* (Santiago, 1990), and Teresa Valdes and Maria Weinstein, "Las Pobladoras y el estado," *Proposiciones 21: Género, Mujer y Socledad* (Santiago, 1992).

62. Schneider, *Shantytown Protest*.

13

Brazilian Workers and Democracy

Anthony W. Pereira

In the past fifteen years or so, after years of government repression, a labor movement has revived in Brazil. Its renewed strength, says Anthony Pereira in this selection, is signified by the growing number of trade unions to be found in the country and their militancy. Pereira argues that much of the progressive politics in Brazil can be laid to the support and encouragement of the left by an ever more organized labor force, especially in the past twenty years.

This rather surprising situation, given the challenges of global capitalism and neoliberalism in Brazil, leads Pereira to ask a couple of important questions. First, why does labor count so heavily in the country's politics? Second, how has organized labor helped democracy to flourish in Brazil? In discussing these questions, Pereira startlingly notes that Brazilian workers found themselves with a few unforeseen advantages over the workers of other countries. These advantages helped to change the labor movement from one dependent upon the state to one that is finding its way independently, freed from the restrictive associations of the past with government bureaucracies. It also has meant new demands, new leadership, and new relationships with other sectors of society. The latter has been critical because, as Pereira explains at length, the relationship between a democratic labor movement and workers' identity is a close and important one for the movement. The new problems faced by workers in Brazil indicate clearly that changes in the character of work have had potentially negative effects on the ability of workers to sustain themselves, that is, to reproduce a working class, unless the identity of the working class itself undergoes significant change.

Working-class collective action may appear to be in decline. In many advanced capitalist countries, the industrial working class has shrunk, rates of unionization have dropped, unions have lost power, and parties representing labor have slipped in popularity. At the same time, new scholarship has questioned the universality of class-based collective action, insisting that it is contingent, socially constructed, and historically specific. The relevance of class to contemporary politics, even its very existence, is questioned more and more forcefully. It may be that those who study labor movements will soon study not working-class collective action but, in the words of a college administrator, "the movement of labor from one place to another."[1]

Yet class identity and working-class collective action as a form of politics are not in decline everywhere. Taking one powerful indicator of such action—the formation of trade unions—we find that the percentage of workers in trade unions actually increased even in advanced capitalist countries such as Sweden, Italy, and Canada between 1970 and 1990.[2] And in many so-called newly industrializing countries, trade union growth has been explosive in the last few decades.[3]

Brazil is one of those countries. Its trade unionists have become not only numerous, but militant: Since the late 1970s unions have played a key role in opposing the military regime that was reformed into a civilian one in 1985, in dismantling state controls over labor, and in challenging neoliberal economic reforms. The weight of the organized working class has increased mightily in Brazil over the last quarter-century, in terms of both its sheer numerical strength and its role as a political actor.

Organized labor has also been a key element in the growth of support for left-wing parties since Brazil returned to a system of multiparty competition in 1982. These parties include the Democratic Labor party, or Partido Democrático Trabalhista (PDT); the Socialist party, or Partido Socialista Brasileiro (PSB); the Communist party, or Partido Comunista do Brasil (PC do B); and most significantly, the Workers' party, or Partido dos Trabalhadores (PT). All of these parties have appealed strongly to the organized working class in their rhetoric and programs and all, save the PDT, increased their representation in the national congress in the 1994 elections. Together, they control one-fifth of the seats in the lower house, the Câmara dos Deputados.

In the historiography of Latin American labor, Brazil has often been considered a backward giant, its working class comparatively small and fragmented, its labor movement relatively tame. Brazilian labor no longer fits this image. The labor movements of Argentina and Chile, once seen as far more class-conscious and militant than their Brazilian counterpart, now seem weaker in comparison.

This essay explores two questions that concern the organized working class in Brazil. First, what accounts for the increase in its relative political weight, both inside the country and in comparison to other labor movements in the region? Second, what role has organized labor played in the construction of Brazilian democracy, and what role can it reasonably be expected to play in the future?

In dealing with the first question, I argue that the Brazilian working class may have gained critical mass at a more favorable time than did its counterparts in the Southern Cone. In the second and third sections, I explore the relationship between the labor movement and democracy in Brazil. I point out that the "new unionism" renewed forms of working-class representation but encountered serious internal obstacles to the radical fulfillment of its project. In the third section I point out that, despite their recent gains, Brazilian trade unions face severe challenges from the restructuring of global capitalism and the government's implementation of neoliberal reforms. The organized working class constitutes an important core of opposition to those reforms but is unlikely to join a ruling coalition at the national level in the near future; it will, however, play an important role in leftist governments at the local and state level.

I. Structure and Timing in the Emergence of Brazilian Labor

Brazil may now have more unionized workers than any other country in the Americas. The size of its unionized work force has risen from roughly 3.7 million in 1960 to perhaps as many as 16.13 million, or around twenty-five percent of the labor force, in 1995. This exceeds the percentage in the United States and places Brazil among the small group of Western Hemisphere countries with a quarter or more of their workers in unions (Table 1).[4] The rates of unionization in these countries are low when compared with those in Western Europe but they are high in the context of Latin America.[5]

Brazil's union density rate is an estimate, because no comprehensive survey of union membership has been undertaken since the 1988 constitution allowed the unionization of public-sector employees. The estimate is a conservative one, however. For example, the largest confederation in the Brazilian union system, that of the agricultural workers, alone claims almost ten million members. Perhaps more significant than static comparisons are trends: Unionization rates have been declining in recent years in many parts of the Americas, but they have risen dramatically in Brazil.

The figures presented here refer to union membership rather than to unions' capacities for organization and action. Although the latter cannot be inferred from the former, it is hard to deny that Brazilian unions not only grew in size and number but increased their power, especially in the 1980s. How does one account for their late, recent rise as a political force?

The beginnings of an answer can be found in what some scholars call structurism—an explanation that recognizes the interaction between structure and agency.[6] One form of structurism is provided by Erik Olin Wright. He argues that "the more coarse-grained and abstract the *explanandum*, the more likely it is that general systemic factors, such as class structure or the dynamics of capitalism, will play an important explanatory role."[7] In other words, the degree to which structure forms a part of explanations of events has much to do with whether one is explaining long-term, fundamental shifts or more detailed instances of political timing, sequence,

Table 1. Estimates of Labor Force and Unionized Labor Force, Selected Countries in the Americas, 1995

Country	Labor Force (Millions)	Percent Unionized	Unionized Labor Force (Millions)
High unionization (25 percent and above)			
Argentina	13.13	30	3.99
Brazil	64.50	25	16.13
Canada	13.90	29	4.03
Jamaica	1.08	40	0.43
Mexico	26.20	25	6.55
Trinidad & Tobago	0.51	35	0.18
Venezuela	7.54	25	1.89
Medium unionization (between 10 and 25 percent)			
Costa Rica	1.19	15	0.18
Chile	5.22	13	0.66
Dominican Republic	3.24	10	0.32
El Salvador	1.77	18	0.32
Panama	0.95	11	0.11
Peru	8.00	18	1.44
United States	105.00	15	15.70
Uruguay	1.39	12	0.17
Low unionization (under 10 percent)			
Belize	0.03	8	0.00
Bolivia	3.54	6	0.20
Colombia	11.50	8	0.92
Ecuador	5.00	8	0.40
Guatemala	3.21	7	0.23
Haiti	2.72	5	0.14
Total/average	**152.76**	**17**	**53.99**

Sources: Diane Lewis, "Cracks in Union's Ceiling," *Boston Globe*, June 22, 1995, 47; U.S. Department of Labor, *Directory of Foreign Labor Organizations* (Washington, DC, 1986); U.S. Department of Labor, *Foreign Labor Trends* (Washington, DC, various countries and years); World Bank, *Workers*, 210.

and particular moments.[8] This insight, which might have been a truism during the heyday of grand social-science theorizing, is rejected by many contemporary post- and antistructuralists. It is, however, the starting point of the analysis offered here.

In Latin America, the obvious structural constraint on class formation is the uneven pace and geographical spread of capitalist development. But Brazil's late working-class formation is not simply a result of late capitalist growth. Another important factor is the nature of development.[9] Brazil lacked significant mineral enclaves in the late nineteenth and early twentieth centuries. This kind of enclave could lead, as with nitrate fields and copper mines in Chile, to a relatively isolated, cohesive working class that gained considerable power due to the strategic importance of the enclave in the national economy, a power that was enhanced when workers could invoke nationalist claims against foreign owners.[10] In contrast, Brazil's development was broad-based rather than enclave-oriented and its main exports in the late nineteenth and early twentieth centuries were agricultural goods such as coffee and sugar produced under domestic ownership.

In contrast to working-class formation, the consolidation of Brazil's central state came early. The establishment of the Portuguese, and later of an independent monarchy in the early nineteenth century, began a long and gradual process of state centralization and bureaucratization that was well advanced by the 1930s when labor was initially incorporated by the state. At the moment of incorporation, the relative balance of power greatly favored the state vis-à-vis the working class. In the words of one observer, the corporatist labor structure created by the Brazilian state was "a highly successful attempt to control, not to say petrify, the process of class formation, by which we mean development of differentiated collective identities and autonomous political organization."[11]

For these reasons, Brazil has often been placed in a second tier, behind such countries as Argentina, Chile, and Cuba, in the historiography of Latin America labor. There was militancy, but not as much as in the other cases; more integration than resistance; and more potential than actual achievement. For a long time, the Brazilian working class was also small, surrounded by an economy that was still essentially agrarian. In 1950, for example, despite the existence of large working-class communities in São Paulo and Rio de Janeiro, manufacturing workers represented only 9.4 percent of the total work force. In Argentina and Chile, in contrast, such workers represented 24.5 and 19.0 percent of all workers, respectively.[12]

All of this has changed during the last few decades, as steady growth (interrupted only by a few years in the 1980s) has expanded the size of the working class. This is especially true of the state of São Paulo, where roughly half of Brazil's industrial labor force is employed.[13] Brazilian capitalism is more dynamic than that of its neighbors; in fact, few countries in the world except perhaps Japan and South Korea have experienced an equivalent degree of economic growth in the twentieth century. After the Brazilian "miracle" of 1969–1974, and continued growth in the rest of the 1970s, Brazil's working class "caught up" to the working classes of its neighbors in terms of its relative size. By 1980, the relative size of the industrial labor forces in the so-called ABC countries were roughly comparable: 16.0 percent in Brazil, 21.0 percent in Argentina, and 15.6 percent in Chile.[14]

However, structural change does not engender uniform effects, as post- and antistructuralists correctly point out, and as static social-scientific models often fail to recognize. The timing of structural change is important; late industrialization, for example, takes place in different global circumstances than early industrialization. In this sense, the Brazilian working class seems to have reached a "critical mass" at a far more favorable political juncture than its counterparts did in Argentina and Chile. In the latter two countries, the relative size of the working class reached its height in the middle of the Cold War, in the 1950s and 1960s.[15] Peronist unionism in Argentina between 1969 and 1973, and again under the junta of 1976–1983, and unions that had been linked to [Salvador] Allende's Popular Unity government in Chile after the coup of 1973 received the full brunt of military repression from regimes that asserted that unionism and terrorism were more or less synonymous. In contrast, the relatively small size of the working class influenced the most combative elements of Brazil's armed Left to seek revolution in the countryside rather than in urban communities of industrial workers. Brazilian unions were thus spared both the ideological enmity of free-market radicals such as the "Chicago boys" in Chile and Finance Minister Martinez de Hoz in Argentina, but also the large-scale violence toward unionists that accompanied their rule.[16]

The Brazilian working class attained a critical mass, comparable to that attained in Argentina and Chile in the 1950s and 1960s, when the Cold War was on the wane in the 1980s. Though debt burdens, state fiscal deficits, and low growth rates caused economic hardship, the 1980s were a much more favorable time for labor in Latin America than the preceding three decades. The collapse of authoritarian regimes and political liberalization were immensely positive political factors, opening up opportunities for labor that had been inconceivable before.

The structural growth of the Brazilian working class can thus be combined with an argument about sequence and world historical time to suggest that there are "relative advantages to backwardness" in class formation as well as economic development.[17] In Brazil, but not in Argentina or Chile, trade union membership expanded quietly within the cocoon of corporatist labor structures under the military regime, which also increased the size of the state sector, maintained import-substitution policies, and avoided radical free-market adventures. In the 1980s, Brazilian labor emerged in much healthier shape than did its counterparts to the south and east.

The tremendous surge in strikes in Brazil in the late 1970s and 1980s illustrates the vibrancy of Brazil's labor movement.[18] Between 1976 and 1987, Brazil lost more work days in strikes per hundred-thousand workers than many other countries with reputations for combative labor movements, including Spain, Italy, the United Kingdom, and Germany.[19] In answering the broad, abstract question of why the Brazilian labor movement evolved from a relatively weak and subordinated one into one of the strongest in Latin America, the question of timing seems crucial.

II. The New Unionism

If the increase in the size of the working class and the timing of that increase expanded the opportunities for working-class collective action in the Brazil of the 1980s, they certainly did not determine the nature of such action. Traditional class analysis that assumes that classes have "interests" that result automatically from class structure and that function necessarily and a priori as the basis for mobilization has been discredited. Classes are now seen by most scholars as a "point of arrival" rather than a pre-given "point of departure."[20] Moreover, "class" itself refers to at least three distinct phenomena: a common position in the economic structure (class as position), a shared identity (class as a cultural creation), and a collective political project (class as actor).[21] These three aspect of class are related to one another in complicated and varied ways, and the existence of the first in no way assures the existence of the second or third.

What did Brazilian workers demand when their political voice was raised in the late 1970s and 1980s? Among other things, many of them demanded a "new unionism." In this, they were part of a movement that occurred throughout Latin America. Unions long subordinated either to political parties or state bureaucracies were captured by "new unionists" who were willing to engage in militant action as they sought both to represent the rank and file more effectively and to challenge the corporatist institutions of labor control.[22] Brazilian "new unionists" or *auténticos* (authentics) are broadly comparable to the *clasistas* (classists) of Argentina and the *jovenes* (young ones) in Chile.[23] Some scholars have associated the new unionism with late, dependent capitalist development and repressive political regimes. In facing regimes that deny labor freedom to organize, unions are forced to reach out to other institutions—churches, community associations, and political organizations—that can provide protective environments in which workplace militancy can be developed. In the process, unions are politicized, absorbing new demands from outside the workplace and forming broad alliances that go beyond workplace issues. Such a "social movement" orientation is said to characterize, for example, both Brazilian and South African unionism.[24] In this kind of orientation, unions struggle not only for narrow workplace demands but for their autonomy as organizations and the democratization of society as a whole. In Latin American countries such as Mexico, Argentina, and Chile, new unionists' demands for autonomy were directed mainly against a dominant political party or parties, whereas in Brazil, and other countries that have traditionally lacked strong and enduring parties, new unionists' central demands were for more independence from state bureaucracies, and specifically from labor ministries.

Brazilian trade unions operate within a corporatist structure that has not been altered fundamentally since it was established in the 1930s, despite several changes of national regime. The key features of this system are *unicidade* (only one union allowed per category of worker in a given territory); a mandatory union tax (*imposto sindical* or *contribuição sindical*) deducted from employees' pay and passed on to unions by the state; and a hierarchy of union organizations, ranging from the local union in a county through state federations and national confederations. Like most other Latin American union structures, Brazil's is a mandatory closed shop, enforced through a state-controlled, hierarchical, corporatist, and bureaucratic structure. Thus, the political opportunities available to unions fluctuate with changes in the composition of the national regime.[25]

Some observers have seen the new unionism as a phenomenon limited to Brazil's industrial workers in and around São Paulo, with some tenuous and limited applicability to other sectors of the economy and regions of the country. However, the new unionism has represented new kinds of demands, new forms of leadership, and new internal and external relationships within and around a variety of Brazilian trade unions scattered throughout the country. In the 1980s, many different trade unions began to make more numerous and complex demands, evolving from an orientation focused mainly on wages to include working conditions and decisions about hiring and firing. Elections within unions produced new leaders who communicated more intensely with members and were more engaged in party politics than their predecessors. The new unionism was not restricted to industrial São Paulo; it clearly spread to the thousands of mostly small unions in less-industrialized parts of the country that sprang up in the 1970s and 1980s.[26] For example, a study of unions in Pernambuco, far from the industrial core of Brazil's economy, found that the relationships between union members and leaders changed under the impact of the new unionism in both urban and rural unions.[27]

Most analysts have generally seen the achievement of the two major goals of the new unionism—authentic workplace representation and reform of corporatist labor institutions—as complementary.[28] However, the two major goals of new unionists have often been in considerable tension. Corporatist labor controls contained carrots as well as sticks or, in the Colliers' words, "inducements" as well as "constraints."[29] Rank-and-file members often benefited from the health, recreational, and sometimes housing programs that were part of the corporatist arrangements. In the absence of a welfare state that could provide such benefits on a universal basis, these union programs were a vital part of organized labor's "social wage." However, new union leaders frequently argued that administering these programs turned them into social workers and prevented them from engaging in their real tasks of workplace organizing and political engagement. So when such leaders questioned "welfarism," or *assistencialismo*, they often encountered resistance from within the rank and file, as well as from the old-style compromised leadership.[30] In such situations, new unionists' desire to authentically represent the rank and file compelled them to preserve bureaucracies that, in their eyes, diluted union militancy.

In addition, many union leaders, especially those who organized poor workers (such as those in agriculture), worried about their unions' financial viability if the mandatory union tax were eliminated. As the debates over the new unionists' platform proceeded, it became clear that only the strongest, best-established unions could expect to be successful without state support. The demands of the new unionists were subsequently muted to preserve peace within the labor movement as a whole.

These divisions help to explain why reform of Brazil's corporatist union structure has been only gradual and piecemeal since the return to civilian rule in 1985. In the 1988 constitution, many state controls over unions, like the requirement that unions be recognized by the Ministry of Labor and the Labor Ministry's prerogative arbitrarily to replace union leaders and interfere in union finances, were eliminated. In addition, the legal work week was reduced from forty-eight to forty hours, and the right to strike was extended to all workers, including those in "essential" public services. However, *unicidade* and the union tax were preserved.

Mirroring the new unionism, critics outside the union movement have attacked corporatist labor institutions as holdovers of a retrograde and authoritarian past. Brazil's President Fernando Henrique Cardoso, a former opponent of the military regime who took office in January of 1995, has echoed these criticisms and pledged to end *unicidade* and the union tax. This would allow workers freedom to form new unions representing the same category of workers in the same area, threatening the sixty-year monopoly of representation enjoyed by Brazil's official union leaders.

Such a reform contains significant advantages. It would do away with unresponsive leaders who do little for their membership because their financial support is automatically extracted from workers by the state. It would allow for more spontaneous creation of unions at the local level and a more pluralistic kind of bargaining between employers and employees. However, it also threatens to weaken existing unionism without putting anything constructive in its place. Nowhere is this fear more pronounced than in rural unions, which are more dependent upon state-collected resources than most of their urban counterparts.

Technocratic members of the Brazilian government have reasons of their own to support the reforms. They argue that Brazil's labor centrals, which represent a minority of relatively powerful unions, promote bargains that benefit their member unions at the expense of unorganized and poorer groups in society. They would prefer that wage bargaining take place only at the enterprise level, allowing bargains to reflect the productivity gains and degree of organization of workers at the workplace. However, this could keep unions divided and weak and concentrate the gains of growth rather than share them more equitably. Chile is an example of what could go wrong. The old labor structure was dismantled by [Augusto] Pinochet and replaced by a much more "flexible" and decentralized system in which the rate of unionization is low: thirteen percent in 1993 compared to thirty-five percent in 1973, on the eve of the Pinochet coup.[31] Reform atomized and marginalized trade unions; it did not empower them.

Not surprisingly, members of the trade union movement, as well as sympathetic outside observers, have very different reactions to the president's proposed reforms. Some favor them, on the grounds that *unicidade* and the mandatory union tax impede the free formation of unions.[32] Officially, this is the position of the largest and most militant trade union central, the Central Única dos Trabalhadores (CUT), as well as, interestingly enough, the major São Paulo employers' association, the Federação das Indústrias do Estado de São Paulo (FIESP). However, it is not clear that such a reform would benefit unions outside leading economic sectors such as steel and automobiles. Others, mindful of the advantages of corporatist structures for relatively weak unions outside of the economy's industrial core, support more modest reforms. While applauding the dismantling of state controls over unions that was achieved in the 1988 constitution, they argue that the mandatory union tax and *unicidade* are vital elements in a strong, political labor movement.[33] This is the position of the smallest union central, the Central Geral dos Trabalhadores (CGT). The Força Sindical, generally seen as a labor central that is more dynamic than the CGT and more conservative than the CUT, is divided on the issue.[34] The end of military rule—so far, at any rate—has not produced a consensus within organized labor for a thorough restructuring of state-trade union relations in Brazil.

III. Prospects for Social Democracy

Despite its contradictions and limitations, the new unionism has succeeded in democratizing trade unions and, in part, the wider society. But the new unionism has represented an essentially negative power, the power of organized labor to oppose and defy the state. A different question altogether is whether the organized working class can form part of a ruling coalition in Brazil, in the same way that unions in Western Europe were an important pillar of support for social-democratic governments.

This section explores that question. First, it charts the decline of the political significance of the new unionism after the transition to civilian rule in 1985. Then it examines the challenges trade unions face both from broad changes in global capitalism and from the government's neoliberal policies. After exploring the relationship between the organized working class and the government elected in 1994, the section concludes with an assessment of the prospects for a social-democratic outcome in Brazil.

The political significance of the new unionism was at its height under the military regime. In the late 1970s, its leaders protested the military regime's manipulation of inflation data to push down wages and its suppression of the right to strike. As the movement gathered momentum, it challenged and successfully removed the most arbitrary of the state's claimed rights to intervene in union affairs. The repressive policies of the military regime forced unions into political confrontations with the regime itself, not just particular employers or government policies. In the process, the new unionism attracted support from other segments of society and came to symbolize opposition to the military regime's despotic power. However, its "social movement" characteristics diminished as the transition to civilian rule proceeded, repression eased, the activities of political parties and other organizations increased, and the main links between the state and unions were preserved.

This is not to say that trade unions in Brazil have ceased to be political. The CUT, which is linked to the Partido dos Trabalhadores, still takes political positions on a variety of issues.[35] It also continued in its tradition of broad-based organizing when in 1995 it admitted the rural labor confederation, the Confederação Nacional dos Trabalhadores na Agricultura (CONTAG), the largest confederation in the Brazilian labor system, into its ranks—a significant increase in the representative powers of the central.

However, organized labor is increasingly drawn into relatively narrow and nonpolitical bargains that affect only a relatively small segment of full-time, permanent workers. The present Brazilian government's stated goal of limiting wage increases to the firm level, and then only on the basis of productivity gains, further undercuts the broad "social movement," or even sectoral, nature of past union collective action. Like unions in many other places, those in Brazil are often forced to engage in defensive battles to preserve past gains. They face severe challenges from two related developments: the nature of late-twentieth-century capitalism and the government's adoption of neoliberal reforms.

As Charles Tilly suggested, globalization—the transnationalization of economic activities such as investment, production, and marketing—generally hurts labor's rights.[36] However, Brazilian unions are also affected by trends that cannot all be subsumed under the rubric of globalization. In many advanced capitalist countries, unions have been waning in power because of such factors as declines in plant size; the growth of the service sector and the flight of manufacturing industry; increased labor and consumer market differentiation, leading to greater individualism and an erosion of working-class identities; a decline in centralized bargaining mechanisms; the disappearance of traditional working-class communities; and even the erasure of traditional worksites and the destruction of work as a face-to-face collective experience, through the increasing use of "virtual" offices, home offices, and small workshops located in homes.[37]

Brazil is not immune to these trends. It seems marked for more industrial growth, but that growth seems unlikely to create the number of jobs that earlier growth in the capitalist core did. Observers of Brazilian labor are already seeing a steady rise in the number of "sub-proletarians": informal, temporary, part-time, subcontracted workers who have far less secure positions in the labor market than the full-time, formal-sector employee.[38] Traditional forms of solidarity built up over many years within stable working classes are eroded by such labor market trends. In Michael Hanagan's terms, the working-class's power of self-reproduction declines.[39]

Furthermore, the Brazilian economy is one of the most inegalitarian in the world. The top 10 percent of its income earners earns 51.3 percent of the national income, while the bottom 20 percent receives only 2.1 percent.[40] In the absence of major compensatory programs, neoliberal policies are likely to exacerbate that inequality. The very poor lie outside the organized working class which the unions seek to mobilize. By "taking care of business" only at the firm level, unions risk alienating themselves from popular movements and representing a shrinking reservoir of relatively privileged workers. Merely extending the old model of union organizing to new groups of workers—the preferred strategy of most union movements— will probably not be enough to halt labor's decline. Concerned observers of unions therefore call for a rethinking of traditional conceptions of organizing and the formation of more broadly based alliances to fight for the rights of less-privileged workers.[41]

Another threat to labor comes in the form of neoliberal economic policies of privatization, trade liberalization, regional integration, and state fiscal austerity. Throughout the 1980s, Brazil remained a heterodox outcast from the "Washington consensus" on the need for such reforms. But under the Cardoso government that took office in 1995, a political coalition in favor of these policies seems to be emerging. In Brazil, such prescriptions are particularly damaging to the union movement, because unions, particularly those affiliated with the largest and most militant labor central, the CUT, have made great inroads in organizing public-sector employees since such organizing was legalized in 1988. But the reforms also strike more generally at the gains in job security, wages, and benefits that the organized working class has achieved since 1979.

The architects of Brazil's neoliberal program may succeed in maintaining significant support despite that program's threat to the historic gains of organized workers. This is due in part to the fact that strong working-class identities do not automatically translate into support for specific national political programs, as many analysts have previously supposed.[42] There is an important difference between labor militancy and political radicalism, and one does not necessarily lead to the other.[43] Working-class identities often legitimate only workplace, trade, or community conflicts rather than extensive class conflict or support for particular left-wing parties.[44] Michael Mann further cautions that it is rare that a working-class self-definition single-mindedly drives anyone, and most individuals are simultaneously members of other associations that complicate and sometimes oppose class identity. When collective action on a class basis occurs, a relatively small number of militants are usually persuading larger numbers of people to make their class identity a fundamental issue.[45]

In his survey of working-class movements in twentieth-century Europe, Mann criticizes political scientists' and sociologists' obsessive reduction of national politics to the presumed objective interests of different classes. Provocatively labeling this "classturbation," he points out that conservatives successfully mobilized many workers against socialism by appealing to religious, nationalist, or technocratic identities, overriding appeals to class coming from left-wing parties.[46]

The point is relevant to contemporary Brazil. While religious and nationalist appeals seem to be limited in the contemporary political climate, the government of Fernando Henrique Cardoso clearly promotes itself in technocratic fashion as a government of the best and the brightest and the agent of modernization.[47] Such an appeal undoubtedly has resonance for many workers, reinforced by the apparent technical skill involved in the Real Plan, which reduced inflation from fifty percent per month in June 1994 to less than three percent the next month, and kept it at about that level for over a year and a half.[48] This is despite the fact that, outside of the upper classes, the Real Plan seems to have mainly benefited the very poor by reducing inflation and the middle class by allowing a consumption boom based on an overvalued exchange rate—rather than benefiting working-class people, who face instead tighter job markets, more job insecurity, and lower real wages. Furthermore, there is some plausibility to the government's claim that its privatizations should instead be called "publicizations," because some state-owned enterprises have served the interests of small, well-organized groups of public employees and private firms more than they have the general public.[49]

The government promotes itself as social-democratic rather than neoliberal. This claim may be technically correct in that the president's own party (one of three in his electoral coalition) is *called* the Social Democratic party or Partido Social-Democrático Brasileiro (PSDB). However, as French Prime Minister Georges Clemenceau once said of the Brazilian constitution, this social democracy "enjoys a chiefly theoretic authority."[50]

The PSDB, unlike its European counterparts, has in fact a very tenuous relationship with the labor movement.[51] Like other Latin American social-democratic parties, its main base of support seems to be the progressive middle class, especially in the industrial heartland of São Paulo.[52] And the party's victory in the presidential election of October 1994 was due in large measure to its alliance with a party dominated by large landowners from the clientelistic and impoverished northeast (the Liberal Front party, or Partido Frente Liberal [PFL]), and the smaller and misleadingly named Labor party, or Partido Trabalhista Brasileiro (PTB)—another party with little connection to the trade union movement.

The validity of these assertions can be seen by referring to Tables 2–4, which suggest that Brazil's government was not elected by the organized working class. Tables 2 and 3 show the economic and social geography of the country. The data indicates that the south and southeast regions have the highest living and educational standards, as well as the work force with the best pay and benefits. Not surprisingly, it is in these regions that the working class is most organized. The north and northeast regions of the country, in contrast, have much lower living and educational standards, as well as relatively impoverished and unprotected work forces. The agrarian northeast in particular has much lower median incomes, a higher percentage of workers earning less than the minimum wage, and more workers without workers' cards (and hence without the entitlements of retirement pay, labor law protection, and paid holidays that such cards represent). Infant mortality and illiteracy rates are also strikingly higher in the northeast, and life expectancy is lower.

Table 2. Selected Economic Indicators by Region, Brazil, 1980–1989

Region	Per Capita Industrial Production	Percent of Work Force in Agriculture	Monthly Median Income (U.S.$)	Percent of Work Force Earning Min. Wage or Less	Percent of Work Force without Worker's Card
Northeast	1.5	39.5	107.1	44.7	58.2
North	1.5	7.4	217.0	21.6	47.9
Southeast	11.7	12.2	265.3	20.9	34.2
South	6.2	30.6	212.4	18.5	31.7
Center-West	1.2	21.4	235.3	25.9	50.4
Brazil	6.7	23.2	209.3	27.2	40.7

Table 4 gives a political profile of Brazil based on votes for candidates to the lower house of Congress (Câmara dos Deputados) in the elections of October 1994. The table shows that it is precisely the most affluent areas with the best-organized working class—the south and southeast—where the percentage of votes for left-wing parties is highest. Conversely,

Table 3. Selected Social Indicators by Region, Brazil, 1980–1989

Region	Infant Mortality	Life Expectancy	Percent Illiterate	Percent Nonwhite	Percent Out-migration
Northeast	121.4	51.6	42.8	70.9	19.5
North	72.3	64.2	20.1	73.7	7.4
Southeast	74.5	63.6	15.7	31.7	13.6
South	61.8	67.0	15.4	16.3	14.5
Center-west	70.3	64.7	22.1	49.2	13.2
Brazil	87.9	60.1	23.9	42.7	15.5

Sources: Tables 2 and 3: Instituto Brasileiro da Geografia e Economia, *Anuário Estatístico do Brasil* (Rio de Janeiro, 1987/88 and 1991); Bertha Becker and Claudio Egler, *Brazil: A New Regional Power in the World Economy* (Cambridge, 1992), 122. Infant mortality figures are for 1970–1980 and refer to deaths per 1,000. Life expectancy is for 1980. Illiteracy data is for 1989 and refers to people five years old and over. The nonwhite population is for 1989 and is the percent of the economically active population ten years old or older that is nonwhite. Out-migration refers to the percent of native-born people residing outside the region of their birth. The industrial production figure is based on the 1980 census. The figures on the work force are for 1989 and refer to the economically active population ten years old and over. The worker's card is a document that is signed by employers and legally entitles employees to retirement and health benefits and the protection of the labor law.

Table 4. Percentage of Congressional Seats (Lower House) Going to Candidates from Parties Supporting Winning Presidential Candidate Fernando Henrique Cardoso and Candidates from Left-Wing Parties, 1994 Election, by Region

	Percent of Seats for Winning Coalition[a]	Percent of Seats for Left-Wing Parties[b]	Ratio of Winning Coalition Seats to Left-Wing Seats
Northeast	49	17	2.88 to 1
North	29	11	2.64 to 1
Southeast	34	25	1.36 to 1
South	25	30	0.83 to 1
Center-West	22	20	1.10 to 1
Brazil	36	21	1.71 to 1

[a]Parties Supporting Fernando Henrique Cardoso: Social Democratic party (PSDB), Liberal Front party (PFL), Brazilian Laborist party (PTB).
[b]Left-Wing Parties: Workers' party (PT), Communist party (PC do B), Democratic Labor party (PDT), Socialist party (PSB), and Green party or Partido Verde (PV).
Source: Leôncio Martins Rodrigues, "As Eleições de 1994: Uma Apreciação Geral," in *Dados* 38 (January 1995): 78, 87.

the proportion of votes for the Left is lowest in the impoverished north and northeast. Turning to the ratio of seats for the winning coalition to seats for left-wing parties, we can see that the highest ratios of support for the winning coalition can be found, again, in the impoverished north and northeast. The lowest ratios (leaving aside the center-west) are in the affluent south and southeast.

These election results present a curious picture of the basis of support for the Cardoso government. While the government's rhetoric portrays a modernizing, technocratic elite anxious to move Brazil firmly into the global economy and the twenty-first century, its political support is based most heavily in the least-modern, most-depressed parts of the country. Several members of the government were prominent opponents of the military regime, but the geography of the government's support closely resembles that of the military regime itself. And while the government depicts itself as interested in administrative efficiency and reform, and as a "social-democratic" friend of labor, its main bases of support are regions characterized by oligarchic control of land, clientelistic political practices, and a fragmented and weak working class. Through their support for leftist parties, large sections of the organized working class stand as a major element of opposition to the government's neoliberal reforms.

If we know what it opposes, it is not clear what alternative project the organized working class might support in Brazil. The Left parties do not seem to have articulated a clear programmatic alternative to neoliberalism. That does not mean, however, that there is no alternative. It seems terribly misleading to assume that the only choice lies between implementing neoliberal reforms, thus making many workers worse off, and not implementing them, thereby discouraging investment and also reducing workers' living standards. It is exactly this dichotomy—and the implication that opponents of neoliberalism must therefore desire a return to the discredited import-substitution policies of the past—that supporters of neo-liberal reform use in presenting their policy preferences as unavoidable.

One possible alternative is what Ian Roxborough calls "open market social democracy," which would involve a commitment to equity-led growth, peak-level negotiations between unions and employers, industrial policy, and redistribution through tax and interest-rate policy.[53] Is it likely that the organized working class could form part of a ruling coalition capable of implementing this kind of social democracy in Brazil?

I believe that the answer is no, due to the nature of both the trade unions and the political parties of the Left in Brazil. First, for peak-level bargaining to work, the trade unions must represent a sizable portion of the national work force. But only twenty percent of Brazilian unions belong to a labor central, and many informal-sector workers lie outside of the unions altogether. The government, therefore, has no incentive to recognize the centrals as interlocutors. Instead, it prefers to isolate and weaken the centrals and the unions most active within them, as it did when it refused to yield to the demands of oil workers. The strike by those workers in May–June 1995, in part to protest plans to end the state's monopoly of the oil sector, was defeated.

Second, unions are unlikely to reinvent themselves so as to include informal and precariously employed workers. Like many other institutions, unions have powerful inertial tendencies that tend toward the status quo even in the face of major changes in the external environment. Given the structure of most unions, leaders still continue to face strong incentives to cater mainly to the demands of their full-time, stable members, even if the number of those members declines. In countries where union membership has expanded, it is mostly through the application of the traditional model of organization to previously non-unionized workers, which targets the public sector, services, women, and so on. This is also the most likely scenario in Brazil. However, the formal-sector working class is not expanding fast enough for unionization rates to increase as dramatically in the future as they have over the last three decades. The growth in unions' numerical strength is undoubtedly slowing down.

Of the leftist parties, the most plausible contender for national power is the Partido dos Trabalhadores, whose president until 1995 was Luís Inácio da Silva, a former São Paulo metalworker and trade unionist known as "Lula." The party was founded in 1980 in São Paulo by trade unionists, progressive Catholic activists, and intellectuals on the Left, and has generally done well in urban areas where organized labor is strong, especially among automobile workers, bank employees, public-sector employees, and parts of the middle class. As its name implies, the Partido dos Trabalhadores (PT; Workers' party) has given primacy to class identity but at the same time organized people around other identities such as religion, gender, and race in creative combinations that vary considerably from region to region.

Offering itself as an alternative to the clientelistic practices of traditional Brazilian parties, the PT attempted not so much to "speak for" social movements and trade unions as to allow them to "speak for themselves" through the party. In an election that surprised almost everyone, its candidate made the second round and almost won the presidency in 1989. Its candidates have won mayoral elections in major cities such as São Paulo and Porto Alegre; reelection in the latter city came partly on the basis of an image of efficient and clean municipal administration, rather like the former image of the Italian Communist party. The PT currently holds ten percent of the seats in the lower house of Congress and six percent of the Senate seats, as well as the governorships (in coalitions with other parties) of the federal district (Brasília) and the state of Espírito Santo. The PT also narrowly missed winning the governorship of the southern state of Rio Grande do Sul in 1994.

However, the PT's presidential candidate, Lula, was soundly defeated in 1994, mainly as a result of the successful implementation of the anti-inflationary Real Plan, and he is unlikely to run for president again. In choosing a new presidential candidate, the party will face major questions about its future direction. Does the party want to retain its historic links to the trade unions? To what extent may it reduce those links, in the style of the contemporary British Labour party, and transform itself into another party of the ill-defined electoral center? The party's choice of José Dirceu as president in August 1995—a former activist in the student, rather than the labor, movement—may indicate that some in the PT would like to take the "British" road (although the president will not necessarily be the party's presidential candidate in the 1998 elections). The attempt by some PT leaders to distance themselves from the oil workers' strike is another indication of this tendency.[54]

The likelihood is that, whatever possible internal reconfiguration the party engages in, the PT will remain an implausible contender for national power for a large number of capitalists. The weight of its historic conflict with the Brazilian right is too heavy for it to be remade into a centrist party trusted by capital overnight. If it does become a national ruling party in the long term, it may well do so by distancing itself from the trade unions in the style not just of the British Labour party but also in the manner of French and Spanish socialism. Either outcome, therefore, is unlikely to result in the kind of social democracy alluded to above. Either the retention of an organic link with the organized working class will keep the PT in its accustomed oppositional role, or the party's remaking into a centrist and "loyal" opposition party will involve a weakening of ties to trade unions and a commitment to peak-level bargaining.

To say that the organized working class is unlikely to get real social democracy at the national level anytime soon is to comment on only one aspect of Brazilian politics. Trade unions in Brazil retain significant power, and the electoral performance of the PT in 1994, measured by the increase in its congressional delegation and the unprecedented capture of two governorships, was the best it has ever managed. At the municipal and state level, therefore, the prospects for experiments in social democracy are bright, and far better than those in most advanced capitalist countries where trade unions have a longer tradition.[55]

In addition, the organized working class in Brazil retains a considerable ability to awaken the nation to the need for economic redistribution and social recognition of those excluded from the benefits of capitalist growth. This was symbolized in January 1995. Incoming President Fernando Henrique Cardoso had promised in his inaugural address to make social justice the "number one objective" of his government. However, in what was a lamentable beginning to his administration, he vetoed a proposed increase in the very low minimum wage and approved a major hike in his own and congressional representatives' salaries. One of the few entities to react to these measures was the metalworkers union of São Paulo, which entered a legal action against the salary increases. "This increase is immoral," said union president Paulo Pereira. "In a moment of sacrifice, when the whole population has its salaries frozen, the executive, legislature, and judiciary should be the first to give the example of containing costs."[56] As in the late 1970s, during the heyday of the new unionism, a representative of organized labor demanded accountability from those who claimed the mantle of political leadership, appealed to the moral sense of the nation, rebuked an abuse of state power, and called for the construction of a more participatory and egalitarian political system.

Conclusion

The decline of working-class collective action is not universal. The Brazilian working class has emerged as a political force to be reckoned with only in the last two decades; this is an example of late working-class formation. In broad terms, the emergence of the working class can be explained with reference to the dynamism of Brazilian capitalism. However, timing has also been important, because unlike workers in Argentina and Chile, the Brazilian working class did not gain critical mass at the height of the Cold War. This suggests that there may be some "relative advantages of backwardness" in class formation as well as economic development.

In Section II, I argued that the "new unionism" did represent something genuinely new and was not limited to the industrial south of the country. It represented a major advance for democracy within a union structure originally designed to facilitate state control over unions. However, in the absence of a fully developed welfare state, new unionists are limited in the time they can spend on workplace organizing and political activity, because they are forced to administer the kinds of social services that their members want but that they might prefer to be rid of. The new unionism therefore compromised one of its goals—the end of "welfarism"—in order to fulfill another, that of authentic representation.

In Section III, I pointed out that, despite tremendous recent gains in unionization, the number of workers organized in Brazil is still relatively small. While Brazilian capitalism, reflecting global economic processes, produces a larger class of "sub-proletarians" with insecure positions in the labor market, unions represent a relatively privileged segment of the work force. The government's neoliberal policies of privatization and trade liberalization are also likely to increase the number of "sub-proletarians" in the work force.

In the second part of Section III, I argued that, while presenting itself as social democratic, the government elected in 1994 has tenuous links to the organized working class and is better described as neoliberal. Contrary to the modernizing self-image of neoliberalism, the government's strongest bases of support are in the relatively impoverished and agrarian north and northeast of the country. Leftist parties opposed to the government's project of neoliberal reforms are strongest in the south and southeast, precisely where the working class is best organized. Many organized workers thus appear to be rejecting the technocratic appeals of the government.

Brazilian trade unions are unlikely to become the support base of a genuinely social-democratic national government anytime soon. This is due to the nature of both the unions and the Left parties that many of them support. However, there are many opportunities at the local and state level for the organized working class to ally with leftist parties and create social-democratic governments. The fate of the neoliberal reform process that has accelerated in recent years may ultimately rest with whatever success these local experiments enjoy.

Notes

1. Quoted in Leon Fink, *In Search of the Working Class: Essays in American Labor History and Political Culture* (Urbana, 1994), x.

2. Admittedly, the trend was negative in Australia, Britain, France, the U.S., and Japan over the same period, while in Germany it was constant. *The Economist* 336 (July 1–7, 1995): 54.

3. For example, the number of firm-level unions in South Korea more than tripled between 1965 and 1992, from 2,255 to 7,676; World Bank, *Workers in an Integrating World: World Development Report 1995* (New York, 1995), 84.

4. U.S. Department of Labor, *Foreign Labor Trends: Brazil, 1991–1993* (Washington, DC, 1993), 1–2. For other, older estimates of unionized workers in Brazil, see Leôncio Martins Rodrigues, *O Declínio do Sindicalismo Corporativo* (Rio de Janeiro, 1991), 19. Estimates of rates of unionization vary in Brazil depending on whether one counts the number of workers formally included in trade unions and subject to the mandatory union tax, or only those who pay additional, voluntary union dues. Needless to say, the latter number is smaller than the former.

5. Even in 1980, union density rates in Austria, Belgium, Great Britain, Denmark, Italy, Norway, and Sweden exceeded fifty percent; Michael Mann, "Sources of Variation in Working Class Movements in Twentieth Century Europe," *New Left Review* 212 (July/August 1995): 20.

6. Michael Hanagan, "New Perspectives on Class Formation: Culture, Reproduction and Agency," *Social Science History* 18 (Spring 1994): 87.

7. Erik Olin Wright, "Class and Politics," in *The Oxford Companion to Politics of the World*, ed. Joel Krieger (Oxford. 1993), 149.

8. Wright gives an example. He concedes that in trying to explain the specific temporal sequence of the introduction of social security laws first in Britain, then in Canada, and later in the United States, economic or class factors are of little relevance, and political factors are primary. But if one wants to know why no industrialized societies had social security in the 1850s, but all had it in the 1950s, class structure and transformations of the capitalist economy would loom large in the answer. Wright, "Class and Politics," 149.

9. Michael Hall and Hobart Spalding, "The Urban Working Class and Early Latin American Labor Movements, 1880–1930," in *The Cambridge History of Latin America*, vol. 4, ed. Leslie Bethell (Cambridge, 1986).

10. Charles Bergquist, *Labor in Latin America: Comparative Essays on Chile, Argentina, Venezuela, and Colombia* (Stanford, 1986).

11. Bolivar Lamounier, "Brazil: Inequality Against Democracy," in *Democracy in Developing Countries*, vol. 4, *Latin America*, eds. Larry Diamond, Juan Linz, and Seymour Martin Lipset (Boulder, 1989), 134.

12. Jean Carrière, Nigel Haworth, and Jacqueline Roddick, eds., *The State, Industrial Relations and the Labor Movement in Latin America* (New York, 1989), 3.

13. Salvador A. M. Sandoval, *Social Change and Labor Unrest in Brazil Since 1945* (Boulder, 1993), 24.

14. Carrière, Haworth, and Roddick, *The State*, 3. I use these figures for illustrative purposes, without meaning to imply that only industrial workers constitute the working class.

15. The percentage of the labor force in manufacturing peaked in 1950 in Chile and in 1960 in Argentina. From Carrière, Haworth, and Roddick, *The State*, 2–3.

16. About forty percent of those killed during Argentina's dirty war, for example, were trade unionists; Paul Buchanan, "State Terror as a Complement of Economic Policy: The Argentine *Proceso*, 1976–1981," in *Dependence, Development and State Repression*, ed. George Lopez and Michael Stohl (New York, 1989), 54–55. The unionists became a target of repression partly because of the association between the guerrilla left and the dissident trade union movement which, in the eyes of one historian "did great damage to the workers' cause"; James P. Brennan, *The Labor Wars in Córdoba, 1955–1976* (Cambridge, 1994), 360.

17. Alexander Gerschenkron, *Economic Backwardness in Historical Perspective* (Cambridge, 1962), 151, 157, 169.

18. Sandoval, *Social Change*, 153–95.

19. Eduardo Noronha, "A Explosão das Greves na Decada de 80," in *O Sindicalismo Brasileiro nos Años 80*, ed. Armando Boito (São Paulo, 1991), 125.

20. David Slater, "Power and Social Movements in the Other Occident: Latin America in an International Context," *Latin American Perspectives* 21 (Spring 1994): 13–14.

21. Ira Katznelson argues that class formation should be seen as involving four distinct aspects—the creation of economic categories, experience, disposition, and collective action. Katznelson, "Working-Class Formation: Constructing Cases and Comparisons," in *Working-Class Formation*, ed. Ira Katznelson and Aristide Zolberg (Princeton, 1986), 14. I have collapsed his categories of "experience" and "disposition" into "class as cultural creation." Michael Mann, for his part, seems uninterested in the cultural aspects of class, treating class only as a set of economic positions and as a collective political actor; Mann, "Sources of Variation," 15. Culture is important, because class politics are frequently as much about recognition as they are about redistribution; see Nancy Fraser, "From Redistribution to Recognition? Dilemmas of Justice in a 'Post-Socialist' Age," *New Left Review* 212 (July/August 1995): 70.

22. Margaret Keck, "The New Unionism in the Brazilian Transition," in *Democratizing Brazil*, ed. Alfred Stepan (Oxford, 1989), 260.

23. See George Reid Andrews, "Latin American Workers," *Journal of Social History* 21 (Winter 1987): 323; Brennan, *The Labor Wars*; Daniel James, *Resistance and Integration: Peronism and the Argentine Working Class, 1946–76* (Cambridge, 1988); and Peter Winn, *Weavers of Revolution* (Oxford, 1986).

24. Gary Marks, *Unions in Politics* (Princeton, 1988); Gay Seidman, *Manufacturing Militance: Workers' Movements in Brazil and South Africa, 1970–1985* (Berkeley, 1994).

25. Sandoval, *Social Change*.

26. Rodrigues, "O Declínio," 18-19. Rodrigues points out that seventy percent of Brazilian unions have fewer than five thousand members, and thirty-seven percent have fewer than five hundred. His data also show the recent fast growth in the number of unions outside the relatively industrialized and urbanized south and southeast of the country. In terms of national politics, the impact of this rapid unionization is diluted by the fact that only twenty percent of all unions are affiliated with a labor central.

27. Jorge Ventura, *New Unionism and Union Politics in Pernambuco, Brazil in the 1980s* (Ph.D. dissertation, London School of Economics, 1992).

28. See, for example, Armando Boito Jr., "The State and Trade Unionism in Brazil," *Latin American Perspectives* 21 (Winter 1994): 7–23.

29. David Collier and Ruth Collier, *Shaping the Political Arena* (Princeton, 1992).

30. This point is made in passing in Keck, "The New Unionism," 283–84. However, while it is marginal in her analysis, I see it as a major tension within new unionism, especially in light of further deterioration of public health services due to cuts in government budgets during the last ten years in Brazil.

31. Joseph Collins and John Lear, *Chile's Free-Market Miracle: A Second Look* (San Francisco, 1995), 69.

32. Examples of this kind of argument are Armando Boito Jr., *O Sindicalismo Brasileiro nos Anos 80* (São Paulo, 1991); and Angela de Castro Gomes and Maria Celina D'Araújo, "A Extinção do Imposto Sindical: Demandas e contradições," *Dados* 36 (1993): 317–52.

33. Examples of this argument are Scott Martin, *Forward or Backward? Corporatism and Industrial Restructuring in Brazilian Autos* (New York: Paper presented at "The Politics of Inequality," a conference sponsored by Columbia University, March 3–6, 1994); and Roberto Mangabeira Unger, *A Alternative Transformadora: Como Democratizar o Brasil* (Rio de Janeiro, 1990), 332. For a debate about the political implications of different labor law regimes, see Tamara Lothian, "The Political Consequences of Labor Law Regimes: The Contractualist and Corporatist Models Compared," *Cardozo Law Review* 7 (Summer 1986): 1001–73; Stanley A. Gacek, "Revisiting the Corporatist and Contractualist Models of Labor Law Regimes: A Review of the Brazilian and American Systems," *Cardozo Law Review* 16 (August 1994): 21–110; and Tamara Lothian, "Reinventing Labor Law: A Rejoinder," *Cardozo Law Review* 16 (March 1995): 1749–63.

34. This discussion draws from "Fiesp e Sindicatos Filiados a CUT Apoiam fim da Unicidade Sindical," *Folha de São Paulo*, October 11, 1994, 1–5, as well as an article against the end of *unicidade* by Antonio Neto, "Unicidade versus Pluralidade Sindical" in *Folha de São Paulo*, October 21, 1994, 2–2. Neto is the president of the CGT.

35. As for the other labor centrals, the declining CGT is identified with more conservative, U.S.-style business unionism, and the relatively new Forca Sindical identities itself as a similar kind of "unionism of results." Data from 1991 indicates that at that time, sixty-five percent of those unions affiliated with a central were affiliated with the CUT, while twenty-nine percent were tied to the CGT; Rodrigues, "O Declínio," 19. Since then, the latter figure has undoubtedly declined, with the Forca Sindical growing but still remaining smaller than the CUT.

36. Charles Tilly, "Globalization Threatens Labor's Rights," *International Labor and Working Class History* 47 (Spring 1995): 1–23. I use here globalization in a narrower, more economic sense than does Tilly. For objections to Tilly's argument, see the comments by Immanuel Wallerstein, Aristide Zolberg, Eric Hobsbawm, and Lourdes Benería in the same issue, 24–55. For the argument that globalization merely provides opportunities and constraints, and does not necessarily harm labor, see World Bank, *Workers*; for a discussion of globalization as it affects labor in Latin America, see Anthony Pereira and Cliff Welch, "Labor and the Free Market in the Americas: Introduction," *Latin American Perspectives* 84 (Winter 1995): 3–9.

37. The decline in plant size and growth of the service sector affect union organizing because small plants and service workers are generally harder to organize than manufacturing workers in large plants. Some of these reasons are presented in *The Economist* 336 (July 1–7, 1995): 54.

38. Ricardo Antunes, "A Centralidade do Trabalho Hoje" (Paper delivered at the Latin American Studies Association meeting, Washington, DC, 1995), 1.

39. Hanagan, "New Perspectives," 80–81.

40. World Bank, *Workers*, 221. The existence of a large informal sector may mitigate these inequalities to some extent, but even after taking that into account, Brazilian income inequality appears to be of epic proportions.

41. Ricardo Antunes, "Os Sindicatos da CUT Estão em Xeque," *Brasil Agora* (June 10–23): 5; Carlos Vilas, *Back to the 'Dangerous Classes'? Capitalist Restructuring, State Reform and the Working Class in Latin America* (New York, Columbia University/Institute of Latin American and Iberian Studies Paper on Latin America #34, 1993), 37.

42. Whether they acknowledge it or not, most students of the working class use some conception of identity. Michael Mann describes working-class identity as "the definition of self as working class, as playing a distinctive role in common with other workers in the economy." Mann, *The Sources of Social Power*, Vol. 2 (Cambridge. 1993), 27.

43. This point is made persuasively by Brennan, *The Labor Wars*, 352.

44. An example of this phenomenon is the sugar zone of the northeastern state of Pernambuco, where in the 1994 elections the majority of workers strongly supported the socialist *caudillo* candidate Miguel Arraes for governor, but did not support Arraes' choice of presidential candidate, Lula, of the Workers' party.

45. Mann, *The Sources of Social Power*, 2:27–28.

46. Mann, "Sources of Variation," 51–53.

47. The government's supporters are apt to agree with such a characterization. For example, José Arthur Giannotti, a prominent academic supporter of Cardoso, entitled his article lamenting a setback in Cardoso's campaign as "A Step Backward in the Search for Rationality" (*Folha de São Paulo*, September 11, 1994, 1–3). Cardoso himself entitled an article about his presidential candidacy "The Maturity of a Great Country" (*Folha de São Paulo*, October 2, 1994, 1–3).

48. There are some questions as to how long the government will be able to maintain the balancing act represented by the Real Plan. The indications are that in 1995, the costs of the Plano Real will include a recession and, possibly, a negative trade balance.

49. Less plausible is the government's claim that private monopolies will serve the public interest better than public ones, or that trade liberalization will transform state-dependent and parasitic capitalists into dynamic, entrepreneurial ones.

50. Quoted in James Bryce, *South America: Observations and Impressions* (New York, 1916), 412.

51. One of the few links it does have is through Francisco Urbano de Araújo, a member of the PSDB and president of the agricultural workers' confederation CONTAG.

52. One observer writes: "In Europe social democracy was the fusion of reformist policy with the political organization of the working class. In Latin America these two elements have often developed separately, with reformist policies being advocated by technocratic elites and with the working-class movement often being committed to political vehicles which, however reformist they may have been in practice, were characterized by strident 'rejectionist' ideologies of one kind or another." From Ian Roxborough, "Neo-Liberalism in Latin America: Limits and Alternatives," *Third World Quarterly* 13 (Autumn 1992): 436.

53. Roxborough, "Neo-liberalism in Latin America," 432–33. See also Carlos Castañeda, *Utopia Unarmed: The Latin American Left After the Cold War* (New York, 1993).

54. It should be said that the PT has never had a trade union bloc vote within its party organization in the style of the British Labour party, but has been constituted instead by local organizations (núcleos and directórios) open to all party members. Trade unionists have been important members of the various levels of party leadership, although they are outnumbered by middle-class professionals. An interesting exploration of the PT's relationship to trade unions and other social movements, and the electoral dilemmas that this presents, can be found in Diane Davis, "New Social Movements, Old Party Structures: Discursive and Organizational Transformations in Mexican and Brazilian Party Politics," in *Social Change and Neo-Liberalism in Latin America*, ed. Roberto Patricio Korzeniewicz and William Smith, forthcoming.

55. For a discussion of the prospects for the Latin American Left in local and state politics, see Jonathan Fox, "The Crucible of Local Politics," *NACLA Report on the Americas* 29 (July/August 1995): 15–19; for a telling account of PT administration of two small towns in the northeastern state of Ceará, see Bill Nylen, "The Workers' Party in Rural Brazil," same issue, 27–32.

56. President Cardoso's inaugural speech is reprinted in " 'Vou Governar para Todos,' Promete FHC," in *O Estado de São Paulo*, January 2, 1995, A8. The union's legal action is recounted in "Sindicato Quer Suspender Aumento" in *O Estado de São Paulo*, January 19, 1995, A4.

14

Looking Ahead
Workers and Radical Christianity

Michael F. Jiménez

One of the concerns that arise when organized labor reaches out to sympathetic sectors of society is the possibility that the labor movement will be so changed by the effort as to be compromised. As the global economy has evolved, so have the conditions under which working people—industrial, nonindustrial, or agricultural—have sought to maintain their identity and their movement. One of the institutions that has long held great appeal as a source of moral support for rural workers has been the Catholic Church. In this selection, Michael Jiménez provides an example of what labor may move toward as an identity. He looks at a "natural" ally of the workers, the radical Christian movement that has grown in strength over the past forty years in Latin America. What is important for an understanding of the identity of workers is the principle that, as was the case from the start of the century, they did not live in isolation, and the labor movement did not carry out its activities in isolation from the environment in which workers lived. That environment was influenced not only by family but also by neighbors and local institutions. Jiménez offers a reminder of the cultural conditions under which the labor movement grew— and its views were formed—in three critical periods: the late 1950s and early 1960s, the mid-1960s through the 1970s, and the 1980s. He also traces the rise of radical Christianity and suggests its importance for workers in general.

"And heaven. What is heaven?" Literary phrases from what seemed another life altogether—the strict life of the seminary—became confused on his tongue: the names of precious stones: Jerusalem the Golden. But these people had never seen gold.

He went stumbling on. "Heaven is where there is no *jefe*, no unjust laws, no taxes, no soldiers, and no hunger. Your children do not die in heaven."

Graham Greene, *The Power and the Glory*

In 1981 liberation theologian José Porfirio Miranda argued that the parable of the weeds in Matthew was a clear guide for a radical politics in the modern world. According to the Mexican mathematician and union adviser, Jesus' explanation that "the farmer sowing seeds is the Son of Man, the field is the world, the good seed the citizens of the Kingdom" was an injunction to achieve justice and freedom in the present.[1] This earthly incarnation of the Kingdom of God was a central pillar of resistance to capitalism among middle- and lower-class groups in Latin America in the last third of the twentieth century, from human rights activism in the Southern Cone to Central America's revolutionary insurrections.

These radical Christian initiatives were part of the third major episode of radical democratic politics in the region since independence. The first, during the middle decades of the nineteenth century, involved movements of artisans, peasants, and the provincial petty bourgeoisie as the remnants of the colonial order were dismantled and Latin America was tentatively connected to the world economy. By the early twentieth century such links had been firmly established, resulting in challenges by rural communalists, proletarians, artisans, and middle-class rebels to foreign and domestic export capitalists and an increasingly powerful state. The most recent opposition occurred between the 1960s and 1980s when the rural and urban poor, organized workers, and middle-class groups fought the rise of authoritarianism following an extended crisis in national capitalism. In each case, the major strain of resistance was a radical democratic politics characterized by a faith in human improvement and sociability as the basis for achieving freedom and equality through decentralized government and sustained citizen participation in civil society.

Religion played an important role in each of these oppositional movements. During the first and the second periods, they contained a powerful strain of anticlericalism resulting from the Catholic church's collaboration with the upper classes; nonetheless, a political theology of sorts and folk religiosity informed these protests. However, the church was in a more ambiguous relationship to political and social conflict after the middle of this century, almost simultaneously promoting and containing a radical political Catholicism. By the 1970s a wide variety of protest movements had grown out of what one of their major sympathizers referred to as the "radical incompatibility of evangelical demands with an unjust and alienating society."[2]

This article focuses on the social origins and nature of contemporary radical Christianity in Latin America. It will argue that the ideals and norms of radical Christians represented a rebirth of radical democratic politics during the three decades after the middle of this century. The approach considers the rise of radical Christianity principally as the outcome of changing class relations and ideologies in Latin American capitalism since World War II. It began as a middle-class protest against a failing national capitalism in the 1950s and early 1960s and crystallized in middle- and lower-class resistance to authoritarian rule after the mid-1960s. While locating institutional and theological transformations within the social consequences of the mid-twentieth-century crisis in Latin America, this article does not discount the significance of changes within the Catholic church (or other denominations).

National Capitalism in Crisis and the Christian Response

Returning from Europe to the headquarters of the Economic Commission on Latin America (ECLA) in Santiago, Chile, in 1958, Celso Furtado made what he thought would be a short stopover in Rio de Janeiro. But the stay of the economist and ECLA program administrator in Brazil became an extended one as he remained to direct the recovery of the country's drought-stricken and economically backward northeast region. By mid-1959 Furtado had secured the establishment of a semiautonomous regional planning authority, SUDENE, to implement major reforms. In so doing, he forged a coalition of middle-class reformists, progressive clerics, leftist unionists, enlightened elites, and the increasingly militant rural poor that encouraged private investment and expanded social benefits in the region. Soon thereafter Albert Hirschman opined that Celso Furtado, to whom he referred as a "master reform-monger," was working "for 'controlled' social transformation, not for a revolution with its unpredictable consequences and huge costs in terms of human lives and liberties."[3]

The Catholic church was a key player in the northeast Brazilian reformist coalition in the early 1960s. After meeting with economists and government officials in May 1956, the northeastern bishops recommended that the central government coordinate a long-term development policy to meet the mounting crisis. Although insisting that they had "no technical and temporal solutions to the problems of an economic and social nature," the bishops argued that the church could "help set the obviously important methods and techniques of development in the context of the natural requirements of Christian humanism."[4] Three years later the bishops forcefully reiterated their support for a coherent approach to the region. After SUDENE's founding, the Catholic hierarchy threw its resources behind Furtado's reforms. The principal tools of this Catholic modernization program were community education and rural unionization campaigns staffed by mostly middle-class Catholic youth.[5] Similar processes were occurring elsewhere on the continent, most notably in Chile. There a Christian Democratic coalition of the middle classes and segments of the rural and urban poor led by Eduardo Frei first competed in the 1958 elections and came to power in 1964 under the slogan "Revolution in Liberty."[6]

This wedding of Christian mobilization and economic and social reform emerged just as the structure of national capitalism set in place in the 1930s and 1940s began to unravel. After the collapse of the international trade and financial networks in the early 1930s, Latin America's elites outside the Caribbean basin sought a balance between reliance on foreign exports and domestic industrialization. A coalition of oligarchs, manufacturers, the middle classes, and workers provided the social underpinnings for the new order. By the middle 1950s, national capitalism had generated relatively dynamic economies with a small but growing middle class. Moreover, political stability accompanied economic prosperity. Within a decade after the war, only a handful of tropical dictators ruled in contrast to an overwhelming majority of elected republican governments.

Yet this apparently democratic and prosperous national capitalism was becoming severely fractured by the late 1950s as growth rates slowed, inflation increased, and income gaps widened. Reduced earnings from international trade and exhausted monetary reserves led to growing dependence on foreign capital and rising indebtedness. Internal markets for domestic manufactures remained shallow due to persistently uneven income distribution. Finally, high inflation eroded national capitalism from within. This was partly due to the growing population pressures on rigid, monopolistic systems of production, especially in still landlord-dominated countrysides. But it was also the consequence of the political design of national capitalism, a balancing act among the industrial and financial elites, the middle classes in the bureaucracy and service sector, and organized segments of the proletariat. In this "buyoff" politics, conflict was managed through deficit financing. "Successive rounds of 'illusory' wage and price increases" served as a substitute for civil war, as Hirschman has noted, in which everyone, except the rural and urban poor, was a winner, at least in the short term.[7]

As national capitalism stalled in the late 1950s, elites and the middle classes alike grew increasingly anxious. Labor unrest in Mexico, Argentina, and Brazil, and the substantial showing of the Chilean left in the 1958 presidential election signalled the initial destabilization of the balancing act. The rural poor were also responding more aggressively to expanding commercial agriculture and claiming a place for themselves within national capitalism. Socialism in Cuba following the victory of radical nationalists in 1960 reenergized dormant revolutionary impulses throughout the region. The middle classes were growing increasingly disillusioned with republican institutions' seeming inability either to contain claims from below or to prevent slippage in their economic position. Although they had been early advocates of national capitalism, the middle classes had always felt vulnerable to the vagaries of the balancing-act arrangements in the quarter century after the Great Depression. Their deep-seated ambivalence about politics was informed by an adherence to classical liberalism even as they conceived of the state as the ultimate guarantor of order and stability. In short, while believing in the market, they had tried to avoid the consequences of its historically erratic behavior in their societies. As the crisis deepened, the middle classes drew close to military leaders and technical experts expected to transcend the cacophony of contending ideas, cliques, programs, propaganda, regions, and, finally, classes. Seeking refuge from the contentiousness of national capitalism, they helped to lay the foundations for the following quarter century of authoritarian rule.

While the middle classes were becoming depoliticized after midcentury, two strains of protest among them converged in the late 1950s and early 1960s, leading to a substantial, though short-lived, effort to repair national capitalism through independent economic development and social progress. In the decade following the war, academics and bureaucrats sharply criticized the region's economic organization. The "structuralists" proposed to revivify national capitalism by diversifying exports, accelerating industrialization, and creating strong domestic markets through income redistribution policies such as agrarian reform and progressive taxation. This position found cogent expression in the United Nations-sponsored Economic Commission on Latin America (ECLA). Its director, the Argentine economist Raul Prebisch, oversaw the creation of a continental network of policy makers who sought to balance "the will for economic transformation . . . independence vis-à-vis the state . . . and social reform."[8] During most of the 1950s, however, the structuralists were voices crying out in the wilderness, confronting the hostility of the United States and the absence of allies for their strong medicine of fundamental economic reorganization. They remained planners without politics.

By the late 1950s, however, a coalition appeared to embody politically the structuralist critique. As the United States adopted a more favorable attitude towards reform, especially following the Cuban Revolution, elites throughout the continent began to implement parts of the ECLA program. The coalitions inherited from the 1930s and 1940s were revived, now including the rural poor and the growing unorganized urban populations. In several places, the church's hierarchy and a substantial segment of its middle-class clientele helped to give life to the new order. Many middle-class Catholics were determined to rescue national capitalism by first legally instituting major structural reforms and expanding welfare benefits to the majority of the population. This modernization program would be complemented by massive mobilization of the continent's urban and rural masses to incorporate them into a renovated national capitalism as a healthy, educated, and responsible citizenry. Furtado's reform campaign on the national level and its implementation in the Brazilian northeast by a progressive coalition, including the church and middle-class Catholics, seemed to foreshadow the future.

Christian developmentalism originated in the interwar period among middle-class Catholics in their encounter with modernity. Following World War I, a distinctly antimodernist Catholic politics had been inspired by rightist French publicists. But this reactionary posture did not survive the depression years, as church leaders cut deals with the leaders of national capitalism, competed aggressively with the left among the proletariat, and reached out to the middle classes through the Catholic Action movement. A sweeping ecclesiastical reorganization in the 1950s, leading to a regional bishops' council (CELAM), reflected a renewed confidence and sense of purpose among the church leadership after midcentury. The reformist impulse within Latin American Catholicism was given further warrant by the papacies of John XXIII and Paul VI and Vatican Council II. These institutional changes also provided the context for a sustained dialogue between middle-class Catholics and the structuralists. Further intellectual groundwork was laid with the ascendancy in the early 1950s of French Catholic commentators on modernization such as Louis Lebret and François Houtart. By the decade's end, Roger Vekemans, a Belgian priest, was shepherding Catholic intellectuals into a conversation with Prebisch's experts in Santiago de Chile and elsewhere.[9] Such dialogues gave a fillip to the Catholic middle-class initiatives such as the Christian Democrats in Chile, the COPEI in Venezuela, and church-sponsored activists in the Brazilian northeast and in other countries. Structuralism was thereby given a political incarnation, one inoculated against leftist entreaties and designed to create a disciplined citizenry responsive to a rational and just order planned from above by middle-class reformers.

While the structuralist critique and Catholic middle-class activism converged in the late 1950s and early 1960s, dissenting voices denied the prospect of a humanized capitalism. A handful of middle-class Catholic activists, inspired by such French Catholic intellectuals as Emmanuel Mounier, offered a more radical Christian vision. Quarreling with the alleged determinism of the developmentalist project, they argued that history—and by implication a Christian politics—did not constitute the fulfillment of some particular model, but was rather more contingent, open to definition through the lived experience of a free and equal citizenry. This proposition denied the apparent developmentalist assumption that Latin Americans were objects of change to be harnessed for the purposes of economic growth. These thinkers and activists also sharply criticized a reformism defined and led primarily by the middle classes. In the Brazilian northeast, the philosopher and educator Paulo Freire allowed that by gaining knowledge of the origins and nature of their condition— "conscientization"—lower classes could represent themselves in history and achieve liberation on their own terms.[10] Dissident Chilean Christian Democrats Jacques Chonchol and José Silva Solar suggested the more concrete political alternative of a communitarian society based upon autonomous workers' councils.[11] Such challenges remained largely muted in the late 1950s and early 1960s. Yet clearly, on the eve of prolonged authoritarian rule, a segment of the Catholic middle class had set out a radical Christian agenda for social change and politics far more inclusive, accountable, and participatory than that proffered by the developmentalist mainstream.

Christians and the Challenges of Authoritarian Rule

The reformist projects of the early 1960s were cut short by the severe fraying or complete collapse of national capitalism in Latin America's most industrialized countries. Beginning in Brazil and continuing in the region through the early 1980s, the program of independent industrialization, income redistribution, and social mobilization from above was largely dismantled. In its stead came an economic and political restructuring by a coalition of domestic and foreign business interests, their powerful praetorian and bureaucratic partners, and the usually compliant middle classes. The results were tightened connections with the world economy, widened opportunities for outside investors, and a shift from the production of nondurable consumer goods to more capital-intensive industrialization. These changes were accompanied by lowered wages and reduced benefits for proletarians and containment of the expectations of those farther below. The alliance of foreign and domestic corporations with the state achieved high rates of growth in a number of cases but masked growing dispossession in the countrysides, immiseration in the cities, and eventually growing economic insecurity of the middle classes. In Central America, by contrast, the 1960s were a period of economic prosperity and political openings caused by propitious international economic conditions and promptings toward reform by the United States.

The new order in South America required depoliticizing the middle and lower classes. In some cases, such as Colombia and Mexico, the balancing act continued but with greater elite control over mobilization. In the Southern Cone, republican institutions underwent political triage, bringing public life to a standstill. Throughout the 1960s and into the early 1970s lower-class organizations such as industrial and service-sector unions and the more recently established peasant leagues were savagely repressed, culminating in the 1973 Chilean military coup against the government of Salvador Allende. Likewise, reformist parties, which had been the linchpins of national capitalism, suffered political interdiction, while other predominantly middle-class institutions, such as universities, were purged and restructured. What began as the neutralization of the buyoff system's principal players became an elite offensive against their own people characterized by torture, murder, and disappearances. Nonetheless, regardless of the role of corporate and bureaucratic interests in the ensuing repression, it also reflected the triumphant antipolitics of middle classes unable to make common cause with those below them, whom they did not know or understand and so deeply feared.

Throughout the early 1970s opposition to the new forms of Latin American capitalism was largely ephemeral. Organized resistance by peasants and proletarians was sporadic and ineffective in most places, save Bolivia and Chile. Among the middle classes, a handful of students, professionals, and others participated in armed uprisings emulating the Cuban insurrection. While expecting to topple elite rule through armed uprisings, these guerrilla movements neither reinvigorated weak leftist movements nor ignited massive popular rebellions and were soundly defeated in most places.

Dissident Christians often played a major role in these movements. In Brazil many Christian activists involved in reform efforts during the early 1960s joined guerrilla operations later in the decade. The Colombian priest, Camilo Torres, was the exemplar of this response. Having failed to create a popular, left-wing movement, this young sociologist and university chaplain joined the rebels only to perish in his first armed encounter in February 1966. Only a handful of other priests followed his activist example, but by the decade's end various lay and clerical networks—such as the Golconda group in Colombia, Argentina's Third World Priests, and the Chilean Christians for Socialism—had established close links with revolutionaries. Although taking some initiative among the lower classes, their principal targets were disaffected middle-class university students and professionals. Some groups embraced a "theology of revolution," an amalgam of Marxism, national liberation ideology, and Christian concepts of just war. But the "revolutionary" Christian option was shortlived, handily cut short by government repression and the church hierarchy's checkmating of its dissidents.[12]

However, even as ecclesiastical authorities contained threats from the left, in several countries the Catholic church was on the defensive against authoritarian regimes. The church leadership initially had welcomed military rule, but growing anxiety about the endurance and depth of repression brought the institution into conflict with the new order. The distancing between the elites and the traditionally compliant church began as the church became the principal guardian of human rights. With unions, political parties, and other institutions immobilized, diocesan peace and justice commissions provided legal assistance to the victims of state terrorism, and many bishops increasingly made public their criticism of military rule.

Defense of human rights, however, led to major transformations in the Latin American church during the 1960s. In the first place, the church became the refuge of developmentalism. This occurred most notably in Brazil, where initial support for civil liberties broadened into a network of Catholic-sponsored public health projects, literacy and education programs, cooperatives, and research institutes. The majority of the region's bishops decided to allow the church to become a surrogate for development, a position that received its clearest expression at the 1968 regional conference in Medellín, Colombia, where the bishops declared a "preferential option for the poor." In this way, the developmentalist alternative was kept alive through middle-class lay and clerical organizing among the poor, more or less shielded by the hierarchies. However, it also meant that the church was converted into an adversary of the new order, leading to kidnappings, murders, and harassment of priests, nuns, and their lay collaborators.[13]

Within this context of generalized repression and the targeting of the church by the upper classes and their military collaborators, radical Christianity crystallized as a major force in Latin America by the early 1970s. For Catholic activists involved in the human rights movements and church-sponsored developmentalist programs, the once-marginal radical discourse began to have greater resonance. For example, the now widely known educational and community development methods of Paulo Freire provided the framework for a democratic communitarian ideal challenging authoritarianism and liberalism alike. At the same time, these Christian dissidents evolved a more coherent diagnosis of the Latin American crisis as they encountered a regional renaissance in political economy that became known as *dependismo*. Although initially an internal reassessment among developmentalists, as the decade progressed their self-criticism was complemented by several streams of thought: a revived indigenous leftist tradition, exemplified by the Peruvian José Carlos Mariátegui; the critiques of global capitalism emanating from the North Atlantic; and European "critical Marxism," which cracked open the long-standing communist hegemony on the left. As the Brazilian Fernando Henrique Cardoso would later insist, *dependismo* was not a theory of social change but rather a general approach designed to break the rigid hold of Marxism and developmentalism on the Latin American imagination. It encouraged "a constantly renewed effort to reestablish a tradition of analysis of economic structures and structures of domination, one which would not suffocate the historical process by removing it from the movement which results from the permanent struggle among groups and classes."[14] This reformulation of Latin American radical thought occurred in the context of the Cuban revolution, whose leader called on the continent's revolutionaries to cease "waiting for a liberal, progressive, anti-imperialist bourgeoisie" and to break into history.[15]

The stage was set for a major debate within the Latin American church on the relationship between religion and politics. A decade earlier Vekemans had led middle-class modernists into a conversation with the structuralists. In the middle and late 1960s Ivan Illich and other figures ushered disillusioned Christian developmentalists into a dialogue with the *dependistas*.[16] The predominantly developmentalist posture of the hierarchy and its middle-class clientele was now challenged from within by those insisting that national capitalism was bankrupt. The result was a new theological position first articulated by Gustavo Gutiérrez, a Peruvian cleric and community activist. As early as 1964 Gutiérrez laid the foundations of what would evolve into a theological critique based on praxis, a constant dialogue between reflection and action. Following the arguments of the communitarians of the 1940s and 1950s, Gutiérrez insisted that a properly lived Christian life was not simply a mechanistic response to a theology or philosophy outside of history, but depended on the contingencies of the lived reality of human beings. Over the succeeding half decade, Gutiérrez's early reflections led him to assert that circumstances in Latin America had caused the ground to be taken from under Christian developmentalism, thereby making a more radical vision both theologically and politically imperative. In July 1968, while preparing for the regional bishops' conference later that year, he argued that revolution—understood as profound structural changes achieved through the agency of the *pueblo* (the people)—rather than development was the principal historical task for Latin Americans.[17] With the savagery of authoritarian regimes increasingly directed at clerics and even upper levels of the hierarchy, Gutiérrez and other radical Christians acquired considerable influence within the ecclesiastical structure. Thus the Medellín declaration, though strongly affirming developmentalism, also provided the impetus for pushing beyond reformism to a more radical posture.

Dissident middle-class groups within the church thus charted a course supportive of lower-class claims and not unsympathetic to revolutionary movements. Yet they were agnostic about traditional leftist prescriptions based on Marxist-Leninist theory. Although indulgent of rebel priests who defied bishops and connected themselves to guerrilla movements, Christian radical democrats distanced themselves from the "theology of revolution," considering it lacking in spiritual and political discernment. When Camilo Torres foreswore clerical duties and moved into opposition to the Colombian elites, Gutiérrez was distressed, reminding his fellow Louvain graduate that "if we can't celebrate the Eucharist until we have attained the perfect society, then we shall have to wait till we get to heaven, in which case the Eucharist will be superfluous."[18]

The widespread radicalization of Latin American Catholics in the 1960s was a response to the perceived inadequacies of both developmentalism and leftist revolutionary doctrines. This radicalism was initially cultivated among middle-class lay and clerical intellectuals. But it achieved concrete social expression among the lower classes through church-sponsored community development programs expanding in numbers and scope as national capitalism collapsed. The *comunidades eclesiales de base* (Christian base communities) were originally intended to assure the fealty of the poor to a church threatened by Protestantism and the left in the 1950s and 1960s. But they rapidly evolved into an affirmation of Catholic support for lower-class mobilization along developmentalist lines, with middle-class managers providing doctrinal training and technical assistance to lower-class neighborhoods and organizations. These communities represented only a small portion of the region's poor and were concentrated in Brazil. Yet the middle-class encounter with the poor in these contexts, together with its absorption of the radical critique of national capitalism, generated a call for a new kind of politics for and by the "people."[19] In this way, the communitarian alternative, which had been at the margins of Christian developmentalism before the mid-1960s, began to have greater salience, infused with vitality by the church's reform efforts at the local level and an influential leftist intellectual response to authoritarianism.

The Rise of Radical Christian Politics

By the mid-1970s the new authoritarianism seemed fully consolidated. In the Southern Cone, the coming to power of the Chilean military in 1973 seemingly ended serious challenges to the new order in the region's most industrialized societies. For the remainder of the decade, the widespread repression in the more industrialized societies—the so-called "dirty wars"—were intended to complete the depoliticization process begun in the mid-1960s. At the same time, Central America's brief flirtation with developmentalism was cut short by its racketeering elites, exemplified by the 1972 coup in El Salvador that denied power to the elected Christian Democrats. Elsewhere, as in Colombia and Mexico, republican institutions were rapidly eroding under authoritarian pressures.

Yet the solidity of absolutist rule was illusory. The global economic crisis caused the "miracle" economies to stumble badly, and the North Atlantic powers clearly lacked the resolve and resources to promote modernization abroad. As growth rates slowed and standards of living declined, the coalitions of bureaucrats and corporations upholding authoritarian rule began to show major fissures. In addition, despite the extraordinary repression, there was a dramatic revival of resistance among the middle and lower classes, leading to the eventual restoration of republican institutions in most of the Southern Cone, save Chile, and a severe crisis of oligarchical rule in Central America. Thus by the early 1980s the savage despotism of generals, bureaucrats, and businessmen that had prevailed for almost two decades seemed weakened.

In the face of deepening authoritarianism and its subsequent decline, the Catholic church confronted a serious dilemma. By sponsoring developmentalist programs, ecclesial leaders had helped give rise to radical initiatives, making their organization a target of sharp repression from above and threatening it from within. After 1972 members of the hierarchy opposed to radical Christians coalesced around the chairman of the regional bishops' conference, Colombian Bishop Alfonso López Trujillo. This group was less interested in a conservative retrenchment than in assuring the security of the organization and solidifying reformist alternatives. Assisted by the Vatican, the group sought to contain the influence of the radical theologians, to more carefully manage the activities of the church at the local level, and, finally, to lock out radical advisers of the 1979 regional conference in Puebla, Mexico.[20] Although individual bishops and much of the Brazilian hierarchy remained sympathetic to radicalism, by the early 1980s a coalition of moderate and conservative groups had reasserted control over the institution and were redefining the relationship between religion and politics along more liberal lines.

Widespread repression and church caution were fertile ground for the refinement and extension of the principal themes elaborated by Gutiérrez and others in the 1960s and early 1970s. A cadre of theologians, philosophers, and social scientists—working within the Catholic church and increasingly among Protestant denominations—created a large opus that acquired global influence. While resulting in neither a coherent theology nor a systematic political theory, their work did provide the outlines for a Christian school of radical democratic political thought. There were three principal elements of what became known as the "theology of liberation."[21] First, these radical Christians analyzed Latin America under capitalism. From critical works on national security doctrine to analyses of the "idolatries" of capitalist culture, these studies represented a full-scale assault on the market-centered, possessive individualism that had underlain both developmentalism and right-wing authoritarianism. Second, these radical Christian publicists identified the church itself as a historic collaborator with the elites and, moreover, as an undemocratic institution requiring "reinvention" as proposed by the Brazilian theologian Leonardo Boff.[22] Finally, these religious thinkers groped toward a definition of citizenship for the radical Christian. In a complex intertwining of Biblical exegesis and a rereading of early church history, they laid down a code of conduct for the authentic Christian radical based on lived solidarity with the poor within the context of communal life, in Gutiérrez's words, "feeling and living as Christ—presented in exploited and alienated man."[23] Three decades after Freire, Chonchol, and other middle-class dissidents were first inspired by modern social Catholic theology and the initial dialogue with Marxism, their democratic communitarian vision had became a powerful ideological weapon in the struggle of Christians against elite power, inside and outside the church.

The renaissance of Christian political theology oriented towards radical democracy coincided with a resurgence in social mobilization beginning in the mid-1970s. Liberation theology captured the imagination of middle-class groups chafing under authoritarian rule and everywhere re-engaging in politics. In the Southern Cone, struggles against military dictatorships were spearheaded by a human rights activism that, whether sponsored by the church or not, was usually guided by a pacifist radical Christian ethic. Organizations such as Adolfo Pérez Esquivel's Justice and Peace Service in Argentina, led largely by the middle classes, played critical roles in this process.[24] A major consequence of this repoliticization was the increased efficacy of middle-class reformist parties such as Christian Democrats and Radicals lobbying for republican restorations in Chile and Argentina. Further important products of the authoritarian era's "catacomb culture" were various social movements such as feminism and environmentalism. Study groups and activist organizations born amid the official terror focused on creating a series of publics with a vision that was antihierarchical, communitarian, and libertarian.[25] Either explicitly or implicitly shaped by a radical Christian idealism, such movements experienced growing friction with ecclesiastical authorities seeking to contain an activism gone rapidly beyond the political and cultural agenda set by the church and the middle-class managers of redemocratization in the early 1980s. For example, there was growing criticism from various quarters of the increasingly political and feminist radicalism of Argentina's most visible human rights movement, the Mothers of the Plaza de Mayo.[26]

In Central America, the largely middle-class-led leftist insurrections provided a very different context for radical Christian commitment. A radical democratic sensibility similar to that of the Southern Cone had been cultivated during the 1970s by foreign missionaries, Jesuits, and sympathetic bishops such as El Salvador's Archbishop Oscar Romero. Yet as middle-class clerics and lay people grounded in an antiauthoritarian Christian radicalism joined revolutionary organizations, they encountered a rejuvenated "theology of revolution" echoing Camilo Torres and seemingly more compatible with Marxist-Leninist impulses within the insurrectionary movements. While providing a distinctive ideological challenge to such movements, these radical democratic Christians now directly confronted the problems of achieving power and building new societies.[27] The result was a tendency for the Central American radical Christians to seek common ground with the leftist revolutionaries, exemplified by Nicaragua's "popular church" and by campaigns to solidify an independent Christian base of support for that country's revolutionary regime.[28]

While the middle classes reasserted themselves politically in the late 1970s, there was also growing and increasingly coherent opposition among the rural and urban lower classes. Latin America's peasants demonstrated growing confidence by making claims against the state and upper classes. From the Brazilian northeast to the Colombian and Peruvian Andes and to Central America, rural mobilization, derailed in the late 1960s and early

1970s, was rekindled through unionization, land invasions, agrarian re-form lobbying, and cooperativist networks. In most places this involved a constant and sometimes violent wrestling with government bureaucra-cies over services and confrontations with recalcitrant local elites. Rural activism in Central America often led to support for insurrectionary move-ments as repressed peasant militants sought refuge in leftist revolution-ary organizations. In either case, peasant opposition was strongly influenced by radical Christian militants within the church. Base commu-nities as well as church-sponsored cooperatives and unions created in the 1960s primarily as surrogates for social reform and as an evangelical net to capture peasant loyalties were propelled into more openly political roles in the 1970s.[29] Middle-class radical Christian influence and the relative autonomy of these organizations from ecclesiastical control helped gen-erate a radical agrarian program, which combined land reform, adequate state services, and autonomous communalism. Yet their growing activism also emerged from the capacity of the rural poor themselves to fuse tradi-tional ideologies and forms of everyday resistance with the resources and strategies proffered by both Catholic radicals and other leftist organizers in the countryside.

Similarly in cities throughout the continent, emergent community organizations were strongly influenced by radical Christianity. The first wave of migrants from the countryside after World War II had scarcely been touched by the developmentalist interlude, but by the 1970s the ur-ban poor were becoming more capable and willing to make demands. The growing coherence of protest among the mass of casual laborers and petty entrepreneurs was reflected in rent strikes, squatter settlements, neighbor-hood groups pressuring for educational and health services, and sustained participation in civic protests against repression and cost-of-living in-creases. The organizational skills and ideological coherence of this urban opposition, like that of the peasants, matured during the repression and collapse of developmentalist programs. But it too was given a distinctive shape and direction by clerics and lay pastoral agents, who promoted egali-tarian and participatory democracy within parish clubs and neighborhood associations. Again, as with the rural poor, local institutions were a source of leaders and a clientele for leftist movements, even as these impover-ished city folk maintained a certain distance from the party politics of middle-class reformers and radicals alike.

Finally, radical Christianity was one of several radical democratic ideologies shaping proletarian activism from the mid-1970s onward. Dra-matic changes in the labor market and within unions prepared the way for a new vocabulary and new organizational forms among the organized working class, especially in the most industrialized countries. The rapid expansion of services and the public sector challenged the predominance of the traditional proletarian core in manufacturing and transportation, making a large segment of wage earners less subject to the disciplines of older trade unionism. Moreover, syndicalist reformers pressing for internal democracy undercut labor collaborators with the corporations and the state as well as leaders tied to the old populist or leftist parties, such as the Peronists in Argentina and communists elsewhere. This breakdown of traditional syndicalism, together with growing economic pressures, contributed to increased strike activity, participation in civic shutdowns, and worker initiatives to revivify old leftist coalitions or to build new ones. An exemplary case of this latter effort was the formation of the Brazilian Workers' party in 1979, in which industrial trade union militants, middle-class leftists, and Christian activists created a small but powerful voice for democratic socialism in that country. Radical Christians were deeply involved in both internal reform efforts and the political campaigns of this working-class revival, finding entry through the human rights movement and the crossover participation of Christian base community members in union activity.[30] Although radical Christianity was only one of several radical democratic influences in this process, this political Catholicism played a significantly more militant role among the working classes than it had earlier under the Christian Democrats and church-sponsored unionism in Latin America and Europe in the nineteenth and twentieth centuries.[31]

During the last third of the twentieth century, Christianity has played a major role in the radical democratic opposition in Latin America. The religious themes of this resistance merged in uneven ways and in different contexts, yet were marked by several common characteristics. In the first place, radical Christianity provided the touchstone for a critique of Latin American reality, pointing toward a vaguely defined democratic socialism. While its Marxist-inspired language was compatible with traditional leftist visions among the middle-class and proletarian militants, its religious symbols resonated with the language and forms of traditional lower-class protest. Thus to the extent that the surviving moral economy of folk Catholicism was oppositional, it appears to have intermingled with the more programmatic radicalism of liberation theology.[32] Second, radical Christianity involved the reassertion of collective life among various social classes. The insistence on participation, democracy, and accountability within its organizations presented a distinctive challenge to the hierarchical and authoritarian bases of the region's culture and politics. Comparing the "congregational" ideal within Christian base communities to Puritanism, Daniel Levine has argued that "the results can be explosive . . . [as] the legitimacy of the established order is called into question, and new bases for common action are built at the grass roots."[33] Third, to the extent that they articulated broader national visions, these groups proposed major structural transformations leading to some form of democratic socialism. On this score, the efforts to reconcile freedom and equality in Catholic social thought—including liberation theology—coincided with secular leftists' uneasiness in the 1970s with contemporary models of revolutionary change. Finally, radical initiatives in Latin America were based on the intertwining of diverse class interests and visions. In what Charles A. Reilly has referred to as religious populism, radical democracy focused on organizing by and for the "people of God"—the poor and those in solidarity with them.[34] In this way, a Christian resistance jettisoned the elitist design of mid-twentieth-century Latin American politics, whether of old leftist-party vanguards or the middle classes' faith in their ability to instruct and guide their fellow citizens toward liberal democracy.

The Dilemmas of Radical Christianity

The radical democratic movements of the late twentieth century, influenced by a militant social Christianity, represented the rebirth of a revolutionary tradition that had flourished in Latin America during the half-century before the Great Depression. In response to the rapid and dramatic economic and social changes accompanying export capitalism in those years, there was widespread resistance by the lower and middle classes to oligarchical rule and to occasional foreign intervention. The three major streams of protest were petty bourgeois jacobins; various segments of the rural poor, most notably Indian communalists in the region's mountain corridors; and artisans and the emergent proletariat strongly influenced by anarchism and anarcho-syndicalism. From the Cuban Wars of Independence to the Mexican Revolution and the sustained labor activism of immigrant workers in the Southern Cone, the decades before the Great Depression were the most turbulent years in the history of Latin America since the early-nineteenth-century wars of independence.

Several major principles guided these turn-of-the-century revolutionary movements.[35] First, the people were to represent themselves through their own institutions rather than being represented by a vanguard party or class. Thus the *pueblo*, in their unions, villages, and social clubs, were the central actors in the remaking of their world. Second, uneasy with positivist views of history proffered by elites, reformers, and some revolutionaries, radical democrats understood history as a process without a predetermined course or end. For them, the contingency of history led to excitedly voluntarist and occasionally apocalyptic movements. Finally, radical democrats profoundly distrusted power. Especially among proletarians and peasants (less so, significantly, among the middle classes), the attractions and demands of powerholding were anathema. For the libertarian socialists, in particular, revolution meant as much the psychological re-creation of the revolutionaries themselves as the sweeping away of elite rule. Internal democracy and intensive education on the dangers of the will to power were central features of their communities. Significantly, religious themes abounded in these movements, from the solicitations of the Zapatista rebels to the Virgin of Guadalupe to anarchist praise for the "vagabond carpenter from Galilee."[36]

By midcentury, few traces remained of the radical democratic crusades before the Great Depression save some isolated noncommunist leftist intellectuals, a few labor unions, and a smattering of radical democratic parties, the most important being the Chilean Socialists founded in 1933. This was partly due to ferocious and effective official repression of radical democratic communities. Furthermore, following the Russian Revolution, the impetus for a more disciplined and institutionalized revolutionary opposition gained ground, especially among proletarians, through the emergent communist parties. Moreover, as national capitalism evolved from the 1930s, lower-class claims in the most industrialized societies were channelled through a rickety liberal democracy and, through default, by charismatic nationalists like Juan Perón. But libertarian socialists, and much less peasant rebels or middle-class jacobins, proved unable to translate their communalist ideology into organized and disciplined movements. The ebb and flow of radical protest between enthusiastic struggle and retreat into community, as well as a fundamental mistrust of power, simply could not sustain a politics designed to assume control over their societies and fundamentally transform them. Even the energy and genius of José Carlos Mariátegui in Peru could not break the impasse between the emergent revolutionary left—with its organizational imperatives and determinism—and the voluntarist radical democrats. At the time of his death in 1930, this labor organizer, essayist, and revolutionary tactician was groping for a position between the necessity to achieve power in order to transform society and the conviction that power needed to be dissolved as the basis for human relations if a genuinely revolutionary society was to be born.[37]

A half century after Mariátegui died, another Peruvian, Gustavo Gutiérrez, his fellow liberation theologians, and radical Christian activists in human rights organizations, unions, base communities, and revolutionary movements confronted similar dilemmas. They were seeking to construct a radical project that would be inclusive, yet discerning of the reality of class relations; voluntarist, yet requiring discipline and rigor; trusting in the instincts and will of the people, yet recognizing the necessity for organization. As we have seen, in the context of a failed national capitalism and the rise of authoritarianism, the church not only became the reformers' haven, but also allowed its own vision of community and human solidarity to serve as the basis for repoliticizing Latin American societies and relegitimizing claims by ignored and repressed social groups. Yet the radical Christians often seemed hesitant or unprepared to construct a politics beyond the struggle for better local conditions or, in national terms, beyond the defeat of dictators. The hope for a new day, inspired by memories of martyrs and the near mystical spirituality of struggle, was accompanied by a narrowed political horizon, a hesitation to engage in the compromises, coalition-building, and discipline needed for effective governance. Like the libertarian socialists before them, they tended to see politics not as the acquisition and management of power, but as its dissolution in personal relations and social life.

The limits of radical democracy are rooted in the nature of capitalist change in Latin America in the nineteenth and twentieth centuries. The region's shifting and uneven economic and social transformations have constantly undermined the creation of the structural bases for either a liberal democratic politics or a welfare state based on lower-class support. They have also repeatedly generated radical democratic alternatives, but presented such initiatives with extraordinary obstacles. Certainly in late-twentieth-century Latin America, powerful states, complex and corporate-dominated economies, and influential foreign interests make any such revolutionary project a difficult prospect. Paradoxically, these difficulties have been compounded by the fact that the region's most recent episode of radical democratic politics originated inside or close to the Catholic church, within which, as Sheldon Wolin has written, there has been "a continuing tension between the untransfigured realities of political and social existence and the promise of a 'new heaven and a new earth.' "[38]

This contradiction, long subject to careful church management, became more salient in Latin America after midcentury as Catholic militants became major opponents of the dominant order. The hierarchy early on asserted itself in order to protect its organization and to find common ground with liberal developmentalism. But radical Christians had more difficulty resolving the conflict between the turning inward—into self and community—and the demands of citizenship. There was a powerful tendency to define their actions not merely as organizing society and seeking human perfection in the present but, more important, as a prospectus for the future. According to Gutiérrez, a radical Christian life, like that of Jesus Christ, should be eminently spiritual, "an anticipation . . . a confidence that the communion of life that does not yet exist among us can become a reality."[39] But such a posture, while inspiring land invasions, strikes, and other mass actions, could just as easily lead to a retreat from the public realm into an exclusively personal spirituality or the comfort of a supportive community of the like-minded.

There were those who were deeply concerned by the seemingly inherent limits of radical Christianity. Leonardo Boff insisted that "it is not enough to say that one is open to transcendence. The decisive thing is to organize a just society so that it will live transcendently."[40] Such a task, he argued, required what he called "political sainthood," or "prayer united with political sagacity . . . mystical theology articulated with a critical analysis of society."[41] In this way, the Brazilian theologian insisted that by locating the Kingdom of God in this world, the radical Christian ideal needed to be informed by a wise and measured use of power. In short, Boff's view suggested an optimistic scenario for radical Christianity in Latin America in its ability to assure freedom and justice in the redemocratizing Southern Cone and revolutionary Central America alike.

The viability of "political sainthood" has been an open question in Latin America during the closing decades of the twentieth century. Some expected that base communities and other radical Christian organizations could be "intermediate institutions" between civil society and the state, which was just the medicine needed by the Southern Cone's convalescing republicanism to keep alive prospects for liberal democracy. Others hoped that radical Christians could give a more libertarian and spiritual shape to revolutionary movements. But though radical Christians had brought Latin America to the gates of the promised land, perhaps they, like Moses, could not enter it. Their politics, deeply critical of powerholding and driven to reconcile freedom and social justice, might have been too threatening to both liberals and revolutionaries; and their spirituality, so intertwined with this worldliness, may not have been sufficient for the ever larger numbers of Latin Americans turning to the succor of Protestant evangelicals. In conclusion, if we extend the analogy with the English Revolution suggested by Levine, Latin America's radical Christians may not have had much in common with the Puritans, who created a state church and provided the ideological foundation for a new social order in seventeenth-century England. Rather they may have been closer to the Levellers, Diggers, and Ranters who, with their apocalyptic popular religiosity, tentative organizational life, and ambivalence about formal, sustained struggle within civil society, helped usher in the new order but were, in the end, repressed and silenced.[42]

Notes

1. José Porfirio Miranda, *Communism in the Bible* (Maryknoll, NY, 1981), 13.

2. Gustavo Gutiérrez, *A Theology of Liberation*, trans. Sister Caridad Inda and John Eagleson (Maryknoll, NY, 1973), 145.

3. Albert O. Hirschman, *Journeys towards Progress: Studies in Economic Policymaking in Latin America* (New York, 1963), 90. On this episode, see also Joseph Page, *The Revolution That Never Was: Northeast Brazil, 1955–1964* (New York, 1972), and Furtado's recollections, "Modernización versus desarrollo: Un reportaje da Celso Furtado," *Crítica y utopia* 4 (March 1981): 95–104.

4. Cited in Emmanuel DeKadt, *Catholic Radicals in Brazil* (Oxford, 1970), 75.

5. For a portrait of these activists, see Luis Alberto Gómez de Souza, *A JUC: Os estudiantes Catolicos e a política* (Petropolis, 1984); and Scott Mainwaring, *The Catholic Church and Politics in Brazil, 1916–1985* (Stanford, 1986), chap. 4.

6. Michael Fleet, *The Rise and Fall of Chilean Christian Democracy* (Princeton, 1985), chaps. 1–3.

7. Hirschman, *Journeys towards Progress*, 220–23.

8. Adolfo Gurrieri, "José Medina Echavarria: An Intellectual Profile," *CEPAL Review* (December 1979): 156. For ECLA's history, see Joseph L. Love, "Raul Prebisch and the Origins of the Doctrine of Unequal Development," *Latin American Research Review* 14 (1980): 45–72; and Fernando Henrique Cardoso, "The Originality of a Copy: CEPAL and the Idea of Development," *CEPAL Review*, Part 2 (1977): 7–32.

9. For a portrait of this process, see David E. Mutchler, *The Church as a Political Factor in Latin America* (New York, 1971).

10. Freire's principal works are *Pedagogy of the Oppresed* (New York, 1970) and *Education for Critical Consciousness* (New York, 1973). For an evaluation of his work and its impact, see Denis Collins, *Paulo Freire, His Works, Life, and Thought* (New York, 1977), and Daniel J. Schipiani, *Conscientization and Creativity: Paulo Freire and Christian Education* (Baltimore, 1984).

11. Jacques Chonchol and Julio Silva Solar, *Hacia un mundo comunitario: condiciones de uno política social-cristiana* (Santiago, 1951).

12. On Torres, see John Gerassi, ed., *Revolutionary Priest: The Complete Writings and Messages of Camilo Torres* (New York, 1971). For further materials on the theology of revolution, see Samuel Silva Goday, *El pensamiento cristiano revolucionario en América Latina y el Caribe* (Salamanca, 1981), and a book of documents edited by Alain Gheerbrant, *The Rebel Church* (Middlesex, Eng., 1974).

13. On this process, see Brian H. Smith, "Churches and Human Rights in Latin America," in *Churches and Politics in Latin America*, ed. Daniel H. Levine (Beverly Hills, 1979), 155–94; Edward L. Cleary, *Crisis and Change: The Church in Latin America Today* (Maryknoll, NY, 1985); and Penny Lernoux, *Cry of the People*, 2d ed. (New York, 1982). For a portrait of the Medellín meeting, see Hernán Prada, *Crónica de Medellín* (Bogotá, 1975). The bishops' report is available in English in the Second Annual Conference of Latin American Bishops, *The Church in the Present Day Transformation of Latin America in Light of the Council* (Washington, DC, 1970).

14. Fernando Henrique Cardoso, "The Consumption of Dependency Theory in the United States," *Latin American Research Review* 12 (1977): 10.

15. Fidel Castro is cited in Andre Gunder Frank, *Latin America: Underdevelopment or Revolution?* (New York, 1969), 407.

16. On Illich, see Roger Bastide, "Sociology of Latin American Religions: The Contribution of CIDOC," *Crosscurrents* (Fall 1976): 363–72. See Mutchler, *Church as a Political Factor* for a broader discussion of these changes.

17. On Gutiérrez, see Robert McAfee Brown, *Gustavo Gutiérrez* (Atlanta, 1980), and Rossino Gibellini, ed., *Frontiers of Theology in Latin America* (Maryknoll, NY, 1979), 311–13.

18. Cited in Walter J. Broderick, *Camilo Torres: A Biography of the Priest-Guerillero* (New York, 1975), 257.

19. The literature on CEBs is vast and growing. For an introduction, see Cleary, *Crisis and Change*, chap. 5, and Phillip Berryman, *Liberation Theology* (New York, 1986), chap. 4.

20. On the debate between developmentalists and radicals within the church, see exchanges in CELAM, *Liberación: Diálogos en el CELAM* (Bogotá, 1974), and *Socialismo y socialismos en América Latina* (Bogotá, 1977). On Puebla, see Phillip Berryman, "What Happened in Puebla," in Levine, ed., *Churches and*

Politics, 55–86; and John Eagleson and Philip Scharper, eds., *Puebla and Beyond* (Maryknoll, NY, 1979).

21. A range of writings by liberation theologians can be found in Gibellini, ed., *Frontiers of Theology*, and Sergio Torres and John Eagleson, eds., *Theology in the Americas* (Maryknoll, NY, 1976).

22. Cited in J. F Regis de Morais, *Os Bispos e a política no Brasil* (São Paulo, 1982), 151.

23. Gustavo Gutiérrez, *We Drink from Our Wells: The Spiritual Journey of a People* (Maryknoll, NY, 1985), 160.

24. On the human rights movements, see Carolyn Cook Diboye, "The Roman Catholic Church and the Political Struggle for Human Rights in Latin America," *Journal of Church and State* 24 (Autumn 1982): 497–524.

25. Elizabeth Jellin, "Los movimientos sociales en la Argentina contemporanea: Una introducción a su estudio," in Jellin, ed., *Los nuevos movimientos sociales* (Buenos Aires, 1985), 39. See also Scott Mainwaring and Eduardo Viola, "New Social Movements, Political Culture, and Democracy: Brazil and Argentina," *Telos* 61 (Fall 1984): 17–54.

26. On the Mothers of the Plaza de Mayo, see John Simpson and J. Bennett, *The Disappeared and the Mothers of the Plaza* (New York, 1985), and Lisa Baldez, "In the Spirit of Antigone: The Mothers of the Plaza de Mayo" (unpublished ms., Princeton University, 1986).

27. For an introduction to this question, see Phillip Berryman, *The Religious Roots of Rebellion: Christians in Central American Revolution* (Maryknoll, NY, 1984), and Tommie Sue Montgomery, "Liberation and Revolution: Christianity as a Subversive Activity in Central America," in *Trouble in Our Backyard*, ed. Martin Diskin (New York, 1984), 75–100.

28. On Nicaragua, see Michael Dodson, "Nicaragua: The Struggle for the Church," in *Religion and Political Conflict in Latin America*, ed. Daniel H. Levine (Chapel Hill, 1986), 79–105. Opposing views are Conor Cruise O'Brien, "God and Man in Nicaragua," *Atlantic Monthly* 257 (August 1986): 50–72, and Humberto Belli, *Breaking Faith: The Sandinista Revolution and Its Impact on Freedom and Christian Faith in Nicaragua* (Westchester, IL, 1985).

29. For materials on the relation between church organizing and peasant rebels, see Berryman, *Religious Roots of Rebellion*, part II, and Jennie Pearce, *Promised Land: Peasant Rebellion in Chalatenango, El Salvador* (London, 1986), chaps. 3–4.

30. For materials on radical Christianity and proletarians in Brazil, see Scott Mainwaring, "Brazil: The Catholic Church and the Popular Movement in Nova Igaucu, 1974–1985," in Levine, ed., *Religion and Political Conflict*, 124–55; José Alvaro Moises, *Licoes de liberdade e de opressão: O novo sindicalismo e a política* (Rio de Janeiro, 1982); and L. E. Greenhalg et al., *Fe e participão popular* (São Paulo, 1984). On Chile, see Brian Smith, "Chile: Deepening the Alliance of Working Class Sectors to the Church in the 1970s," in Levine, ed., *Religion and Political Conflict*, 156–86. For a critique of the Workers' party, see Emir Sader, "The Workers' Party in Brazil," *New Left Review* 165 (September/October 1987): 93–103.

31. For example, see Molly Nolan, "Economic Crisis, State Policy, and Working Class Formation in Germany, 1870-1900," in *Working-Class Formation: Nineteenth-Century Patterns in Western Europe and the United States*, ed. Ira Katznelson and Aristide R. Zolberg (Princeton, 1986), 352–96.

32. The issue of "popular religion" and its relation to politics is the subject of intense debate but very few careful studies. An optimistic view is in Juan Carlos

Scannone, "Evangelization of Culture, Liberation, and 'Popular' Culture: The New Theological Synthesis in Latin America," in *The Church and Culture since Vatican II*, ed. Joseph Gremillion (Notre Dame, 1985), 74–89; more skeptical is Mark J. Osiel, "Going to the People: Popular Culture and Intellectuals in Brazil," *Archives Européennes de Sociologie* 25 (1984): 245–75.

33. Daniel H. Levine, "Religion, the Poor, and Politics in Latin America Today," in Levine, ed., *Religion and Political Conflict*, 15. For a suggestive treatment of "anticipatory" radical communitarianism, see the seminal article on North American utopianism: Arthur Bestor, Jr., "Patent-Office Models of the Good Society: Some Relationships between Social Reform and Westward Expansion," *American Historical Review* 58 (April 1953): 505–26.

34. Charles A. Reilly, "Latin America's Religious Populists," in Levine, ed., *Religion and Political Conflict*, 42–58.

35. On the libertarian socialists who had the most accessible ideological articulation, see two general histories: David Viñas, *Anarquistas en América Latina* (Mexico City, 1983), and Alfredo Gómez, *Anarquismo y anarcosindicalismo en América Latina* (Madrid, 1980), and the following monographs: John Hart, *Anarchism and the Mexican Working Class, 1860–1931* (Austin, TX, 1978); Peter Blanchard, *The Origins of the Peruvian Labor Movement, 1883–1919* (Pittsburgh, 1982); and Peter DeShazo, *Urban Workers and Labor Unions in Chile, 1902–1927* (Madison, 1983).

36. Antonio Díaz Soto y Gama's phrase cited in Hart, *Anarchism and the Mexican Working Class*, 124.

37. On Mariátegui, see Jesús Chavarria, *José Carlos Mariátegui and the Rise of Modern Peru, 1890–1930* (Albuquerque, 1979).

38. Sheldon Wolin, *Politics and Vision* (Boston, 1960), 98.

39. Gutiérrez, *We Drink from Our Wells*, 160.

40. Cited in Berryman, "What Happened at Puebla," 162.

41. Leonardo Boff, "The Need for Political Saints," *Crosscurrents* (Fall 1980): 384.

42. For Puritans and other groups in the English revolution, see Christopher Hill, *The World Turned Upside Down* (Middlesex, Eng., 1985), and "God and the English Revolution," in *The Collected Essays of Christopher Hill*, ed. Hill (Amherst, 1966), 2:321–42.

15

Latin America's
New Social Landscape
Who Will Be the Workers?

Kenneth M. Roberts

Setting his analysis of Latin American society in a framework of conflict between labor and capital, in this selection Kenneth Roberts reviews seven outstanding studies on labor:

> María Lorena Cook, *Organizing Dissent: Unions, the State, and the Democratic Teachers' Movement in Mexico* (1996)
>
> Paul W. Drake, *Labor Movements and Dictatorships: The Southern Cone in Comparative Perspective* (1996)
>
> Javier Martínez and Alvaro H. Díaz, *Chile: The Great Transformation* (1996)
>
> Anthony W. Pereira, *The End of the Peasantry: The Rural Labor Movement in Northeast Brazil, 1961–1988* (1997)
>
> Ronn F. Pineo, *Social and Economic Reform in Ecuador: Life and Work in Guayaquil* (1996)
>
> Eduardo Silva, *The State and Capital in Chile: Business Elites, Technocrats, and Market Economics* (1996)
>
> Barbara Weinstein, *For Social Peace in Brazil: Industrialists and the Remaking of the Working Class in São Paulo* (1996)

The purpose that unites these works is the authors' intention to examine the condition of the present labor movement in various parts of the region. Thus, Roberts looks at labor in general in the context of today's global economy. The identity of workers seems to be at the center of these seven works, and this focus leads Roberts to make some suggestions about the changing character of the workers in Latin America at the turn of the twenty-first century. He speculates about the meaning of class and how it is intimately tied to the issue of identity. This selection is an excellent way in which to end a consideration of work, protest, and identity in Latin America, and it provides a useful point of departure for further discussion.

Although class actors have occupied a permanent place in Latin America's turbulent twentieth-century political landscape, they have not been a focus of continuous scholarly attention. For a variety of reasons, class themes largely disappeared from the mainstream scholarly agenda during the 1980s. At least partly in reaction against the class-tinged structural determinism of theories of dependency and bureaucratic authoritarianism, dominant approaches to the study of democratization eschewed class analysis in order to emphasize institutional engineering and the contingent construction of elite-level political accords (O'Donnell and Schmitter 1986; Higley and Gunther 1992).

In similar fashion, the study of neoliberal economic reforms typically turned the spotlight on global market forces, international financial institutions, and technocratic state elites rather than on domestic class actors (Haggard and Kaufman 1992). Even scholars who retained an interest in (or a commitment to) social reform and the empowerment of subaltern sectors increasingly questioned the transformative potential of traditional class actors, such as labor unions, and directed attention to grassroots popular organizations and other "new social movements" as agents of cultural and political change (Slater 1985; Escobar and Alvarez 1992).

In recent years, however, there has been a modest revival of interest in class relations and class actors in Latin American scholarship. Several influential works have stressed the enduring theoretical significance of class relations in the shaping of political regimes (Collier and Collier 1991; Rueschemeyer et al. 1992), while first-rate studies have dissected the political beliefs and behavior of workers (Ranis 1995; Middlebrook 1995; Buchanan 1995), capitalists (Payne 1994), and peasants (Anderson 1994) in different Latin American societies. The books reviewed here continue this revival of interest in themes related to social class. Although they do not all focus directly on class actors, they all shed light on various dimensions of evolving class relations in Latin American societies, both historically and in the more contemporary era of neoliberal transformation. In so doing, they provide important insights into the social foundations of the region's incessant political change.

This essay is organized around two broad themes that stand out in the works reviewed here. The first is the interactive relationship between class actors and their social and political environment. Class actors are invariably shaped and constrained by the economic structures and political institutions in which they are embedded; characteristics such as the size, cohesion, organizational forms, and strategic orientation of class actors bear the indelible imprint of their surroundings. Several of the books reviewed here, however, suggest that this relationship is interactive rather than unidirectional, because class actors are political agents who seek to influence their structural and institutional environment in varying levels of competition, conflict, and cooperation with alternative sociopolitical actors. Understanding this reciprocal causation is fundamental to any explanation of the role of class actors in the political process.

As for the second theme, these books highlight the heterogeneity of interests and identities that are likely to exist in any particular social class, regardless of objective class positioning in the structure of productive relations. Political expressions of class interest are thus contingent, contested, and socially constructed through a process of struggle that is both endogenous and exogenous to any given class category. These books demonstrate that this process of social construction—of articulating common interests and identities—is never-ending, although it is often associated with a parallel process of disarticulation, in accordance with [Joseph A.] Schumpeter's characterization of capitalist development as creative destruction.

The Interaction between Class Actors and Their Environs

Because class actors seek to exercise political influence, their organizational strength is a matter of obvious interest. This is especially the case for labor movements, which must counteract by weight of numbers and collective action the structural power that capitalists derive from their control of investment resources. Organizational strength, however, is not a purely endogenous matter, as it is heavily conditioned by structural and institutional forces. This point is driven home in Ronn F. Pineo's *Social and Economic Reform in Ecuador: Life and Work in Guayaquil,* which explores the limits of social reform in Ecuador at the turn of the century. Pineo's detailed analysis of social and economic development in Guayaquil helps explain the structural and historical factors that caused Ecuador's labor movement to become "one of the most feeble in Latin America" (p. 157).

Drawing from Bergquist's (1986) model of the linkages between leading export sectors and the character of national labor movements, Pineo traces the impact of Ecuador's cacao-based agroexport model of development on Guayaquil's social formation. The export of cacao concentrated wealth in the hands of small commercial and landed oligarchies, yielded few spinoffs in either transport infrastructure or industrial processing, and left behind a minuscule middle class and proletariat. There was no large, strategically located body of workers with the political or economic leverage needed to threaten the export trade, and domestic ownership of the cacao industry prevented workers from mobilizing around nationalist themes.

With a huge glut of cheap labor, attributable to the steady migration of indigenous workers from the sierra to the coast, and with most workers employed in temporary positions, a fluid work force relied primarily on individual mobility rather than collective action for economic improvement.

As a labor movement began to emerge in the early decades of the twentieth century, it was led by artisans and workers in the service sector and
was heavily dependent on the financial and political support of liberal
allies in the state. The collapse of the cacao market in 1922 engendered a
powerful spurt of militant labor mobilization, but a general strike was
crushed by military repression in a Guayaquil massacre from which the
labor movement never fully recovered.

In the aftermath of the massacre, militant labor organizations were
disbanded, and the union movement lost its state support and the capacity
to monitor the concessions it had won during earlier stages of mobilization. Although Pineo does not explore the broader comparative and theoretical implications of his case study, it stands in stark contrast to the
patterns of labor incorporation in most of the Latin American countries
studied by Collier and Collier (1991), and it helps in understanding both
the endurance of oligarchic domination in Ecuador and the relative weakness of organized labor in that country's populist experience under José
Velasco Ibarra.

Whereas Pineo explains how patterns of dependent development and
political repression constrained the Ecuadorean labor movement during
an earlier, agroexport phase of development, other recent works explore
the impact of later stages of capitalist modernization on class actors. In
*The End of the Peasantry: The Rural Labor Movement in Northeast Bra-
zil, 1961–1988*, Anthony W. Pereira chronicles the transformation of rural lower-class collective action in Pernambuco during a tumultuous period
of economic and political change. Pereira's account artfully synthesizes
structural and institutional approaches to explain the demise of peasant
leagues, with their emphasis on land distribution claims, and the rise of
rural unions with a focus on wages and benefits following the 1964 military coup in Brazil. In addition to political repression, the peasant leagues
were doomed by the figurative "end of the peasantry," as accelerated capitalist development modified the class structure of northeast Brazil, diminishing the relative importance of land-hungry tenants, sharecroppers,
and landless peasants. With "depeasantization" came commercialized
smallholders and rural wage laborers in the sugar industry, who organized in unions under the institutional strictures of Brazilian corporatism.
Following Paige (1975), Pereira argues that patterns of collective action
are structured by the relations of production in agriculture; as capitalist
modernization proceeds, revolutionary struggles over land ownership yield
to reformist union movements that bargain over wages and benefits.

One of Pereira's most provocative findings is that economic and institutional change strengthened rural unions' capacity for collective action despite political repression under bureaucratic-authoritarian rule. As
he explains, local rural unions gained new political appeal and organiza-

tional resources when they were chosen as financial conduits for the military government's new health and retirement programs. These institutional innovations, however, also reshaped the rural union movement. They incorporated the unions into the state's restrictive corporatist framework; they created a leadership caste that was highly dependent on state subsidies; and they encouraged the unions to prioritize wages and welfare benefits in their daily operations. Consequently, although the national union CONTAG (the National Confederation of Agricultural Workers) retained a principled commitment to land redistribution in its formal declarations, in practice its state and local-level affiliates were preoccupied with wage and benefit issues. As Pereira states, "The welfare programs . . . empowered a new category of professional union leaders, connected to the state, with a high degree of influence over their members, but with little interest in challenging the existing distribution of property rights" (p. 75).

Although the rural unions were capable of militant collective action—the agricultural workers in Pernambuco declared the first rural strike in the nation against the military regime in 1979, and they struck eight more times in the subsequent ten years during the negotiation of annual contracts—their militancy did not target the structure of property ownership in the countryside, as did that of the pre-coup peasant leagues.

The impact of authoritarianism on labor movements is also a central concern of the excellent studies by Paul W. Drake and María Lorena Cook. The most valuable contribution of Drake's *Labor Movements and Dictatorships: The Southern Cone in Comparative Perspective* is its cross-regional comparative analysis of labor movements under authoritarian rule in southern Europe, Brazil, and the Southern Cone of Latin America. All the dictatorships Drake studies arose in contexts of class conflict and adopted antilabor positions. Nevertheless, authoritarian rule affected labor movements in very different ways. Where labor was a relatively weak actor before authoritarianism, as it was in Portugal, Greece, and Brazil, "containment coups" led to authoritarian regimes that "enveloped labor in official corporatist organizations" (p. 33) in order to ameliorate class conflict while trying to industrialize their societies. Industrialization, however, created structural conditions that encouraged labor movements to gain strength, while corporatist institutions "offered the outlawed labor parties official structures to infiltrate" (p. 33). According to Drake, "As the working class grew in size, strength, and expectations, it became more militant—and in some cases more radical—than it had been before the coup" (p. 33). In contrast,

> rollback or reactionary coups took place to incapacitate stronger labor movements in Spain, Uruguay, Chile, and Argentina. The Southern Cone governments meshed a policy to atomize and shrink the proletariat with an economic program that reduced industry and employment. Their free-

> market labor strategy to disassemble and disable unions matched their free-market economic strategy. . . . Not surprisingly, the debilitated labor movements became less militant and more moderate than they had been before the coups in the Southern Cone. (p. 33)

Like Pereira, Drake sees a strengthening of Brazilian unionism under bureaucratic-authoritarian rule, although he focuses more on the success of the "new unionism" in organizing inside and outside state corporatist institutions in the urban industrial sector than on its activities in the agricultural sector. By analyzing the structural, institutional, and political constraints faced by labor movements, Drake uses his theoretical framework to help differentiate Brazil's experience from that of its Southern Cone neighbors. In those countries, labor emerged from authoritarianism both politically and economically weakened.

Both authors provide a useful check on tendencies to accept facile generalizations about the negative impact of authoritarian rule on labor movements. Drake does, however, perceive more generalizable structural effects of the global trend toward market liberalism, which he sees as weakening labor unions (p. 192). Although he acknowledges the resilience and perseverance of labor movements and their partisan affiliates in the face of authoritarian repression and economic restructuring, he is cautious when assessing their political leverage, arguing that they "were much more successful at outlasting these regimes than at battling them" (p. 192). He concludes that capitalist authoritarianism successfully foreclosed socialist development options and circumscribed the potential for democratic social reforms, thus contributing to the growing moderation of contemporary labor unions and leftist parties in Latin America.

In *Organizing Dissent: Unions, the State, and the Democratic Teachers' Movement in Mexico*, Cook also explores the impact of an authoritarian political system on organized labor. More specifically, she seeks to explain how a dissident, democratically organized teachers' movement could emerge and survive within an official union structure that is thoroughly integrated into the corporatist, authoritarian framework of a single-party-dominant political regime.

One of the most valuable contributions of Cook's study is her adoption of a social movement theoretical framework to analyze dissident teachers' unions. Too often, scholars of social movements and organized labor have talked past one another; the literature on "new social movements" has often portrayed unions as calcified remnants of "old" social movements at best, or as co-opted junior partners of establishment institutions at worst. Cook's study builds a bridge between scholars in the two fields and demonstrates that unions can adopt organizational features that are generally attributed to new social movements, such as participatory and democratic organizational structures and a collective identity that emphasizes political autonomy. Indeed, Cook argues persuasively that inter-

nal democratic practices are not merely naive expressions of political ideals. Instead, internal democracy in this case was both a means and an end,
as it "proved to be a functional strategy for the movement's survival."
Democratic practices helped to manage factionalism while providing a
number of additional benefits:

> the strengthening of a grassroots defense against the movement's en-
> emies through a sense of "ownership" of the movement by its members,
> the facilitation of mobilization, the reduced likelihood of co-optation,
> the generation of new leaders, the creation of political consciousness,
> and the expansion of horizontal alliances. (p. 265)

Cook's study, however, does not attribute movement success solely to
endogenous organizational characteristics; rather, success is contingent
on the interaction between a movement's organization, its strategy, and its
external environment. Theoretically, she crafts a political process model
of movement dynamics, drawing from Tarrow (1994) and other scholars
who emphasize the political opportunity structures that shape and con-
strain social movements. In contrast to most of the literature, she employs
this model to analyze a social movement in an authoritarian context in
which a corporatist state seeks to close off organizational space and co-
opt or repress autonomous forms of sociopolitical organization.

One of the fruits of this approach is Cook's ability to show the fluid
character of Mexico's long-standing system of corporatist labor control,
which she characterizes as an "unstable equilibrium" (p. 34) plagued by
internal contradictions between the interests of state institutions, official
union leaders, and their rank-and-file constituents. Dissent springs from
the tensions between official unions' contradictory roles as both instruments of government objectives and representatives of constituent interests. That dissent becomes rapidly politicized when even economistic
demands cannot be effectively articulated without internal democratic
reforms to make unions more representative.

Cook uses the political process model to explain how proposed education reforms triggered the sudden emergence of the dissident teachers'
movement at the end of the 1970s; how the closing of political space led
to the movement's demobilization in the mid-1980s; and how the 1988
elections and conflicts between President Carlos Salinas and traditional
labor bosses provided a context for the resurgence of the movement at the
end of the 1980s. She also provides a comparative analysis of the dissident movement in different states, demonstrating the relative advantages
of organizational strategies that rely on legal forms of mobilization and
demand articulation rather than illegal and highly confrontational challenges to the authoritarian state. In the end, Cook's case study of Mexico's
most important dissident labor movement provides a revealing, micro-
level portrait of the political and economic changes—and the responses

from civil society—that have eroded Mexico's corporatist, authoritarian system of governance.

Cook, Drake, and Pereira all perceive labor movements as important actors in the struggle to democratize political regimes and civil societies, yet they are all guarded in their expectations for significant union impact on democratic policy making in contemporary Latin America. It is indicative of unions' predicament, perhaps, that these authors point to different factors when assessing the limits of labor's political leverage. For Drake, structural changes in the regional and global economies have diminished the relative size and political weight of organized labor. For Cook, democratization of the political system can be a two-edged sword for a dissident labor movement. Although democratization opens organizational space and new channels for representation, the institutionalization of union access may also produce bureaucratic organizational forms with oligarchic leadership structures. It may endanger political cohesion and autonomy, and ultimately may undermine grassroots mobilizational capacity. Pereira, by contrast, emphasizes the coordination problem faced by the rural union movement in representing the diverse, and not always congruent, interests of different sectors of the rural poor.

These concerns are buttressed by the analyses of social and political change contained in the two books on Chile: Javier Martínez and Alvaro Díaz's *Chile: The Great Transformation* and Eduardo Silva's *The State and Capital in Chile*. Both books are devoted to understanding the nature and consequences of the capitalist revolution that transpired in Chile under the military regime of General Augusto Pinochet, following the overthrow of socialist president Salvador Allende in 1973.

For a relatively short and highly readable account that cuts through the myths surrounding Chile's free-market "miracle," there is no better source than the book by Martínez and Díaz, two of Chile's most prominent social scientists. The authors argue persuasively that the dynamism of the neoliberal economic model imposed by Pinochet and his Chicago School technocrats was predicated on a series of socioeconomic reforms implemented by the military regime's socialist and Christian Democratic predecessors. Agrarian and other reforms undertaken by the Allende and Frei governments transformed paternalistic, precapitalist social relationships; undermined traditional elites that impeded economic modernization; and provided the military regime with the political autonomy required to restructure Chilean capitalism for a new era of export-led growth. This argument has major implications for comparative research. It suggests that the Chilean model—which has been embraced by international financial institutions and emulated by governments throughout Latin America and the developing world—may not be easily replicable. As Martínez and Díaz state, "The task of neoliberalism was made considerably easier by the radical nature of the reforms carried out by the two previous governments" (p. 135). That observation casts doubt on the generalizability of the Chilean experience.

Indeed, Martínez and Díaz challenge conventional interpretations of Chile's economic success, which they characterize as a capitalist revolution but not a free-market one. The authors provide substantial evidence of the numerous ways the Chilean state under Pinochet intervened in the marketplace to shape the course of capitalist development, including the manipulation of tariffs, interest and exchange rates, prices, and wages. In their words,

> There is a false, albeit widely accepted, idea that neoliberalism in Chile involved a state that intervened in a "subsidiary" fashion only when private enterprise was not effective, and that markets were left to function freely or savagely (depending on one's viewpoint) without interference of the state. The idea that the neoliberal state worked only to liberate markets, while withdrawing progressively from the economy, takes no account of the real role of the state in Chile between 1973 and 1990. On the contrary, the state was highly interventionist. . . . (pp. 65–66)

However Chile's capitalist revolution is interpreted, Martínez and Díaz leave little doubt that it has fundamentally transformed Chilean society, including the structure of class relationships. Echoing Drake, they document the structural weakening of labor as a political actor, a weakening attributable to the deindustrialization of the Chilean economy during the first decade of neoliberalism, the repression of organized labor, the reform of the labor code designed to emasculate unions and create more flexible labor markets, and the fragmentation of a "precarious" work force that is increasingly engaged in subcontracting activities or temporary forms of employment. Although Martínez and Díaz hold out the possibility that labor movement strength could be revived as a result of political democracy and the increase in wage labor since the mid-1980s, they argue that the balance of power in Chilean society has swung decisively in favor of capital, as a result of social and economic restructuring. The redistribution of economic resources from the state and labor to capital has reinforced the structural power of dominant classes in Chilean society, particularly the elite sectors tied to finance and to international trade and capital flows.

For Martínez and Díaz, however, this process of restructuring contains a basic paradox: although capitalist elites were the primary beneficiaries of the neoliberal revolution, they were not its political agents. This analysis characterizes Chile's economic transformation as a revolution from above, directed by a technocratic state elite operating with relative autonomy from the capitalist class that undermined Allende's experiment in democratic socialism and ushered the military into power. The authors portray Chile's traditional capitalist class as a reactive and defensive elite, too closely wedded to state protectionism to initiate reforms leading to a competitive marketplace, and too weak to block the policy initiatives of ideological technocrats committed to the restructuring and modernization of Chilean capitalism.

The problem with this argument is that it does not adequately capture the dynamic diversity within Chile's capitalist class, the range of interests that compete for expression among its different fractions, or the personal and organizational bonds that linked economic elites to the state and the policy-making process under the Pinochet regime. It is precisely these factors that form the centerpiece of Eduardo Silva's revealing study of the state and capital during Chile's neoliberal revolution.

Like Martínez and Díaz, Silva believes that Chile's economic transformation has enhanced the political leverage of capitalist elites and narrowed the parameters for democratic social and economic reform. Unlike them, however, he argues that capitalist and landowning elites were important actors in the design and implementation of the neoliberal model. What sets Silva's analysis apart is his effort to disaggregate the capitalist class "as a first step toward examining intraclass conflict and its impact on the formation of more fluid policy coalitions than those found in classic interpretations of the bourgeoisie in Latin America" (p. 19).

Drawing from previous efforts by Jeffry Frieden (1991) and Peter Gourevitch (1986) to disaggregate social groups, Silva develops a categorization that differentiates capitalist class fractions according to their possession of fixed or liquid assets, their orientation toward domestic or international markets, and their degree of international competitiveness. Whereas these various fractions could unite against the shared threat to propertied interests posed by Allende's program of socialization, they had very different interests at stake in the process of economic restructuring under the military regime. Capitalists holding fixed assets in noncompetitive sectors and producing for domestic markets were directly threatened by the neoliberal model, whereas those holding liquid assets tied to international markets were highly favored. The latter, in turn, provided an important domestic class constituency for the Pinochet regime and played an active role in formulating the neoliberal model through the close ties between prominent financial conglomerates and leading figures among the Chicago Boys.

Silva's book is most effective at tracing the interplay between public policies and shifting state-capitalist coalitions during the period of military dictatorship. The initial period of gradual economic adjustment was associated with more mainstream technocratic advisers and a broad capitalist coalition. The period of "radical" neoliberalism after 1975 saw the ascendance of the Chicago School technocrats and internationally oriented conglomerates with liquid assets. With the financial collapse of 1982 and the onset of mass antiregime protests in 1983, the Pinochet re gime shifted to a more "pragmatic" neoliberal model that offered various forms of state support for industrial and agricultural producers, thus helping to restore a broad capitalist coalition behind the regime and block the emergence of an opposition movement with business support.

Silva makes a compelling case that capitalist support for Pinochet was not predicated solely on the regime's adoption of favorable policies or on capitalists' fear of the Chilean left; it was also solidified by establishing institutional channels by which Chilean capitalists and their representative associations could gain direct access to the policy-making process. Capitalists' structural power in the aftermath of widespread privatizations and their privileged access to policy arenas weighed heavily on the new democratic regime that took office in 1990. This pressure largely ensured that social reforms would stay within the parameters of pragmatic neoliberalism.

Silva's work is a leading example of the analytical leverage that can be obtained by focusing on the interaction between state and societal actors—in this case, the policy coalitions forged between state technocrats and fractions of a dominant bourgeoisie. As he argues, to ignore these relationships "generates a certain measure of hubris about the relationship between market economics and social equity; it blinds observers to the limitations that Chile's system of interaction between capital and state places on social reform policy; and, hence, it conceals the true nature of the state and society under construction in Chile" (p. 2). Ultimately, Silva's analysis of state-capital relations in Chile has more in common with Peter Evans's (1995) portrayal of East Asian-style "embedded autonomy" than with the image of an economic revolution directed by an insulated and omniscient technocratic vanguard.

The final work reviewed here, Barbara Weinstein's *For Social Peace in Brazil*, also focuses on the political agency of capitalists, albeit at an earlier phase of political and economic development. The parallels and contrasts between Weinstein's and Silva's accounts of capitalist agency are instructive. Both scholars challenge the traditional assumption that Latin American bourgeoisies are so politically and economically weak that they lack a modernizing project of their own, and must therefore rely on the state as the engine of development. Like capitalists and technocrats in Chile, the São Paulo industrialists studied by Weinstein sought to modernize backward productive structures and contain the political threat posed by a potentially militant working class. The methods they chose, however, were strikingly different. Like their Chilean counterparts, they promoted technological modernization to enhance economic efficiency and competitiveness, but within a macroeconomic framework of state-protected import-substitution industrialization. And whereas Chilean workers were disciplined by a combination of state repression, market competition, economic dislocation, and social fragmentation, the Brazilian industrialists chose to envelop workers in a network of education, vocational training, and social welfare designed to socialize workers to accept a shared vision of class harmony wrought by economic rationalization.

Weinstein weaves an intricate and fascinating tale of the creation and evolution of SENAI (the National Service for Industrial Training) and SESI (the Industrial Social Service), two public agencies founded by the Vargas and Dutra administrations in the 1940s but financed and operated by associations of industrialists. The two agencies reflected the modernizing vocation of leading São Paulo industrialists who sought to rationalize productive relations and implement scientific management principles inspired by Taylorist and Fordist principles. In the process, the industrialists hoped to transform both the capitalist and working-class self-images, in an industrial culture that had been molded by clientelism and apprenticeship.

SENAI and SESI were committed to the establishment of an industrial hierarchy and social discipline in the workplace, but they also believed in the "social functions" of capital. The two agencies sponsored a wide variety of activities, ranging from vocational training to health and education programs, domestic instruction for housewives, and recreation. These programs were designed to create a better-educated, better-trained, and more "cultured" labor force that would be more efficient in the workplace and more resistant to the appeals of communist agitators and other labor militants. Although SENAI encouraged labor organization when corporatist controls contained union militancy, both agencies ultimately collaborated in the state's coercive labor practices during periods of heightened class conflict, both before and after the installation of bureaucratic-authoritarian rule in 1964.

Weinstein is most effective at conveying the tensions and ambiguities between the two agencies' missions of economic modernization, social control, and social welfare. She also provides a nuanced interpretation of their social and political impact. Although they contributed to the consolidation of a "hegemonic discourse" that premised "all discussions of social welfare on rapid economic development and the attendant notions of heightened productivity, rational organization, and technological progress" (p. 340), they did not succeed in disciplining the Brazilian capitalist class to support their activities or to embrace their integrated notion of socioeconomic modernization. Likewise, although SENAI and SESI were able to induce individual workers to take advantage of their services, they had limited success in their mission of social control, as organized labor in Brazil proved resistant to the industrialists' vision of depoliticized social harmony. In reference to the "new unionism" that arose under military rule in the late 1970s, Weinstein says, it is worth noting the leading role played by skilled workers, a surprising number of them SENAI graduates, in the insurgent labor movement. By the mid-1980s, the presidents of the four most militant metallurgical workers' unions in São Paulo were all tool-and-die makers trained by SENAI. And the two most prominent figures to emerge from the new union movement over the last fifteen years—Jair Meneghelli and, of course, Luiz Inácio Lula da Silva—were both SENAI graduates. (p. 341)

In the end, Weinstein's account demonstrates the complexity of the historical process by which classes are socially constructed, and the difficulty of imposing any particular political blueprint on such a process. Indeed, many of the works reviewed here shed light on the fluid, heterogeneous, and contested nature of class interests and identities. These issues merit additional consideration.

Social Heterogeneity and the Construction of Class

Although all these books take class actors seriously, most of them avoid blanket generalizations about the political or economic interests and behavior of specific social classes. Instead, they analyze the interplay between different class fractions or subgroups as they compete to define collective interests and construct (or refine) collective identities.

With respect to capitalists, this heterogeneity is clearly present in the work of both Silva and Weinstein. Indeed, it is a centerpiece of Silva's analysis, which explains capitalists' policy preferences in terms of objective economic interests derived from differential locations in the sphere of production and unequal access to global capital flows. Even in the context of a relatively autonomous and highly technocratic authoritarian state, macroeconomic policy shifts were shaped and constrained by the coalitional dynamics and conflicts of interest that existed between competing fractions of the bourgeoisie. Weinstein's analysis, on the other hand, places more emphasis on the role of ideology and political discourse in the efforts of a class vanguard to rationalize productive relations, modify both elite and mass-level economic behavior, and construct a hegemonic bourgeois class whose self-interest would be synonymous with that of the nation. The ambitious designs of this class vanguard, however, were obstructed not only by the competing identities of Brazilian workers, but also by the inertia of traditional productive relations and the collective action problems of sympathetic capitalists, who were reluctant to bear the financial costs associated with an integral process of modernization.

Likewise, the books on labor movements reviewed here provide ample evidence of the diversity and tensions that exist within the working classes of Latin America. Three principal sources of differentiation can be identified in these books. The first source is structural in nature, and refers to the divergent interests and identities of workers who occupy distinct positions in the structure of productive relations. This is seen most clearly in Pereira's account of the rural labor movement in Brazil. Pereira traces the rise and decline of different types of lower-class collective action as the political agenda shifts in accordance with changes in the rural class structure and national political institutions. He also shows how different sectors of the rural poor define their interests and collective identities in different ways, and he provides a thoughtful discussion of the problems of representation this creates for a national confederation like CONTAG, which tries to speak for a variety of commercial smallholders, rural wage laborers, and land-hungry peasants. Ultimately, he argues, CONTAG represents these social categories very unevenly, giving precedence to the interests and identities of smallholders and the rural proletariat over those of squatters, migrants, and landless peasants. The volumes by Drake and Martínez and Díaz suggest that the problem of structural differentiation is likely only to grow as market liberalization proceeds.

A second line of division in labor movements is institutional in nature, differentiating union officials from their rank-and-file constituents. This cleavage can be found in the union movements studied by Pereira and Weinstein in Brazil, a country with a long tradition of corporatist control and state co-optation of union leaders. It is a central analytical theme in Cook's study of the dissident teachers' movement in Mexico, which defined its core identity in opposition to the official union leadership. Like structural differentiation, this institutional cleavage raises serious questions about the representativeness of established labor unions, and puts union democracy at the forefront of labor's agenda, especially in countries with state corporatist traditions of labor control.

The final set of cleavages is more political in nature: it relates to the different partisan loyalties, ideological predispositions, and strategic orientations that exist within and between sectors of national labor movements. In Mexico, loyalty to the PRI was a defining feature of the official teachers' federation, whereas dissident unions had political ties to diverse leftist parties or articulated claims for organizational autonomy. Weinstein's analysis suggests that conservative sectors of the Brazilian labor movement were inclined to accept industrialists' vision of "social peace" and economic modernization, preventing SENAI and SESI from becoming pure instruments of social control, whereas leftist sectors were hostile to the notion of class collaboration in a joint project of economic rationalization. Likewise, union movements in Brazil and Mexico faced divisive strategic choices over the relative efficacy of confrontational and collaborative tactics in their relationships with state institutions, as can be seen most clearly in Cook's study of the teachers' movement.

Two final points are worth noting regarding the social construction of class in modern Latin America. First, it is the nature of modern capitalism that workers are more dependent on collective action than on capitalists to defend their interests in both the workplace and the political arena. As such, the aforementioned intraclass cleavages place significant constraints on the political leverage of labor movements in contemporary Latin America. The current power imbalance between capital and labor is unlikely to be redressed unless workers find ways to organize across these divides and find strength in their diversity.

Second, the works reviewed here provide numerous examples of how the construction of new class interests and identities may coincide with the disarticulation or deconstruction of old ones. Thus the rise of rural labor unions in Brazil followed in the wake of the demise of peasant unions, with corresponding changes in the patterns of collective action and the content of collective demands. Likewise, democratic union structures have emerged in the cracks of declining corporatist institutions in Mexico and Brazil, while political repression and economic restructuring in the Southern Cone have caused militant, mass-based labor movements to evolve into smaller, more moderate, and largely economistic union organizations. If, as Schumpeter claims, capitalism is a force for creative destruction, this applies not only to the sphere of production, but to the domain of class relations and social organization as well.

References

Anderson, Leslie. 1994. *The Political Ecology of the Modern Peasant: Calculation and Community*. Baltimore: Johns Hopkins University Press.

Bergquist, Charles. 1986. *Labor in Latin America: Comparative Essays on Chile, Argentina, Venezuela, and Colombia*. Stanford: Stanford University Press.

Buchanan, Paul G. 1995. *State, Labor, Capital: Democratizing Class Relations in the Southern Cone*. Pittsburgh: University of Pittsburgh Press.

Collier, Ruth Berins, and David Collier. 1991. *Shaping the Political Arena: Critical Junctures, the Labor Movement, and Regime Dynamics in Latin America*. Princeton: Princeton University Press.

Cook, María Lorena. 1996. *Organizing Dissent: Unions, the State, and the Democratic Teachers' Movement in Mexico*. University Park: Pennsylvania State University Press.

Drake, Paul W. 1996. *Labor Movements and Dictatorships: The Southern Cone in Comparative Perspective*. Baltimore: Johns Hopkins University Press.

Escobar, Arturo, and Sonia E. Alvarez, eds. 1992. *The Making of Social Movements in Latin America: Identity, Strategy, and Democracy*. Boulder: Westview Press.

Evans, Peter. 1995. *Embedded Autonomy: States and Industrial Transformation*. Princeton: Princeton University Press.

Frieden, Jeffry. 1991. *Debt, Development, and Democracy: Modern Political Economy and Latin America, 1965–1985*. Princeton: Princeton University Press.

Gourevitch, Peter A. 1986. *Politics in Hard Times: Comparative Responses to International Economic Crises*. Ithaca: Cornell University Press.

Haggard, Stephen, and Robert Kaufman, eds. 1992. *The Politics of Economic Adjustment: International Constraints, Distributive Politics, and the State*. Princeton: Princeton University Press.

Higley, John, and Richard Gunther, eds. 1992. *Elites and Democratic Consolidation in Latin America and Southern Europe*. Cambridge: Cambridge University Press.

Martínez, Javier, and Alvaro H. Díaz. 1996. *Chile: The Great Transformation*. Washington/Geneva: Brookings Institution/United Nations Research Institute for Social Development.

Middlebrook, Kevin. 1995. *The Paradox of Revolution: Labor, the State, and Authoritarianism in Mexico*. Baltimore: Johns Hopkins University Press.

O'Donnell, Guillermo, and Philippe Schmitter. 1986. *Transitions from Authoritarian Rule: Tentative Conclusions about Uncertain Democracies*. Baltimore: Johns Hopkins University Press.

Paige, Jeffery M. 1975. *Agrarian Revolution: Social Movements and Export Agriculture in the Underdeveloped World*. New York: Free Press.

Payne, Leigh A. 1994. *Brazilian Industrialists and Democratic Change*. Baltimore: Johns Hopkins University Press.

Pereira, Anthony W. 1997. *The End of the Peasantry: The Rural Labor Movement in Northeast Brazil, 1961–1988*. Pittsburgh: University of Pittsburgh Press.

Pineo, Ronn F. 1996. *Social and Economic Reform in Ecuador: Life and Work in Guayaquil*. Gainesville: University of Florida Press.

Ranis, Peter. 1995. *Class, Democracy, and Labor in Contemporary Argentina*. New Brunswick: Transaction.

Rueschemeyer, Dietrich, Evelyne Huber Stephens, and John D. Stephens. 1992. *Capitalist Development and Democracy*. Chicago: University of Chicago Press.

Silva, Eduardo. 1996. *The State and Capital in Chile: Business Elites, Technocrats, and Market Economics*. Boulder: Westview Press.

Slater, David, ed. 1985. *New Social Movements and the State in Latin America*. Amsterdam: CEDLA.

Tarrow, Sidney G. 1994. *Power in Movement: Social Movements, Collective Action, and Politics*. Cambridge: Cambridge University Press.

Weinstein, Barbara. 1996. *For Social Peace in Brazil: Industrialists and the Remaking of the Working Class in São Paulo*. Chapel Hill: University of North Carolina Press.

Suggested Readings

Jeremy Adelman, ed. *Essays in Argentine Labor History, 1870–1930*. Houndsmills: Macmillan, 1992.

James P. Brennan. *The Labor Wars of Córdoba, 1955–1976: Ideology, Work, and Labor Politics in an Argentine Industrial City*. Cambridge: Harvard University Press, 1994.

Jonathan C. Brown. *Workers' Control in Latin America, 1930–1979*. Chapel Hill: University of North Carolina Press, 1997.

Norman Caulfield. *Mexican Workers and the State: From the Porfiriato to NAFTA*. Fort Worth: Texas Christian University Press, 1998.

Elsa M. Chaney and Mary García Castro, eds. *Muchachas No More: Household Workers in Latin America and the Caribbean*. Philadelphia: Temple University Press, 1989.

Aviva Chomsky. *"A Perfect Slavery": West Indian Workers and the United Fruit Company in Costa Rica, 1870–1950*. Baton Rouge: Louisiana State University Press, 1996.

Ruth Berins Collier and David Collier. *Shaping the Political Arena: Critical Junctures, the Labor Movement, and Regime Dynamics in Latin America*. Princeton: Princeton University Press, 1991.

María Lorena Cook. *Organizing Dissent: Unions, the State, and the Democratic Teachers' Movement in Mexico*. University Park: Pennsylvania State University Press, 1996.

Paul Drake. *Labor Movements and Dictatorships: The Southern Cone in Comparative Perspective*. Baltimore: Johns Hopkins University Press, 1996.

Steve Ellner. *Organized Labor in Venezuela, 1958–1991: Behavior and Concerns in a Democratic Setting*. Wilmington: Scholarly Resources, 1993.

Edward C. Epstein, ed. *Labor Autonomy and the State in Latin America*. Boston: Hyman Unwin, 1989.

Ann Farnsworth-Alvear. *Dulcinea in the Factory: Myth, Morals, Men, and Women in Colombia's Industrial Experiment, 1905–1960*. Durham: Duke University Press, 2000.

John D. French. *The Brazilian Workers' ABC: Class Conflicts and Alliances in Modern São Paulo*. Chapel Hill: University of North Carolina Press, 1992.

———. *Globalizing Protest: The Fight for Workers' Rights in World Trade*. Durham: Duke University Press, 2000.

John D. French and Alexandre Fortes. *Urban Labor History in Twentieth-Century Brazil*. Albuquerque: University of New Mexico Press, 1998.

John D. French and Daniel James, eds. *The Gendered Worlds of Latin American Women Workers: From Household and Factory to the Union Hall and Ballot Box*. Durham: Duke University Press, 1997.

Linda Fuller. *Work and Democracy in Socialist Cuba*. Philadelphia: Temple University Press, 1992.

Jeffrey Gould. *To Lead As Equals: Rural Protest and Political Consciousness in Chinandega, Nicaragua, 1912–1979*. Chapel Hill: University of North Carolina Press, 1990.

Gerald Greenfield, ed. *Organized Labor in Venezuela*. Westport, CT: Greenwood Press, 1990.

Jim Handy. *Revolution in the Countryside: Rural Conflict and Agrarian Reform in Guatemala, 1944–1954*. Chapel Hill: University of North Carolina Press, 1994.

Mark Healy. *In the Spirit of Battle: Shaping the Political Arena and the Great Uruguayan Exception*. Durham: Duke University Press, 1996.

Daniel James. *Doña María's Story: Storytelling, Personal Identity, and Community Narratives*. Durham: Duke University Press, 2000.

Margaret E. Keck. *The Workers Party and Democratization in Brazil*. New Haven: Yale University Press, 1992.

Thomas M. Klubock. *Contested Communities: Class, Gender, and Politics in Chile's El Teniente Copper Mine, 1904–1951*. Durham: Duke University Press, 1998.

Deborah Levenson-Estrada. *Trade Unionists against Terror: Guatemala City, 1945–1985*. Chapel Hill: University of North Carolina Press, 1994.

David J. McCreery. *The Sweat of Their Brow: A History of Work in Latin America*. Armonk: M. E. Sharpe, 2000.

Kevin J. Middlebrook. *The Paradox of Revolution: Labor, the State, and Authoritarianism in Mexico*. Baltimore: Johns Hopkins University Press, 1995.

June Nash. *I Spent My Life in the Mines: The Story of Juan Rojas, Bolivian Tin Miner*. New York: Columbia University Press, 1992.

David S. Parker. *The Idea of the Middle Class: White-Collar Workers and Peruvian Society, 1900–1950*. University Park: Pennsylvania State University Press, 1998.

Jorge Parodi, trans. James Alstrum and C. Conaghan, ed. Catherine Conaghan. *To Be A Worker: Identity and Politics in Peru*. Chapel Hill: University of North Carolina Press, 2000.

Vincent C. Peloso. *Peasants on Plantations: Subaltern Strategies of Labor and Resistance in the Pisco Valley, Peru*. Durham: Duke University Press, 1999.

Peter Ranis. *Argentine Workers: Peronism and Contemporary Class Consciousness*. Pittsburgh: University of Pittsburgh Press, 1992.

David Sowell. *The Early Colombian Labor Movement: Artisans and Politics in Bogotá, 1832–1919*. Philadelphia: Temple University Press, 1992.

Steve Stein, comp. *Lima obrera: 1900–1930*. 2 vols. Lima: Ediciones El Virrey, 1986, 1987.

Mary Turner, ed. *From Chattel Slaves to Wage Slaves: The Dynamics of Labour Bargaining in the Americas*. Bloomington: University of Indiana Press, 1995.

Mary K. Vaughan. *Cultural Politics in Revolution: Teachers, Peasants, and Schools in Mexico, 1930–1940*. Tucson: University of Arizona Press, 1997.

Barbara Weinstein. *For Social Peace in Brazil: Industrialists and the Working Class in São Paulo, 1920–1964*. Chapel Hill: University of North Carolina Press, 1996.

Cliff Welch. *The Seed Was Planted: The São Paulo Roots of Brazil's Rural Labor Movement, 1924–1964*. University Park: Pennsylvania State University Press, 1999.

Joel Wolfe. *Working Women, Working Men: São Paulo and the Rise of Brazil's Industrial Working Class, 1900–1955*. Durham: Duke University Press, 1993.

In addition to the above works, a student might dig deeper into labor history by making use of the following bibliographies: John D. French, *Latin American Labor Studies: An Interim Bibliography of Non-English Publications (1989)* (Miami: Center for Labor Research and Studies, Florida International University, 1989); John D. French, *Latin American Labor Studies: A Bibliography of English-Language Publications through 1989* (Miami: Center for Labor Research and Studies, Florida International University, 1989); and Ian Roxborough, "The Urban Working Class and Labor Movements," in Leslie Bethell, ed., *The Cambridge History of Latin America*, Vol. 11, *Bibliographic Essays* (Cambridge: Cambridge University Press, 1995), 617–34.

Suggested Films

The following videos depict the life of ordinary working people in a variety of settings—some socially chaotic and others less intense, some rural and others urban. Migration and immigration, workers' protest and organization, and politics at the national level are among the issues found here.

"La Ciudad" [The City]. Four vignettes about Latin American immigrants in New York City, filmed by David Riker for PBS, 1993–1997; broadcast September 22, 2000

Alpaca Breeders of Chimboya (Peru), 30 mins., First Run
Battle of the Titans (Venezuelan oil workers), 54 mins., www.filmakers.com
Chile's Roots (Mapuche and Aymara), 50 mins., First Run
Coffee: A Sack Full of Power, 52 mins., www.filmakers.com
Coffee Break! (Nicaragua and Honduras), 27 mins., www.filmakers.com
Coffee Is the Gold of the Future (Colombia), 52 mins., First Run
El Crucero (Nicaraguan labor, women, 1984), 59 mins., Facets
El Grito (Peruvian sugar workers form union), 84 mins., Facets
I Spent My Life in the Mines (Bolivia), 40 mins., www.cinemaguild.com
La Tigra (female identity as seen through macho culture), 80 mins.,
    Facets
Las Nicas and *Home Life* (women, work, life in Estelí), 45 mins. and
    27 mins., Facets
Made on Rails: A History of the Mexican Railroad Workers (1920s and
    after), 40 mins., www.cinemaguild.com
Peru: Between the Hammer and the Anvil, 52 mins., www.films.com
Population Explosion and Industrialization (Latin American lifestyles),
    30 mins., Facets
Prayer for the Weavers (Mexico: Chiapas women weavers) by Judith
    Gleason, 35 mins., Filmakers Library, www.filmakers.com
Rebellion in Patagonia (1920s repression of rural worker strikes),
    107 mins., www.cinemaguild.com
Savage Capitalism (Brazilian mining and ecology), 86 mins., Facets
Solo, The Law of the Favela, 54 mins., First Run/Icarus, www.frif.com
Stories from Cuscatlán (El Salvador), 52 mins., Icarus, www.frif.com
The Dark Light of Dawn (Guatemalan Human Rights Commission),
    28 mins., Facets
The Havana: Cigar of Connoisseurs, 59 mins., Facets, rentals@facets.org

Trinkets and Beads, 52 mins., First Run/Icarus, http://www.newday.com
Txai Macedo (Brazilian rubber workers), directed by Marcia Machado
 and Tal Danai, 50 mins., Icarus, www.frif.com
Up to a Certain Point (Cuban dockworker in love), 72 mins., Facets

About the Contributors

ALEJANDRO DE LA FUENTE is assistant professor of Latin American and Caribbean history at the University of Pittsburgh. He is the author of *A Nation for All: Race, Inequality, and Politics in Twentieth-Century Cuba* (2001). His research interests include comparative slave systems and comparative race relations. He is currently working on a book on slavery in colonial Cuba.

JEFFREY D. NEEDELL is associate professor of history and Latin American studies at the University of Florida. The author of *A Tropical Belle Epoque: Elite Culture and Society in Turn-of-the-Century Rio de Janeiro* (1987) and numerous articles, he is currently researching the origins and development of the Brazilian monarchy as it relates to specific social and economic groups, political party organization, and ideology. His most recent work appeared as "Party Formation and State-Making: The Conservative Party and the Reconstruction of the Brazilian State, 1831–1840," in *Hispanic American Historical Review* 81 (2001).

ANTON ROSENTHAL is an associate professor at the University of Kansas where he teaches history and sociology. He has published articles in the *Journal of Latin American Studies*, *Radical History Review*, *Studies in Latin American Popular Culture*, and other journals in addition to chapters in two books. His most recent essay is "Spectacle, Fear and Protest: A Guide to the History of Urban Public Space in Latin America," in *Social Science History* (Spring 2000). He is completing a study of streetcars, labor, and public space in early twentieth-century Montevideo. In 2000 he received the Byron T. Shutz Award for Distinguished Teaching.

ANN FARNSWORTH-ALVEAR, assistant professor of history, University of Pennsylvania, teaches Latin American gender and social history. She has published articles on gender and labor in an anthology and in several journals, including *Signs: Journal of Women in Culture and Society*. Her book, *Dulcinea in the Factory: Myths, Morals, Men, and Women in Colombia's Industrial Experiment, 1905–1960* was published in 2000. Her current research interests include the impact of U.S. capital and culture on the Chocó as well as identity and subjectivity in rural Colombia.

DAVID S. PARKER is associate professor of history at Queen's University, Kingston, Ontario. He has published *The Idea of the Middle Class: White Collar Workers and Peruvian Society, 1900–1950* (1998) as well as articles in several journals and anthologies. His current research interests focus on concepts of honor and dueling, and he is at work on a book about dueling, political culture, and the law in nineteenth- and twentieth-century Uruguay.

MARC BECKER is an assistant professor of Latin American history at Truman State University in Kirksville, Missouri, where he teaches courses on ethnic identities, revolutions, and peasants. He has published a number of articles and a book, *Mariátegui and Latin American Marxist Theory* (1993). His next book on the history of Indian and peasant movements in twentieth-century Ecuador is forthcoming. Becker is a founding member of the Ecuadorian Studies section of the Latin American Studies Association (LASA) and president of "NativeWeb," an Internet website dedicated to indigenous issues around the world. He is currently beginning research on the debates over ethnicity in the Andean region within the Communist International.

MIGUEL TINKER-SALAS is an associate professor of history and chair of Latin American studies at Pomona College. He has published on the Mexico-U.S. border, including *In the Shadow of Eagles: Sonora and the Transformation of the Border during the Porfiriato* (1997). He is currently finishing a manuscript that analyzes the political transformations, social relations, and cultural interactions that resulted from contacts between Venezuelans, North Americans, and other foreigners working in Venezuela's oil camps.

MARÍA DEL CARMEN BAERGA is assistant professor in the History Department at the University of Puerto Rico, Río Piedras, where she teaches courses on gender, labor, and Latin American history. She is the editor of *Género y trabajo: La industria de la aguja en Puerto Rico y el Caribe hispánico* (1993) and has contributed chapters to several books, including *La mujer en Puerto Rico* (1987). Her current research interests include the racialization of the working classes in Puerto Rico during the late nineteenth and early twentieth centuries.

CATHERINE LEGRAND is associate professor of history at McGill University. Her most recent work includes participation in the editing (with Gil Joseph and Ricardo Salvatore) of *Close Encounters of Empire: Writing the Cultural History of U.S.-Latin American Relations* (1998) and contribution of an article for that volume, along with a number of articles on the politics of violence and on resistance on plantations in various journals. She continues to work on banana society in Colombia and on sugar and the Canadian connection in the Dominican Republic.

NORMAN CAULFIELD is associate professor of history, Fort Hays State University, Fort Hays, Kansas, where he teaches Mexican, Latin American, and U.S. history. His most recent publication is *Mexican Workers and the State: From the Porfiriato to NAFTA* (1998). Currently on a two-year leave from his professorship, he is working in the Secretariat of the Commission for Labor Cooperation, an office created by NAFTA, where his research focuses on globalization and workers in North America.

RACHEL MAY is an associate professor of Latin American studies and comparative human rights in the Interdisciplinary Arts and Sciences program at the University of Washington, Tacoma. Her book on violence and popular movements in Guatemala, *Terror in the Countryside: Campesino Responses to Political Violence in Guatemala, 1954–1985*, was published in 2001. Her current research is on the Argentine militant movements of the 1960s and 1970s and on peace processes and post-terrorist transitions in the Southern Cone and Central America.

THOMAS MILLER KLUBOCK is associate professor of history at the State University of New York, Stony Brook. His book, *Contested Communities: Class, Gender, and Politics in Chile's El Teniente Copper Mine, 1904–1951* (1998), examines the history of Chilean copper miners during the twentieth century. He is currently at work on a book about labor and the environment in Chile's temperate rainforests.

ANTHONY W. PEREIRA, associate professor of political science at Tulane University, is the author of *The End of the Peasantry: The Emergence of the Rural Labor Movement in Northeast Brazil, 1961–1988* (1997) and chapters in a variety of anthologies. His articles have appeared in several journals familiar to Latin Americanists, Africanists, and others involved in problems of Third World development. His research interests include the rule of law and military justice in Brazil.

MICHAEL F. JIMÉNEZ was assistant professor of Latin American history at the University of Pittsburgh. He died in 2001. His many articles on Colombian peasants, coffee, and related themes are well known. His book *Struggles on an Interior Shore* is forthcoming.

KENNETH M. ROBERTS is associate professor of political science at the University of New Mexico. He is the author of *Deepening Democracy?*

The Modern Left and Social Movements in Chile and Peru (1998). His current research focuses on the transformation of party systems and political representation in modern Latin America.